K. INDRAPALA

THE EVOLUTION OF AN ETHNIC IDENTITY

THE TAMILS IN SRI LANKA c. 300 BCE TO c. 1200 CE

PUBLISHED BY
MV PUBLICATIONS
FOR
THE SOUTH ASIAN STUDIES CENTRE
SYDNEY
2005

The Evolution of an Ethnic Identity:

The Tamils in Sri Lanka c. 300 BCE to c. 1200 CE

ISBN 0-646-42546-3

Printed in Sri Lanka
by
Unigraphics (Pte) Ltd,
732, Maradana Road, Colombo 10.

Published by MV Publications

For The South Asian Studies Centre

Sydney, 2005

To the innocents who lost their lives
as a direct consequence of
misinterpretations of history

K. Indrapala took his first degree from the University of Ceylon (now University of Peradeniya) in 1960 and, from that time until 1975, lectured in history in that university. He took his doctorate from the University of London. In 1975, he was appointed Foundation Professor of History in the new Jaffna Campus of the University of Sri Lanka , which later became the University of Jaffna. In 1977/78, he was a Japan Foundation Fellow and Visiting Professor at the Tokyo University of Foreign Studies, Tokyo. In 1984, he was appointed Foundation Professor of Southeast Asian Studies at the Tamil University, Thanjavur. He now lives in Australia.

CONTENTS

ACKNOWLEDGEMENTS

This book is the product of knowledge and skills acquired over a lifetime. Many people have contributed immensely to this acquisition through their devoted instruction, ungrudging guidance and timely assistance. I wish to record my sincere thanks to all of them.

First of all, I owe much to my parents and my teachers at Jaffna College who helped me to develop a broad outlook and to free myself from parochial constraints, and thus prepare for a better understanding of history and archaeology.

In a deeper sense, I owe a great debt of gratitude to those who initiated me into the study of history, archaeology and languages. Many of them are now no more but live on in my mind and I feel it my duty and pleasure to record here my unforgettable gratitude to them - those who initiated me into the study of different languages and thus helped me widen my horizons and understand the history and cultures of various peoples with a perspective that would have been difficult to develop without familiarity with their languages: Poet Sagara Palansuriya (who initiated me into the study of Sinhala when I was ten years old), Dr. Klaus Matzel, Rev. Nanavasa Thero, Prof. Kailasanatha Kurukkal, and Mrs. S. Sasaki; two scholars who helped develop my interest in epigraphy: Prof. K. Kanapathi Pillai (Professor of Tamil, University of Ceylon) and Prof. Tennekoon Vimalananda (Senior Lecturer in Archaeology, University of Ceylon and later Professor at the Vidyalankara University, Kelaniya); Shri K. G. Krishnan (Senior Epigraphist, Office of the Government Epigraphist for India, Mysore) who gave me further training in epigraphy; and, Prof. W. J. F. LaBrooy (Head, Department of History, University of Ceylon) who made me to turn my attention to the history of the Tamils of Sri Lanka when I was interested in medieval south Indian history and gave me encouragement in my academic pursuits. And I also fondly remember another scholar who was not one of my teachers but from whom I learnt much - Dr. James T. Rutnam, who first encountered me as a critic of my views and remained an admirer and staunch supporter, giving me encouragement in my researches.

Archaeology has been a source of immense pleasure in my life. There were many who were responsible for some of the best moments in my experiences in this field and helped me gain first-hand knowledge of much of the material discussed in this work. I thank them all: Dr. P. C. Sestieri (UNESCO Adviser to the Government of Ceylon), under whose supervision I entered the fascinating world of archaeological excavations in 1957 at Anuradhapura; Dr. Vimala Begley (University of Pennsylvania Museum Project) who gave me the unique opportunity of participating in the entire excavation project at the megalithic site of Pomparippu in 1970 and in the excavation at Kantarodai for a brief period in the same year; Dr. P. L. Prematilleke (Senior Lecturer and later Professor of Archaeology, University of Peradeniya), who took me in the late 1960s and early 1970s to study various archaeological sites, including Medirigiriya (where he located a Cōḷa inscription in 1969) and Bundala (where Siran Deraniyagala was conducting an excavation for prehistoric material in 1972); Dr. R. Nagaswamy (Director of Archaeology, Tamil Nadu), who took me in 1977 to various places of archaeological importance in Tamil Nadu and helped me to study the sites, including Gangaikonda-cholapuram, Darasuram and Mamallapuram; Dr. P. Ragupathy (Lecturer at the University of Jaffna and later, Professor, Utkal University of Culture, Bhubanesvar), who, with his uncanny knack for detecting archaeological material in unusual places, located the site of the Anaikoddai megalithic burials and provided me with the singular opportunity in 1980 for the unforgettable experience of conducting a salvage excavation and stumbling upon very valuable artefacts, including the Anaikoddai seal, and the first complete megalithic burial in the Jaffna District; and, Prof. Senake Bandaranayake, who gave me the chance to be associated with the UNESCO-Cultural Triangle Project at Sigiriya in its early stages in the 1980s.

A number of persons helped me in various ways in the course of my explorations for inscriptions from 1967 to 1978. Among them were some who, out of their enthusiasm for archaeological finds, located inscriptions and guided me to those locations. N. Tambirasa, A. Kandiah and S. Ganeshalingam deserve special mention. I offer my grateful thanks to them.

Successive Archaeological Commissioners in Sri Lanka have been most helpful in granting me permission to take estampages of inscriptions and to publish photographs of estampages. I wish to record my gratitude to all of them: Dr. Raja H. de Silva, Dr. W. Saddhamangala Karunaratne and Dr. W. H. Wijepala (the present Director-General of Archaeology).

In the last three years, while writing this book, several friends have given me valuable help: Mugunthan Gunasingam, Inoka Jayasena, Pavithra Kailasapathy, Noboru Karashima, Sirinimal Lakdusinghe, Sumith Nakandala, M. A. Nuhman, K. Rajan, Gowtham Reddy, Murali Reddy, V. S. Sivalingam, Y. Subbarayalu and S. Subbulakshmi. My thanks are due to all of them. M. Gunasingam (Librarian, Charles Sturt University, Bathurst) provided invaluable help in the preparation of this book by tracking down articles and other publications and urged me on to complete the work. For all this, I am deeply indebted to him. Kulasegaram Sanchayan, showing sincere dedication and a desire for perfection, gave very valuable assistance in the final stages of the preparation of the draft and the typesetting of the book with his amazing expertise in computer technology. To him I say a special ‘Thank you’.

And finally, I cannot fail to mention the unseen ways in which those near and dear to me provided sustenance throughout this work: Harini, Dharini, Chandra, Aravindan, Meghana, Maya, Vivek and Priya who, in their own way, provided inspiration and support through difficult times and encouraged me to complete this work. I always felt that I owed it to them and to my numerous friends and wellwishers to undertake this task and complete it. I express my sincere gratitude to all of them.

ABBREVIATIONS

ASCAR	*Archaeological Survey of Ceylon Annual Report*
BCE	Before the Common Era
BP	Before Present (see Glossary)
CE	Common Era (same as Christian Era)
Cv	*Cūḷavaṃsa*
Dv	*Dīpavaṃsa*
EHP	Early Historic Period
EI	*Epigraphia Indica*
EIA	Early Iron Age
ET	*Epigraphia Tamilica*
EZ	*Epigraphia Zeylanica*
JRASCB	*Journal of the Royal Asiatic Society Ceylon Branch*
JRASSLB	*Journal of the Royal Asiatic Society Sri Lanka Branch*
Mv	*Mahāvaṃsa*
SISL	South India-Sri Lanka
UCHC	*University of Ceylon History of Ceylon*

A NOTE ON TRANSLITERATION

The transliteration of Tamil words has been done, as a rule, in accordance with the system adopted by the *Madras Tamil Lexicon* (MTL) and in scholarly writings on south Indian history, such as those by K.A. Nilakanta Sastri. However, there are some exceptions to be noted:

1. Placenames in current use are transliterated in the way they are written in contemporary official records and maps: for example, Tamil Nadu (not Tamiḻnāṭu), Thanjavur (not Tañcāvūr). When these occur in an original text that is being quoted, the MTL system is used. In the case of Cōḻa territorial names, such as those ending in –maṇḍalam, vaḷanāḍu and nāḍu, the forms commonly used in academic writings on south India are adopted.
2. Personal names, especially those of kings, have been transliterated in the way they appear in most scholarly writings. This particularly applies to names of Sanskrit origin: for example, Rājendra (not Rācēntiraṉ or Rājēntiraṉ). The following forms are used for the three well-known ancient south Indian lineages: Cōḻa, Pāṇḍya and Cēra.
3. Names of religions that are still popular are written without transliteration: for example, Saiva (not Śaiva), Vaishnava (not Vaiṣṇava).

The transliteration of Sanskrit, Pali and Sinhala words follows the standard practice adopted in academic publications on South Asia.

PREFACE

This book has long been overdue. Over forty years ago, in 1962, when, as a junior member of the teaching staff of the university at Peradeniya (then known as the University of Ceylon, now the University of Peradeniya), I was planning my postgraduate research, the late Prof. W. J. F. LaBrooy, my revered teacher and, at that time, Head of the Department of History at the university, advised me to research into the early history of the Tamils of Sri Lanka for my doctoral dissertation, as he considered this aspect to be a serious gap in the known history of the island. (In hindsight, I now think that this advice had something to do with the controversy over the omission of the section dealing with the early history of the Tamils from the university's publication *History of Ceylon,* Volume I, Pt. II, released in 1960.)[1] In October 1963, I enrolled as a postgraduate student at the School of Oriental and African Studies of the University of London and commenced my research on the ancient settlements of the Dravidian-speakers in Sri Lanka. I was fortunate to engage in this research in a department headed by Prof. Bernard Lewis (still a leading specialist in Middle Eastern history), under the overall supervision of the late Prof. A.L. Basham (then the foremost British historian of ancient India) and the guidance of Dr. Johannes de Casparis (then Reader in History at the SOAS and later Professor at the University of Leiden), whose profound knowledge of South and Southeast Asian history as well as expertise in Indian and Indonesian epigraphy became invaluable for my training. My thesis was completed in October 1965.

Work on this thesis opened my eyes to the paucity of material relating to the early history of the Tamils in Sri Lanka and to the great need for archaeological work in the regions settled by the Tamils. The thesis was completed with the material that was available in the early 1960s. 'As long as excavation work remains undone', I pointed out, 'much that is relevant to our study will be wanting… Even the inscriptions and literary works that we have used have proved to be inadequate in the reconstruction of a satisfactory history of the settlements and in the solution of many important problems' (p. 21). The thesis was presented as the first major attempt to bring together all the available evidence on the subject. The fact that it was in no way a complete study was admitted: 'In view of these limitations and difficulties, while we may claim to have added something to our knowledge of the history of the Tamils of Ceylon, the account presented here is inevitably incomplete and not always definite. We have often been led to state our conclusions in hypothetical terms' (p. 23).

Needless to say, that dissertation is now completely out of date. My own perspectives and interpretations have changed since its completion. More importantly, significant developments, both in terms of archaeological research and changing historical perspectives, have taken place in the last four decades. The work of a whole new generation of Sri Lankan scholars has not only helped to unearth much evidence relating to Sri Lanka's prehistory and protohistory, but also brought to bear new approaches and interpretations on the study of the country's past. The researches of Sri Lankan as well as foreign anthropologists and sociologists have also immensely assisted in the understanding of the island's past. The advances in knowledge that have resulted from these developments have made it possible to attempt this study of the early history of the Tamils of Sri Lanka and the evolution of their separate identity.

In times of human conflict, whether communal, national or international, history, together with its sister discipline of archaeology, is always among the first casualties. In South Asia, with its long and chequered history and multi-ethnic population, every other person with some education seems to consider herself or himself as an authority on history and tends to pay scant respect to the views of specialists, if those views do not agree with what she or he holds to be the truth. Through a process of selective quoting, with no regard for the nature of the source, favourable views are put forward. I have no doubt that a number of general readers will show unusual interest in this book. Many are likely to view what is said here in the light of contemporary prejudices. To them, I wish to say that Sri Lanka has been, from time immemorial, the home of various ethnic groups. There have been political and social conflicts among them but the kind of ethnic consciousness and destructive prejudices that have surfaced in the twentieth century and continue to plague the island were not part of Sri Lanka's pre-colonial history. The first kings that we know of in the centuries before the Common Era were not all of the same ethnic group or religious persuasion. Neither were the last kings of the island before the European invasions.

The political ideologies pursued by opposing groups in times of conflict affect not only ordinary people but sadly also intellectuals, some of whom go to great lengths to interpret history and archaeology to support the views they favour. This was seen in Germany, Japan and other countries during the Second World War. Regrettably, it would appear that, in the last three decades, a number of Sri Lankan scholars, both young and old, in the universities of Sri Lanka as well as in universities outside, have been responding to the current political and ideological environment in a disappointing manner. History has been enlisted and mobilised to fight the issues of our day. Some academic historians have become willing recruits for this battle.

The manner in which history is being 'used' in fighting contemporary issues is a matter for concern. That there is a need to go back to the distant past and drag historical figures and mould them into heroes of the present is not a healthy sign. This situation is best summed up by a distinguished Sri Lankan scholar, who, though not a professional historian, wrote a better general history of Sri Lanka than some academic historians have done in the recent past. His words are very relevant indeed to the present state of affairs:

> … the legendary heroes once created to satisfy the old needs are still resorted to in the entirely different circumstances of the present. That cultures have their mythical heroes is not surprising, indeed it would be strange if they should lack them. There is a slight distinction to be drawn, however, between this and the need for heroes… To have invented what was once required is surely the normal and economical satisfaction

> of desires, to be met with in the history of individuals and communities. But to insist on satisfying a recurring need at all times in the same old ways is surely an indication of deep seated malaise. To be, at the present time, dependent on the mythopoeic creativeness of ages long past is to argue an inability to face up to the demands of the contemporaneous. When we continually cry for a cause, for a hero whom we could follow, when we need the sustenance of legendary forefathers, we are most probably showing symptoms, not only of angry unhappiness, but also of retarded adolescence. (E. F. C. Ludowyk, *The Story of Ceylon*, London 1967: 33)

This is not a situation that is peculiar to Sri Lanka. We live at a time when in many countries history has become a weapon in the hands of political activists. A very distinguished historian of our time, Eric Hobsbawm, has expressed serious concern, as a university teacher and historian, about this development. His comments are worthy of note by those who are engaged in genuine historical research:

> History is the raw material for nationalist or ethnic or fundamentalist ideologies, as poppies are the raw material for heroin addiction. The past is an essential element, perhaps the essential element, in these ideologies. If there is no suitable past, it can always be invented. ... The past legitimizes. The past gives a more glorious background to a present that doesn't have much to celebrate...
>
> I used to think that the profession of history, unlike that of, say, nuclear physics, could at least do no harm. Now I know it can. Our studies can turn into bomb factories like the workshops in which the IRA has learned to transform chemical fertilizer into an explosive. This state of affairs affects us in two ways. We have a responsibility to historical facts in general, and for criticizing the politicoideological abuse of history in particular. (*On History*, New York 1997: 5, 6)

Referring to some modern day attempts to revise history on the basis of new myths, Hobsbawm warns us that 'These and many other attempts are not merely bad intellectual jokes. After all, they can determine what goes into schoolbooks' (p. 7). Again, Hobsbawm's views are worthy of note:

> Myth and invention are essential to the politics of identity by which groups of people today, defining themselves by ethnicity, religion or the past or present borders of states try to find some certainty in an uncertain and shaking world by saying, 'We are different from and better than the Others'. They are our concern in the universities because the people who formulate those myths and inventions are educated people: schoolteachers lay and clerical, professors (not many, I hope), journalists, television and radio producers. Today most of them will have gone to some university. Make no mistake about it. History is not ancestral memory or collective tradition. It is what people learned from priests, schoolmasters, the writers of history books and the compilers of magazine articles and television programmes. It is very important for historians to remember their responsibility, which is, above all, to stand aside from the passions of identity politics even if we feel them also. After all, we are human beings too. (pp.7-8)

A leading Sri Lankan scholar and university teacher, Prof. Sudharshan Seneviratne, who is in a far better position than I am to assess the Sri Lankan situation, has already warned us about the dangers facing historical and archaeological research there:

> The future of both historical and archaeological studies in Sri Lanka is at cross roads facing a dilemma of priorities, choices, resource persons, attitudes and, above all, quality of research. It is indeed reasonable to question the extent to which a new breed of charlatans and political animals in these disciplines are responsible for the emergence of [an] ahistorical attitude

> and an anti-historical bias in schools, at seats of higher education and the country in general. 'Anti-Orwellian' historians in this country who have slithered their way through 'corridors of power` have not only compromised the very fundamentals of intellectual decency but are now in the process of subverting the study of history for personal ends and political expediency. (*The Island*, Colombo, 4 August 2001)

Another leading Sri Lankan academic who has repeatedly expressed similar concern about this unfortunate development in historical writings is Prof. Leslie Gunawardana:

> A trend which appears to be gathering strength is represented by some researchers in the field of archaeology and history who see in their work the fulfilment of a duty to highlight the splendour of the Sinhala or the Tamil group as the case may be, and to bolster the claims of one's own group to disputed territory. While it has led to a growth of interest in research related to ethnic studies, this development has brought in its wake a noteworthy relaxation of intellectual rigour in research. (Gunawardana 1994: 213)

In Hobsbawm's view, 'history is engaged on a coherent intellectual project, and has made progress in understanding how the world came to be the way it is today' (1997: x). My aim here is to explore the past in order to understand how the Tamils of Sri Lanka (as well as the Sinhalese) came to be what they are. Their political claims that have led to the current conflict are to be judged in terms of accepted universal human rights and not in terms of their past in the island. The deeper one delves into Sri Lankan history the more one will find how much the Tamils and the Sinhalese have in common. They have a shared history and culture; and a common descent. In the cogent words of that distinguished Sri Lankan archaeologist Prof. Senerat Paranavitana, 'the vast majority of the people who today speak Sinhalese or Tamil must ultimately be descended from those autochthonous people [of the prehistoric period] of whom we know next to nothing' (*UCHC*, I, 1: 96-97). As that eminent Cambridge scholar and renowned historian of science, Prof. Joseph Needham, rightly remarked, together they had achieved an admirable hydraulic civilization in the island about a thousand years ago.* Together they could attain great heights in the future.

---

* Discussing one of the finest achievements in ancient hydraulics in his monumental work on the science and civilization of China, Prof. Joseph Needham (1900-1995) judged 'that the achievements of the Indian civil engineers in ancient and medieval times are quite worthy to be compared with those of their Chinese colleagues', but concluded that 'it was never in India that the fusion of the Egyptian and Babylonian patterns achieved its most complete and subtlest form. This took place in Ceylon, the work of both cultures, Sinhalese and Tamil, but especially the former' (*Science and Civilization in China*, IV, Cambridge 1971: 368).

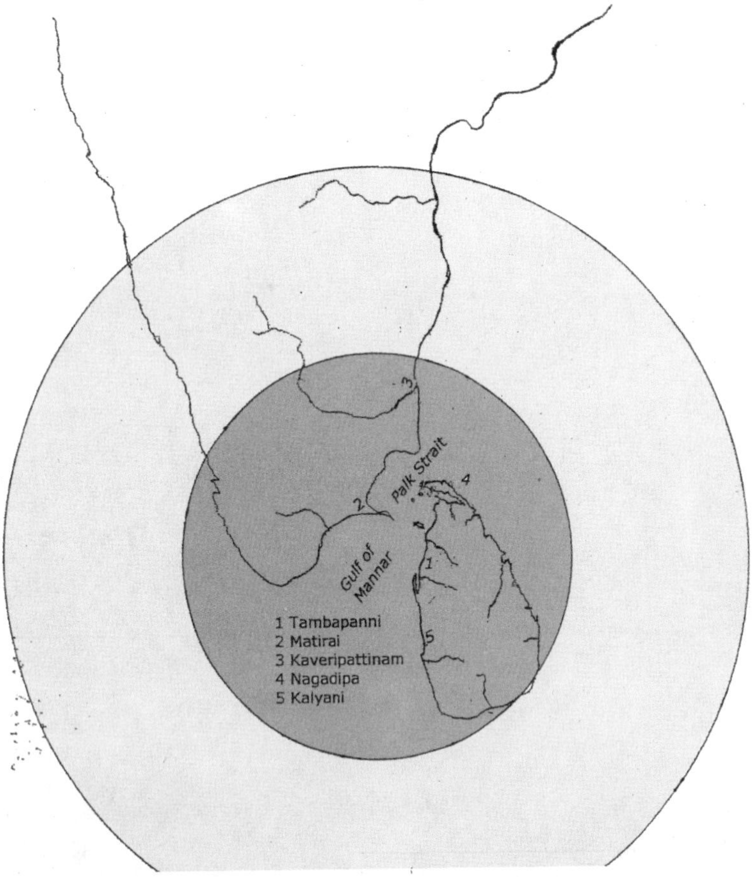

Map 1. The South India - Sri Lanka Region (SISL)

INTRODUCTION

"Political pressures on history, by old and new states and regimes, identity groups, and forces long concealed under the frozen ice-cap of the Cold War, are greater than ever before in my lifetime, and modern media society has given the past unprecedented prominence and marketing potential. More history than ever is today being revised or invented by people who do not want the real past, but only a past that suits their purpose. Today is the great age of historical mythology. The defence of history by its professionals is today more urgent in politics than ever. We are needed.." Professor Eric Hobsbawm, *Interesting Times: A Twentieth–Century Life*, London 2002: 296.

Sri Lanka is a country with a very long history of human settlement. Over several millennia, people of different cultures have been settling here and it is a process that has gone on until the end of colonial rule and the island's emergence as a newly independent country in the middle of the twentieth century. From prehistoric times, its people have been, to use a contemporary term, multicultural. From the myriad cultural groups that were there in the protohistoric period, about 2500 years ago, two major ethnic identities, the Sinhalese and the Tamils, began to evolve in the early historic period. There were also other minor ethnic groups who were assimilated, in course of time, into one or the other major group. Later, with the arrival of the Muslim traders, a third significant ethnic identity evolved. This group is now known as the Muslims of Sri Lanka. European rule from the sixteenth century added another important ethnic group, the Burghers. In the time of European domination, under the Dutch, another minor group, the Malays, was brought from the islands of Indonesia. And finally, colonial rule and economic exploitation of the country by the British resulted in one more significant ethnic identity, the Tamils of Indian Origin, emerging here.

Sri Lankan Tamil Ethnic Identity

Ethnicity

To trace the evolution of the major ethnic identities of the early historic period is a forbidding task. To begin with, one is confronted with the problem of definition. In a world where ethnic consciousness has assumed greater proportions than perhaps ever before, ethnic terms are very commonly used but remain hard to define. The ethnic conflict in Sri Lanka has helped to publicise the name 'Tamil' in many parts of the world in a manner that the Dravidian movement in Tamil Nadu could not achieve. But has that helped to define a Tamil? We hear of the Arab-Israeli conflict several times a week, but who is an Arab? In fact, the problem relates to almost every ethnic name. Such is the complexity of defining an ethnic group.

Ethnicity is a social attribute and not a physical one. A convenient definition of the *ethnos*, the ethnic group, accepted by historians and archaeologists, is quoted by the archaeologist Colin Renfrew: "a firm aggregate of people, historically established in a given territory, possessing in common relatively stable peculiarities of language and culture, and also recognizing their unity and difference from other similar formations (self-awareness) and expressing this in a self-appointed name (ethnonym)."[1] Agreeing with this definition, Renfrew points out that this "allows us to note the following factors, all of them relevant to the notion of ethnicity: 1. shared territory or land, 2. common descent or 'blood', 3. a common language, 4. community of customs or culture, 5. community of beliefs or religion, 6. self-awareness, self-identity, 7. a name (ethnonym) to express the identity of the group, 8. shared origin story (or myth) describing the origin and history of the group."[2] This definition is useful in the study of the Sri Lankan situation.[3]

Ethnic identities in the modern world are based on self-perception. This is the guiding principle in the identification of the different ethnic groups. There are, however, various indicators of ethnicity, although it is not always easy to use these to identify a person's ethnic group. Language, for instance, is one such indicator but it does not apply to every case. While the Sinhalese language is, without argument, an indicator of Sinhalese ethnicity, it is not possible to use the Tamil language in a similar manner as an indicator of Tamil ethnicity. The speakers of the Tamil language in Sri Lanka are not a single homogeneous ethnic community. Among the Tamil-speakers, there are three main groups, the Sri Lankan Tamils, the Tamils of Indian Origin and the Sri Lankan Muslims, each perceiving itself as a separate ethnic group. Yet another small group, the Colombo Chetties, which considered itself as a part of the Sri Lankan Tamils until the last decades of the twentieth century, now wishes to be identified as a community distinct from the Sri Lankan Tamils. Not all speakers of the Tamil language consider themselves Tamils. The Muslims of Sri Lanka, the vast majority of whom speak Tamil as their mother tongue, do not consider themselves to be Tamils. And there are also some who do not speak Tamil but consider themselves Tamils.

Subject of this book

This book is concerned with the Tamils who lived in Sri Lanka in the early centuries of its history and with the evolution of an ethnic community speaking the Tamil language in the northern, northwestern and eastern regions of the island whose descendants in modern times perceive themselves as an ethnic identity that is different from the Tamils of south India as well as other ethnic groups in Sri Lanka.

It is not suggested here that ethnic consciousness and ethnic identities prevailed in the ancient period as they do in our time. The ethnic labels, such as Dameḍa, Iḷa and Barata, occurring in the ancient inscriptions referred to groups that represented what has been described as archaic ethnicity. These groups no doubt had features that distinguished them from one another. These features would be hard to identify with the available evidence. It is unlikely that at that stage language was a distinguishing feature. As pointed out by Leslie Gunawardana, it will be difficult to claim that a strong feeling of ethnic consciousness bound the members of each group together in the modern sense.[4] Indeed the ethnic divisions in society found in modern Sri Lanka are not applicable to the society of the Early Historic Period (EHP).

Tamiḻ and Damiḷa

In the Tamil language, the earliest occurrences of the word *Tamiḻ* are in the poems of the anthology known as the Sangam literature and in the grammatical work *Tolkāppiyam*, dating back to the centuries immediately before the Common Era. In these occurrences, the word is used to denote a language, an ethnic group and a country. About the same time, derivatives of this name were used in the Prakrit languages (*Tramira* in the Hathigumpha inscription of the second century BCE, and *Damiḷa* in an early inscription from Amaravati) to refer to an ethnic group. The Pali *Akitti Jātaka*, also datable to a period BCE, refers to the *Damiḷaraṭṭhaṃ* (the country of the *Damiḷa*). It is clear from these references that in the period of the earliest Brāhmī inscriptions of Sri Lanka there was in south India an ethnic group using *Tamiḻ* as its descriptive term.

A section of the population of Sri Lanka in the historical period has been designated *Demaḷa* and *Ḍamiḷa* in the major Sinhala and Pali chronicles respectively. In the Sinhala inscriptions of the ninth and tenth centuries the related term *Demeḷ* occurs. There cannot be any dispute about the relationship of these terms to the words *Tamiḻ* and *Tamiḻar* in the Tamil language, denoting that language and the people associated with that language (although language may not have been the only distinguishing feature of this group). That these terms are the forerunners of the modern Sinhalese term *Demaḷa* (often Sanskritised as *Draviḍa* in literary usage) and that they refer to the same ethnic group cannot also be contested. Scholars have also accepted that the Prakrit form of this name is *Dameḍa*, occurring in the Brāhmī inscriptions of Sri Lanka datable to about the second century BCE.[5] In some of these early records, the variant *Dameḷa* is found to occur. The origin of a separate Tamil ethnic group in Sri

Lanka, whatever its characteristics over the centuries, will have to go back to this early *Dameḍa* group.

Until very recent years, serious historical research was not directed at the origin and evolution of either the Sinhalese or Sri Lankan Tamil communities. Historians have tended to base their writings on the assumption that the people of the island at the dawn of its history were Sinhalese and that, at a later time, the Tamils and other communities came to share the country. Sri Lankan historiography of the nineteenth and the early twentieth century is largely responsible for this oversimplification of the ancient history of Sri Lanka.

Sri Lankan Historiography

Colonial constructions

Modern scientific research into the island's ancient history was an area that was very seriously neglected almost to the end of the colonial period. Whereas in the Indian subcontinent, the early establishment of universities in the middle of the nineteenth century provided the facilities for the training and employment of Indian historians, and the growth of a vibrant nationalist movement in the final decades of the nineteenth century gave an impetus to the development of historical and archaeological research as well as a national interest in the past, at least among the English-educated intelligentsia, Sri Lanka did not have a single university until about six years before gaining independence from Britain, and lacked serious scholarly interest in research into the ancient history of the island till the second quarter of the twentieth century. This is not to deny the interest shown in the archaeological remains in the ancient cities that lay in ruins, in the epigraphic records and in the Pali and Sinhala chronicles by both Sri Lankan and European scholars.

European writers had no doubt shown an interest in the history of the island from the time the Portuguese began their rule in the sixteenth century. The Portuguese priest, Fernao de Queyroz, was among the first to write a notable history of Sri Lanka in a European language in the seventeenth century.[6] Joao Ribeiro was another Portuguese historian who wrote a history of the island.[7] In the eighteenth century, a similar interest in the history of the island was shown by some Dutch writers. Notable among them was Philippus Baldaeus.[8] These accounts have very little about the ancient history of Sri Lanka.

It is in the nineteenth century, under British rule, that Europeans, particularly British officials, evinced a keen interest in the traditional history of the island as told in the local chronicles. The European discovery of the Pali and Sinhala chronicles, the publication of early translations of the *Mahāvaṃsa* and the acquisition of information relating to the ancient ruins led to the first serious British attempts to write the early history of Sri Lanka in the middle of the nineteenth century. It was in these early colonial writings, largely based on the uncritical acceptance of the local chronicles, that a new perspective of the ancient history of the island began to develop. The view that the Sinhalese were the 'proper inhabitants' of the island in ancient times and that the Tamils were invaders came to dominate colonial historical writing. Before long, the Sinhalese were identified with the 'Aryans' and the Tamils with the 'Dravidians'. In recent years, several anthropologists and historians have shown how this perspective came to be developed in colonial writings.[9]

Sri Lankan history was hardly taught in the schools until the end of British rule. The only major institution where history was taught at the undergraduate level, namely the Ceylon University College in Colombo, was affiliated to the University of London and prepared students for examinations in British and European history. There were only a couple of school textbooks on the history of Sri Lanka, even as late as 1930. These were written by historians of British origin.[10] The demand for school textbooks in the early years of independence, in the nineteen-fifties, led to the publication of a few books on Sri Lankan history by school teachers.[11] The only exception to these school books was the *Early History of Ceylon* written by G. C. Mendis, an academic in the Ceylon University College.[12]

These writings were all based on the Pali and Sinhala chronicles which inevitably set the tone for the Sinhalacentrist approach that has remained a hallmark of Sri Lankan historiography until recent years. Even as late as the nineteen-eighties, some of the authoritative works dealing with the entire history of Sri Lanka ('from its legendary beginnings to the author's own day') could only begin with the 'Aryan colonisation' as told in the chronicles and dismiss the original inhabitants of the island as of no significance because the 'Aryan' colonists 'either absorbed, swept away or pushed into the remoter regions of the island the original inhabitants whom they encountered.'[13]

In these writings, the view that Sri Lankan history began at a single moment with a single event and flowed in one continuous stream into modern times has been dominant.[14] In this linear view, echoes of modern nationalism could unmistakably be heard. Sri Lankan history was seen as the exclusive domain of a single ethnic identity which was from time to time threatened by another from across the Palk Strait. As David Ludden has argued, 'we must now separate the academic study of pre-modern history from contemporary efforts to construct modern cultural boundaries' and 'We need to separate the study of collective identities and everyday experience in the past from our current cultural politics of national identity.'[15]

The Paranavitana Factor

The establishment of the first university in Sri Lanka, the University of Ceylon, in 1942, provided the opportunity to take the first step towards serious academic research into the island's past. Courses in Sri Lankan history were introduced and the first student to conduct a doctoral research in ancient Sri Lankan history was enrolled.[16] There was, however, only one specialist in ancient Sri Lankan history on the staff of the university (G. C. Mendis) and the foundation chair of history went to a specialist in ancient Indian history (H. C. Ray).[17]

While the young Department of History of the new university was struggling to establish itself, with hardly any significant research output until the 1950s, there was one department of the government that enjoyed a great reputation for its researches into the ancient past of Sri Lanka. This was the Archaeological Survey of Ceylon. The Commissioner of Archaeology, who headed this department, was Senarat Paranavitana, the first Sri Lankan to hold that position. A self-made scholar, he had a profound knowledge of the archaeology of Sri Lanka as well as of several languages and wrote prodigiously, earning a wide reputation as an authority on ancient Sri Lanka. The university did not have a department for archaeology and could not boast of anyone in its Department of History with scholarship comparable with that of Paranavitana. When Paranavitana retired from the post of Commissioner in 1957, he was appointed Research Professor of Archaeology in the University of Ceylon and nearly everyone in the young university looked up to him with awe and admiration.

It was about this time that the university felt its responsibility to satisfy a long-felt need in the country, namely, to bring out an authoritative history of Sri Lanka. But strangely, there was no one in the university's Department of History who could take up the challenge of editing the first volume of the proposed history dealing with the ancient period. The university turned to the newly appointed Professor of Archaeology to take on this task.

Though undoubtedly an eminent archaeologist of the historical period and the foremost Sinhalese epigraphist of the time, Paranavitana was hardly the historian fitting the role of editor of what was intended to be the pioneer historical publication of the university providing to the new nation an authoritative history. An indefatigable researcher and prolific writer, he wrote almost all the major chapters of the first volume covering the history up to the end of the fifteenth century. Thus, he was in a position to use his perspectives and provide a history largely based on the monastic chronicles and his interpretation of the archaeological material. For more than a decade, what he wrote remained the only authoritative history of ancient Sri Lanka.

This situation, which may be termed the Paranavitana factor, had a tremendous influence on a whole generation of Sri Lankan students and general readers. His reputation as a great scholar was further enhanced by the history he wrote. Many researchers, young and old, disagreed with several of his views and theories in private but were not willing to go public.

The impact of the Paranavitana factor on the teaching and writing of Sri Lankan history is yet to be fully researched.[18] As one who had followed the undergraduate courses in ancient Sri Lankan history in the University of Ceylon (the only university in the island until 1959) in the late 1950's and had worked as a member of the teaching staff of the Department of History there throughout the 1960's, the present writer is in a position to say that the influence of the Paranavitana factor was enormous.

The extent of this influence could be gauged from some of the notable publications on Sri Lankan history in the 1960s and early 1970s. One instance of this is the perpetuation of the Aryan myth. While the notion that the 'Aryans' had colonized Sri Lanka in the centuries before the beginning of the Common Era was prevalent even before the publication of the *University of Ceylon History of Ceylon*, Paranavitana's chapter on the 'Aryan Settlements: The Sinhalese' gave the theory a much-needed authority.[19] For the next two decades after its publication, even the leading young historians of the university, who were trained in the modern historical method in some of the established western universities, found it difficult to discard the theory of an 'Aryan' migration and settlement, although they were writing more than a decade after the Aryan myth of the Nazis and their mentors had been completely jettisoned by modern western historians.[20] The Paranavitana factor also had its impact on perceptions of the history of Tamils in the island.

The Peradeniya School

It was against this backdrop that a school of Sri Lankan scholars, who may rightly be called the Peradeniya school, emerged in the university at Peradeniya. They were without doubt under the shadow of Paranavitana's figure that loomed large above them. They had reservations about many of his theories and views but were unwilling to air any criticism openly. Then came, in the 1960s, Paranavitana's strange revelations about the existence of a vast amount of ancient historical information, covering a good part of the ancient world from Greece to the Southeast Asian islands, in the form of what he termed 'interlinear inscriptions', on several stone slabs in Sri Lanka.[21] The Peradeniya school hesitated to accept this but felt reluctant to reject it openly. It took a while before the Sri Lankan scholars, both historians and archaeologists, rejected Paranavitana's claims.[22] The 'interlinear inscriptions' were finally declared as non-existent records. This made a big dent in Paranavitana's reputation and helped to check the influence of the Paranavitana factor.[23] By the 1970's, the Peradeniya school was well on its way to break new paths.

It is a matter of good fortune that at a time as the one that Sri Lanka has passed through in the last two decades, there were some scholars of exceptional ability and scientific frame of mind who, with their profound knowledge of history, archaeology and other related disciplines as well as an outlook that took into account both the Sinhala and Tamil sources, stood at the frontline of the battle against the charlatans and pseudo-scholars who had been striving hard to undermine the admirable directions that the Peradeniya school had begun to give to Sri Lankan historical research. Undoubtedly, the leading light of the Peradeniya school was Leslie Gunawardana.[24] Another eminent scholar, Sudharshan Seneviratne, though not a product of Peradeniya, joined the Peradeniya school and helped to break the insularity of Sri Lankan archaeology. His most significant contribution came in the form of his monumental research, *Social Base of Early Buddhism in South East India and Sri Lanka*, paving the way for important re-interpretations concerning the earliest phase of Sri Lankan history.[25] In this connection, two other scholars from outside the Peradeniya school, Senake Bandaranayake and Siran Deraniyagala, deserve special mention for their contributions to raising the standard of archaeological and historical scholarship in Sri Lanka. The present work benefits from the researches of all these scholars.

Ethnic conflict and history writing

The high standards of historical scholarship set up by the Peradeniya school, however, could not prevent ethnic and nationalist bias creeping into scholarly writings and, with the intensification of the ethnic conflict in the island, unashamedly blowing up into ugly proportions. Long before the birth of the Peradeniya school, the growth of nationalist sentiments at the beginning of the twentieth century was accompanied by the sowing of the seeds of ethnic bias in the nascent historical writings of that time. As the possibility of gaining greater political rights from the colonial power came into the view, the past became important in staking claims to a larger share of the cake. Since the country was clearly multi-ethnic, establishing who was present first was seen as crucial in these claims. As usual in such circumstances, history and archaeology as well as linguistics were called to the aid of the contenders. Ethnic bias in historical writings was sometimes subtle, at other times crude. But with an open conflict breaking out in the 1970s, ethnic bias in some writings became ugly.[26]

The comments of Leslie Gunawardana on this situation are worthy of note as they give an indication of the seriousness of the problem:

> With the intensification of the ethnic conflict and the accompanying polarization within the academic community, scholars have been coming under increasing pressure to develop representations of the past which lend legitimacy to the claims of the ethnic group to which they belong. While they have been expected to challenge representations of the

> past in works of writers in rival ethnic groups, it has become difficult and, in certain situations, even risky for them to challenge or to be critical of representations being utilized by their own ethnic groups. This development brought in its wake a notable relaxation of intellectual rigour in research.[27]

Any objective reader of the recent historical writings on Sri Lanka will not fail to see that the ethnic conflict between the Sinhalese and the Tamils has thrown up a breed of pseudo-historians who are seriously undermining the traditions that the Peradeniya school has been seeking to establish. When one looks at the pseudo-historical writings on ancient Sri Lanka, one is reminded of similar writings in Europe in the period of nineteenth century nationalism. As the pungent comment of the British historian Norman Davies on the latter seems to apply almost wholesale to the current Sri Lankan experience, it is worth quoting it at length:

> … present-day nations and regimes have a strong inclination to believe that they and their forebears have 'possessed' their present territory since time immemorial. Belief in the unbreakable bond between 'Blood and Soil' was one of the most powerful psychological motors of nineteenth century nationalism. Europeans were thoroughly indoctrinated with the notion that every inch of ground within their national frontiers was eternally 'theirs' and hence inherently 'French' or 'German' or 'Polish' or whatever. …prehistory and archaeology have inevitably developed in an intensely political context. Nationalism has never been far beneath the surface. Immense efforts have been made to discover a past to which modern people could relate, and, where necessary, to exclude those elements of the past that were politically inconvenient.[28]

Historians admit that 'history is inextricably bound to contemporary politics.' This is true of identity history as it is of any other. The past becomes an essential argument in the debates on contemporary issues. In this respect, the words of the veteran historian of our times, Eric Hobsbawm, are worth pondering upon:

> ...all human beings, collectivities and institutions need a past, but it is only occasionally the past uncovered by historical research. The standard example of an identity culture which anchors itself to the past by means of myths dressed up as history is nationalism. Of this Ernest Renan observed more than a century ago, 'Forgetting, even getting history wrong, is an essential factor in the formation of a nation, which is why the progress of historical studies is often a danger to nationality'. For nations are historically novel entities pretending to have existed for a very long time. Inevitably the nationalist version of their history consists of anachronism, omission, decontextualization and, in extreme cases, lies. To a lesser extent this is true of identity history, old or new.[29]

Scholars recognize that the past is not just a subject for academic study. 'The past is politically highly charged, ideologically powerful and significant' and almost everyone has some interest in it. Archaeologists admit that 'Increasingly archaeology plays an important role in the definition of national identity' and that in many countries 'the ancient past is used in some ways to legitimate the present and is drawn upon to reinforce a sense of national greatness and identity'. Following on this, 'nationalist aims, sectarian objectives, and political agendas are often served by the partisan interpretation and presentation of what is alleged to be the cultural heritage.'[30] The political and ideological uses of the past, particularly in the last few decades in countries where ethnic conflicts and identity concerns have led to violent eruptions, have put academic historians and archaeologists under great pressure. And, as often happens in times of major conflicts, some (or too many?) of them have unwittingly fallen victims to political pressures.

It is all too easy to fall into the trap of ethnic bias unwittingly in times of ethnic conflict. The biased statements of the historians are often seized upon by the non-professionals and turned into propaganda. As Hobsbawm says, historians 'have a responsibility to historical facts in general, and for criticizing the politico-ideological abuse of history in particular'. He spells out this responsibility in the following words: 'To insist on the supremacy of evidence, and the centrality of the distinction between verifiable historical fact and fiction, is only one of the ways of exercising the historian's responsibility' and adds a second responsibility: 'The deconstruction of political and social myths dressed up as history has long been part of the historian's professional duties, independent of his or her sympathies.' Hobsbawm has an advice and a warning that need to be heeded by young historians in conflict-torn Sri Lanka at a time when the country appears to have taken the first steps towards reconstruction. The advice is: 'Historians, however microcosmic, must be for universalism, not out of loyalty to an ideal to which many of us remain attached but because it is the necessary condition for understanding the history of humanity, including that of any special section of humanity. For all human collectivities necessarily are and have been part of a larger and more complex world. A history which is designed *only* for Jews (or African-Americans, or Greeks, or women, or proletarians, or homosexuals) cannot be good history, though it may be comforting history to those who practise it.' And the warning is: 'Unfortunately, as the situation in large parts of the world at the end of our millennium demonstrates, bad history is not harmless history. It is dangerous. The sentences typed on apparently innocuous keyboards may be sentences of death.'[31]

There is no need to give any prominence to the writings of pseudo-historians and fringe archaeologists who have emerged on both sides of the ethnic divide. Readers will understand if these writers have not been taken seriously in any discussion in this work. As Sudharshan Seneviratne has rightly pointed out, 'such lumpen intellectuals … belong in the dustbin of history.'[32] But there is the need to be concerned about their misrepresentations of history. Some of these are based on misinterpretations of significant literary and archaeological sources of ancient Sri Lankan history. It is important to set our faces against such unscientific misrepresentations of the past.

PLATE 1.
The skeletal remains of an Early Iron Age chief (*Ko*) from Anaikoddai, Jaffna District.
This is the only known burial of an EIA chief anywhere in the SISL region. The name and the non-Brahmi symbols used by the chief are engraved on the signet ring buried with the skeleton. (Excavated in 1980 by a team from the University of Jaffna headed by the author.)

***Photo**: December 1980. Courtesy: P. Ragupathy.*

PLATE 2.
The Brahmi inscription and the non-Brahmi symbols on the seal belonging to an Early Iron Age chief, from Anaikoddai. See Appendix VIII.

Photo: February 2005, by K. Sanchayan.

PLATE 3.
An Early Iron Age potsherd from Kantarodai, Jaffna District, with a Brahmi graffito. See Appendix VI.

***Photo:** 1970, University of Pennsylvania Museum Project. Courtesy: Department of Archaeology.*

Who came first?

With regard to the attempts to establish which ethnic group was in Sri Lanka before the others, it would not be out of place to quote the view of one of the most renowned historians of ancient India, Romila Thapar, in respect of similar controversies in India into which she herself has often been dragged:

> One of the current debates relating to the beginnings of Indian history involves both archaeology and linguistics, and attempts to differentiate between indigenous and alien peoples. But history has shown that communities and their identities are neither permanent nor static. Their composition changes either with the arrival of new people in an area, and the possible new technologies that are introduced, or by historical changes of a more local but far-reaching kind…To categorize some people as indigenous and others as alien, to argue about the identity of the first inhabitants of the subcontinent, and to try and sort out these categories for the remote past, is to attempt the impossible. It is precisely in the intermixture of peoples and ideas that the genesis of cultures is to be found. Such arguments arise from the concerns of present-day privilege and power, rather than from the reading of history.[33]

Indeed it is contemporary political motives rather than historical evidence that lie behind the arguments about the ethnicity of the first inhabitants of Sri Lanka. What has become a matter of concern for the future of historical scholarship is that some professional historians and archaeologists are unable to free themselves of such bias.

Mahānāma

In this unfavourable climate of the ethnic conflict, as one would expect, history has been distorted and ancient historical sources have been unfairly used or condemned. One of the notable victims of this unfair treatment is Mahānāma, the author of the *Mahāvaṃsa*, the

Pali chronicle that forms the main source for the ancient history of Sri Lanka. Many have been indulging in what Sudharshan Seneviratne has termed 'Mahāvaṃsa-bashing'. While, on the one hand, Sinhalacentrist writers have 'used' Mahānāma to present their own misrepresentations of history, anti-Sinhalese extremists, on the other, have 'abused' Mahānāma without even reading the *Mahāvaṃsa.* In between, some others who have engaged in anthropological and archaeological as well as historical research are also guilty of unfairly judging the work of Mahānāma.[34]

The *Mahāvaṃsa* should be given credit for what it is and not be criticised for failing to be what it ought to be.[35] Mahānāma was not writing history the way we in contemporary society want it. The *Mahāvaṃsa* may be described as a chronicle of that famous Buddhist institution Mahāvihāra.[36] It tells us about its foundation and the rulers who patronized this institution. It chronicles some of the main events in the kingdom of these patrons, the domain they controlled from Anuradhapura. This domain was, in the period covered by the *Mahāvaṃsa,* never the whole country now known as Sri Lanka. Whatever information we glean about other matters from the *Mahāvaṃsa* is incidental – about other Buddhist and non-Buddhist institutions, other religions (like Jainism), and other kingdoms in the island.[37]

Using the *Mahāvaṃsa* as their main source, most historians of Sri Lanka tend to consider this work as a chronicle of the whole island. That they do this is not the fault of Mahānāma. The author is quite clear as to his purpose and audience. He wrote the chronicle for "the serene joy and emotion of the pious" (*sujanappasādasaṃvegatthāya kate*).[38] He was not an official scribe recording the events of his monarch's reign for the benefit of posterity.

Mahānāma has followed a chronicle style for his account of the reigns of all rulers, except one, after Devānampiya Tissa, the founder of the Mahāvihāra monastery, to Mahāsena, in whose time the monastery was destroyed. The exception is the reign of Duṭṭhagāmaṇī Abhaya. The account of this reign is the one most misinterpreted in the context of relations between Sinhalese and Tamils. This section of the *Mahāvaṃsa* deviates from the rest of the work in style and content. The manner in which it is introduced gives the impression that it is a later interpolation. It may well be that this section was not written by Mahānāma.[39] Even if it were the work of the same author, there is no ground for accusing Mahānāma for the anti-Tamil misrepresentations of the twentieth century for which the section on Duṭṭhagāmaṇī has been used. It will be shown later in this work that Mahānāma (or whoever was the author of the section on Duṭṭhagāmaṇī), far from being the Sinhalese nationalist chronicler who presented Duṭṭhagāmaṇī as a great Sinhalese hero, has been quite fair in his account of the conflict between two rulers, one of whom happened to be an adventurous Tamil prince and the other an ambitious Sinhalese prince. What was important for the author was that one was a great Buddhist whose benefactions, especially to the Mahāvihāra fraternity, made him worthy of being treated as an epic hero. However, he had great admiration for the just rule of the other, Eḷāra, including this king's patronage of Buddhism, and did not conceal his amazement that someone who was not a Buddhist could rule with such justice towards 'friend and foe' alike. He could only explain the miraculous powers attributed to Eḷāra in popular myths to the king 'being free of the blemish of resorting to injustice.'[40] These are not words from someone who intended to portray Eḷāra as an enemy of the Sinhalese people.

The account of the Duṭṭagāmaṇī - Eḷāra conflict in the *Mahāvaṃsa* has formed the basis of twentieth century perceptions of the relations between the Sinhalese and the Tamils in ancient Sri Lanka. Interested persons have been reading into it the ideas of their time. Even reputed scholars seem to have been carried away by the nationalistic feelings of their time when they used the *Mahāvaṃsa* account of the above conflict in writing the history of ancient Sri Lanka. Perhaps the best example for this is Paranavitana's chapter entitled 'The Triumph of Duṭṭhagāmaṇī' in the *University of Ceylon History of Ceylon*.[41] This detailed account of Duṭṭhagāmaṇī's battles follows closely the account of the *Mahāvaṃsa*. The vivid narrative in the *Mahāvaṃsa* reads like an eyewitness account.[42] It is not possible to assume that such eyewitness descriptions of the battles had been preserved from the time of Duṭṭhagāmaṇī and that the author of the *Mahāvaṃsa*, writing nearly six centuries later, made use of eyewitness accounts for his narration. Following the epic style of the Sanskrit *kāvya*, the author of the *Mahāvaṃsa* was only recreating the battles with his knowledge of contemporary warfare or epic wars.[43] It would be hard to accept the *Mahāvaṃsa* description of the campaigns of Duṭṭhagāmaṇī as historically reliable.

Further, Paranavitana describes the battles waged by Duṭṭhagāmaṇī as 'a campaign of liberation' aimed at 'delivering the Sinhalese from foreign domination'. These are ideas that belong to a period closer to our time than to the early historic period in which Eḷāra and Duṭṭhagāmaṇī, like many other rulers in the island at that time, were waging battles for territorial power. The *Mahāvaṃsa* author, far from portraying the reign of Eḷāra as a period of foreign domination from which the Sinhalese were waiting to be liberated, expresses in unequivocal terms that it was a time of just rule and that the king, though not a Buddhist himself, followed the tradition (*cāritaṃ anupālayaṃ*) of patronizing the Buddhist Sangha and considered himself as deserving the death penalty when he had accidentally damaged a Buddhist monument.[44] Mahānāma is not to be blamed for the interpretations given by Paranavitana and others. Duṭṭhagāmaṇī's time was a period when chieftains in the whole region, in Sri Lanka and south India, were engaged in bloody battles against one another in a bid for territorial expansion and extension of power. The conquest and rule of Anuradhapura by a chieftain from some part of south India was no more foreign than that of a chieftain from Rohaṇa.

It must not be forgotten that Mahānāma presents both the victor and the vanquished as noble humans. Duṭṭhagāmaṇī is portrayed as one who displayed great nobility in victory, not only through a deep feeling of remorse at the killing of many humans in battle but also through an act, unparalleled in Sri Lankan history, of honouring his enemy in death by building a *cetiya* (shrine) at the spot where he was cremated and ordaining worship.[45] What is of even greater significance for the defence of Mahānāma is the fact that this pious author deviates for a moment from the narration of historical events to tell the reader something that was happening even in his own time (more than six centuries later) in regard to Duṭṭhagāmaṇī's injunction to his people to worship the Eḷāra monument. 'And even to this day the princes of Lanka, when they draw near to this place, are wont to silence their music because of this worship' are the words with which Mahānāma cnds his account of the conflict between Duṭṭhagāmaṇī and Eḷāra. Would the author of the *Mahāvaṃsa* have gone out of his way to say this if he had considered Eḷāra as an alien intruder whom the people were happy to see dead?

The assumption forming the basis of Paranavitana's statements is that the people of the kingdom ruled by the Anuradhapura kings and the inhabitants of Rohaṇa and other southern chiefdoms were all Sinhalese and that any ruler other than a Sinhalese in control of Anuradhapura or other chiefdoms was a foreigner. As will be seen later, such an assumption is not supported by archaeological or epigraphical evidence. In the centuries before the Common Era, there were many ethnic groups in the island and one of them was the group known as the Dameḍas in inscriptions and Damiḷas in the Pali chronicles, identified without any controversy as the Tamils. It is possible that many of the ethnic groups were large enough to have their own chiefdoms. The leaders of these chiefdoms as well as others who were influential could have aspired for the kingship at Anuradhapura. Sena and Guttaka, the first Tamils mentioned in the Pali chronicles as having gained power at Anuradhapura, were from a merchant family and are not even described as invaders (although modern writers unquestioningly assume that they were from outside Sri Lanka, presumably because they are referred to in the chronicles as Tamils and sons of a trader).

The chiefdoms and kingdoms that arose in Sri Lanka and south India in the centuries before the Common Era were in a common region of cultural, social, economic and political interaction. It was a time when the more powerful chieftains and kings were attempting to gain power in neighbouring territories. Just as princes from

Rohaṇa aspired for control of Anuradhapura, those in the Cōḷa capital aspired to defeat the rulers at the Pāṇḍya capital in south India. There were times when some of them crossed over to Anuradhapura with the same motive. Such dynastic conflicts are all too well known to ancient historians and are not to be interpreted as 'foreign invasions'. As for the ordinary people, they were not supporters or opponents of one side or the other in these political games. If contemporary writers have attempted to read ideas and prejudices of their times in the ancient chronicles, the authors of the chronicles are not to be blamed for that.

Recent Archaeological Discoveries

In recent years, many notable developments have taken place in Sri Lankan archaeology and these have no doubt helped immensely in shaping the perspectives adopted in this work. The most significant work relating to the uncovering of the past in the last four decades has been undoubtedly in the area of archaeological excavations. The interest shown by scholars in some western, particularly American, universities, together with the establishment of departments of archaeology in the universities of Sri Lanka, and the expansion of the government Department of Archaeology, culminating in the UNESCO-Cultural Triangle Project in the ancient cities, have contributed to this situation. The universities and the Department of Archaeology were fortunate in having a good team of skilled archaeologists whose work provided a silver lining to the dark clouds that hung over historical research on account of the ethnic conflict in the island.

The result of this recent archaeological research has no doubt been the unravelling of new evidence relating to the prehistoric, protohistoric and early historic periods. For the first time, evidence relating to the megalithic burials of the centuries before the Common Era was discovered in the Northern Province, particularly in the Jaffna peninsula, and for the first time data from the earliest levels of settlement was uncovered through excavations at Anuradhapura.

Among the major archaeological projects that helped to extend the frontiers of our knowledge of Sri Lanka's ancient past in the last four decades were the following: the University of Pennsylvania Project headed by Vimala Begley and including Bennet Bronson and K. A. R. Kennedy in 1970 under which excavations were conducted at Pomparippu (in which the present writer had the good fortune to participate for the full period of the excavations) and at Kantarodai; Siran Deraniyagala's excavations at Anuradhapura from 1972 to 1990; the UNESCO-Cultural Triangle Project beginning from 1981; P. Ragupathy's archaeological work in the Jaffna District in 1980-81; the University of Chicago Project headed by John Carswell and including Martha Prickett under which excavations were conducted at Mantai in 1980-84; the excavations in 1988-91at Ibbankatuva conducted by a team from the Post-Graduate Institute of Archaeology of the University of Kelaniya, headed by Senake Bandaranayake; and the excavations at Salgaha Watta (Anuradhapura) carried out by the British Anuradhapura Project (Robin Coningham, F.R. Allchin et al) in 1990-91. Needless to say, all the discoveries and researches resulting from these projects have helped in the adoption of new perspectives in the writing of this work.[46]

Unfortunately in Sri Lanka, as in many other countries, archaeological interpretations have often been made in a political context. In some of the most important archaeological writings, one sees a 'simplification of the archaeological material and a tendency to play into the hands of those who seek a narrow-minded interpretation'.[47] While the archaeological material shows a diversity in protohistoric cultures in the island (and in south India, too), there have been attempts to use this material to discover a homogeneous past. The following comment about the work of some archaeologists in India and Japan is applicable to the pursuits of certain scholars in Sri Lanka, too:

> In trying to get at the 'Indian behind the artefact' however, aracheologists are often lured into the trap of equating their archaeological classifications to groups of people. The device

most often employed is ethnicity, and the result is an unhealthy pre-occupation with the ethnic group...A large part of the archaeological endeavour becomes oriented towards the search for ethnic origins, a dubious pursuit that often has been – and continues to be – hi-jacked and manipulated for contemporary political expediency, not least in Japan.[48]

The comments of Norman Davies, in relation to the work of some archaeologists in Central Europe, also seem quite relevant here:

> Prussian archaeologists would prove beyond question that the prehistoric monuments of Prussia's eastern borderlands were indisputably Germanic. A few decades later Polish archaeologists working with identical material established that the selfsame monuments were indisputably, and *ab origine*, Slavonic. Neither side paused to ask whether those monuments were not, at least in part, Celtic.[49]

Viewing the conflicting claims of Sri Lankan archaeologists, an archaeologist from outside, Robin Coningham, was prompted to make the following comment recently:

> Claims and counter-claims of an Indo-Aryan or proto-Dravidian linguistic foundation for the island (Deraniyagala 1992: 747; Ragupathy 1987: 202) ignore the fact that linguistic changes can occur without recourse to population changes.[50]

Epigraphical Discoveries

In the absence of a systematic epigraphical survey, inscriptions outside the ancient cities have generally been chance discoveries. This is particularly true of Tamil inscriptions. However, some exploration work undertaken by the present writer in the 1960s and 1970s in the northern and eastern parts of Sri Lanka helped to bring to light significant Tamil inscriptions of the eleventh and twelfth centuries. For the first time, Tamil inscriptions of the Cōḻas were discovered in the Northern Province in this period. Among the new Tamil inscriptions discovered in the Eastern Province was one that provided information about the political arrangements made by the Cōḻas to rule the conquered territories of the island in the eleventh century. In the Northern Province, a Brāhmī potsherd inscription and an interesting Brāhmī inscription on a steatite seal were discovered, making them the earliest written records found so far in the Jaffna peninsula.[51] In the 1980s and 1990s, more inscriptions relevant to this work have come to light in the area of the UNESCO-Cultural Triangle Project and elsewhere.

Epigraphical researches in the last three decades have also resulted in some important re-interpretations of the evidence of early Brāhmī inscriptions in Sri Lanka. The views of W. Saddhamangala Karunaratne on the similarities between the Tamil-Brāhmī script of south India and the early Brāhmī script of Sri Lanka and those of Sudharshan Seneviratne with regard to the interpretation of certain terms in the Sri Lankan Brāhmī inscriptions in the light of evidence from Tamil sources have been very relevant to the present study.[52] The contributions of Iravatham Mahadevan, one of the leading Indian epigraphists of our time and indisputably the foremost authority on Tamil-Brāhmī inscriptions, have also helped to use the evidence of the earliest epigraphs in south India and to understand the flow of influences not only from south India to Sri Lanka but also in the opposite direction.[53]

An interesting aspect of the epigraphical research in recent years is the attention focused on graffiti found on potsherds. In recent decades, a large number of interesting inscribed potsherds with Brāhmī letters and non-Brāhmī symbols have been discovered at archaeological sites in south India and Sri Lanka. Some have been found even in distant Middle Eastern ports frequented by traders from this region. Much attention has been focused on these finds. These hitherto less utilized sources provide interesting evidence of cultural and economic interaction between south India and Sri Lanka and the long distance trade relations of this region with the Graeco-

Roman world. Recently K. Rajan and Osmund Bopearachchi made the first serious attempt to compare the graffiti marks found on pottery from a site in Tamil Nadu with those from a site in Sri Lanka revealing remarkable similarities.[54] Scholars studying the pottery graffiti from various sites in Tamil Nadu have claimed in recent years that some of the graffiti reveal unmistakable evidence of the script and language of the Sri Lankan Brāhmī inscriptions.[55] In the northern part of Sri Lanka, P. Pushparatnam has brought to light a number of potsherds with Brāhmī writing, including some read as Tamil-Brāhmī inscriptions.[56] Perhaps the most exciting discovery of potsherds with Brāhmī writing comes from Anuradhapura where Siran Deraniyagala, F. R. Allchin and Robin Coningham have unearthed potsherds with Brāhmī writing going back to a period before the Asokan records.[57]

Recent Advances in Other Fields

Classical Studies

Recent researches into the material relating to Sri Lanka in the ancient Greek and Latin writings have also thrown fresh light on the ancient history of the country. In this respect, the publications of D. P. M. Weerakkody, an erudite and discerning Sri Lankan scholar of Western Classics, deserve very special mention.[58] Another Sri Lankan scholar, Osmund Bopearachchi, has also made valuable contributions in this field in recent years.[59]

Numismatics

Notable evidence relating to the present study has also come from numismatic sources. Again, Osmund Bopearachchi (together with Rajah Wickremasinghe) has brought to light Graeco-Roman as well as Indian and Sri Lankan coins of the early historic period of the island. These are of great significance to the study of Sri Lanka's ancient history. Among these are coins with early Brāhmī legends in Tamil, the like of which had not been discovered earlier.[60] Ancient coins bearing relevance to the present study have also been found by P. Pushparatnam in the Northern Province.[61]

Historical Linguistics

The enormous interest in anthropological and sociological researches in Asian societies evinced by European and American universities in the last four decades has led to important studies on Sri Lanka by American, European and Sri Lankan scholars. These studies have helped to provide new perspectives for historical research. While there has been a similar surge in linguistic studies, very little in the field of historical linguistics and comparative philology has been accomplished. These latter are areas of great relevance to the study of the island's past, especially for the identification of the elements that played an important part in the evolution of the Sinhala language and people. In recent decades a few linguists have made some notable investigations in this direction. The work of M. H. Peter Silva, James Gair, M. W. Sugathapala de Silva and W. S. Karunatilleke are noteworthy. Like M. H. Peter Silva (who was able to take W. F. Gunawardhana's pioneering work of the 1920s much further with better scientific training in the 1960s), and C. E. Godakumbure before him, M. W. S. de Silva and James Gair, in the course of their valuable contributions to Sri Lankan linguistics in the last quarter of the twentieth century, have pointed out Dravidian elements in ancient Sinhala and, what is more important, recognized that a language or languages that did not belong to either the Indo-Aryan sub-family or the Dravidian family existed in the island before Tamil and Sinhala came to be spoken there.[62] Regrettably very little scientific investigation has been undertaken in regard to the languages spoken in the island before the spread of Prakrit and Dravidian languages. No doubt the lack of evidence relating to the prehistoric languages has been a serious handicap to such research. But advances in historical linguistics may help to identify those elements in Sinhala and Tamil that go back to the prehistoric languages.

That there were prehistoric languages unrelated to the Indo-Aryan or Dravidian families is undeniable and yet this is conveniently ignored in the discussion of the language of the earliest inscriptional records of Sri Lanka. Many obscure words in these epigraphs are traced strenuously to Indo-Aryan roots or, increasingly in some recent studies, to Dravidian without much effort. The possibility that some at least of these words may derive from the languages of the Mesolithic people is not even considered. Not only to the evolution of Sinhala but also to the development of Tamil, these early languages would no doubt have made some contributions. As Gair has rightly pointed out, 'it is often overlooked in this regard that there was clearly some other, apparently non-Dravidian, language (or languages) spoken on the island before the advent of Sinhala. ' In his view, the role of the earlier language or languages 'may well have been more than is generally recognized'.[63] M. W. S. de Silva has also drawn attention to 'a high-frequency segment of the Sinhalese vocabulary, especially words for parts of the body and the like: e. g. *oluva* 'head', *bella* 'neck', *kakula* 'leg', *kalava* 'thigh', etc., which are neither Sanskritic nor Tamil in origin'.[64] For the moment the historian has to await the researches of historical linguists to know something about these contributions by prehistoric languages.

Archaeology of the Living Body

We are living in exciting times. There are amazing developments in practically every field of study. Archaeology is one of those sciences in the forefront in this respect. The thrilling advances in genetics have already begun to help the archaeologist with DNA evidence in identifying origins and distribution of human populations. Already in some countries, the evidence of mtDNA variation and Y-chromosome, for instance, is being used in the investigation of language replacement that took place several centuries ago. Before long, it may be possible to apply these scientific methods to find answers to some of the questions relating to the origin and evolution of the ethnic communities in Sri Lanka. Already some studies have been undertaken in this direction.[65] However, these are not included in this work. Genetic evidence is a growth area of archaeological research and there is much work to be done in this field before meaningful use could be made of such evidence.

Concepts

An island close to a subcontinent: a unique development

Sri Lanka's physical feature as an island and its distance from the Indian subcontinent are undoubtedly two of the geographical factors that have had a great influence in shaping the island's history. Islands that are close to extensive landmasses or subcontinents, if they are at a distance that helps to maintain contacts with the mainland but are not close enough to be overwhelmed by influences or populations from that mainland, are continuously at the receiving end of settlers and influences from that mainland as well as from other directions but evolve a distinct identity which they tend to guard jealously. The process of assimilation of settlers and cultures goes on throughout history. Where more than one ethnic or cultural identity has emerged, assimilation into the major identity continues, even if there are conflicts between that and other identities. This is seen in the history of major island countries like Britain, Japan and Sri Lanka.

The difference that distance from a mainland makes to the history of an island or group of islands can be seen in the contrast between Sri Lanka's history and the history of the Maldive Islands. The latter country has been at the receiving end of major influences from south India, particularly Kerala, and Sri Lanka.[66] The Maldives has also received significant influences, especially religious, from West Asia. But its distance from the Indian subcontinent has allowed it sufficient freedom to develop its own language (from a dialect of Sinhala) and a homogenous culture. If Sri Lanka were located at that distance from India, its history may have been comparable to that of the Maldives.

Sea as a unifier: the area of SISL as one cultural region

One of the basic concepts adopted in this study is that of the sea separating Sri Lanka and south India as a unifier and the lands on either side of it as parts of a single cultural region. In the core of this region would be Sri Lanka, Kerala and Tamil Nadu. At the periphery would be the southern parts of Karnataka and Andhra Pradesh. The Maldives would also be within this region but at the periphery. For the sake of convenience, this region is referred to here as the South India-Sri Lanka (SISL) region *(Map 1)*. It will be shown that migrations and cultural influences were flowing across the narrow sea in both directions from prehistoric times. Until the emergence of major polities embracing large parts of this region, it is not proper to speak of the movement of people or flow of influences or political incursions from one part to another as foreign. These were interactions within the region. As Sudharshan Seneviratne has emphasized, the island's 'close proximity to the southern fringe of the subcontinent made for the incorporation of Sri Lanka into the cultural vortex of the neighbouring landmass.'[67] The acceptance of this geographical reality will help to view the events of the prehistoric and protohistoric period in this region with a different perspective – a perspective that does not treat south India as foreign in relation to Sri Lanka.

Language replacement: Renfrew's theory of Elite Dominance

An important concept used in this study relates to language replacement in the Early Iron Age (EIA). Clearly the prehistoric languages spoken by the Mesolithic people in Sri Lanka were replaced, no doubt gradually, in the protohistoric period. For a long time historians of Sri Lanka have assumed that there was a total change of population at the beginning of the protohistoric period as a result of a significant migration. Recent developments in archaeology go against such an assumption. As the archaeologist Colin Renfrew has pointed out, 'one of the most striking shifts in archaeological thought in the past few years has been the realization that there have been far fewer wholesale migrations of people than had once been thought.'[68] Earlier, language change was often attributed to population change. Archaeologists now accept that language change can occur without population change. In his seminal work, *Archaeology and Language*, Renfrew presents his challenging models of language change. One of them is the now well-known model of elite dominance.[69] Renfrew describes this model as follows:

> It assumes...the arrival from outside the territory of a relatively small group of highly-organized people, speaking a dfferent language, who because of their military effectiveness are able to dominate the existing population, and bring it into effective subjection. The two languages will then exist side-by-side for some time, with many of the population, probably both the indigenous and the immigrant, becoming bilingual. In some circumstances the newcomers will be assimilated and their foreign language forgotten. In others it is the language of the newcomers which prevails, while that of the original population, although they were the more numerous, dies out. That is a case of language replacement.[70]

Other scholars have argued that there is also the possibility of language replacement occurring as a result of prolonged trade contact. The archaeologist Coningham has pointed out this possibility and drawn attention to the argument of the linguist Sherratt that 'trade networks involving directional exchange' could have led to slow language replacement.[71] While admitting that 'it is still unclear which process, or combination of processes, were the cause of Sri Lankan language replacement', Coningham has argued that all of Renfrew's models for linguistic change 'may have performed a function in the process of language replacement.'[72]

The concept of elite dominance resulting from long-distance trade contacts is adopted here to explain the gradual language replacement that took place in Sri Lanka in the protohistoric period. Long-distance trade with western and eastern India brought Prakrit-speakers while trade interests as well as other factors led to the dominance of Tamil-speakers in certain parts of the island. One cannot agree more with Coningham's comment that 'there is no reason to suppose that the processes at work in one part of the island were the same as in other parts.'[73]

Evolution of major identities: a local development

The Sinhalese are an ethnic identity that evolved in Sri Lanka through the assimilation of various segmentary/ tribal and ethnic communities that occupied the island at the beginning of the EIA, about five or six centuries before the Common Era. Long distance trade brought traders who spoke Prakrit, the *lingua franca* of the South Asian region at that time. Shortly before the third century BCE, it is possible that Buddhist and Jaina monks, too, arrived in the island in the wake of trade. This would have strengthened the position of Prakrit as the language of the elite. Later, the adoption of Buddhism by the ruler at Anuradhapura and the people under his rule, the organization of a strong Buddhist church and the use of Prakrit as the written language of the elites helped to forge different communities together and to evolve a common language with elements from the local languages. The diversity of cultures in the island created the need for the use of Prakrit as the unifying language. As can be learned from the history of many other countries, such as Britain, language in this early period cannot be equated with ethnic group. Those who argue in favour of 'Indo-Aryans' settling in Sri Lanka assume that the Prakrit-speakers who came to the island were the people who introduced the Indo-Aryan languages to north India. It is often forgotten that in the subcontinent, too, Indo-Aryan languages spread through a process of language replacement among myriad cultural groups that were already settled there.[74]

The Tamils of Sri Lanka evolved as a second ethnic group. Their evolution was parallel to that of the Sinhalese. The earliest inscriptions and the early Pali chronicles attest to the presence of the Tamils (Dameḍas/Damiḷas) in the EIA. The spread of cultural influences from the Tamil-speaking region of south India, possibly including the spread of the Tamil language, in the same period, is evidenced by archaeology. It would appear that Tamil-speaking traders formed the elite in northern Sri Lanka and their dominance began the process of replacing the local language or languages by Tamil. The proximity of northern Sri Lanka to Tamil Nadu and the frequent rise of dominant political entities there reinforced the local Tamil-speaking population in considerable numbers, thus working against the total assimilation of the Tamils into the majority Sinhalese group. The Tamils who lived in the southern parts of the island were assimilated into the Sinhalese population. This is a process that has continued until modern times. In the northwest, north and east, however, various ethnic groups, including the Telugus, Keralas, Kannadas, Sinhalese and, later, even some Malay (Javaka) elements, came under the dominant influence of Tamil-speakers and contributed to the evolution of a distinct Tamil community there.

Continuity of population: dates back to the Mesolithic period

While the spread of the Prakrit and Tamil languages as well as the introduction of Buddhist and Hindu religions have been instrumental in bringing about major cultural changes, it cannot be denied that there has always been a basic continuity of population. While there is much to be done in this area of biological continuum, the few scholars who have already carried out some investigations in this field have reported the existence of a basic continuity of population.[75] The archaeological and anthropological evidence that points to the substantial genetic continuity from prehistoric times would mean that the prehistoric people of Sri Lanka are the common ancestors of the modern-day Sri Lankans. In that sense, the origins of the two major ethnic groups go very much deeper than the time when Prakrit and Tamil influences began.

A wider context: South Asia and Southeast Asia

The developments in ancient Sri Lanka have to be viewed in the wider context of South Asian and Southeast Asian history. For a long time, scholars have been writing about the events and developments in the protohistoric and early historic periods in Sri Lanka without reference to parallel developments in neighbouring south India or Southeast Asia. Such an insular approach had affected the interpretations given and inhibited a proper understanding of the developments. Fortunately, this trend has begun to change in recent years. In this respect, the researches of Sudharshan Seneviratne, in particular, and Leslie Gunawardana have thrown new light on the early history of the island. These two scholars have viewed the developments in Sri Lanka in the larger background of South Asia with special focus on south India. They both have used Sinhala and Pali sources together with Tamil sources and combined archaeological field work in south India and Sri Lanka in a manner not previously attempted by other historians of the island. Consequently they have succeeded in bringing new perspectives to the study of Sri Lankan history.

As much as the South Asian background is important for a better understanding of developments in Sri Lanka, the Southeast Asian context is of significance especially in the prehistoric and protohistoric periods. The movement of people in prehistoric times and the development of long distance trade dominated by Prakrit-speakers from western and eastern India, linking South Asia and Southeast Asia, did not bypass Sri Lanka. When one considers the westward movement of Austroasiatic-speakers and Austronesian-speakers from Southeast Asia in prehistoric times, one is inclined to think that these migrations had also touched Sri Lanka. Austronesian-speakers had crossed the Indian Ocean and gone as far as Madagascar. 'That some element of these', as Senake

Bandaranayake says, 'must have reached the shores of Sri Lanka is very likely'.[76] After all, it is now recognized that Southeast Asia 'served, over a timespan of at least 40,000 years, as the ultimate source-region for the populations of Australia and the Pacific Islands: populations as diverse and as anthropologically significant today as the Aboriginal Australians, the Melanesians, the Micronesians and the Polynesians'.[77] Siran Deraniyagala and W. G. Solheim looked for evidence relating to prehistoric Austronesians along the east coast of Sri Lanka but faced negative results.[78] The evidence on this score is still elusive. But the possibility of Austroasiatic (Munda) speakers having entered Sri Lanka appears to be on firmer ground. That they had entered northwestern and eastern India from mainland Southeast Asia is now well established. They seem to have penetrated as far south as Tamil Nadu. Scholars have claimed that the Munda languages had made a significant contribution to the development of Tamil.[79] Siran Deraniyagala is inclined to accept the possibility of the language of the ancient Veddahs of Sri Lanka belonging to the Munda subfamily.[80]

Main conclusions

The main conclusions resulting from this study may be summarised as follows:

1. The southernmost parts of India, comprising mainly the modern Indian states of Kerala and Tamil Nadu and the southern parts of Karnataka and Andhra Pradesh, together with Sri Lanka formed a single cultural region (referred to in this study as the SISL region), with the Palk Strait/Gulf of Mannar as a unifier, in the prehistoric and protohistoric periods. Even after the emergence of states, there was always a two-way flow of influences, particularly in art, religion and technology, between south India and Sri Lanka. The admirable achievements in hydraulic engineering especially were the result of the transfer of technology between the two areas.

2. The two ethnic communities, Sinhalese and Sri Lankan Tamil, are ultimately descended from the Mesolithic people who occupied almost all parts of the island in prehistoric times.
3. There was no large-scale migration of either Prakrit-speakers or Tamil-speakers in the protohistoric period and there was no displacement of the Mesolithic people by newcomers.
4. Trade was the most important single factor responsible for the arrival of Prakrit-speakers from western and eastern India.
5. Prakrit-speaking traders came not only to Sri Lanka but also to south India (the SISL region) early in the first millennium BCE. By the end of that millennium, their trade had extended into Southeast Asia.
6. The rise of urban centres, and chiefdoms around them, at the ports on either side of the Palk Strait/Gulf of Mannar (particularly Tambapaṇṇi and Matirai) was the result of the long-distance trade stimulated by Prakrit-speaking traders. In the early centuries CE, a similar impact was felt in the ports of mainland Southeast Asia, leading to the rise of new chiefdoms whose rulers embraced elements of Sanskrit culture in much the same way as the lineages in the south Indian (Matirai) and Sri Lankan (Tambapaṇṇi) chiefdoms did.
7. The Mesolithic people spoke different languages, all of which were replaced as a consequence of elite dominance, in the EIA and Early Historic Period (EHP), by a Prakrit language in most parts of the island, especially in the south and the centre, and by Tamil in the northwest, north and northeast. Prakrit, as the *lingua franca* of South Asian trade, had an edge over Tamil from the very beginning. There were advantages in adopting this as an elite language and as a language of communication among different linguistic groups.
8. The evolution of the two identities as Sinhalese and Tamil, assimilating many small social and cultural groups, reached completion by 1200, although further assimilation,

development and changes would continue in the later centuries. From about this time, there is a marked geographic division between the two identities.

CHAPTER 1

PEOPLING OF THE REGION

The Common Gene Pool

"The higher culture, including the languages, brought to these regions by the Sinhalese as well as the Tamils, was adopted in varying degrees by the people of a Stone Age culture who were there before their arrival. Thus, the vast majority of the people who today speak Sinhalese or Tamil must ultimately be descended from those autochthonous people of whom we know next to nothing." S.Paranavitana, 1959, *UCHC*, I, 1: 96-97.

"It needs to be borne in mind, however, that there would have been unimpeded gene-flow between southernmost India and Sri Lanka (in both directions) from the Palaeolithic onwards, and that future research will probably reveal a whole range "of genetic clusters in the prehistoric populations of this region..." Siran Deraniyagala 1996: 3.

The Prehistoric Period

The Indian subcontinent

The story of humans in the landmass that we now call the Indian subcontinent goes back to possibly more than one million years. For the greater part of this period, more than 99% of that time, the country that we now call Sri Lanka formed part of that land mass.[1] It will not be proper to discuss the peopling of this part of the land mass with the geographical perspectives of our times, namely that of Sri Lanka as a separate country. It was about 7000 years BP that the last separation between India and Sri Lanka appears to have occurred.[2] 'The island', as K.A.R. Kennedy has described, 'is essentially a detached portion of the South Indian Deccan.'[3]

Although human activity on the subcontinent began nearly a million years ago, the spread of humans across this vast area was slow; and, for several hundred thousand years, these early humans were in the Old Stone Age. Archaeologists are not agreed on absolute dates. As in other parts of the world, there were different phases of development, from the Palaeolithic, through the Mesolithic to the Neolithic and Chalcolithic. After a very long period of evolution, there emerged in the Indus Valley the well-known civilization usually referred to as the Harappa Culture.

The beginning of the Harappan civilization is dated to about 2600 BCE.[4] As the most extensive of the ancient civilizations, this covered almost the whole of the Indus plain and extended down to western India as far as Kathiawar. By the time of this civilization, the people who were to form the basic elements of the future population of the subcontinent had spread to various parts of the region. There is no evidence so far to suggest that cultural influences spread to the SISL region from the area of the Harappan civilization before its disappearance. It is the activities of the people of the Palaeolithic and later periods in the areas lying to the east of the region of the Harappan Culture that had an impact on the SISL region.

Palaeolithic Period

Archaeologists have discovered evidence relating to hunter-gatherers of the Palaeolithic period in various parts of the subcontinent outside the area of the Harappan civilization. Indeed, the whole subcontinent is rich in artefacts belonging to the Stone Age. Palaeolithic culture in South Asia was similar to that of many other parts of the world. A simple summary of the evidence relating to the Palaeolithic period as given by F.R. Allchin and Bridget Allchin, two leading archaeologists who have studied the prehistory of South Asia almost throughout the second half of the twentieth century, is as follows:

> ...the Palaeolithic industries of the Pleistocene can be divided into three major groups, on the basis of the shape, size and methods of manufacture of the principal artefact types. The Lower Palaeolithic is characterized by hand axes, cleavers, chopping tools, and related artefact forms. Middle Palaeolithic industries are characterized by smaller, lighter tools based upon flakes struck from cores, which in some cases are carefully shaped and prepared in advance; the Upper Palaeolithic by yet lighter artefacts, and parallel-sided blades and burins.[5]

Not much can be learned about these early humans other than about their obvious activities of hunting and gathering. The techniques employed by them to make their stone tools were basically very similar to those found in West Asia, Europe and Africa. The majority of the Lower Palaeolithic artefacts were made of quartzite. Some developments began to occur in the Middle Palaeolithic period which was 'a time of regional and local diversity both in terms of stone technology and artefact types'. In the Upper Palaeolithic period, the stone industries 'represent a marked and fairly consistent change in methods of making stone tools'.[6]

Mesolithic Period

The Palaeolithic industries lasted for a very long time and about ten thousand years ago we see the beginning of new stone industries. This is generally referred to as the Mesolithic. This and other stone industries of the Holocene period represent a further development of the Palaeolithic industries, particularly microliths. By this time, there were settled communities in some parts of the subcontinent and it appears that Mesolithic communities of hunters, fishers, gatherers and pastoralists co-existed with settled communities up to the beginning of the Iron Age (about 1000 BCE) and in some places even later.[7]

In most parts of the subcontinent, except the far south, the Mesolithic Phase was succeeded by the Neolithic. In this phase, agriculture and domestication of animals assumed greater importance and revolutionised the life of the prehistoric people, leading to more settled living patterns. Important Neolithic sites have been found in the Swat Valley, the Kashmir Valley, the Belan Valley of Uttar Pradesh and in the Godavari and Krishna Valleys of peninsular India. A few Neolithic sites have come to light in northern Tamil Nadu.

The ethnic composition of the people who were in various parts of the subcontinent in the prehistoric period was not identical. Ethnologists believe that several groups moved into the subcontinent at different times. The earliest of these seems to be the Negrito type. The next important group was the Proto-Australoid, followed by the Mediterranean. In the north and northeast, the Mongoloid type was very prominent. A few decades ago, it was believed that 'the Proto-Australoid were the basic element in the Indian population' and that the languages they spoke belonged to the Austroasiatic family.[8] This view may now need revision.

Southeast Asia

The Southeast Asian background is as important as the South Asian background for a proper understanding of human settlement and flow of influences in the prehistoric period in SISL. In fact, the prehistory of Southeast Asia is considered to be of importance for the world for several reasons. According to prehistorians, the 'population of Southeast Asia around 40,000 years ago may have been predominantly Australo-Melanesian'.[9] The Negrito people who today occupy only the Andaman Islands and some parts of Malaysia, Thailand and the Philippines, 'seem to represent the modern members of an Australo-Melanesian population which may once have occupied much of the region' of Southeast Asia.[10] Since the Negritos were present in the Indian subcontinent in prehistoric times, their presence in Southeast Asia is of significance. Some of the Australo-Melanesians of Southeast Asia moved away to settle in Australia and New Guinea about 40,000 years ago. These movements are considered as 'the earliest known human sea crossings anywhere in the world'. In Peter Bellwood's words,

'Southeast Asia also provided the source-region and early environmental backdrop for the most extensive diaspora of a single ethnolinguistic group in the history of mankind – that of the speakers of the Austronesian languages, who by the early centuries CE had spread more than halfway around the world to Madagascar and Easter Island.'[11] Prehistoric movements from mainland Southeast Asia are also important for an understanding of the spread of the Austroasiatic languages, particularly Munda, in South Asia. It is now widely accepted that these languages had spread to eastern India and beyond before the spread of Indo-Aryan languages.

The population movements and developments in Southeast Asia in prehistoric times are also significant for South Asian prehistory for an understanding of some economic aspects, especially the spread of certain important plant foods. Bellwood believes that the northern part of Southeast Asia may 'hold the key to the domestication of rice', one of the most important plant foods in early south India and Sri Lanka. Southeast Asia may have also been the area where many other major plant species, including bananas, sugarcane and certain yams were domesticated.[12] In all probability, the coconut was introduced to SISL from Southeast Asia in the prehistoric period.

South India

It is in the background of the prehistory of south India that the movement of humans into Sri Lanka can be understood. In the Palaeolithic period, Sri Lanka was connected to the Indian mainland by land. 'Land connections with the mainland,' as Siran Deraniyagala has asserted, 'would of course have been of prime importance for prehistoric human settlement of the island prior to the advent of seafaring'.[13] Even after the final separation of the island around 5000 BCE, there were 'intermittent land bridges which permitted the movements of fauna from the Indian mainland into Sri Lanka.'[14]

The discovery of several Palaeolithic sites confirms the presence of humans in the southern part of the subcontinent for many millennia. Evidence of Palaeolithic industries has been found in all the states of south India. Practically all the districts in Andhra Pradesh have yielded Palaeolithic tools. In Karnataka, too, evidences of Lower, Middle and Upper Palaeolithic industries have been brought to light. In Tamil Nadu, however, Palaeolithic remains are neither abundant nor widespread. One of the main Palaeolithic sites in this state is Attirampakkam. In recent years, more evidence of Palaeolithic industries has been uncovered. However, it cannot be claimed that the prehistory of this area has been satisfactorily researched so as to arrive at definite conclusions. A number of young archaeologists are now working in this field and it may not be long before we find out more about prehistoric south India. In the present state of our knowledge, it is possible to say that the northern parts of peninsular India have yielded evidence of Palaeolithic, Mesolithic and Neolithic phases. However, the southern part of peninsular India, particularly southeastern Tamil Nadu and Sri Lanka have not as yet yielded artefacts comparable with those from the northern parts of the subcontinent. As V. Selvakumar, one of the younger archaeologists working on the prehistory of Tamil Nadu, has concluded, 'at this stage of research nothing can definitely be said about the presence of the pre-Mesolithic industries in Tamil Nadu until more clear-cut stratigraphical and topographical evidences are available'.[15]

Nonetheless, it must be added that some south Indian archaeologists have claimed that there is clear evidence of Palaeolithic industries in some parts of Tamil Nadu. Though Selvakumar is of the view that there is no clear evidence for the Lower Palaeolithic phase, Rajan has reported the discovery of a site belonging to this phase in the Dharmapuri District, while Raman has claimed that artefacts showing characteristics of the Middle Palaeolithic phase were found in T.Pudupatti and Sivarakottai.[16] In Kerala, too, the occurrence of prehistoric cultural evidences has been reported in various locations. On this basis it is claimed that the Kerala region was inhabited since the Lower Palaeolithic period (more than 300,000 years ago, in the Indian context).[17]

The discovery of Neolithic sites in some parts of Tamil Nadu has also been reported.[18] However, in the extreme south as well as in Sri Lanka the cultural phases described as Neolithic and Chalcolithic do not seem to occur. Instead, the Mesolithic phase appears to have lasted till the beginning of the Iron Age. Mesolithic sites are fairly widespread in south India, including Kerala, where there is clear evidence of the Mesolithic culture in such sites as Tenmalai (situated on a spur in the Western Ghats). Those in Tamil Nadu have received attention in recent decades and at least two areas have been studied in detail.

One of these is the Pamban coast in the Tirunelveli District (opposite the northwestern coast of Sri Lanka) where a large number of Mesolithic sites, known as the *Teri* sites, have been studied since the last quarter of the nineteenth century. F.E. Zeuner and B. Allchin, who carried out extensive studies at these sites nearly fifty years ago, have dated the Mesolithic occupation here to 4000 BCE.[19] Investigating these sites nearly three decades later, R.A.M. Gardner was inclined to assign them to an earlier period.[20] An interesting feature of the microliths from the *Teri* sites is worth noting here, as it also applies to microliths found in Sri Lanka. D.P. Agrawal has drawn attention to this feature:

> The teri microliths are made both from chert and quartz; the former is more dominant. Discoids, crescents and points are the main tool types. The pressure flaking used on some almond shaped points and other tools has no parallels in India but only in Ceylon. In Ceylon, Beli-lena Athula, a Mesolithic site, has been dated to c. 6000 BC… and may indicate a similar age for the *teri* sites.[21]

Siran Deraniyagala has given an earlier date to this site.[22]

The second area lies to the north of the *Teri* sites, in the Gundar Basin. The Mesolithic sites here have been studied by Selvakumar less than a decade ago. These sites have been tentatively dated by him to a period more than 5000 years ago (Early- to Mid-Holocene) which is comparable to the date given by Gardner for the *Teri* sites.[23] Though crescents and points as well as blades, triangles, choppers and scrapers have been found in the Gundar Basin sites, there is no clear evidence for the use of the pressure-flaking technique.

Several other Microlithic sites have been identified north of the *Teri* sites in southern Tamil Nadu, mainly in the area between the Vaippar River and the Kaveri. No systematic study has been carried out in the sites of this area. They seem to share certain characteristics of some of the *Teri* sites. Evidence of pressure-flaking has also been reported.[24] The Mesolithic, according to Selvakumar, 'is the earliest, well represented cultural phase' in southern Tamil Nadu.[25] In the present state of our knowledge, this may be a safe conclusion, but one cannot ignore the scattered evidence, however small, of a Palaeolithic culture in southern Tamil Nadu and Sri Lanka, which was connected by land to the former in the period to which that culture belongs.

Movement to Sri Lanka

The pre-separation phase

For several thousand years, humans had been walking over to the southernmost tip of the subcontinent that later became the island of Sri Lanka. It would be very misleading to say that 'the first settlers from India had reached Sri Lanka at least as early as one million years ago', when in fact geographically there were no two separate regions that could be described as India and Sri Lanka.[26] This would amount to projecting modern perspectives into prehistoric times. Whoever they were, these early humans no doubt first spread to areas that now form the State of Tamil Nadu, among other areas in southeast India, before they spread to the area now forming Sri Lanka. They should, therefore, be counted among the ancestors of the modern-day people of the states of south India as well as of Sri Lanka.

Until the emergence of political entities that could fit the description of states in this region, it would be unwise to talk of separate countries. In this region of south India and Sri Lanka, it would appear that humans were roaming about for many millennia before the present island of Sri Lanka separated from the mainland. Even after that, the narrow sea dividing the two areas was indeed a unifier than a divider. Siran Deraniyagala's comment in this respect is worthy of note:

> The Palk Strait separating Lanka and India is only ca. 11 m at its deepest. Hence a slight eustatic drop in sea level would create a land bridge between the two countries, and this is likely to have occurred on numerous occasions during the Quaternary, the last being estimated at ca. 7,000 BP. The crossing of the Strait by sea-craft over the last 50,000 years is also a possibility, by analogy with the settling of Australia over a wider expanse of sea. It is thus clear that prehistoric human traffic to and fro between India and Lanka would have been commonplace, leading to complex patterns of miscegenation between groups.[27]

Even when the final separation of the Sri Lankan islands from the mainland occurred, the connections with south India were not severed. 'The islands off the Jaffna peninsula...would undoubtedly have served as "stepping stones" for people crossing the Palk Strait during phases of high sea level when the land connection between India and Sri Lanka would have been severed, as it is today, with the springboards for such migration being the Tinnevelly coast of south-eastern India and the north-western seaboard of Lanka.'[28]

Early Humans in Sri Lanka

Today we are in a position to get a far better view of Sri Lanka's prehistoric scene than we were about four or five decades ago, thanks to the pioneering and dedicated work of the Deraniyagalas. P.E.P. Deraniyagala, the father, gave the first clear view of the prehistoric scene through his discovery and identification of the

'Ratnapura' and 'Balangoda' cultures. Inspired by the father and following his footsteps, Siran Deraniyagala devoted nearly three decades to find more prehistoric sites and put the available pieces of the jigsaw in place, enabling us to see the main portions of the picture. His major work, *The Prehistory of Sri Lanka* (1992), has laid the firm foundations for a comprehensive study of Sri Lanka's prehistoric past.

Siran Deraniyagala, who is at present without doubt the leading prehistoric archaeologist of Sri Lanka, has presented well attested evidence to show that humans were present in the island for a very long period, spreading out to almost every part, before the Holocene period which covers the last 10,000 years. He has concluded that the 'present radiometric evidence indicates that man was certainly in Lanka by ca. 28,500 C BP, probably by 74,000 – 64,000 TL BP and earlier during the last interglacial at ca. 125,000 BP'.[29] In his view, 'There is secure evidence of settlements in Sri Lanka by 130,000 years ago, probably by 300,000 BP and possibly by 500,000 BP or earlier'.[30] It would appear that some sites have yielded more reliable evidence for the presence of humans about 125,000 years ago: 'By about 125,000 BP it is certain that there were prehistoric settlements in Sri Lanka ...The evidence stems from excavations conducted in coastal deposits near Bundala.'[31]

The passage of these humans to the region of Sri Lanka was through south India. For these prehistoric inhabitants, south India and Sri Lanka would have been one common territory. As Siran Deraniyagala has pointed out, 'there would have been unimpeded gene-flow between southernmost India and Sri Lanka (in both directions) from the Palaeolithic onwards'.[32] These early nomadic people cannot be considered to have been a homogeneous group. Deraniyagala believes that 'future research will probably reveal a whole range of genetic clusters in the prehistoric populations of this region'.[33]

These early peoples of Sri Lanka lived in a Stone Age culture, the Palaeolithic or Old Stone Age. Not much is known about them. The excavations at Bundala have yielded some information about them. 'These people made tools of quartz (and a few on chert) which are assignable to a Middle Palaeolithic complex...Apart from such tools, no other vestiges of their culture have survived the ravages of time and tropical weathering: we do not know what these people looked like, although it can be guessed that they were early Homo sapiens sapiens akin to anatomically modern South Asians. Even the sizes of their settlements are not known due to the limited scale of the evaluation excavations; surface indications are ca. 50 square metres or less per site. That they lived by hunting and gathering is obvious and it is probable that this conformed to the pattern discernible in the activities of their descendants some 100,000 years later.'[34]

It can be surmised that these early people and possibly others who continued to move into the Sri Lankan area from south Indian regions would have contributed to the widespread population of the next phase, the Mesolithic Period. Whether some of the movements were from Southeast Asia is hard to determine. Since Australo-Melanesians moved out of Southeast Asia to far-off lands as early as 40,000 BP, undertaking some of the earliest known crossings across the Indian Ocean, it is possible that these people were among those who moved to the SISL region in the Palaeolithic period.

Mesolithic Phase

The Mesolithic phase (the Middle Stone Age) which followed the Palaeolithic extended over a very long period. For the greater part of that period, Sri Lanka was joined to the mainland and, therefore, it stands to reason to treat the beginnings of this culture as something common to southern Tamil Nadu and Sri Lanka, the core of the SISL region. It is at this stage that we are able to trace clearly the common origins of the culture and population of this core region. The archaeological record is certainly clearer in this phase.

While Siran Deraniyagala has given us for the first time a very comprehensive account of this arachaeological record, Robin

PLATE 4.
The Andhra connection: Amaravati style dolomite Buddha image from Chunnakam, Jaffna District. Circa 5th-6th century. Now in the Anuradhapura Archaeological Museum. See p.209.

Courtesy*: Department of Archaeology.*

PLATE 5.
The Pallava connection: Mamallapuram style rock relief sculpture at Isurumuniya, near Anuradhapura.

***Photo**: March 2005, by the author. **Courtesy**: Department of Archaeology.*

Coningham has provided a good overall summary of the evidence available at present:

> ...the evidence of habitation prior to the Iron Age and the early historic period is very well attested: indeed, over 75 sites have been identified (Deraniyagala 1992). The wide distribution of such sites within the island suggests that most of the island's ecological zones were being exploited...while the wide spread of dates suggests that this broad-based pattern of subsistence activities was established prior to the Holocene and continued in some areas up to relatively recent times. A number of these sites are shell middens, situated in the coastal regions and representing open-air nodes of marine resource exploitation...Inland, excavated and dated sites abound...One of the best preserved inland open-air sites is the habitation midden at Ballan-bandi Palassa...Additional sites of importance are the caves of Batadomba-lena and Beli-lena Kitulgala. The former site yielded evidence of occupation between c. 26,500 and 9500 cal. BC, with an associated faunal record which included mollusc, giant squirrel, porcupine and monkey (ibid.: 314), while the latter yielded giant squirrel, porcupine, flying squirrel, rodent, an unidentified bovid and a large number of concentrations of molluscan shells (ibid.: 315-316).[35]

As already noted, the tool technology of the Mesolithic people of Sri Lanka (whose culture is also known as the Balangoda culture) had much in common with that of the Mesolithic people of southern Tamil Nadu. Archaeologists and anthropologists have commented on the close similarity between the microlith tools used by the Mesolithic people in Sri Lanka and those found in the south Indian sites, including sites in Karnataka.[36] There is remarkable similarity particularly between the tools of the *Teri* sites of the Pamban coast and those of Sri Lanka. Kennedy's summary of these similar features is worthy of being quoted:

> The occurrence of bifacial pressure flaked tools, geometric microliths made on flakes and blades, and the preference for quartz as a medium of manufacture are features characteristic of the Tirunelveli teri sites and sites in Sri Lanka. In both areas blades are short and thick and cores tend to be amorphous.[37]

Agreeing with Kennedy, Sudharshan Seneviratne observes:

> The primary artefacts of this culture consist of stone and bone implements. The high intensity of well-manufactured microliths and the primary use of quartz (chert to a lesser extent and jasper very rarely) are notable features associated with this culture complex. In the subcontinent the parallel techno-cultural elements are found in southern Tamilnadu.[38]

From all evidence, the Mesolithic phase was a period of close cultural interaction and movement of people between southern Tamil Nadu and Sri Lanka, the core of the SISL region. It would appear that the ground was prepared in this period for the major developments that took place in the first millennium BCE with the arrival of the EIA culture and of influences that flowed from long distance trade. There were Mesolithic communities that were active on the northwest coast of Sri Lanka and the southeast coast of Tamil Nadu. There is evidence that they shared the microlithic technology that they used. They were engaged in fishing chanks and other marine products. They were, in this respect, prepared for the chank fishery and pearl fishery that would emerge as major economic activities in the EIA. There was, however, no transition to either a Neolithic or a Chalcolithic phase as in some parts of the Indian subcontinent. It would appear that before any such transition, these Mesolithic people of the SISL encountered superior cultural influences that inauguarated the EIA.

The Mesolithic people

Before the arrival of new cultural influences, the Mesolithic culture appears 'to have spread over various physical and environmental zones with the exception of the northern peninsula and the lower Mahaweli basin of north east Sri Lanka'.[39] In the picturesque language used by Siran Deraniyagala, the Mesolithic folk appear 'to have settled in practically every nook and corner of Sri Lanka ranging from the damp and cold High Plains such as Maha-eliya (Horton Plains) to the arid lowlands of Mannar and Vilpattu, to the steamy equatorial rainforests of Sabaragamuwa'.[40] The absence of chert and quartz as well as surface water supply in the Jaffna peninsula seems to be the reason for the failure of this area to attract Mesolithic people.[41]

Archaeological evidence indicates clearly that the core area of the SISL region had a population that shared common characteristics. The evidence of physical anthropology seems to support the view that the people of this area shared common physical features. An examination of some of the skeletal remains from the burials in the next phase, the EIA, in southern Tamil Nadu, particularly Tirunelveli, has revealed evidence of a physical type that was common to the SISL region in the Mesolithic period. However, it is unlikely that the Mesolithic population was a homogeneous one.

Physical anthropology also lends support to the view that there was a biological continuum from the Mesolithic times to the present day. A leading researcher in the physical anthropology of south India and Sri Lanka, K.A.R. Kennedy, after examining the skeletal record for Mesolithic and Iron Age sites in peninsular India and Sri Lanka, states that 'comparative morphometric studies reveal close genetic ties between certain ancient and modern populations of the area' and that 'various *degrees* of biological affinity are suggested by both morphometric and immunological-genetic studies of the contemporary populations of peninsular India and Sri Lanka'. In his view, 'The aboriginal population Sri Lanka, the Veddas, appear to have a close affinity with the Mesolithic inhabitants of the island, as represented in a skeletal record dating from the late Pleistocene to the middle Holocene'.[42]

Chronology

Although archaeologists have not yet settled the question of dates with regard to the prehistoric phases, as already mentioned, it is now established that humans associated with microliths, that is people of the Mesolithic phase, were present in Sri Lanka as early as 28,500 years BP. In fact, it is claimed that migrations of these people could have taken place much earlier, even prior to 75,000 BP. Kennedy's summary on this question is a useful starting point:

> The geological and climatic factors that encouraged the migration of Pleistocene fauna from India to Sri Lanka also affected hominid populations which established a Mesolithic culture on the island. The date of the original settlement is unknown, but recent excavations yielding microlithic tools and human skeletal remains testify to the presence of anatomically modern *Homo sapiens* at the upland cave site of Batadomba lena by 28,500 years BP (Kennedy and Deraniyagala 1989). In the lowermost levels of the cave were found geometric microliths, the earliest occurrence of this type of tool in South Asia...Confidence for the Sri Lankan dates comes from thermoluminescent dating of ca. 28,500 years BP...However, migrations could have taken place before the last (Eem) interglacial period, for if dated correctly the evidence from Bundale-Patirajawela indicates settlement prior to 75,000 – 65,000 years BP.[43]

These dates have implications for the sites on the Tamil Nadu side. So far the sites on the Pamban coast (Tamil Nadu) have not been dated earlier than the Holocene, that is not prior to 10,000 years BP, although, as already discussed, Gardner is inclined to date the Teri sites to a period as early as the last glacial (before 10,000 years BP).[44] Compared with the Mesolithic phase in many other parts of the world, the Sri Lankan date is very early. Since the Mesolithic people could not have migrated to Sri Lanka from any other part of the world except through the south of the Indian mainland, further studies may lead to the revision of the south Indian dates.

A Neolithic Phase?

Archaeologists agreed for a long time that the Mesolithic Phase was directly succeeded by the iron using culture and that there was no intervening Neolithic or Chalcolithic culture in Sri Lanka.[45] The Mesolithic culture was considered to be a non-pottery culture with no use of metals.[46] But recent excavation work, especially that at Dorawaka-kanda by W.H. Wijayapala, seems to call for a revision of this view.[47] There are indications at this site of pottery, along with stone tools, being used as early as about 4300 BCE. The discovery of a few pieces of copper-working slag at Mantai (datable to about 1800 BCE) is also taken to point to a Chalcolithic phase in Sri Lanka.[48] These discoveries have to be followed up and one has to await the uncovering of further evidence to support any theory of a Neolithic Phase in the island. For the present, the Mesolithic Phase appears to have been succeeded by the EIA.

Language

The languages spoken by these prehistoric peoples are unknown and will be hard to identify. Historical linguistics relating to the languages of Sri Lanka is yet to make any significant advance in the direction of identifying a prehistoric linguistic substratum. Until then one can only speculate. As Siran Deraniyagala has succinctly stated, 'The prevalent indigenous language(s) of Sri Lanka at the advent of Indo-Aryan Prakrits constitutes an unknown: it could be Vadda (?Munda), Dravidian, or some other linguistic group.'[49] Given the nature of prehistoric populations, it is almost certain that more than one language was spoken in Sri Lanka. Survivals of these languages are likely to be found in Sinhalese and Sri Lankan Tamil.

Pre-modern and modern Sinhala grammarians have recognised that there is in the Sinhala language a category of words that are 'indigenous'. The author of the oldest Sinhalese grammar, *Sidatsañgarāva*, written in the thirteenth century, and Munidasa Kumaranatunga, the founder of the modern Heḷa school, have recognised this category in which these scholars obviously see words that exclusively belonged to the early Sinhala language.[50] As mentioned earlier, M.W.S. de Silva and Gair (and D.E. Hettiarachchi before them) have indicated that there was a language (or languages), unrelated to Indo-Aryan or Dravidian, spoken in the island at an early date.[51] But research in this area still awaits to be done.

Some have hinted at the possibility of a language or languages of the Munda subfamily being among the languages spoken by the Mesolithic people. But there is as yet no definite evidence on this score. Munda languages are spoken in the northeastern and eastern regions of the subcontinent. The separation of these languages (which are not spoken outside the subcontinent today) from the other Austroasiatic languages, namely those of the Mon-Khmer subfamily, is considered by linguists to have taken place in prehistoric times, possibly some 4000 years ago. This would mean that the eastward movement of Austroasiatic speakers from the Southeast Asian mainland and the spread of the ancestral Munda languages in the Indian subcontinent took place some time in the second millennium BCE or before. It would not be surprising that, not long after this, some of these languages spread to Sri Lanka as well. These are matters that remain to be settled in the future by archaeologists and historical linguists adopting an interdisciplinary approach.

The best and most commonly used survival of this ancient Austroasiatic connection appears to be the very name of the island. *Laṅkā* (Tamil *ilaṅkai*) does not seem to belong to either the Indo-Aryan or Dravidian languages. It has survived in place-names right along the eastern part of the subcontinent, from Assam to Andhra Pradesh.[52] It appears to have been a generic name for 'island', as indeed it is in Telugu to this day. The occurrence of this name in the Godavari Delta prompted some scholars to argue that the Lanka of the *Rāmāyaṇa* was not Sri Lanka but an island in the Godavari Delta. Some two thousand years ago, there were places with the name Laṅkā on the Tamil Nadu coast, too. In the earliest literature of the Tamils, namely the Sangam poems, there are references to places with '*ilaṅkai*' as an element in their names (such as Māvilaṅkai and To<u>n</u>māvilaṅkai).[53] In later centuries, inscriptions refer to a place named Uttaralaṅkā (Lanka in the North) in south India.[54] About the time of these records and later, Sri Lanka is referred to in Tamil literature and inscriptions as Teṉṉilaṅkai (Lanka in the South).[55] It will not be surprising if historical linguists identify the name Laṅkā as of Austroasiatic origin.

Whatever the languages spoken in the prehistoric period, what is of importance for a proper understanding of the early phase of Sri Lankan history is the recognition that the speakers of these prehistoric languages were never annihilated by newcomers. Archaeologists have so far not met with evidence of either a mass migration of people at the end of the Mesolithic period or annihilation of the existing population. The arguments of anthropologists about a biological continuum from prehistoric times lend support to Paranavitana's assertion that 'the vast majority of the people who today speak Sinhalese or Tamil must ultimately be descended from those autochthonous people of whom we know next to nothing.'[56] No dispassionate student of Sri Lankan history and archaeology can escape this conclusion.

It was among these peoples, about a thousand years before the Common Era, that superior cultural influences from the north and possibly from the west began to spread, bringing about major transformations, including the emergence of the first states. The spread of new cultural influences, including that of new languages, has often been taken as an indication of new migrations and the displacement of earlier inhabitants. Ancient historians and historical linguists are now inclined to reject such theories.[57]

The Mesolithic culture that prevailed in Sri Lanka until about 1000 BCE was one that was common to the whole SISL region. There was a free flow of humans and their cultural traits across various parts of this region. The whole region shared a common technology. Even the languages spoken by the Mesolithic people would have been common to the whole region. In such an environment, any new development or cultural intrusion experienced in south India would have sooner or later impacted on Sri Lanka as well. The dawn of the first millennium BCE saw such an intrusion that was to have far-reaching effects for the whole SISL region in shaping its history.

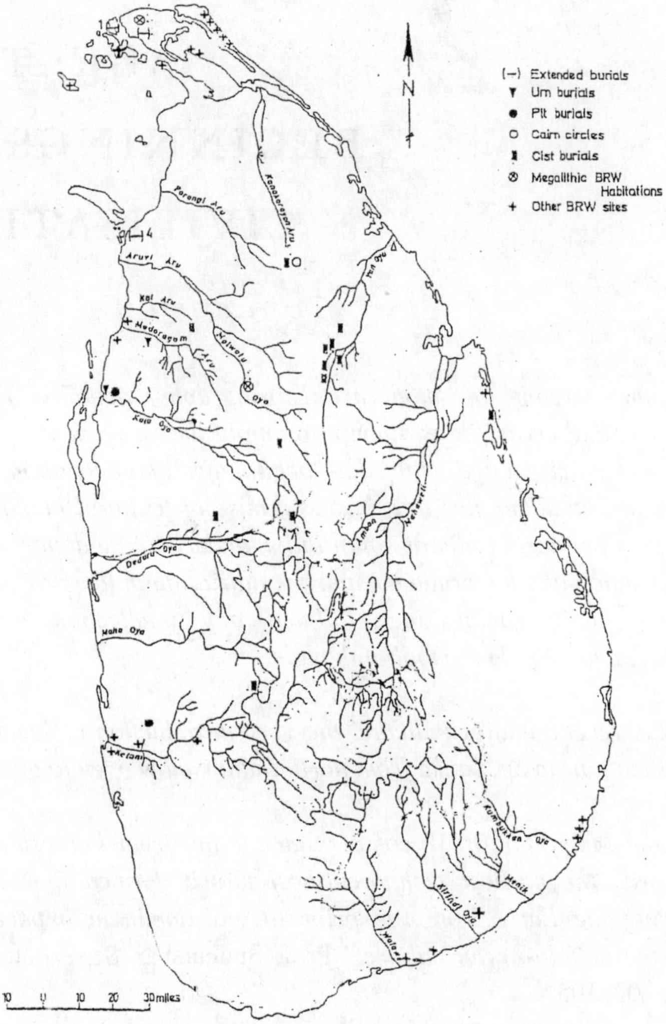

Map 3. **Sri Lanka**: Early Iron Age sites
(after Sudharshan Seneviratne)

CHAPTER 2 THE EARLY IRON AGE: THE BEGINNINGS OF CIVILISATION

Conception and Birth

"...one stream of modern historiography actually faced a 'conceptual crisis' in its attempt to unfold the antecedents of culture dynamics associated with the 'beginnings of civilization' in Sri Lanka. The adherence to a basic premise of 'cultural implantation' either from north India or south India, underlining a donor-recipient interaction and the crude compartmentalization of language-cultural zones along racial lines, diluted any intellectual credibility associated with this school of thought.

"...as recent studies indicate, the very introduction of 'elements of civilization' to Sri Lanka from north India is now open to question.

"...the Megalithic-BRW complex emanating from Peninsular India ... was the earliest techno-cultural matrix formed in Sri Lanka during the Early Iron Age prior to any dominant impact of the northern Indo-Aryan culture." Prof. Sudharshan Seneviratne 1992: 99, 102, 105.

Dawn of a New Age

New Cultural Elements

The origins of the ethnic group now known as the Sri Lankan Tamils go back to the period referred to as the Early Iron Age. The

Mesolithic people of the island came under new influences in the first millennium BCE, more specifically in the Early Iron Age (circa 900-300 BCE). The far-reaching developments in this period were to determine the evolution of the two main ethnic groups of historical times.

Towards the end of the second millennium BCE new cultural elements were introduced into peninsular India from the western side. A number of important questions relating to the new culture still remain unanswered. We still lack the evidence to answer these questions satisfactorily. In recent decades, much work has been done to throw fresh light on the main elements of the new culture and its spread across the Indian peninsula and Sri Lanka. Much more remains to be done.

Since the introduction of iron is associated with this new culture, it has been often referred to as the Iron Age culture, although the name 'Megalithic culture' is more popular. Some objections to equating the two names have been raised. It has been pointed out that, on the basis of the megalithic mortuary trait associated with the new culture, 'it is misleading to refer to a Megalithic culture, as several scholars are apt to, since this mortuary trait is not necessarily a concomitant of the Early Iron Age of peninsular India or Sri Lanka'.[1] This is no doubt a valid objection. The term 'Iron Age culture' is, therefore, preferred in this study.

The significance of the spread of this new culture in the SISL region cannot be over-emphasized. As summarized by Sudharshan Seneviratne, without dispute one of the leading authorities on the subject, some of the main elements of civilization introduced by the new culture were:

> a basic metal technology, i.e. iron, a potter's wheel, the plough, paddy cultivation, dam and tank irrigation, a greater degree of craft specialization, the ability to harness the environment with greater efficiency, the establishment of new settlements and the definite beginnings of a sedentarized

village culture, the emergence of petty exchange centres and the relative expansion in the exchange network, prelude to a greater demographic expansion, the emergence of petty chieftaincies, the introduction of the horse, new burial types (megalithic) and pottery types (characteristic BRW, all black ware, red ware and the russet-coated painted ware).[2]

The Mesolithic societies of SISL were fundamentally transformed by the arrival of these elements. The transformation took place over several centuries.

Use of Iron

The arrival of iron was no doubt an event of great economic consequence, leading on to important socio-political and cultural changes. The introduction of iron in north India, in particular the Indo-Gangetic plain and the upper Gangetic basin, is associated with the Painted Grey Ware Culture at the beginning of the first millennium BCE. The distribution of the Painted Grey Ware covers a wide area, as far north as even the Himalayas and to the south up to Ujjain in Madhya Pradesh. 'The sites of this culture are located along river banks. The distinctive features of the ware are the superior quality of the paste formed of well-levigated clay and the fine thin well-burnt fabric. On the grey surface of the body are painted linear and dotted patterns in black. Instances of red-on-grey and black-on-black and bichrome painted designs are also attested.'[3] This ware, in its upper levels, is associated with another type called the Northern Black Polished Ware which is of a superior quality and belongs to the period from about 400 BCE to the third century CE.[4]

The coming of the Iron Age in south India is associated with what is now widely known as the Megalithic Black-and-Red Ware Culture. This culture is associated with burials that are often grouped in small clusters, although sometimes they extend over large areas. Some of the burials contain urns with partial or complete skeletal remains or ashes collected after cremation. Other burials are without urns. Megaliths or large stones are not always found with the burials.

Different types of burials are seen in different geo-physical areas. As summarized by Sudharshan Seneviratne, 'the chamber tombs in the laterite zone of Kerala, the passage chambers in the granite zone of Karnataka, cists and dolmens in the Palani hills of Tamilnadu clearly point to the constructional base of these tombs', while 'Urns and other burial types having no stone appendage are generally concentrated on river banks, alluvial and other soil regions suitable for irrigated agriculture'.[5] In Sri Lanka, there is a large concentration of urn burials at Pomparippu, while some of the burials in other parts of the island are associated with cists and dolmens. The grave goods consist of offerings that include food items, ornaments and tools as well as weapons. Often the offerings are kept in the characteristic Megalithic Black-and-Red Ware.

The arrival of this new culture and the introduction of the use of iron led to very important developments in the region. In Seneviratne's words, 'this culture made significant contributions and innovations to introduce elements of civilization' in south India and Sri Lanka.[6]. In the core of the SISL region, on either side of the Gulf of Mannar, the first major chiefdoms arose around the exchange centres of Matirai and Tambapaṇṇi.[7] Through the latter centre, as well as others along the western, northern and northeastern coast the new culture spread into the interior of Sri Lanka.

With regard to the time and space of these introductions and innovations, Seneviratne believes that the 'time factor approximately extends within a span of eight centuries (c. 1000 to 200 B.C.)' and that 'the culture spread over a relatively wide geographical area (present Andhra Pradesh to Sri Lanka)'.[8] It is in this period that we see the emergence of a Tamil-speaking ethnic group in the far south of the Indian peninsula.

The Megalithic Folk

There is controversy among scholars over the origins of the Early Iron Age Megalithic Culture and the people who were responsible for its spread in peninsular India. Several scholars have tended to identify these people as speakers of a Dravidian language or languages, while a few have suggested an Indo-Aryan origin.[9] As far as the archaeological evidence is concerned, there is nothing to identify the language or languages of those who brought this culture to south India. Written records are not available here before the third century BCE. Nor are there clearly identified survivals of the early languages through oral traditions. There have been some studies of the human remains from the burials but the results seem to indicate a hybrid population. A summary of the findings of these studies by Thapar and Rahman is as follows:

> Studies of the human remains obtained from some of the excavated burials (Zuckerman, 1930; Sarkar, 1960, 1972; Gupta and Dutta, 1962), indicate besides an autochthonous Australoid type, a brachy-mesocephalic people similar to the Scythio-Iranian stock as encountered in Necropolis B and in the deposits of period III of Tepe Hissar. It is postulated that the great migration of these Scythio-Iranians took place between 2000 and 1000 BC from the Ukraine region. Studies of the head forms from the different types of megaliths have shown on the other hand that the jar burial people, like the one at Adichchanallur in the extreme south, appear to possess head forms falling within the dolichocranial range verging towards the hyperdolichocephalic. The megalithic builders seem to be a hybrid population.[10]

In the present state of our knowledge, the earliest date at which definite evidence of the spread of the new culture is visible in peninsular India is about 1200 BCE.[11] The origins of this culture as well as the route it followed before entering peninsular India are still unsettled matters.[12] Research on the spread of this culture points to its entry first into northwest Deccan (Maharashtra). From there it spread to southern Deccan (Karnataka). It then spread along the Krishna basin into Andhra Pradesh up to the eastern coast and into the lower plains along the Godavari and Pennar. In the spread of the Megalithic-BRW culture of the Early Iron Age, the Karnataka region played an important role. It was an area from where cultural diffusion into Andhra and Tamil Nadu took place. And, it was from Tamil Nadu that this culture spread into Sri Lanka.

Iron Age in Tamil Nadu

Routes of intrusion

The intrusion of the new culture into Tamil Nadu was from southern Karnataka. The intrusion extended into Kerala as well. The Bangalore and Kolar Districts in southern Karnataka have a large number of Iron Age burial sites. The burials in the Dharmapuri and North Arcot Districts of northern Tamil Nadu are an extension of the Karnataka burial complex. These northern Tamil Nadu burial sites are mainly close to the banks of the upper Kaveri, Ponnaiyar and Palar rivers. These rivers flow into Tamil Nadu from southern Karnataka and the spread of the Iron Age culture along these major rivers can easily be deduced. From this fertile region of northern Tamil Nadu, the new culture spread along the banks of the rivers into southern Tamil Nadu, especially the Salem District, and then northwards into South Arcot and Chingleput Districts along the east coast.[13] The major rivers flowing from the west to the lowland plains in the east appear to have marked the routes followed by the new culture. This culture took root in the fertile plains watered by the major rivers, namely Kaveri, Ponnaiyar, Palar and Tambraparni. There is a concentration of Megalithic-BRW sites in the highland, on the banks of the upper reaches of these rivers and their tributaries, showing the flow of this culture from southern Karnataka. In the lowland plains of the east, the Megalithic-BRW sites are mainly located near river banks or irrigation reservoirs. It has been observed that 'there is a tendency for urns/cairns/stone circles/pit burials to be generally associated with areas more suitable for paddy cultivation'.[14]

There is little doubt that the EIA Megalithic/urn burial/BRW culture (hereinafter referred to as the EIA culture) entered Sri Lanka from southern Tamil Nadu. Spreading from the Agastyamalai

(Southern Ghats), the new culture spread to the southeastern coast along the Vaigai, Vaippar, Chittar and Tambraparni rivers. When it arrived at places like Vasudevanallur and Adichchanallur, and the Vaigai plains, it had entered the core area of the SISL region and its spread to Sri Lanka was only a matter of time.

A look at the distribution of the megalithic burials and BRW sites in southern Tamil Nadu helps to trace the routes along which the EIA culture spread to the estuaries of the Tamraparni, Chittar and Vaippar. Near the upper reaches of the Chittar is the urn burial site of Ilanji as well as Courtalam (Kuṟṟālam) where urn burials are associated with cairn circles. Near the upper reaches of the Vaippar are the urn burial sites of Sivagiri, Panaiyur and Vasudevanallur. A significant number of urn burials are found in Sivasailam on the upper reaches of the Tambraparni, at the foothills of Agastyamalai. As this river winds its way to the Pamban Coast, there is the most famous of the southern Tamil Nadu sites, namely Adichchanallur, which was first investigated, along with the neighbouring site of Perumbair, as early as the 1870s.[15] Near the estuary of the river, on the Pamban Coast, more of the EIA urn burial sites are located at places like Kayalpattinam and Korkai. The ancient Koṟkai was, in the centuries immediately before and after the beginning of the Common Era, an important port for long distance trade.

Vaigai Plains

In the Vaigai plains, too, one sees a similar spread of EIA sites. The Vaigai is one of the major rivers of southern Tamil Nadu. Flowing from the Palani Hills, it waters the plains where the major historic urban centre of Madurai dominates the scene. The Vaigai plains constitute an important area associated with very early cultural developments. The western parts of the plains are rich in prehistoric sites. Several sites with microlithic tools have come to light here, indicating habitation by Mesolithic people. 'These Mesolithic sites', in Seneviratne's view, 'were perhaps linked to the Teri sites in Tirunelveli'.[16] The EIA sites of the next phase appear to coincide with the Mesolithic sites. The new Early Iron Age culture was evidently introduced to the Mesolithic settlers. The Megalithic complex, revealing urn burials and stone circles, extends from the Palani Hills towards Madurai, where a cluster of Megalithic burials has been located. These burials help to establish the antiquity of the site and the antecedents to the rise of an important urban centre that later became the capital of the Pāṇḍya lineage.

Kaveri Valley

Another major movement of the EIA culture in Tamil Nadu was along the Kaveri River. Originating in southern Karnataka, this river no doubt facilitated direct movement from the Karnataka region along its upper reaches. In addition, it appears that there were also movements from the west and southwest, which prompted Seneviratne to make this observation: 'The megalithic sites along the lower Kaveri are necessarily vestiges of communities that moved into the lower valley from the north (along the upper Kaveri via Salem district), from the west (across the Kongunadu upland), from the southwest (along the Palani hills) and the south (from southern Tamilnadu).'[17] The modern Tiruchirapalli District, through which the Kaveri winds its way to the Bay of Bengal, is rich in protohistoric sites. Two of the places where these sites are located, namely Karūr and the ancient Uṟaiyūr, were centres of authority of two leading Tamil lineages in the EHP. Karūr was the capital of the early Cēras while Uṟaiyūr was the capital of the early Cōḻas. Further east, there emerged the more famous urban centre of Tañcāvūr (Thanjavur), the capital of the medieval Cōḻas, while at the estuary of the Kaveri, on the eastern coast, there was the ancient port of Kāvēri-paṭṭiṉam (Pukār) which played an important role in the maritime trade of the Cōḻa kingdom for over a thousand years.

To the south of the ancient Kāvēri-paṭṭiṉam is another ancient port of the Cōḻa kingdom, namely Nāgapaṭṭiṉam. It is another place where EIA sites with burials and BRW have been found. They seem to be not as old as the sites further inland. To the south of Thanjavur, in the Pudukkottai District, many EIA sites have been located in areas suitable for rice cultivation.

North of the Kaveri delta, the Ponnaiyar and Palar rivers provided a direct link with the EIA sites of Karnataka. As in southern Karnataka, there are different types of burials in the large number of sites in the regions watered by these two rivers. The burials include cairn circles, dolmenoid cists, sarcophagi, stone circles and urns. There is evidence in these sites of an expansion of population and development of agriculture, including tank irrigation, in the later centuries of the first millennium BCE.

The location of the EIA sites in the eastern plains watered by the Tambraparni, Vaigai, Kaveri, Ponnaiyar and Palar and their tributaries seems to associate the spreading EIA culture with rice cultivation and tank irrigation. It has been suggested that the introduction of tank irrigation and rice cultivation may be attributed to the urn burial folk. As Seneviratne has summed up: 'The southern group [from the fertile plains of Vaigai-Tambraparani] may have mingled with the urn burial group of the middle Kaveri valley (Karur-Tiruchirappalli area) and reached the northeast auxiliary area (South Arcot-Chingleput) to begin extensive paddy cultivation based on tank irrigation and also chosen to live along the coastal belt at places suitable for petty exchange activities, such as Kaveripattinam.'[18]

When the EIA culture reached the eastern coast of Tamil Nadu, particularly the areas around the estuaries of the Tambraparni, Vaigai and Kaveri, it was poised to cross over to Sri Lanka. The sea dividing the island and southern Tamil Nadu was never a separator of the two areas. And once more, it was demonstrated that south India and Sri Lanka formed one cultural region. Once again, Seneviratne's observation summarises the situation as it existed in the EIA:

> The geographical proximity, the similarity between ecological zones, common burial and ceramic traditions, including other grave ware and skeletal remains...indicate a cultural homogeneity between the megalithic monuments of south India and Sri Lanka. It also suggests community movement,

the intrusion of techno-cultural elements (iron, ceramic industry, irrigation) and a new subsistence pattern (based on paddy cultivation) from south India, more specifically from Tamilnadu, well before the 3rd century B.C. period.[19]

Sri Lanka

The area in Sri Lanka directly opposite the Pamban Coast of southern Tamil Nadu, across the Gulf of Mannar, is the northwestern coast, from Puttalam to Mannar. This is the area watered by the Aruvi Aru (Malvatu Oya), Kal Aru, Modaragam Aru, Elapat Aru (a tributary of Kala Oya) and Kala Oya. That this area has a comparatively large number of EIA urn burials and BRW sites yielding artefacts similar to those from the Tamil Nadu coast comes as no surprise. It only reiterates the view that the lands on either side of the Palk Strait and the Gulf of Mannar were part of a single cultural region in the period before the rise of the states. The northwestern coast of Sri Lanka would also have been the earliest in the island to receive the new EIA culture.

The narrow sea separating the coast of Tamil Nadu and the northwestern coast of Sri Lanka being a unifier, the two coasts were the scene of much interaction from prehistoric times. Clearly, Sri Lanka was part of 'the cultural vortex of the neighbouring land mass.'[20] It would appear that the shallowness of the dividing sea as well as certain attractions of northwest Sri Lanka contributed to this situation. Seneviratne comments on the close connections between the two coasts in the following words:

> The Mesolithic techno-cultural complex common to Sri Lanka and southern Tamilnadu clearly indicates the existence of contact between these two physical areas extending to a remote period in antiquity...With the arrival of the iron using groups to the lower Tambapaṇṇi valley and their success in gaining direct access to the marine resources (viz. fish, pearl oyster, chank, coral) in the Gulf of Mannar, it led to a greater

interaction between the two coastal areas gradually resulting in community movement to north west Sri Lanka.[21]

Northwest coast

Beginning in the north of the coast, in the area watered by the Aruvi Aru, and moving southwards to the banks of the Kala Oya, one finds that as many as seven significant EIA sites have so far come to light in this littoral. Not far north of the mouth of the Aruvi Aru is the well-known historical port of Mātoṭa (Mātōṭṭam / Mantai). Though this was a site occupied by Mesolithic folk as early as the beginning of the second millennium BCE, EIA artefacts are hard to come by in its vicinity.[22] Surprisingly, it is the most disappointing of all the northwestern coastal sites. As an urban centre that was built up for several centuries from the EHP, Mātoṭa is no doubt a much-disturbed place for prehistoric and protohistoric research. Investigations have been carried out at this site from the late nineteenth century, but artefacts from the prehistoric and protohistoric periods are disappointingly few. The latest field study, the expedition led by John Carswell of the University of Chicago, occurred in 1980, 1982 and 1984. Unfortunately, owing to unforeseen circumstances, it did not turn out to be a comprehensive investigation as originally planned. Although BRW sherds were unearthed in certain pits, their dates were not settled. Mātoṭa appears to have emerged as a port for long distance trade in the protohistoric period, enjoying a development parallel to that of Koṟkai on the opposite coast. It is a site that is likely to yield important artefacts of the protohistoric period if comprehensive excavations are undertaken.

South of the Aruvi Aru, near the upper reaches of the Kal Aru, is the site of Alutbombuva. It is a cist burial site and is yet to be fully investigated. To the south of the Kal Aru runs the Modaragam Aru and the banks of this river have several EIA sites. One of them, Tekkam, is an urn burial site. This, too, has not been excavated yet. Some BRW sites have been located near the estuary of the Modaragam, especially at Pookulam. Seneviratne is of the view that further investigation along the river 'is bound to reveal more Proto and Early Historic sites'.[23]

The Wilpattu Sites

The best known and the most intensively studied urn burial/BRW site in the island is Pomparippu, one of the first of its kind to be uncovered. Near the mouth of the Kala Oya and connected to some of the other EIA sites by the Elapat Aru, it forms almost the core of the EIA region of northwestern Sri Lanka. It is estimated that there are about 8000 burials in this place and, fortunately, they are in no danger of being destroyed by development projects or extension of settlements as the entire site is safely located inside a national wild life sanctuary (the Wilpattu Sanctuary). Indeed, several other important EIA sites, such as Tekkam, Alutbombuva and Karamban-kulam are also within the wild life sanctuary and offer much scope for future research.[24]

The important EIA site of Karamban-kulam is further inland from Pomparippu but along the Kala Oya.. This is also an urn burial site. Again, it is still awaiting a proper investigation but there is no doubt that it forms part of the urn burial complex covering a large area in the Wilpattu Sanctuary.[25] Kollankanatta is another interesting site close to Pomparippu. BRW sherds have been found here and this site may also turn out to be one of the important EIA locations in the northwestern part of Sri Lanka.[26]

The above sites fall within the core area of SISL and, together with the sites on the opposite coast in Tamil Nadu, provide ample evidence of the close interaction that went on in this region in the EIA. As Seneviratne, whose study of the EIA sites in south India and Sri Lanka is perhaps the most comprehensive on the subject, has rightly stressed, the impetus for the spread of the EIA culture in the northwestern coast of Sri Lanka came from the southeastern coast of Tamil Nadu. 'It is fairly certain', concludes Seneviratne, 'that the burial culture of north-west Sri Lanka received its impetus from [the] urn/cairn burial complex in the Vaigai-Tambapaṇṇi plains, the land of the Pāṇḍyas'.[27] This area of the urn burial complex in the Wilpattu Sanctuary, with Pomparippu as the core, appears to be one of the earliest and most important areas in the island that received the EIA cultural influences from south India in the first millennium BCE. The striking similarities between the Adichchanallur burials on the opposite coast and those of Pomparippu establish beyond any reasonable doubt that the cultural influences reflected by the Pomparippu burials flowed from the Adichchanallur area. This is not surprising as the Mesolithic people of these two coastal areas were in continuous contact for several centuries before the EIA. As soon as the EIA culture arrived in the southeastern corner of Tamil Nadu, the next natural development would have been its spread to the northwestern coast of Sri Lanka.

The Cist Burials

The cist burial complex in Sri Lanka is concentrated in the north-central parts of the island. Seneviratne is of the view that the cist burials in north-central Sri Lanka may have received their impetus from the cist burial complex in Tamil Nadu that extends from Pudukottai to the Chittoor area of Andhra Pradesh.[28] A considerable number of the cist burials known so far are clustered along the banks of the Yan Oya that flows into the Bay of Bengal on the northeastern coast, prompting the conclusion that the impetus for this burial practice entered the island from the northeast. In Tamil Nadu, cist burials were prominent in the territory that later became the Cōḻa kingdom and the flow of influences from this area, particularly the Kaveri delta, to the northeast of Sri Lanka is only a natural development that continued throughout the historical period.

Though an EIA burial site seems to be located near the estuary of the Yan Oya, all the identified cist burials along this river are near the middle reaches. A large number of burials have been uncovered at Tammenna-godella, Gurugal-hinna, Vadigawewa, Kok-ebe, Divul-wewa and Rabewa forming what is referred to as the Yan Oya complex. From here, the cist burial practice seems to have spread to interior places. Not far to the north is the site of Mamaduwa. To the southeast, close to the upper reaches of the Malwatu Oya, is another site, namely Machchagama. The cist burials of Ibbankattuwa and Pin-wewa are further south of this site. Another important cist burial site is located at Kathiraveli, on the eastern coast south of Trincomalee.[29]

Jaffna District

The EIA burial/BRW sites in the Jaffna District, discovered mostly within the last twenty-five years, appear to form a separate complex. There are neither cist burials comparable to the Yan Oya complex nor urn burials similar to the northwestern coast complex. However, a large number of BRW sites, a few extended burials and at least two urn burials have come to light. The oldest and best known site is Kantarodai.[30] Though BRW sherds have been unearthed here, no burials have been as yet excavated. Another important site with extended and urn burials is Anaikoddai.[31] A site with much potential for protohistoric research, it has been partly destroyed in recent years. P. Ragupathy has brought to light another burial site at Karainagar as well as a large number of BRW sites in Kumpuruppitti (Velanai Island), Catti (Velanai Island), Cattirantai (Karainagar Island) and Kottuppanivu (Mannitalai).[32] P. Pushparatnam has reported the discovery of more BRW sites in Mannitalai, Kalmunai, Vettukkatu, Pallikuda, Pallavarayan, Ilavur and other places in the Punakari area of the mainland.[33] He has also excavated recently (2004) a new urn burial site in Catti (Velanai Island). The inspiration for the spread of the EIA culture in the Jaffna District no doubt came from southeastern Tamil Nadu, probably by way of the Jaffna islands and Jambukolapaṭṭana, which later became the main port of the peninsula. The incidental information in the Buddhist *Jātaka* stories, which reflect conditions in the centuries before CE, refers to contacts between Kāvēripaṭṭiṉam on the Tamil Nadu coast and places like Kāradīpa and Nāgadīpa in northern Sri Lanka while the *Mahāvaṃsa*, *Sammohavinodanī* and other Pali texts refer to sailings between the eastern coast of India and Jambukolapaṭṭana in the Jaffna peninsula.[34]

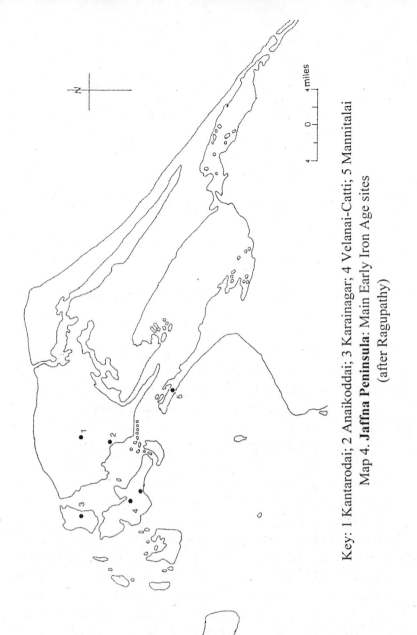

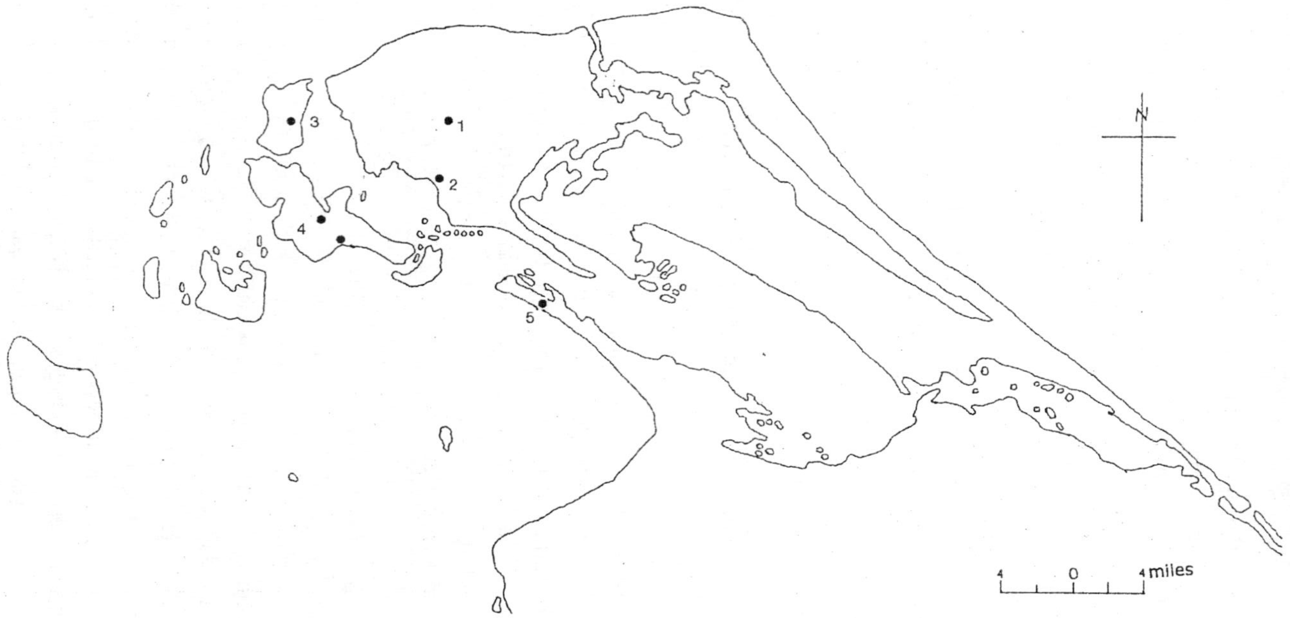

Key: 1 Kantarodai; 2 Anaikoddai; 3 Karainagar; 4 Velanai-Catti; 5 Mannitalai

Map 4. **Jaffna Peninsula**: Main Early Iron Age sites
(after Ragupathy)

The Jaffna peninsula and its offshore islands present a picture different from that of the mainland. So far this area has not yielded any confirmed Stone Age artefact. Archaeologists are of the view that this area was not inhabited in the Mesolithic period.[35] This would mean that the first settlements in the Jaffna peninsula and its offshore islands date from the EIA. The offshore islands, particularly Nainativu, Karainagar (formerly Karaitivu, the Kāradīpa of the *Jātakas*) and Velanai, appear to have played an important part in the spread of the EIA culture into northernmost Sri Lanka from the southeastern coast of Tamil Nadu. The Kantarodai site, which is the only one in the area with radiocarbon dates, reveals that it was settled as early as the sixth century BCE.[36]

As is well known, the Jaffna peninsula is the area referred to as Nāgadīpa (the Island of the Nāgas) in the earliest literary sources. The people known as the Nāgas were the group inhabiting that area in the EIA. They have to be considered as the earliest settlers there. That the Nāgas were also among the people on the opposite coast, in southeastern Tamil Nadu, is known from the earliest Tamil sources and from surviving place-names, including the well-known place-name of Nāgapaṭṭiṉam (the Port-town of the Nāgas). If the credit for the introduction of the megalithic/urn burial/BRW culture to the Jaffna peninsula goes to the Nāgas, it would mean that the story of human settlements in that peninsula began with the south Indian EIA culture. If one is to go by the evidence of the legends in the Pali chronicles and the *Jātaka* stories, the Nāgas were in southern Sri Lanka, too, as far as Kelaniya. The occurrence of a large number of personal names with the element *Nāga* in the earliest cave inscriptions would confirm their presence in different parts of the island. Siran Deraniyagala is also of the view that the Nāgas were protohistoric EIA settlers from India.[37]

Southern Sri Lanka

The three major areas showing a concentration of EIA sites, discussed above, are all in the northern half of the island. In the southern half, especially in the Wet Zone (the southwestern part of the island) such EIA sites are conspicuous by their absence. Two exceptions are the Gal-atara site (a cist burial) and Makevita. A few BRW sites have also been discovered along the Kelani River. In the southern extremity of the island, outside the Wet Zone, some BRW sites have been found near the estuaries of the Walawe Ganga, the Kirindi Oya and the Kumbukkan Oya.[38] In 1996, excavations carried out at Ridiyagama (at the estuary of the Walawe Ganga) by Bopearachchi and others brought to light unmistakable evidence of the spread of the EIA culture in that area. 'We were able to collect', Bopearachchi reports, 'not only at Ridiyagama, but also along the Walawe Ganga, large quantities of early Black and Red Ware, some of which were engraved with early megalithic symbols'.[39] In his view, these 'ceramic types can be dated with certainty back to the fourth and third centuries B.C.'[40]

Anuradhapura

The most important EIA site from the point of view of future history is Anuradhapura, almost centrally placed between the northwestern urn burial sites and the northeastern Yan Oya cist burial complex. Although no burials belonging to this age have so far been identified here, the earliest occupation site uncovered during excavations revealed the presence of BRW pottery and iron technology. Perhaps the most excavated site in Sri Lanka, it has also been established as the largest EIA settlement in the island. It is also one of the earliest EIA settlements with clearly determined dates. Furthermore, it is different from all the other known EIA sites on account of its early urban character.[41]

It will be difficult to reject any links between Anuradhapura and Pomparippu. The latter is by far the most important EIA site with implications for an understanding of some of the early developments after the end of the Mesolithic period. It is easily the largest and possibly one of the earliest urn burial/BRW sites in the island. With an estimated 8,000 burials, in which are the remains of about 12,000 persons, there is no doubt that a large settlement existed in that area. It was possibly in the vicinity of an early urban centre. Looking at the evidence of the earliest historical traditions, one can only think of the first known centre of authority, Tambapaṇṇi. This centre was later supplanted by Anuradhapura, and it would be an interesting pursuit to establish the process by which this happened.

Cultural factors

Seneviratne has drawn attention to the unmistakable evidence for the cultural homogeneity of the coastal sites and the inland sites, comparing the burial ware and other artefacts from these sites. He points to the parallel pottery forms, namely the BRW, found in the sites of the northwest coast (Pomparippu and Kollankanatta) and the inland sites (Anuradhapura and Galsohonkanatta) and concludes: 'From this it is evident that the inland movement was initiated from the northwest region of Sri Lanka, thus forming a homogeneous techno-cultural complex covering the whole of northern Sri Lanka'.[42] He is inclined to think that the population of the northwest expanded towards Anuradhapura because the soil and the terrain there attracted them.[43]

But it would appear that, more than indicating a demographic expansion inwards, the evidence of the EIA sites points to the spread of the new culture inland from the area where it first established itself successfully. It is now known that there was a settlement at Anuradhapura as early as 900 BCE.[44] Lying within only about 70 km from the coast, the settlement at Anuradhapura would have been in contact with the coastal settlement. An internal trade network would have also linked the two areas. When the new culture was transforming the coastal settlement, introducing elements of civilization, the Anuradhapura settlement would not have been left untouched by the new influences. It was an area where a chiefdom would have been established very early; and, the new EIA culture would have spread through the elites in that settlement. Excavations at Anuradhapura seem to indicate that there was an overlap of the Mesolithic phase with the EIA, prompting Seneviratne to suggest that there may have been 'a cultural and a physical fusion between the indigenous Mesolithic people and the iron using Megalithic cultural groups.'[45] Physical anthropologists have indicated that even at Pomparippu biological affinities between the Mesolithic people and the Megalithic people are discernible in the skeletal remains.[46] The new culture, unquestionably, was spreading among an existing population, as one would expect when a superior culture is brought to a new place.

Tambapaṇṇi and Anurādhagāma

The demise of Tambapaṇṇi appears to have been the result of the rise of Anuradhapura. Known in the early stages as Anurādhagāma (Anourogrammon of the Graeco-Roman writers), Anuradhapura seems to have quickly adopted the elementary irrigation technology introduced by the EIA culture and become economically strong. It was also at the receiving end of beneficial influences from the long distance trade with north India and appears to have gained control of the port of Mātoṭa through which that trade passed. Very early, a group that had adopted Prakrit and come under the influence of Sanskritisation was in control of Anuradhapura. If the corpus of Vijaya legends is anything to go by, an elite group of north Indian origin may have gained control of Tambapaṇṇi first and later moved to Anuradhapura. The Paṇḍu connection, reflected in both the Vijaya legends and the Paṇḍukābhaya cycle of legends, seems to preserve the memory of close links between the Tambapaṇṇi rulers and those of Matirai on the opposite coast, namely the Paṇḍu (Sanskrit Pāṇḍya) lineage, who too had come under strong Sanskritic influences.[47] The emergence of Anuradhapura as the most powerful chiefdom in the island appears to have occurred before 300 BCE.

Chronology

Recent archaeological work, particularly the excavations and researches of Siran Deraniyagala, Vimala Begley, Bennet Bronson, Robin Coningham and F.R. Allchin, have helped enormously to determine the dates of some of the EIA sites. Consequently, one is in a better position now to provide a reliable chronology for the EIA in Sri Lanka and to revise some earlier views. A similar scientific dating of various important sites in Tamil Nadu has made it possible to look at the whole region and view developments with a better perspective.

Though not likely to be the earliest of the EIA habitation sites in the island, Anuradhapura has been the focus of investigation by leading archaeologists in the last three to four decades. As a result, it has turned out to be a place where very early dates have been established for EIA artefacts. A number of radiocarbon dates have been secured for the citadel area of Anuradhapura and with the help of these Siran Deraniyagala assigned the period c. 900-600 BC (BCE) for the Protohistoric Iron Age at Anuradhapura in 1992.[48] The early commencement date of c. 900 BCE received confirmation from the excavation conducted by a British team that included F.R. Allchin and Robin Coningham.[49] In recent years, on the basis of more radiocarbon dates, Deraniyagala has claimed that the 'earliest manifestation' of the protohistoric Early Iron Age is radiocarbondated to c. 1000-800 BCE [50] 'It is very likely', in his view, 'that further investigations will push back the Sri Lankan lower boundary to match that of South India' (1200 BCE).[51]

Radiocarbon dates obtained from other sites, too, support the view that the EIA in Sri Lanka began in the early centuries of the first millennium BCE. The Ibbankatuva burial site, for instance, has a radiocarbon date placing it in the eighth century BCE.[52] Some early dates have been obtained at Kantarodai, too, but Deraniyagala is of the opinion that a ' protohistoric Iron Age component is lacking in the sample' used for dating the site.[53] In the case of the important urn burial complex at Pomparippu, despite all the attention focused on it over several decades, absolute dates are still not available. While Begley is of the view that this site is datable to the same period as Arikamedu in Tamil Nadu, Seneviratne favours a date in the first half of the first millennium BCE.[54]

Seneviratne's arguments for a higher antiquity for the northwestern burial complex in comparison with the date for those of the north-central region are worthy of note. 'If the logical direction of the inland movement of the Iron Age culture extended from the north-west to the north-central areas, then the former area may possess a higher antiquity, perhaps a date around c. 600 B.C.' The other point he makes is that 'a date of c.7/6th century B.C. for the earliest intrusions made by the iron using culture in the north-west may indirectly substantiate the C-14 date of 785 B.C. assigned for Korkai' (on the Tamil Nadu coast).[55] But this argument was presented in 1984, before a date closer to 1000 BCE was established by later excavations in Anuradhapura. In the light of the new dates for the EIA in Anuradhapura, if one adopts the first argument of Seneviratne, an even earlier date will have to be assigned for the spread of the new culture in northwestern Sri Lanka.

In the present state of our knowledge, with the few absolute dates that are available for some of the sites in south India and Sri Lanka, it is possible to conclude that the EIA culture, along with the urn and cist burial practices and use of iron technology, had begun to spread in south India about 1200 BCE and had crossed over to Sri Lanka by about 1000 BCE.

Causes of cultural diffusion

Long distance trade

It is generally agreed that the EIA culture was an intrusive one in peninsular India and Sri Lanka. As stated earlier, there is much controversy about the origins of this culture. In the present state of knowledge, it is not possible to arrive at anything conclusive. Whatever the origins, there may have been different forces that combined to bring the various concomitants of this culture to the subcontinent. One of them without doubt was long distance trade. The introduction of this culture as well as the rise of urbanism in the first millennium BCE in the SISL region is directly linked to the development of long distance maritime trade that brought traders from West Asia and the Mediterranean, from Gujarat and the Gangetic Valley.

For a long time scholars have surmised that commercial interests brought traders from the west to the shores of south India at a very early date. From about the end of the second millennium BCE, Mediterranean trade, among other factors, created a new demand for products of the SISL region. The emergence of the Phoenicians, the intrepid long distance traders of this time, seems to have had some link to the beginnings of West Asian trade in the Indian Ocean. The demand for SISL products in the Mediterranean area appears to have provided the stimulus for the emergence of an internal trade network in this region and the exploitation of resources, leading to the establishment and spread of new settlements along the coast as well as in areas close to mineral and other valuable resources.

Pearl trade

One of the most sought after articles of trade was the pearl of the Gulf of Mannar. As for pearl fishery and trade in pearls in the EIA, the archaeological record is scant. Korkai on the Tamil Nadu side of the Gulf and Pookulam on the northwestern coast of Sri Lanka have yielded oyster shells supporting the supposition that pearls were among the articles sought after in the EIA. Greek, Sanskrit and Tamil literary sources of the EHP reveal that the pearls from the Gulf of Mannar were among the best and most valuable in the ancient world.[56] The demand for pearls seems to have begun even before the EHP. It is quite possible that traders from West Asia, like the Phoenicians who were fearless maritime traders at the beginning of the first millennium BCE, had created a demand for pearls from the Gulf of Mannar.[57]

There seems little doubt that pearls from the narrow sea separating Sri Lanka and Tamil Nadu were bought by long-distance traders and taken to North India and possibly West Asia as early as the fourth century BCE. Megasthenes, one of the earliest Greek writers to leave behind valuable notices of Sri Lanka, wrote in the fourth century BCE that the inhabitants of the island were 'more productive of gold and large pearls than the Indians'.[58] No doubt he obtained his information when he was the Greek ambassador at the court of the Mauryan emperor Chandragupta. That the pearls from the Tamil Nadu and Sri Lankan coasts were well known in the Mauryan capital is inferred from the references in the Sanskrit treatise, *Arthaśāstra*, to two types of pearls, namely Pāṇḍya Kavāṭaka and Tāmravarṇika, which names help to identify them as pearls from the SISL region.[59]

While these early Greek and Sanskrit literary sources confirm the emergence of pearl as an important article of trade in the SISL region in the middle of the first millennium BCE, the earliest Tamil literary sources, the Sangam poems, provide vivid allusions to the pearl fishery and those who were engaged in this occupation along the southeastern coast of Tamil Nadu, especially in the area of the ancient port of Korkai.[60] Thus, based upon all this evidence, it is clear that long distance traders came to the ports in the Gulf of Mannar in search of pearls in the later centuries of the first millennium BCE, if not earlier.

Demand for chanks

Another marine product, the chank (Indian conch shell), will no doubt have to be counted as one of the earliest articles in demand among the people of SISL, even during the Mesolithic Period. Anyone familiar with South Asian culture and rituals will know that the humble chank has a variety of uses in traditional life. It is used as a ceremonial trumpet, a libation vessel, a symbol of good omen and an amulet. Since it is considered to be an auspicious object and a charm against evil, the chank is also used for making ornaments such as rings, beads and bangles.[61] These uses of the chank are known in South Asia from very ancient times. It is no surprise, therefore, that it was an important article of trade and barter among prehistoric people in SISL.

The chank is found in large quantities in the shallow waters of the Gulf of Mannar and the Palk Strait. The area abounding in chank oysters extends from there around the southern coast of Tamil Nadu to Kerala. The archaeological record reveals that the chank, like the

PLATE 6.

The Pallava connection: Pallava style relief sculpture at Isurumuniya. Identified as the figure of the Hindu deity Aiyanar by the Dutch art historian , Prof. J.E. Van Lohuizen – De Leeuw. See p.219. 'This work has earned the highest encomiums from art critics; and, in the studied restraint which characterizes the form of the man, the paucity of jewellery which accentuates the plastic form, and in the elongated slender limbs, the work is reminiscent of the sculpture executed under the patronage of the Pallavas of Kanchi.' (Prof. S.Paranavitana).

***Photo:** March 2005, by the author. **Courtesy:** Department of Archaeology.*

PLATE 7.

The Pallava connection: Nalanda Gedige, Nalanda. This is the earliest known building in Sri Lanka 'which was entirely of stone construction' (S. Paranavitana). Late Pallava style – 8th century. '...there is general agreement that it is an entirely "imported" monument in a generally South Indian style' (Prof. Senake Bandaranayake).

Photo*: March 2005, by the author.* ***Courtesy****: Department of Archaeology.*

pearl, featured prominently among the articles associated with the EIA culture in SISL.[62] With the rise of long distance commerce, traders from north India and the interior of peninsular India would have included chanks among their chief merchandise.

Gems and other exotic products

Besides the marine products of pearls and chanks, there were also some mineral and other products from the interior that were already in demand in the EIA. Among these, gems were the most important. That gems were among the more valuable articles of trade in the EHP, becoming important items in the long distance trade of the SISL region, is well known. Very early in its history, Sri Lanka gained the name Ratnadvīpa (Island of Gems) on account of its renowned gems. From the time of Ptolemy, the Graeco-Roman sources refer to the precious stones of Sri Lanka, particularly beryl and hyacinth.[63] The Sangam literature of the Tamils bear ample testimony to the importance of the gem industry in Tamil Nadu. Recent archaeological excavations in Tamil Nadu have provided more evidence about this lucrative industry in the EIA.[64]

There were also a few exotic wild products that brought long distance traders to the SISL ports. Ivory and peacock feather were two such items. For a long time it has been surmised that some of these exotic wild products were sought after by West Asian traders. The reference in the *Bible* to King Solomon's ships bringing ivory, gold, apes and peacock from distant lands has been used in support of this claim on account of the Hebrew words for these items. These words, it has been claimed, are derived from Sanskrit or Tamil, indicating that the items originated from South Asia.[65]

The growth of long distance trade from north India across the Vindhyas through the ancient Dakṣiṇāpatha (the southern route) as well as along the eastern and western coasts gave an impetus to the spread of the EIA culture to the southern tip of the subcontinent and then across the narrow sea to Sri Lanka. By all indications, the interest of Mediterranean traders in the luxury items that were procurable from the SISL region also led to the beginnings of an active and lucrative trade with the west that continued well into the EHP. In addition to helping the spread of the salient elements of the EIA culture in different parts of the SISL region, the Mediterranean and north Indian connections brought new influences that became significant factors in the rise of urbanism and the emergence of states in SISL.

Other economic factors

There were probably other factors, too, that led to the spread of the EIA culture into the southern part of Tamil Nadu and Sri Lanka in the first millennium BCE. Gunawardana suggests that there were also economic reasons other than trade for migration of people from south India in this period. 'South Indian peoples occupying such ecological zones like montane tracts (*kuṟiñci*) and scrubland (*mullai*) were constantly facing shortages of subsistence resources' and, Gunawardana argues, one of the options these peoples faced was 'migration to more favourable ecological zones', including those in Sri Lanka. 'Migrations of South Indian peoples propelled most probably by ecological and demographic pressures ', in his view, 'were among the causes of warfare in ancient Sri Lanka.' His contention is:

> If people from unattractive ecological zones formed the main element among immigrants, it is also likely that dynamic peoples from the coastal (*neytal*) tracts like the *paratavar* were also involved in these activities. As Sumati has pointed out, the *paratavar* were fishermen who later developed into a group which played an important role in long-distance trade, and Seneviratne has drawn attention to evidence which points to the possibility that they were known in ancient Sri Lanka. Collaboration between fishermen/traders and men who wanted to settle down in more productive land would have been essential for the latter to obtain transport across the Palk Strait. Many migrations would have gone unrecorded, but the

chroniclers have preserved traditions about several instances of 'invaders' from South India settling down in the island.[66]

The First Urban Centres

The expansion of the exchange network, the emergence of small exchange centres and the arrival of long distance traders inevitably led to the growth of the first urban centres in the SISL region. It comes as no surprise that the earliest urban centres/ centres of authority that we hear of in this region, from the traditions preserved in the early literary sources, lay on the shores of the pearl and chank-rich Gulf of Mannar. There was Matirai (Madura) on the southeastern coast of Tamil Nadu, presumably near the estuary of the Vaigai River, and there was Tambapaṇṇi on the northwestern coast of Sri Lanka. They were obviously important ports for the trade in pearls and chanks as well as for articles such as ivory and peacock feather from the interior.

Rise of Matirai (Madura)

One of the earliest urban centres in the SISL region, and perhaps the earliest in the core of this region, was Matirai. Its name is suggestive of this. *Matirai* could be derived from the Tamil word *matir/matil*, meaning an outer wall. Matirai would, therefore, mean 'The Walled Area (City)'. Such a name was given presumably because it was the first and only fortified urban area there when it was established. The importance attached to the circumvallation of the emerging urban centre is clearly reflected in the name. The information available about this early urban centre is scanty, in the form of traditions preserved in a later literary source.[67] According to this source, it was the seat of the Pāṇḍya lineage and was destroyed by a deluge. A second city was then built along the coast and was given the name of Kapāṭapuram (Pāṇḍya Kavāṭa in the Sanskrit sources), with a meaning similar to that of Matirai, namely 'The City with Portals'. Kapāṭapuram, according to the same tradition, suffered the same fate as Matirai and the seat of the Pāṇḍyas was then moved interior to another site that was also named Matirai. To distinguish this city from the first Matirai, the latter came to be referred to in Tamil tradition as Ten Matirai (later Ten Maturai, following the Sanskritisation of the name), meaning 'Southern Matirai', and Dakkhina Madhura in the Pali tradition. As Paranavitana has pointed out, it is this city that is referred to in the *Mahāvaṃsa* (in the Vijaya legend) as *Dakkhiṇaṃ Madhuraṃ.*[68]

Rise of Tambapaṇṇi

The earliest known urban centre/ centre of authority on the Sri Lankan coast of the Gulf Mannar was Tambapaṇṇi, again a city about which only fragmentary information is preserved in later literary sources. The Pali chronicles of Sri Lanka, which preserve this information in the form of legends relating to the period before the introduction of Buddhism, indicate that Tambapaṇṇi was a port and the seat of a ruling lineage long before Anuradhapura came into prominence. What happened to this early urban centre, perhaps the first one, in Sri Lanka is not known. But before it disappeared into obscurity, it had succeeded in giving its name to the main kingdom on the northwestern coast and to the island, a name by which people in the Mauryan Empire and the Graeco-Roman world came to know the island. Whether the ruling lineage of Tambapaṇṇi decided to move their seat to the interior, to Anurādhagāma (later Anurādhapura), for reasons similar to those that compelled the Pāṇḍyas to move interior, or whether a separate but more powerful lineage based at Anurādhagāma succeeded in supplanting Tambapaṇṇi and eclipsing it is not easy to determine. What is important is that traditions preserved in the Pali chronicles indicate that some time in the middle of the first millennium BCE Tambapaṇṇi on the northwestern coast of Sri Lanka and Matirai in southern India had emerged as urban centres and the seats of ruling lineages.

In the context of the rise of these two urban centres, one may also consider the significance of the name Tāmbraparṇī/ Tambapaṇṇi. The name Tambapaṇṇi is the Pali form of the Sanskrit Tāmraparṇī and is common to the major river in Tirunelveli (Tambraparni River) and to the ancient chiefdom in northwest Sri Lanka. It is not known whether the area around the estuary of the modern Tambraparni river was also known by the same name in ancient times. If so, this would be comparable to the Irish kingdom of Dal Riata extending from the north of Ireland across the sea to the west of Scotland, which part was known as Dalriada (the difference is merely one of Irish and non-Irish spelling). The sea dividing the two regions was a unifier and indeed for some time the two parts were ruled as one kingdom.[69] One wonders whether the Tambraparni region of Tamil Nadu and the Tambapaṇṇi of Sri Lanka were similarly under one rule at one time. Whether there was a common political authority or not, the populations of the two regions appear to have interacted as people of one kingdom, with their common interests in the pearl and chank fishery in the sea that united them.

The rise of Matirai and Tambapaṇṇi was clearly the result of the exchange network brought about by the spread of the EIA culture. These two ports emerged as important exchange centres, chiefly on account of the chank and pearl fisheries, and rose to the position of seats of chiefdoms. They were linked to the ports of western India and eastern India by coastal sea routes. Traders from north India and from the Mediterranean began to frequent these ports early in the first millennium BCE. In the wake of the north Indian trade came new cultural influences in the form of Sanskritisation, as it happened later when Indian traders went to the Southeast Asian chiefdoms.

Sanskritisation

The pattern of developments in the SISL region in the EIA is similar to that in Southeast Asia in the early centuries of the Common Era. When the EIA dawned in the SISL region, it was untouched by Sanskritic influences in the same way as Southeast Asia was before the Common Era. The development of long distance trade brought north Indian traders whose dominance had made Prakrit the *lingua franca* of South Asian trade. The introduction of Prakrit was without doubt one of the key results of the long distance trade. But there were also other important aspects of north Indian culture that flowed as a consequence of this trade. These were elements of what may be called the process of Sanskritisation.[70]

The process of Sanskritisation is not something that can be easily traced. While archaeology may provide some evidence of north Indian contacts, there are no written records to help trace the developments. What is available to find out something about this process is the body of myths and legends relating to the events of this time as preserved in the literary sources of the EHP. These myths and legends help to establish a pattern in the process of Sanskritisation in the SISL region, a pattern that is seen repeated a few centuries later in Southeast Asia in the wake of long distance trade with that region. These myths and legends are mainly preserved in the Pali chronicles of Sri Lanka, the Buddhist *Jātaka* stories and to a small extent in the earliest Tamil literary works. They later found their way into Sanskrit and Chinese Buddhist writings, too.

The main aspects of this pattern are the arrival of civilized persons (Brāhmaṇas or Kṣatriyas) to the ports by design or by accident, the confrontation between the leaders of the visiting groups and the local elite, the description of the backward locals as non-human creatures, the victory over or reconciliation with the locals, and, most importantly, the marriage of the leader of the visitors with the leading maiden of the local population culminating in the establishment of a north Indian-style ruling lineage in the area of the local people. The ruler adopts the north Indian Brahmanical ideology in the new polity, links his family with an ancient north Indian lineage and introduces Brahmanical rituals and the use of the Sanskrit language by the appointment of Brāhmaṇa court-priests (*purohita*). The elites find it fashionable to adopt Sanskrit/ Prakrit names or to Sanskritise their names. Even place-names get Sanskritised or get altered to new Sanskrit names. Thus, the way is opened for the flow of north Indian cultural practices and ideas at the elite level.

The legends relating to Agastya, Paraśurāma, Kauṇḍinya, Vijaya, Arjuṇa, the Pāṇḍyas, the Cōḷas and the Pallavas show aspects of this pattern with minor variations.[71] The Agastya and Paraśurāma legends deal with Brahmanical leaders coming to south India, subduing places in the south and making their homes there or bringing Brāhmaṇa settlers. The Arjuṇa and Vijaya legends relate to princes from north India venturing into areas in the south, confronting and subduing the backward people there and finally establishing their authority in those areas after marrying local maidens. The Kauṇḍinya legend is very similar to these, except that the hero is a Brāhmaṇa and not a Kṣatriya prince. The local maidens they married are portrayed as non-human beings, a stereotype applied to the people of lands beyond north India who had not come under the influence of Sanskritisation. In the case of the legends associated with the Pāṇḍyas, Cōḻas and Pallavas, one finds that the ancestors of these ruling families of the south are linked to established lineages of north India, thus implying that they came from the north.

The EIA culture and long distance trade ushered in a new age, ending the prehistoric period in the SISL region. While archaeology remains the main and most reliable source for this period, the legends provide some evidence of the far-reaching developments that took place during this period. The emergence of Tambapaṇṇi and Matirai as the centres of two major chiefdoms that later grew into leading kingdoms in this region is to be understood with the help of these sources. Since the legends relating to Tambapaṇṇi found a permanent place in the Pali chronicles of Sri Lanka, details of these legends have been better preserved when one compares their survivfal with the fate of the south Indian legends. For this reason, the Tambapaṇṇi legends are also useful in providing clues to understanding the developments on the Tamil Nadu side.

Tambapaṇṇi and Matirai were two of the coastal centres where the Mesolithic people came into contact with traders. The two places had probably emerged as important exchange centres towards the end of the Mesolithic period. They were therefore places where the intruding EIA culture made an early impact. The new culture, in all probability, helped the chiefs or those wielding authority to assume greater importance and more power. Long distance trade brought about more changes. At first, there was possibly some hostility. It is possible that, at some stage, leaders among the traders, or others who had joined them, gained authority either by marrying into the families of the chiefs or by using their superior military power. Where this did not happen, the chiefs themselves, along with other elites, adopted the culture of the traders and opened the way for Sanskritisation.

Chronology

It is not easy to provide a chronological sequence to these developments. The evidence currently available from archaeology seems to indicate that the EIA culture spread across the SISL region from about the beginning of the first millennium BCE. Long distance trade along the western and eastern coasts of India probably reached an active phase in the early centuries of that millennium, creating a lucrative market in luxury goods in the ports of Sri Lanka and Tamil Nadu by the middle of the millennium. There were no doubt very close relations between the chiefdom based at Tambapaṇṇi and the one based at Matirai. It is indeed possible that at one stage Tambapaṇṇi had authority over the area around the estuary of the Tambraparni on the Tamil Nadu coast. The legends relating to the Paṇḍu family of Tambapaṇṇi may also reveal links with the Pāṇḍyas of Matirai.[72]

Towards the end of the EIA, the centre of power had moved from the northwestern coast of Sri Lanka to the interior centre of Anurādhagāma. Similarly, the Pāṇḍyas had also shifted their centre from the Tamraparni-Vaigai coast to the interior centre, also named Matirai, which had been Sanskritised as Madhura. At the beginning of the third century BCE, by all indications, the two had become centres of small kingdoms.

Common Elements in the Sankritisation legends of South India, Sri Lanka and Southeast Asia

Common elements	Agastya legends	Parasurama legends	Arjuna legends	Vijaya legends	Kaundinya legends
Arrival of Brahmana/ Ksatriya leader	Brahmana rishi	Brahmana leader	Ksatriya leader	Ksatriya leader	Brahmana leader
Existence of non-human local population	Raksasas	Non-Brahmana enemies	Nagas and Nishidas	Yakkhas	Nagas
Resistance by and confrontation with local population	Opposition by Vatapi and Ilvala	Opposition by non-Brahmans	Opposition by Nagas and Nishidas	Leader's entourage tricked and imprisoned	Opposition by Nagas in sea battle
Use of superior knowledge/ power to achieve dominance	Use of mystic powers and superior knowledge	Use of superior weapon *(parasu)* and prowess	Use of superior military skills (archery)	Use of superior power	Use of superior power
Victory and reconciliation	Victory over Raksasas and acceptance as Sage of the South	Victory and acquisition of new lands for settlement	Victory over local population	Subduing of Yakkhas and reconciliation with Yakkha maiden	Victory over Nagas
Marriage of leader to local maiden	Marriage with local princess	-	Marriage with Naga maiden	Marriage with Yakkha maiden	Marriage with Naga maiden
Introduction of Brahmanical ideology	Spread of Vedic knowledge	Introduction of Brahmanical practices		Consecration according to Brahmanical laws	Rule over Naga kingdom and introduction of Brahmanical system

Language and literacy

The establishment of a developed and more sophisticated polity or polities was without doubt accompanied by significant social and cultural developments. These would have included advances in the use of language and literacy. The spread of the advanced EIA culture must have been accompanied by the development of one or more of the languages that were already in use or by the introduction of more advanced languages. Those who were responsible for the spread of the EIA culture would have also spread the language or languages they used. In a similar manner, traders would have also shared this responsibility.

Although there is no dearth of theories about the language or languages associated with the EIA culture, identifying the languages spoken by those who spread this culture and by those among whom this culture spread is one of the most difficult problems confronting scholars. Various theories have been floated ever since the discovery of the archaeological remains of urn burials and megalithic monuments in south India in the nineteenth century. One of the earliest, and still the most popular, theory is that the people who introduced this culture to peninsular India were speakers of Dravidian languages.[73]

Earliest records

Without the aid of written records there is no way of determining the language or languages spoken by any pre-literate society. That the people associated with the EIA culture used some kind of writing system for certain limited purposes may not be disputed. They used a set of characters, commonly referred to as non-Brāhmī symbols or graffiti symbols, which have survived as graffiti marks on sherds of pottery. These characters as yet remain undeciphered. They were in use long before a phonetic script, the well-known Brāhmī, was adopted in peninsular India and Sri Lanka. As long as they remain undeciphered, they cannot provide any clue to the language or languages spoken by the users of these symbols.

We are on firmer ground, however, when we get to the material with Brāhmī writing. Almost all the material with Brāhmī writing in SISL cannot be dated to a period prior to 300 BCE. The only exceptions are the potsherds with Brāhmī graffiti discovered in excavations at Anuradhapura a few years ago and carbondated to the middle of the first millennium BCE. But such material cannot be reliably used to determine the language spoken by the people who lived in Anuradhapura at that time. Graffiti on pots, which were almost always names, were used to indicate ownership and traders inscribed their names on pots to show ownership of the contents.[74] The inscribed sherds from Anuradhapura, valuable though they are for the chronology of the Brāhmī script, are interesting only in providing clues relating to the contacts that the early urban centre of Anuradhapura had with long distance traders as well as for the revelation that the Brāhmī script was known, at least at the elite level, at such an early stage in the history of the region.[75]

Any search for the languages spoken in the EIA will have to begin with the earliest inscriptional and literary records we have. The earliest stone inscriptions in Sri Lanka, datable to about the second century BCE, are all in Prakrit. There are, however, traces of Dravidian-language influence in vocabulary and phonology. The earliest stone inscriptions in Tamil Nadu, also datable to the second century BCE, are in Old Tamil but betray influence of Prakrit. The graffiti on potsherds, whose dates have not been precisely determined but which belong to the EHP, are mostly in Prakrit with a few in Tamil as far as Sri Lanka is concerned. On the Tamil Nadu side the potsherd graffiti are mostly in Tamil with a few in Prakrit. In addition to these, there are also coins and at least one seal with Brāhmī legends. Some of these legends are in Tamil while others are in Prakrit. All these inscriptions are records of the elites – traders, monks and rulers as well as administrators. They reflect the two dominant languages that were used as written languages by the elites in the EHP.

Tamiḻ and Heḷa

In the EHP, on the Tamil Nadu side, there is even more important evidence relating to the linguistic situation that leaves one in no doubt about the evolution of a language that would dominate in the area in historical times. The emergence of Tamil as a developed literary medium is reflected in the large number of poetical works that collectively go by the popular name of Sangam poetry. In Sri Lanka, on the other hand, the establishment of the Buddhist Sangha (Church) and the royal patronage it received led to the language of Buddhism, namely Pali, having an edge over any other as a literary medium. But it took some time before the local monks mastered the new language and the earliest literary output in this medium took place towards the end of the EHP, about 300 CE. However, as a language that was already dead, Pali was not the spoken language. But there was an emerging literary language in which commentaries were written for the Pali canonical texts, a medium through which the monks could communicate with the local people. The name of this language, as known from later sources, has the forms Heḷa and Eḷu (Sīhaḷa in Pali).

Was Heḷa the same as the language of the Brāhmī cave inscriptions? Was it widely spoken in the island in the EHP? Was it the most dominant of the languages spoken at that time or was it the only language of the island people? Definite answers cannot be provided at present for these and other relevant questions. Much work remains to be done by historical linguists before we could say anything definite about the origins and development of Heḷa. None of the commentaries or other literary output in this language dating to the EHP has survived. The few scholars who have worked on the early inscriptions have expressed differing views on the language of these records and generally tended to avoid the issue of its connection with Heḷa.

Sinhalese-Prakrit

It is generally agreed that the Heḷa of the EHP is the older form of the Sinhala language that is known to us through literary works and inscriptions from about the tenth century. *Heḷa* was clearly the name given for their language by the speakers of that language, while *Sīhaḷa* was the name given to it in Pali. The Sanskritised form *Siṃhaḷa* became popular in later centuries. Scholars who have studied the inscriptions from the Brāhmī cave records to those of about the twelfth century are inclined to support the view that some of the distinctive features of the later Sinhala language are to be seen from about the eighth century. The language of the earliest records is a form of Prakrit, often referred to as Sinhalese-Prakrit.[76] It is not fully identifiable with any of the Prakrits of northern India. It shows some features that are similar to those in the Prakrit of western India and others that are akin to the features of the Prakrit of eastern India. As a result, some have claimed that Sinhalese-Prakrit is closest to the Prakrit of western India and some others have claimed a close affinity with the Prakrit of eastern India. Yet another claim is that it is a Western Prakrit which was later 'profoundly modified by a superimposed lingustic substratum of Eastern origin'. At least one scholar has classed it with the Prakrit of the south Indian inscriptions.[77] In view of this divergence of opinions, another scholar has concluded that this Sinhalese-Prakrit is a 'composite language influenced by the sub-continent of India taken as a whole, and not by any particular region'.[78]

It is clear that much remains to be done in regard to the origins of the Sinhala language. For the present, it would appear that Sinhalese-Prakrit was considerably removed from the Indian Prakrits in the second century BCE (when the earliest Brāhmī cave records appear). This would mean that after the introduction of one or more forms of Prakrit in the island, changes had taken place over a considerable period, perhaps two or more centuries. In all probability, the origin of Sinhalese-Prakrit in the island dates back to a time before the arrival of Prakrit-speaking Buddhist monks in the third century BCE.

To trace back the time when Prakrit was introduced to the island will no doubt be a fascinating quest for historical linguists. For the moment, we have to start with the premise that Prakrit was not the language spoken by the Mesolithic people of Sri Lanka. This is a view that will not be contested by serious scholars. As stated earlier, in the present state of our knowledge, we have no evidence about the languages spoken by the Mesolithic people. The spread of the EIA culture and the development of long distance trade with western and eastern India would have, among other innovations, brought new languages to the island. Long distance trade, rather than the EIA culture that came via south India, would be the factor responsible for the introduction of Prakrit, the language of that trade in the first millennium BCE.

When do we get any evidence for the presence of Prakrit-using traders in the island? The earliest evidence we have comes from Anuradhapura and it is carbondated to the middle of the first millennium BCE. This is in the form of fragmentary inscriptions on potsherds. The language of these inscriptions is identifiable as Prakrit. Few and fragmentary though they are and only indicative of restricted use by an elite group of traders, these early epigraphs may be taken to provide evidence of the arrival of Prakrit in the island in the middle of the first millennium BCE or earlier.

Language Replacement

In the light of the above discussion, it is possible to conclude that some time between about 1000 BCE, when the Mesolithic Period draws to a close and the EIA culture begins to spread, and about 500 BCE Prakrit had made its appearance in Sri Lanka. It was a language brought by traders – some from western India, some from eastern India and some others who had settled in the ports of southern India and exchange centres in the interior to exploit the lucrative marine and mineral resources in SISL. Before long it would have become a language used by the local elites and, in course of time, spread among the other inhabitants.

Renfrew's models

This brings us to the question of how a Prakrit language came to be widely used in the greater part of Sri Lanka by about the last quarter of the first millennium BCE, replacing the languages spoken in the Mesolithic Period and paving the way for the emergence of the Sinhala language. Such a phenomenon of linguistic replacement is not something peculiar to Sri Lanka. One sees this in the history of many countries. One of the best examples is what happened in Britain. In recent years, as already mentioned, the archaeologist Renfrew, working on the theme of archaeology and language, has drawn the attention of scholars to his theory of language replacement by proposing some models of language change. This theory is useful for the understanding of the process through which a Prakrit language came to be spoken in Sri Lanka.[79] It rejects the need for population change for language change to occur.

In the Sri Lankan situation, one is reminded of those who base their arguments for population change on the occurrence of the BRW or Northern Black Polished Ware and jump to conclusions. The words of caution from two respected specialists in South Asian archaeology, F.R. Allchin and Bridget Allchin, are relevant here:

> Another source of misconception is the tendency of archaeologists to identify single traits or groups of traits with people. Thus one reads of the first appearance of a certain type of pottery at a given site as evidence of the presence of the Indo-Aryans, that the Painted Gray Ware was the pottery of the Indo-Aryans, etc. While this may be partially true for some traits in special circumstances, perhaps for example with the first arrival of horses in a region, or of a new and different burial pattern, such cultural traits can and almost universally are acquired by one group from another without necessarily having refrence to ethnic origins or language, or other aspects of culture.[80]

Elite dominance

Of the six models that Renfrew has proposed, Elite Dominance is more applicable to the Sri Lankan situation than any of the others. This model, as described earlier, assumes the arrival of a small group of well-organized people, speaking a different language, who are able to establish their dominance over the local population. In this model, the social organization of the incoming group is very important. Renfrew emphasizes: 'They may not be large in number, but in order to bring the pre-existing population into subjection effectively, they must already display, I would argue, what the anthropologist terms "ranking": they must already have a ranked or a stratified social organization.' He argues that 'it is only when a small incoming group is organized in such a way that it can expect to dominate a much larger resident population.'[81]

Given the superior social organization of the small incoming group, this is what happens to the language of the existing population and that of the newcomers: the language of the new arrivals and the language of the local population will exist side by side for some time paving the way for a period of bilingualism. In course of time, the incoming group is assimilated into the local population and either its language prevails and the local language dies out, or the new language is forgotten and the local language prevails.[82]

There is no reason why this model cannot apply to the Sri Lankan situation, although there is no need to rule out the operation of other factors as well. If long-distance traders came to the island from the northern parts of India very early in the first millennium BCE, as indeed they seem to have, their arrival coincided with the spread of the EIA culture via south India. The benefits of the new culture may not have worked so quickly as to bring about the rise of polities powerful enough to resist domination by outsiders. By all indications, the first kingdoms in the island did not emerge before the middle of the first millennium BCE. Even after the emergence of a large and comparatively strong kingdom, in the second century BCE, a leader of a trading group did not find it difficult to seize power and dominate the political scene for some time.[83] It must have been not too difficult for trading groups from northern India to establish themselves in the exchange centres and centres of authority in various parts of the island and gradually gain dominance over the local population.

The resident population was not yet organized socially or politically to resist this domination. Nor did they possess a language or languages that were developed enough to resist replacement by the language of newcomers. Presumably, there were more than one language spoken by the local population which not only would have weakened their resistance but, what is more important, created the need to adopt the language of the dominant minority incoming group as a link language at a time when the internal exchange network and contacts with the long-distance traders were expanding. In these circumstances, it is not difficult to see some features of Renfrew's Elite Dominance model at work. The local languages and the Prakrit of the traders would have existed side-by-side for some time with at least the elite of the resident population becoming bilingual. In the long run, the language of the newcomers prevailed with, presumably, some elements from the local languages.

Combination of different factors

As discussed earlier, Coningham et al have pointed out that all the models 'may have performed a function in the process of language replacement' and that 'Renfrew's models omit the possibility of linguistic replacement through prolonged trade contact'.[84] This is a valid comment. It is very likely that in the Sri Lankan case a long period of contact with north Indian traders was responsible for language replacement. In this connection, Coningham et al have drawn attention to the argument put forward by Sherrat in whose view

> it could be argued that trading networks involving directional exchange …would have created new demands for inter-regional communication, especially between elites. These

> would have provided circumstances for the formation of pidgins and creoles, which because of their association with prestige activities could have slowly gained much wider currency in pre-literate communities.[85]

There is a strong possibility that such a situation existed in Sri Lanka. While long-distance trade appears to have played an important role in language replacement in the island, one cannot disagree with the argument that 'there is no reason why the Sri Lankan linguistic replacement need have been monocausal rather than polycausal'. The southward movement of Jaina, Buddhist and Ajivika monks from north India from about the fourth century BCE, for instance, would have had an impact on Sri Lanka, too, adding another factor that strengthened the position of Prakrit in the island.

The spread of the Prakrit dialects in some parts of India and Sri Lanka is comparable to that of the Indo-European languages in many areas of Europe. Commenting on the latter, the linguist H.R. Robins makes the following observation:

> …the spread of the Indo-European languages resulted, in the main, from the imposition of one of them on the earlier population of the territories occupied. In the historical period, within Indo-European, the same process can be seen at work in the western Roman Empire. Latin superseded the earlier, largely Celtic languages of the Iberian peninsula and of Gaul (France) not through population replacement (the number of Roman soldiers and settlers in the empire was never large) but through the abandonment of these languages by the inhabitants over the generations as they found in Latin the language of commerce, civilization, law, literature, and social prestige.[86]

One thing, however, is clear. There is no archaeological evidence in the island for any mass migration, be it from the north or the south of the subcontinent, or for that matter from any other place, in the first millennium BCE, resulting in the displacement or extermination of the existing population. The Prakrit used in the EHP could only have been the result of a process of slow language replacement.

The South Indian Scene

Arrival of Prakrit

Long-distance trade along the coastal sea routes and across the Deccan no doubt brought Prakrit-speaking north Indian traders to various trade centres in the south in the first millennium BCE. The position of Prakrit introduced by these traders was further strengthened by the Buddhist, Jaina and Ajivika monks who crossed over to the south from about the fourth century. Going by the earliest inscriptions in south India, it would appear that Prakrit had a greater impact in Andhra, Karnataka and northern Tamil Nadu than in southern Tamil Nadu. All the earliest inscriptions in Andhra are in Prakrit. The earliest inscriptions of the Pallavas in northern Tamil Nadu are also in Prakrit. But in southern Tamil Nadu almost all the earliest stone inscriptions are in Old Tamil, some of them showing influence of Prakrit. There are, however, a few potsherd inscriptions from southern Tamil Nadu written in Prakrit.

But Prakrit failed to gain ascendancy in the southern Tamil Nadu region. Well before 200 BCE, the dominance of the Tamil language seems to have led to a process of assimilation and integration of other language speakers into the Tamil-speaking ethnic group, thus paving the way for the evolution of the larger Tamil ethnic group of the EHP. This was, no doubt, a process that went on even in the later centuries. The presence of Munda and other non-Dravidian elements in the Tamil language may have to be explained as the result of the acculturation that took place in the period when the EIA Megalithic culture spread in south India.

Although Prakrit was adopted by the elites for their records in Andhra, it did not succeed in replacing the language or languages of the local people. A local language, Telugu, did finally emerge as the dominant language of Andhra, even though it took more than a millennium for this to occur.

Emergence of Tamil

The southern tip of the peninsula, the area that is now southern Tamil Nadu and southern Kerala, proved to be an exception. It was the only region in peninsular India, indeed in the whole of South Asia, where inscriptions were indited in a language not belonging to the Indo-Aryan sub-family. This may be an indication of the level of development of Tamil at the time Prakrit made its appearance. Historical linguists will no doubt in time find some good reasons for this. Judging by the literary output in Tamil in the EHP, namely the Sangam poems, it would seem that the Tamil language had reached a level of development to be employed as a literary medium in the second half of the first millennium BCE. The contact with Prakrit and Sanskrit appears to have provided the impetus for the development of Tamil. The fact that the Tamil language was firmly entrenched in the far south of the subcontinent and could not be dislodged by Prakrit or even Sanskritised like its neighbouring languages, Telugu, Kannada and Malayalam, had its implications for the linguistic scene in Sri Lanka.

As will be seen in the next chapter, the rise of Tamil as the most dominant language of present-day southern Tamil Nadu may not have occurred later than the middle of the first millennium BCE. It was the time when the EIA culture, with its special features of BRW, urn burials, megaliths and iron tools as well as rice cultivation associated with an early system of irrigation, was spreading in all parts of southern Tamil Nadu and crossing over to Sri Lanka. Speakers of the Tamil language were without doubt associated with this cultural movement. It is possible that there were also speakers of other languages among the recipients, and later distributors, of this culture in this part of south India.

Spread of Tamil into Sri Lanka

When the urn burial practices of Adichchanallur were carried over to Pomaparippu and when the technology of the iron tools and BRW spread from the port of Korkai to the port of Mātoṭa, when the cist burial practices of the Vaigai Valley spread to the north-central plains of Sri Lanka watered by the Yan Oya, when those engaged in pearl fishery and chank fishery in the Palk Strait and the Gulf of Mannar frequented the Pamban Coast and the Puttalam Coast, one cannot imagine the Tamil language not being associated with these activities or being part of this cultural movement. Just as Prakrit, and to an extent Sanskrit, was part of the cultural movement that flowed from north India along with long distance trade, so was Tamil part of the EIA cultural movement that spread from Tamil Nadu to Sri Lanka in the first millennium BCE.

When did the Tamil language (or its ancestor, Proto-Tamil-Malayalam) begin to spread in Sri Lanka? Where was it first introduced? Questions like these are difficult to answer and may probably never get the right answers. There is ample archaeological evidence for the cultural interaction between Tamil Nadu and Sri Lanka from prehistoric times. But, as Renfrew has reminded us, 'the archaeological evidence from an early (and non-literate) period can tell us nothing directly about the languages which were spoken'.[87] We know from the Mesolithic sites near the Tambraparni River in Tamil Nadu and those in Sri Lanka that there was a close interaction between the two areas in the second millennium BCE. But we do not know, and will probably never know, whether an ancestor of the Tamil language was spoken in the Tambraparni River region at that time.

It is only when we get closer to the EHP that we are in a position to say with confidence that the Tamil language had achieved a dominant position among the languages spoken by the protohistoric peoples of Tamil Nadu. Assuming that the earliest of the Tamil Sangam poems were composed about the second century BCE (which is the date favoured by most modern scholars) and assigning a period of two or three centuries for the language to reach the level of a literary medium, the middle of the first millennium BCE seems to be a reasonable date to mark the emergence of Tamil in south India. Tamil-speakers would have been present in Sri Lanka about that time.

As discussed earlier, it is about that time that the first major chiefdoms seem to have emerged on either side of the Gulf of Mannar. Long-distance traders from north India and inter-regional traders from south India would have been major players in the significant socio-political, cultural and economic developments that took place in the SISL region. Sri Lanka appears to have been the focus of new linguistic influences – Prakrit from the north and Tamil from the south – that were to have far-reaching consequences in the history of the island. When the EHP dawns, the picture becomes clear with the availability of literary sources as well as epigraphic material.

Archaeological record

The process of change occurring in the middle of the first millennium BCE has left considerable material traces in the archaeological record, enabling us to infer when this process, which includes linguistic changes, became significant. However, it is to answer the question of where the processes of change began that the archaeological record is on firmer ground. As already seen, it is in the northern third of the island that we see a concentration of material traces of the new cultural influences from Tamil Nadu – the urn burials, the cist burials, BRW, iron technology and the beginnings of rice cultivation with the use of irrigation. The southern two-third of the island has so far yielded relatively few of these material traces, prompting Seneviratne to make this observation:

> ...we have to recognize the fact that by the beginning of the Early Historic period around 3rd Cent. B.C., there was a co-existence of various cultural nuclei in different physical areas of the island. Covering the broadest physical area was the

> Mesolithic element which was also the substratum culture of the island. Then there was the cultural locus that developed primarily in northern Sri Lanka which appears to have had its impetus largely from South India. Another cultural locus developed in south-east Sri Lanka which may slightly post-date the northern locus, but had conclusively emerged as an independent geo-cultural unit at least by the 3rd Cent. B.C. and seems to have had a stronger Indo-Aryan culture element in it.[88]

While the new social and economic landscape created by the spread of the EIA culture was accompanied by the arrival of not merely traders but also artisans and those skilled in exploiting marine and mineral resources, there was no mass migration of settlers either from north India or from south India. There was no displacement of the local population. The newcomers undoubtedly had an advantage over the local people and many of them would have constituted the elite in the new society. The chiefs and other leaders among the local population would have come under the influence of the newcomers and begun to adopt elements of the new culture. The archaeological remains of the new culture need not all be ascribed to outsiders. One cannot agree more with Seneviratne in this respect:

> The introduction of the 'Iron Age' to Sri Lanka has to be viewed more as a transmission of 'culture elements' through periodic contacts established by various groups where they physically and culturally intermingled with each other as well as with the existing Mesolithic people in such areas, in the course of which the latter came to adopt the higher culture elements of the iron using people.[89]

Prakrit and Tamil

By all indications, Prakrit made rapid progress in the major part of Sri Lanka and its position was clearly augmented by the arrival of the Jaina, Ajivika and Buddhist religions. The mission of Mahinda in the third century and the royal patronage that Buddhism received ensured the dominance that Prakrit was to enjoy in the EHP. However, in the northern third of the island, Tamil was a language to be reckoned with. In that part of Sri Lanka at least, it was in competition with Prakrit to replace the languages of the Mesolithic people. The developments in south India were to help Tamil immensely in this contest for dominance as far as the northernmost part of the island was concerned.

Two major developments, one linguistic and the other political, in Tamil Nadu would have strengthened the spread of Tamil in northern Sri Lanka. One was the emergence of Tamil as a literary language that could compete with Prakrit and Sanskrit and hold its own against them. The other was the rise, so close to northern Sri Lanka, of the chiefdom of the Pāṇḍyas which became the centre for the development of Tamil literature. One may add a third factor, namely, the movement of the people known to us from the literary sources as Nāgas to the northern peninsula and the islands. As Seneviratne says, ' the significance of the Nāgas (mentioned in literature) who were concentrated along the northern and the western coast cannot be overlooked in the early social and economic formations of the island and also as agents of a more cosmopolitan culture associated with long distance trade.'[90] The Nāgas of Tamil Nadu, it would appear, were on the way to being integrated into the dominant Tamil-speaking group in Tamil Nadu when Nāga migrations to northern Sri Lanka began. The earliest Tamil poems of the Sangam anthology reveal names of poets with Nāga connections, indicating their assimilation into the Tamil-speaking population. Since the Jaffna peninsula was not settled by Mesolithic people, the Nāgas would have been the first settlers there, paving the way for the area to be called Nāgadīpa. Not only did they bring the new Iron Age cultural elements from south India but may have also introduced the Tamil language along with their own. The dominance of the Tamil language under Pāṇḍya patronage and the assimilation of the Nāgas of Tamil Nadu into the Tamil-speaking population would have been strong influences that led to the demise of the Nāga language and the emergence of Tamil in the northernmost region of Sri Lanka.[91]

As will be seen later, language replacement and the evolution of a major ethnic community were well on their way by the beginning of the EHP. By the end of the third century BCE Prakrit had achieved the position of the written language of the elite. Prakrit names were also universally popular. And what is most important, a major ethnic group, whose language would be the Prakrit-derived Heḷa, had begun to evolve.

Major ethnic groups

This major ethnic group came to be also known as Heḷa. Its composition in the EIA would be impossible to determine. But it may have already included different ethnic groups, with Prakrit as the *lingua franca* uniting all of them. These are again issues for the historical linguist to resolve. What will prove hard to refute is the emergence of a major ethnic group with Prakrit as the principal uniting force. That there was a similar process occurring in northern Sri Lanka, with Tamil as the uniting force, among other sections of the population cannot be easily dismissed. In Tamil Nadu, too, Tamil had emerged as the dominant language of the elite and begun to replace other languages.

Almost to the end of the EIA the SISL region underwent transformation as a single region. The development of wet rice cultivation, a rudimentary tank system and iron technology as well as an internal trade network were common features of development for both Sri Lanka and Tamil Nadu. It is in that background that we see the beginnings of a writing system capable of being a vehicle for maintaining simple records and for inscribing labels on pottery. By all indications at present, the SISL region appears to have received the new script, if it had indeed not developed it, earlier than the other regions of South Asia.

The Brāhmī Script

The origin of this script, now known as Brāhmī, is still an intriguing subject for scholars. More than a century of scientific archaeological work in West Asia and South Asia has failed to provide any clues to the origin of Brāhmī. It makes its appearance suddenly as a well developed writing system which spread rapidly over the whole of South Asia and then began a process of regional development that culminated in the birth of all modern South Asian scripts, except the one used for Urdu.

It is not impossible, in the context of the rapid advances towards urbanization and civilization that were being made in South Asia in the first millennium BCE, for a South Asian community or an intelligent individual to have invented the script. But the fact that all available written material in South Asia shows this script in an advanced, well-tried form, without any evidence of innovative attempts or early forms goes against such an assumption. It is hard to reject the view that Brāhmī was introduced basically in the form in which we see it in the third century BCE (except for certain regional variations) as a fully developed script.

Of the many theories about the origin of Brāhmī, the most convincing is that it was introduced by traders from West Asia. Of all the scripts used in the first millennium BCE, before the date of the earliest Brāhmī records, it is the scripts of some Mediterranean communities that resemble Brāhmī. And of all the Mediterranean traders who might have helped in the invention, the Phoenicians seem to be the most likely. The Phoenicians have been celebrated not only as 'vaunted seafarers and intrepid explorers' but also as 'learned scribes, who passed on the modern alphabet'.[92] There is general agreement among scholars that the modern linear alphabet of the West arose in the Eastern Mediterranean region some time in the second millennium BCE. The Phoenician linear alphabetic script, it is believed, emerged at the end of the second millennium BCE as a result of simplifying and abstracting a system of pictographic character writing that was in use in the Sinai peninsula.

PHOENICIAN AND BRAHMI

Similarities between Phoenician (Byblian) / Phoenician-derived scripts of the Mediterranean region and Brahmi

Phoenician c 1000 BCE	Brahmi	Early Greek c 800 – 600 BCE	Brahmi	Etruscan c700 – 500 BCE	Brahmi

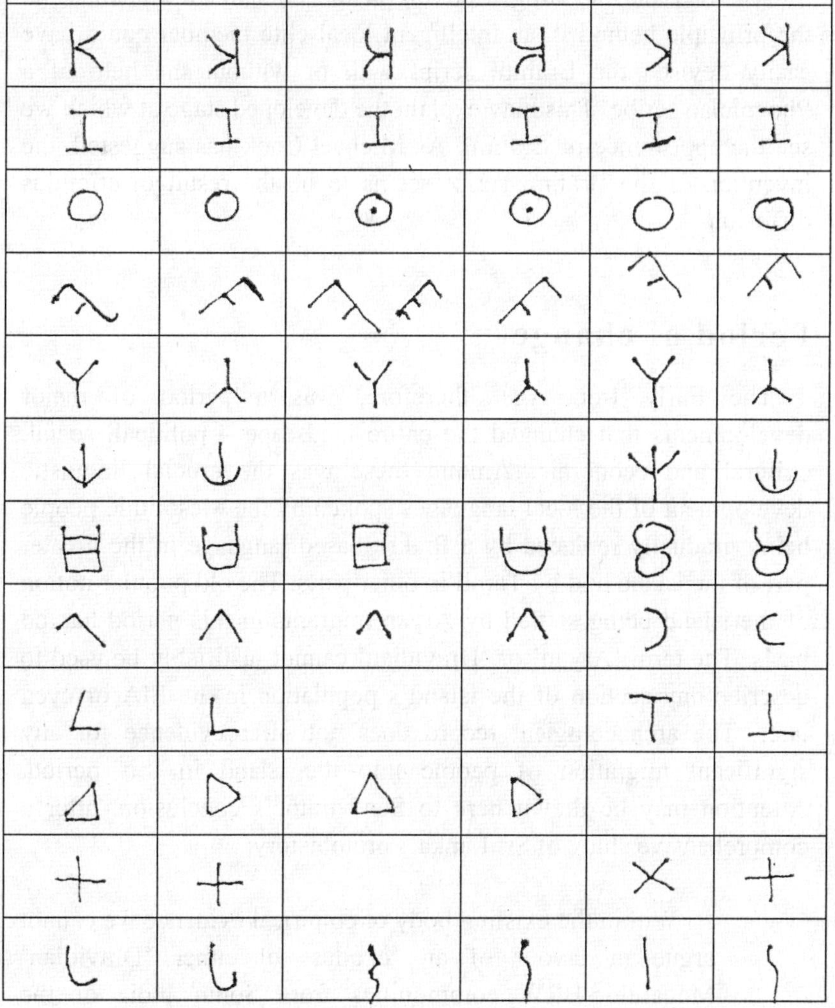

With its twenty-two consonants, the Phoenician alphabet spread quickly in various directions. By the ninth century BCE, the new alphabet had been adopted by many Mediterranean languages such as Hebrew, Aramaic and Ammonite. With Phoenician commercial expansion, the alphabet was exported to areas in the Western Mediterranean as well. If, as argued earlier, the Phoenicians were trading in the ports of the western coast of India early in the first millennium BCE, it will not be surprising that they had inspired the local elite to adopt a system of writing for elementary recording of transactions and labelling. Looking at the Phoenician alphabet and the principle behind it, an intelligent local elite member could have easily devised the Brāhmī script with or without the help of a Phoenician scribe. This may explain the developed stage at which we see the appearance of Brāhmī. As Michael Cook has suggested, the invention of the Brāhmī script seems to be the result of stimulus diffusion.[93]

Period of change

The Early Iron Age, therefore, was a period of major developments that changed the entire landscape – political, social, cultural and economic. Among these was the crucial linguistic development of the local languages spoken by the Mesolithic people being gradually replaced by a Prakrit-based language in the greater part of the island and by Tamil in other parts. The old popular notion of the island being settled by Aryan migrants in this period has no basis. The term 'Aryan' or 'Dravidian' cannot justifiably be used to describe any section of the island's population in the EIA or even later. The archaeological record does not offer evidence for any significant migration of people into the island in this period. Attention may be drawn here to Seneviratne's conclusion, after a comprehensive study of Sri Lanka's protohistory:

> Within the existing body of empirical evidence we cannot argue in favour of an 'exodus' of either 'Dravidian' Megalithic-BRW communities from South India or the

'Aryans' of north west/ east India, who arrived en-masse with a mission to 'civilize' Sri Lanka. Such a view is unscientific not only on account of its racial implications and that it entails an ethnic concept associated with the techno-cultural elements of the formative period, but it also ignores the actual internal and external impetus given to the dynamics of institutional development that provided the infrastructure for the emergence of civilization in Sri Lanka.[94]

CHAPTER 3

ARYAN AND DRAVIDIAN

Imaginary Ancestors

"It is important to note that the Aryan theory was not merely something imposed from above by Orientalist scholars. It was eagerly welcomed by most Sinhala scholars who found the Aryan theory flattering in that it elevated them to the ranks of the kinsmen of their rulers". Prof. Leslie Gunawardana 1994: 197.

Aryan controversy

Few topics are as emotive in South Asian studies as the so-called Aryan controversy. This and, to a lesser extent, the Dravidian controversy have plagued scholarly work in South Asian studies – linguistic, historical and even archaeological – for the past century and a half. Today, the controversy still rages not only among scholars but also among politicians, educationists and media personnel often creating emotional outbursts and heated arguments. The Sanskrit word *ārya*, first occurring in the ancient Indian text *Rigveda* some 3500 years ago (and related to the word *airiya* in the contemporary Iranian text *Avesta*), originally had the denotation 'noble' but, in modern times, acquired the connotation of racial superiority and almost became a dirty word when the Nazis were dominant in Germany. With the explosion of the Aryan myth after the defeat of the Nazis, the controversy surrounding the so-called Aryans became largely a subject of academic interest in the West. But in South Asia, with the success of the nationalist movement in India and the gaining of political independence from Britain, the controversy over the Aryans acquired new dimensions.

The Aryan controversy is a complex one. If one were to describe it in simple terms, it is about the origin and spread of a family of languages in Asia and Europe. As a language was often identified with a particular 'race' of people, this family of languages was also identified with a 'race' of people and the controversy came to include the original home and spread of this 'race' as well. Gradually ideas of racial superiority and original occupation of lands also came to be aspects of this controversy. While there is absolutely no necessity to go into the history and details of this question, a brief account may not be out of place as this has a direct bearing on the myth of the Aryan colonization of Sri Lanka.

The whole controversy begins early in the nineteenth century, largely as the creation of colonial scholarship. When European scholars discovered a close relationship between the languages of Europe and those of northern India, the idea that all these languages were derived from one language and that they all belonged to a single family did not take long to be accepted. Among the names given to this family were Aryan, Indo-Germanic and Indo-European. Of these, the last mentioned, coined in 1813, has come to be widely accepted. However, the name Aryan is still used in common parlance, particularly in South Asia. This name is based on the evidence in the *Rigveda*, acclaimed to be the oldest text in any Indo-European language, wherein we find that the people who composed and used the Rigvedic hymns were the Ārya. Soon it was assumed that all those who spoke the Vedic language and the later languages that were derived from this language were Aryans. These people were differentiated by the name Indo-Aryans, since the speakers of the related languages elsewhere, including those in Europe, were also assumed to be Aryans. In other words, from the beginning of the studies relating to the Indo-European languages, a fundamental flaw was seen and that was the confusion of language with 'race'. That is where the problem really began.

Having equated language with 'race', it was easy for scholars and others to talk about the migration (and invasions) of Aryans in the same breath as the spread of Aryan languages. On the assumption that all the Aryan languages were descended from a single language, linguists began to reconstruct this ancestral language. This reconstructed language was named Proto-Indo-European. Assuming that the speakers of this Proto-Indo-European, the original 'Aryans', migrated to different parts of Asia and Europe from their homeland, scholars also began the search for this original homeland (*Urheimat*). As different theories were propounded, there began a controversy over the identification of the original homeland, the routes of migration and the chronology of this migration.[1]

The Aryan question also incorporated a racial element in it. This was to take an ugly turn in the first half of the twentieth century when politicians stepped in and exploited the researches of linguists and historians in creating the myth of the racial superiority of the Aryans, a development that resulted in terrible consequences under the Nazis in many parts of Europe.[2] Elsewhere, too, a consciousness of superiority arose among people who suddenly found that their language was considered to be a member of the Aryan family, although they were not even remotely related to the 'Aryan race' (or Nordic) that the European politicians had in mind. In the nineteenth century, using the references in the *Rigveda* to the 'fair-skinned' Āryas who fought with the 'dark-skinned' Dāsas or some other evidence, some pictured the Aryans as tall and fair-skinned people. By the first quarter of the twentieth century, politicians had created a myth that made the 'Germanic race' the representative of the pure 'Aryan race'. It was a myth that was based on the assumption, among others, that peoples whose languages are related are also related 'racially'. This Aryan myth has now been exploded. However, the controversy over the original home of Proto-Indo-European still rages.

Current Theories

Recent developments in linguistics and archaeology have had a significant impact on the Aryan question. This has resulted in the

PLATE 8.
A Tamil inscription belonging to Matsyesvaram, from Nilaveli. Circa 10th century.
***Photo** of estampage by author.*

PLATE 9.
A view of the ancient Ganga-tataka (Kantalay) irrigation reservoir, around which grew a flourishing Brahmana settlement (*brahmadeya*) known early in the 11th century as Rajaraja-caturvedi-mangalam (after Cola Rajaraja I), and later re-named as Vijayaraja-caturvedi-mangalam (after Vijayabahu I). In the 12th century, it was known also as Caturveda Brahmapura. The tank submerges an area of 2296 hectares. See pp.215, 233.

Photo: March 2005, by the author.

adoption of new perspectives and the abandoning of some of the old theories. Perhaps the most important work in relating the results of the developments in linguistics and archaeology and reviewing some of the long-held theories about the spread of languages, particularly the Indo-European languages, is that of Colin Renfrew. Questioning the series of assumptions on which these theories have been based, this archaeologist dismisses as 'naïve as well as arrogant' the old theories that explained the spread of the Indo-European (Aryan) languages. According to these old theories, it was the racial superiority of the Proto-Indo-Europeans (or Proto-Aryans) that enabled them 'to expand their territories at a certain point in time and conquer most of Europe and northern India'.[3] In his view, the various attempts hitherto undertaken to locate an original homeland for the Proto-Indo-Europeans have had no sound basis. Strongly supporting the current scholarly view that 'it is a serious mistake to equate race and language', he rejects the arguments based on linguistic palaeontology for the identification of the Aryan homeland.[4] Renfrew also criticizes the manner in which prehistoric archaeology has been used to claim an original homeland for the Aryans. 'The existing homeland theories', he argues, 'make the fundamental mistake of equating the emergence of a new culture complex with the intrusion of a new linguistic group'. He also gives a third reason for rejecting these theories, namely, 'they give absolutely no clear and adequate indication as to *why* there should have been a spread [of the languages] at all'.[5]

Seeking a demographic and economic explanation for the wide uniformity in language seen in Europe, Renfrew links the spread of farming in Europe to the spread of the Indo-European languages. In his view, 'The Indo-European languages of Europe would thus be traceable back to the first farmers of Greece who would themselves have spoken an early form of Indo-European.'[6] It was in Greece that the process of bringing a farming economy began about 6500 BCE. And farming was introduced to Greece from Anatolia. Renfrew concludes that an early Indo-European language was introduced to Greece from Anatolia. On the basis of his model, he identifies 'east Anatolia as part, although not necessarily all, of the early "homeland" of people speaking a very early form of Indo-European, around 7000 B.C.'[7]

Renfrew, however, has found it difficult to explain easily the spread of Indo-European eastwards into Iran and India. He has ventured to suggest some explanations that fit the theory he has presented for the spread of Indo-European in Europe. According to his first hypothesis, 'the arrival of Indo-European speakers in the Indian sub-continent was very much analogous to that in Europe'.[8] This would mean that farming, together with an Indo-European language, spread southeastwards from Anatolia at a very early date (about 6000 BCE) and that, 'from the very earliest farming times...an early Indo-European language was spoken in the Indus Valley and in areas to the north and west.' In Renfrew's view, 'it is difficult to see what is particularly non-Aryan about the Indus Valley civilization, which on this hypothesis would be speaking the Indo-European ancestor of Vedic Sanskrit'.[9] The conclusion drawn from this hypothesis is that the history of the Indo-European languages in north India and Iran dates back to the early Neolithic period in those areas. Admitting the complexity of the problem in regard to the Indian subcontinent, Renfrew suggests an alternative hypothesis as well. This is similar to the old and traditional view that the Indo-European languages were introduced into Iran and the Indian subcontinent by pastoral nomad invaders. Through a process of elite dominance, the languages of the mounted warriors displaced the earlier local languages. Admitting that it is not easy to choose between the two hypotheses, Renfrew also suggests the possibility of a combination of both.[10]

The Aryan Question in Indian History

Until about thirty years ago, it was generally accepted that there was an Aryan invasion of India. Some even attributed the fall of the Harappan civilization to this invasion. Using the evidence of the *Rigveda*, it was argued that the Aryans descended on the subcontinent from the northwest. The Aryan leader Indra, with his title 'Purandara' (Destroyer of Forts/Cities), was seen as one of the invading chiefs who destroyed cities in the Indus valley.[11] In the last few decades, the invasion theory lost support and the current controversy is mainly between those who argue for an Indian homeland and those who support a migration theory.

Migration theory

While it is true that the media and the internet carry an enormous amount of popular material relating to the Aryan controversy, often from persons who are untrained in the disciplines of linguistics, history or archaeology, it must be noted that scholarly interest in the subject is also very much alive today, both in India and in the West. Some of the leading historians and archaeologists, as well as linguists, both in India and the West, now support the view that there was no mass migration into India of the speakers of Indo-European languages but that there was a slow process of migration that resulted in the spread of these languages. On the other hand, there are also scholars who believe that there was no migration and that these languages were indigenous to the Indian subcontinent.

While the invasion theory has now lost support, some of the leading Indian historians and archaeologists are in favour of the migration theory. Among them, perhaps the most notable is Romila Thapar, whose views are summed up below:

> There is virtually no evidence of the invasion and the conquest of northwestern India by a dominant culture coming from across the border. Most sites register a gradual change of archaeological cultures...The borderlands of the northwest were in communication with Iran and Central Asia even before the Harappa culture with evidence of the passage of goods and ideas across the region. This situation continued into later times and if seen in this light the intermittent arrival of groups of Indo-European speakers in the northwest, perhaps as pastoralists or farmers or itinerant traders, would pose little

> problem. It is equally possible that in some cases local languages became Indo-Europeanized through contact.[12]

Though Romila Thapar does not say it in so many words, this leading historian of India is stating views that support the kind of language replacement that Renfrew has put forward. While rejecting the theory of invasion and conquest, she is inclined to support the view that groups of Indo-European speakers arrived in the subcontinent from time to time and inaugurated a process of cultural change. Elsewhere, elaborating on this, Thapar is very emphatic that these Indo-European (Indo-Aryan in India) speakers, when they settled in the subcontinent, found themselves in the midst of people who spoke Proto-Dravidian and Austroasiatic languages. Indo-Aryan eventually became the dominant language. Clearly Thapar implies that there was a process of language replacement that saw the demise of the once dominant Dravidian and Austroasiatic languages, only a few of which survived in isolated pockets.[13]

In one of her most recent contributions, Romila Thapar argues in support of the theory 'that groups of Indo-Aryan speakers gradually migrated from the Indo-Iranian borderlands and Afghanistan to northern India, where they introduced the language'[14] and sums up the consensus among leading historians and historical linguists as follows:

> A two-way relationship is expressed in the language change that is reflected in Vedic Sanskrit. Indo-Aryan was introduced and adopted, so evidently those who spoke it or adopted it associated it with some advantage, such as authority, technological change or ritual power. At the same time Vedic Sanskrit itself underwent changes. Linguistic elements from Dravidian and Austro-Asiatic (for example, Munda) were introduced into Vedic Sanskrit. A period of bilingualism has been suggested when more than one language was used in the communication between various communities. Alternatively, the non-Indo-Aryan languages could have been substratum languages, elements from which were absorbed into Indo-

Aryan. The Vedic corpus is the statement of the dominant group, but this does not preclude the presence of others. These linguistic elements are apparent in Indo-Aryan but are not noticed in cognate languages such as Old Iranian.[15]

Indian homeland theory

There are also scholars who hold the view that the original homeland of the Indo-European speakers is north India. This theory is today connected with contemporary politics in India, particularly to what is widely referred to as the Hindutva ideology.[16] The supporters of this theory, too, use the evidence of the *Rigveda* to argue their case. It must, however, be noted that even some scholars who are not associated with Indian politics are of the view that there is no evidence in the *Rigveda* to support a migration theory. 'As far as I can see', says Colin Renfrew, 'there is nothing in the *Hymns of the Rigveda* which demonstrates that the Vedic-speaking population was intrusive to the area'.[17]

It is interesting that the different views presented to explain the presence or spread of the Indo-European languages in India are based on the same sources – the archaeological remains in the Indus Valley and north India and the *Rigveda*. This is no doubt an indicator of the lack of definite evidence in support of any theory and the extent to which the same evidence lends itself to different interpretations.

Language replacement

As more and more archaeological evidence comes to light, one thing seems to be certain. There was no real invasion of the Indian subcontinent by a people called the Aryans as was believed for a long time. It would appear that the Indo-European language or languages that originally spread in the Indian subcontinent before the emergence of the Prakrits (the languages that were derived from Old Indo-Aryan) did so over a long period of time and came to be spoken by various peoples whose languages became displaced as a result of various factors that favoured the Indo-European speakers.[18]

The origin and spread of the Indo-European languages are issues not likely to be settled easily. The way scholars use the same sources to arrive at opposing views indicates that we have to await the discovery of new evidence for any breakthrough. Whether Indo-Aryan was native to the northwestern region of the subcontinent or whether it spread there through a process of migration and elite dominance, for our purposes what is important is the linguistic development after the period of the Old Indo-Aryan dialects.

Emergence of Prakrits

Perhaps the most notable linguistic development in north India after the period of Vedic Sanskrit and other Old Indo-Aryan dialects is the emergence of the Prakrits or the Middle Indo-Aryan dialects. The Prakrits were the languages spoken by the general population. The speakers of the Prakrits were not new migrants but descendants of the prehistoric peoples of north India. It was not Classical Sanskrit but these Prakrit languages that played an important part in the economic and cultural developments of the first millennium BCE.

As long-distance trade between the north and the south began to develop actively in the first millennium BCE, the Prakrits became the *lingua franca* of this trade. The rise of non-Vedic religions in the middle of that millennium helped to elevate the Prakrits to a position of religious significance on par with that enjoyed by Sanskrit in the Vedic religion. Pali, the most archaic literary Prakrit, became the language of the Buddhist canon, while another literary Prakrit generally known as Arddha-Magadhi became the language of the Jaina canon. It was the Prakrits of the long-distance traders and the Middle Indo-Aryan literary dialects of the Buddhist and Jaina monks that spread to the SISL region in the EIA bringing new influences from the north.

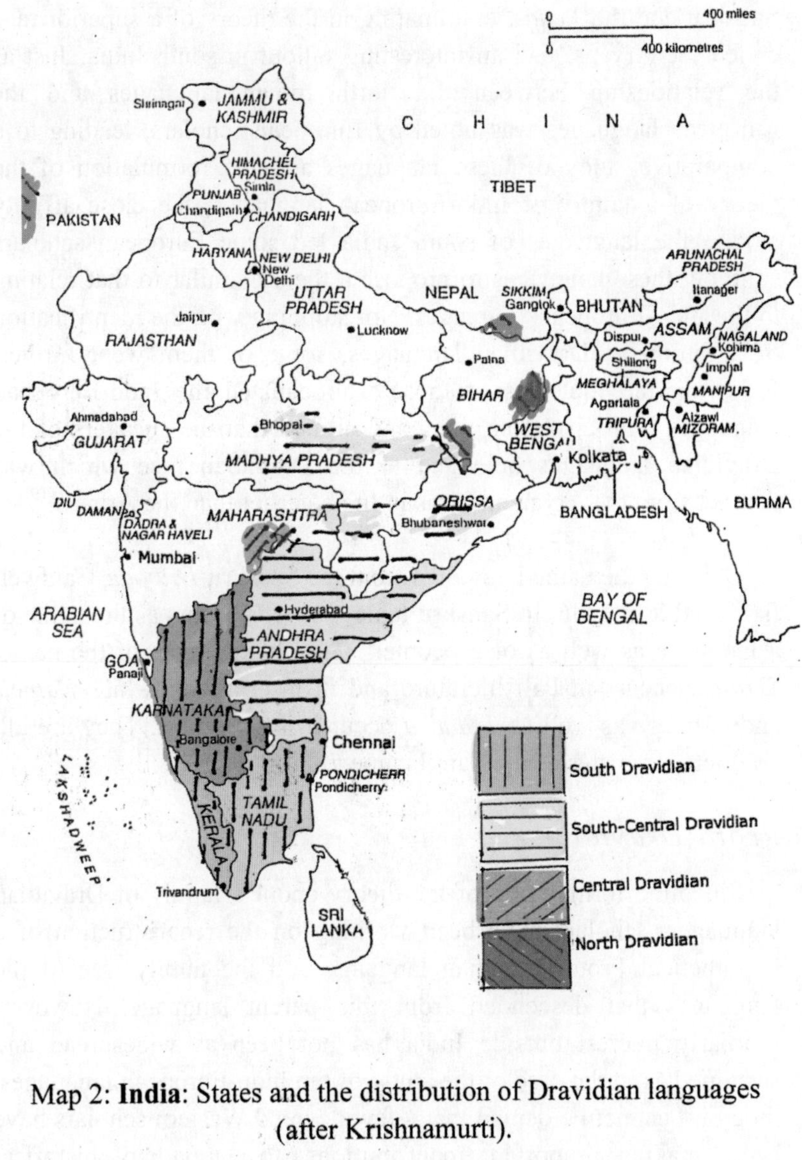

Map 2: **India**: States and the distribution of Dravidian languages (after Krishnamurti).

Dravidian

Identification of the Dravidian Family

The equation of language and race that resulted from the study of Sanskrit and the *Vedas*, culminating in the theory of a superior race called the Aryans, had an interesting fallout in south India. Just as the relationship between the north Indian languages and the European languages was noted by European scholars, leading to a comparative study of these languages and the formulation of the theory of a family of Indo-European languages, the close affinity among the languages of south India led some European scholars studying these languages to propose a theory similar to that relating to the Indo-European languages. Not stopping with the identification of a family of Dravidian languages, some of them went further, following the footsteps of those who equated the Indo-European languages with an Aryan race, and argued that the speakers of the Dravidian languages belonged to the Dravidian race which was distinct from the Aryan and was in India earlier than the Aryans.[19]

Deriving the name Dravidian from the Sanskrit *Draviḍa*, Caldwell first used it in 1856. In Sanskrit texts, *Draviḍa* occurs as the name of a language as well as of a people.[20] The Prakrit form of the name, *Damiḷa*, occurs in Pali literature and in inscriptions, while *Dameḷa* and *Dameḍa* as well as *Tramira* occur in inscriptions. They are all, no doubt, cognates of the Tamil name *Tamiḻ*.[21]

Proto-Dravidian

Since the formulation of the theory about a family of Dravidian languages, scholars have been working on the reconstruction of a hypothetical Proto-Dravidian language and the family tree of the languages that descended from this parent language. However, scholarly interest outside India has not been as widespread and sustained as in the case of the study of the Indo-European languages, though it cannot be denied that a few devoted Western scholars have been making important contributions to Dravidian historical linguistics in the last three decades.[22] Consequently, nothing comparable to the homeland question and migration theories associated with Indo-European is to be seen in Dravidian studies. However, the association of Dravidian with the language of the Harappan civilization has given Proto-Dravidian some significance.[23]

Original home

Outside India and Sri Lanka, no Dravidian language, with the exception of Brahui, has been identified by linguists, although certain affinities with Dravidian have been pointed out in respect of the Uralic and Altaic families as well as Japanese.[24] Some have also claimed affinity between ancient Sumerian (Elamite) and Dravidian.[25] On the basis of these hypotheses, some have even suggested that the original Dravidian-speakers came from some part of Central Asia, passing through present-day Hungary and Turkey, and entered the Indian subcontinent through the northwest. Clearly there is no acceptable evidence for either establishing a relationship between Dravidian and any language outside the subcontinent or identifying the original homeland of the ancestral Dravidian. This has not prevented scholars from speculating on the orginal home of Proto-Dravidian and its spread.

'In recent years,' as Zvelebil has pointed out, 'a hypothesis has been gaining ground that posits a movement of Dravidian speakers from the northwest to the south and east of the Indian peninsula, a movement originating possibly from as far away as Central Asia'. He believes that the Uralic and Altaic connection is 'definitely most probable and most promising'.[26] 'It is possible,' in Zvelebil's opinion, 'that a Dravidian-speaking people …established themselves in northwest India during the 4th millennium BC.'[27] Basing on the views presented by various researchers, Merritt Ruhlen has spelled out this hypothesis relating to movement from outside in a precise manner:

> It would appear that the speakers of Proto-Dravidian originally entered NW India during the fourth millennium B.C. During the first half of the second millennium B.C. Dravidian

> speakers spread from NW India in a southeasterly direction until, around 1500 B.C., three large dialect areas covered most of the Indian subcontinent, and probably portions of Pakistan as well. The following three and a half millennia saw these three broad dialects gradually evolve into the three branches of the Dravidian family.[28]

The Italian scholar Luigi Luca Cavalli-Sforza gives an even earlier date for the movement: 'It is likely that the Dravidian languages were spoken from the western borders of Iran into and throughout the whole of India, and were first introduced by Neolithic cultivators from nine thousand years ago.'[29]

As with the Indo-Aryan homeland question, there is a strong view that the Dravidian languages were indigenous to India. This view is best summed up by a leading Indian historical linguist, Bhadriraju Krishnamurti, in his most recent contribution:

> Most of the proposals that the Proto-Dravidians entered the subcontinent from outside are based on the notion that Brahui was the result of the first split of Proto-Dravidian and that the Indus civilization was most likely to be Dravidian. There is not a shred of concrete evidence to credit Brahui with any archaic features of Proto-Dravidian. The most archaic features of Dravidian in phonology and morphology are still found in the southern languages... For the time being, it is best to consider Dravidians to be the natives of the Indian subcontinent who were scattered throughout the country by the time the Aryans entered India around 1500 BCE.[30]

Distribution of Dravidian languages

Languages belonging to the Dravidian family are spoken today mainly in South Asia, but migrant groups from this region have taken these languages to almost all the developed countries of the world. What is of interest to historical linguists is the presence of some of the minor and less developed Dravidian languages in places outside south India. South India, as is well known, is the place where speakers of the four major Dravidian languages are concentrated, each dominant in a separate linguistic state. Telugu has the largest number of speakers, an estimated 75 million, and is the language of Andhra Pradesh. Tamil, with the oldest literature among the Dravidian languages, spoken by about 65 million people, is the language of Tamil Nadu. Kannada, the language of the state of Karnataka, has about 50 million speakers. Malayalam, the language of Kerala, has an estimated 35 million speakers. Besides these four major languages, about twenty-two other languages have been identified as belonging to the Dravidian family.[31]

Of these minor languages, Gondi, Tulu and Kurukh are each spoken by more than a million speakers. Many of the others are spoken by tribal people. It is noteworthy that some of these are spoken by tribes in north India, in states like Madhya Pradesh, Orissa, Bihar and West Bengal. The only Dravidian language spoken entirely outside modern India is Brahui, which is now spoken in some parts of Pakistan, Iran and Afghanistan. This distribution of Dravidian languages in Pakistan and north India is of significance for tracing the history of the Dravidian family in the Indian subcontinent. Although in modern times the speakers of the major Dravidian languages are concentrated in peninsular India, as the historical linguist Kamil Zvelebil has pointed out, 'It is, however, a well-established and well supported hypothesis that Dravidian speakers must have been widespread throughout India, including the north-west region'.[32]

Whether this means that the Dravidian languages spread into India from the northwest and that their origin has to be sought somewhere in the west or Central Asia is hard to say in the present state of our knowledge.

That a Dravidian language was widely spoken in the Indus Valley at the time of the Harappan civilization and that the inscriptions on the Indus seals are in that language is a theory that has been popular from the time of the discovery of Moehnjodaro and Harappa. One of the first excavators at the site of these ancient cities, Sir John Marshall, was also among the first to suggest that the language of this urban civilization was Dravidian. Since then, a number of scholars have attempted to provide an acceptable reading of the Indus seals. Among them, Henry Heras, Asko Parpola and Yurij V. Knorozov are the foremost scholars supporting the theory that the Indus seals are written in a Dravidian language.[33] In recent years, other scholars like Madhusudan Mishra have read the inscriptions as pre-Vedic Sanskrit. At least one scholar has recently claimed that the language of the seals is neither Indo-Aryan nor Dravidian.[34] Although laudable attempts have been made to decipher the Indus seals using very modern techniques, unfortunately none of the decipherments seems convincing.

For the present, then, any discussion of the early history of Dravidian will have to be confined to the linguistic evidence available in the Indian subcontinent after the Harappan civilization. The earliest evidence for Dravidian takes us to Pakistan (or the northwest of the subcontinent). Leading Sanskritists have shown that the oldest Indian literary text, the *Rigveda*, contains evidence of Dravidian influence.[35] The Dravidian language Brahui still spoken in Pakistan is seen as a survival from the distant past when one or more Dravidian languages were spoken there. Pakistani linguists are now claiming through their researches that the modern Pakistani languages have a Dravidian substratum. All these seem to point to Dravidian being spoken in the region now covered by Pakistan at a very early date.

Dravidian in Pre-Vedic India

For some time, linguists had recognized the existence of Dravidian loan-words in the Vedic Sanskrit of the *Rigveda*. As time went on, more Dravidian influence seems to have been felt on Sanskrit. The post-Vedic texts seem to reflect this influence in various aspects of the language. This has been interpreted to indicate that the Gangetic plain and other parts of north India were already settled by Dravidian-speakers when Sanskrit and the Prakrits spread to those areas. Basing her views on the evidence of historical linguistics, Romila Thapar has argued that Vedic Sanskrit has several non-Indo-Aryan words relating to agricultural processes.[36] It would appear that well before the beginning of the Common Era Dravidian languages as well as languages belonging to other families were replaced by Indo-Aryan Prakrits, paving the way for the emergence of the modern languages of north India. Some pockets of Dravidian languages, however, survived particularly among tribal people who remained outside the pale of Sanskritisation.

In the present state of our knowledge, therefore, it has to be accepted that languages belonging to the Dravidian and Austroasiatic families were already being spoken in north India when languages of the Indo-Aryan family began to spread there some time in the second millennium BCE. Considering the fact that one of the Dravidian languages, Tamil, had developed to the level of a literary medium by the first century BCE, it would appear that languages of the Dravidian family had spread to south India at least a few centuries before that time.

South Dravidian

If, as historical linguists are inclined to give, a date as early as the fourth millennium BCE is to be assigned for the spread of Dravidian languages in the northwestern regions of the subcontinent, it would be reasonable to assume that the spread of these languages in the peninsular part of the subcontinent took place well before the Early Iron Age. To quote Zvelebil's view:

> Between 2000 and 1500 BC, there was a fairly constant movement of Dravidian speakers from the northwest to the southeast of India, and in about 1500 BC three distinct dialect groups probably existed: Proto-North Dravidian, Proto-Central Dravidian, and Proto-South Dravidian.[37]

Krishnamurti gives a slightly different classification of the Dravidian subgroups: North Dravidian, Central Dravidian, South-

Central Dravidian and South Dravidian.[38] It is from South Dravidian, linguists believe, that Tamil, Kannada and Malayalam are descended.

Spread of South Dravidian to Sri Lanka

The languages of the South Dravidian subfamily spread to cover the entire area of the present-day states of Karnataka, Tamil Nadu and Kerala. It was, therefore, a matter of time before one or more of these languages overflowed into Sri Lanka. It is not known, and will perhaps be never known, whether this occurred before the Early Iron Age. As there was always a close interaction among the Mesolithic people of the SISL region, it is quite possible that one or more of the South Dravidian languages spread among the Mesolithic people of Sri Lanka as well. With the spread of the EIA culture in the first millennium BCE, linguistic influences would have also spread from south India.

The spread of the Indo-Aryan Prakrits and one or more South Dravidian dialects is one of the major developments in Sri Lanka in the EIA or Protohistoric Period. It is a development of great significance in the evolution of the two major linguistic ethnic identities of Sri Lanka. The spread of these languages, however, should not be equated with the settlement of 'Aryans' and 'Dravidians' or with any mass scale movement of people from the subcontinent.

Impact on Sri Lankan historiography

Unfortunately twentieth century writings on the history of Sri Lanka have been marred by the impact of the myths relating to Aryan and Dravidian races. In recent years, Leslie Gunawardana has drawn attention to the manner in which the invention of the Aryan and Dravidian myths by Orientalist scholarship in the nineteenth century found its way into the colonial writings on Sri Lanka and paved the way for scholarly, and later popular, belief that the Sinhalese belonged to the 'Aryan race' while the Tamils formed part of the 'Dravidian race'. Beginning with the invention of the 'Aryan' myth early in the nineteenth century, Gunawardana has traced the steps by which an 'Aryan' status came to be claimed first for the Sinhalese language and then for the Sinhalese people.[39] In his words, the new 'Aryan' theory 'was eagerly welcomed by most Sinhala scholars who found the Aryan theory flattering in that it elevated them to the ranks of the kinsmen of their rulers'.[40] From the 1860s belief in this theory has persisted for over a century, making 'a profound impact on Sri Lankan historiography'.[41]

Regrettably, even some of the leading historians of Sri Lanka have been helping to perpetuate this myth of Aryans and Dravidians as recently as the 1980s. Not only did they believe in an 'Aryan colonisation' of the island, they even ventured an opinion on who came first – the Aryan settlers or the Dravidian settlers.[42] Against this background, the relentless researches of Leslie Gunawardana in the 1990s have aided the process of exposing the fallacy of Aryan and Dravidian peoples in Sri Lanka. There is absolutely no case for anyone to talk about the coming of Aryans or Dravidians to Sri Lanka. What happened in the first millennium BCE was the spread of languages belonging to the Dravidian family and the Indo-Aryan sub-family. As discussed earlier, the consensus among leading historians and historical linguists of South Asia is that languages belonging to the Dravidian and Austroasiatic families were prevalent in the Indian subcontinent when languages of the Indo-Aryan sub-family spread there. The former had spread to the far south of the subcontinent by the first millennium BCE. In the context of the interactions that took place between south India and Sri Lanka, the movement of Dravidian and Austroasiatic (particularly Munda) languages into the latter area about the same time would be hard to dispute.

CHAPTER 4

IḶA AND DAMEḌA

Two Little Siblings

"*My own opinion, advanced with due caution but firmly held, is that the question "Where did the Greeks come from?' is meaningless. We can only begin to speak of Greeks after the formation of the Greek language as a recognizably distinct branch of Indo-European.*" Dr. John Chadwick (Cambridge academic and collaborator with Michael Ventris in the decipherment of the Linear B script), *Bronze Age Migrations in the Aegean*, ed. R.A. Crossland and A. Birchall, London 1973: 254)

Protohistory

The Beginning

The dawn of the first millennium BCE, as already discussed, saw the arrival of new cultural influences in Sri Lanka and the commencement of the EIA. If one were to begin at the beginning of Sri Lankan protohistory, one could say that there was no state or kingdom called Sri Lanka, no language called Sinhala or Tamil and no ethnic identity named Sinhalese or Tamil. From the murky darkness of prehistoric life in the Mesolithic period one sees the emergence of new identities in the early centuries of the first millennium BCE.

There were no Sinhalese anywhere at the dawn of the first millennium BCE. And so, they did not arrive in the island from anywhere. To talk of memories brought by 'the Sinhalese, when they migrated to this Island', is like discussing about the time when the French migrated to France or the English migrated to England.[1] One is reminded of the caustic comment made by the British historian Norman Davies about those who talk about the coming of the English to Britain in the fifth century: '...as if the English landed pre-mixed, pre-cooked, and pre-packaged.'[2] As an ethnic identity, the Sinhalese evolved in Sri Lanka and nowhere else. So did their Sinhala language. Their gene pool may take them back to ancestors who lived in the Mesolithic period in Sri Lanka and to others in the Indian mainland. But their story as a new identity in Sri Lanka begins in the Early Iron Age.

The unfolding of this fascinating story will take years of patient and dispassionate toil by a dedicated band of historical linguists, archaeologists and ancient historians. For the moment, one can only scratch at the surface of the hidden mound of evidence and attempt to piece together some fragments to gain a general idea of the whole picture.

Ethnic names

A name of considerable significance in the investigation of the evolution of the Sinhala language and the Sinhalese ethnic group is *Iḷa*, together with its variants *Īḷa, Heḷa, Eḷu, Sīhaḷa, Siṃhaḷa, Salai, Sele* and *Siele* (in different languages). These forms, with the exception of *Heḷa/Eḷu*, occur in sources that are datable to the period between the second century BCE and the fifth century CE. They all refer to an ethnic group and the language spoken by that group, and later also to the land where this group lived, with or without a suffix (*dvīpa/dīpa/diva/diba*) meaning 'island' attached to the name. In the same period, the name *Dameḍa / Dameḷa*, with its variant *Damiḷa* (later, also *Demeḷ*), in some of the sources mentioned above, is used to refer to another ethnic group. This name is of significance in tracing the evolution of the Tamil ethnic group in Sri Lanka.

Iḷa

The origin of the name *Iḷa* (for convenience, this form is being used here without repeating all the variants, as this seems to be the earliest in occurrence in the historical sources) may never be known and is likely to be debated forever.[3] As will be discussed later, the form *Iḷa* appears to be the Prakrit form in vogue in the EHP and possibly also in the EIA. It is probable that this form was also used in Pali before the form *Sīhaḷa* was adopted. The Tamil form *Īḻam* appears to have been derived from the form *Iḷa*, though it is more likely that it was derived from an earlier form with an initial '*s*', namely *Siḷa* (or *Sīḷa)*, for the occurrence of which we have no evidence yet. This latter form is likely to be the origin for the Old Sinhalese names *Heḷa* and *Eḷu*, as well as the Pali form *Sīhaḷa*, the Sanskrit form *Siṃhaḷa* and the ancient Greek forms *Salai/Sele/Siele* (all of which have the initial *s* or its alternative *h*). This is a matter for historical linguists to settle.

Whatever the origin of the name, *Iḷa* is synonymous with and related to the names *Heḷa* and *Eḷu.* As in the case of *Dameḍa/Damiḷa*, this name denoted both an ethnic group and its language. In the present state of our knowledge, it is hard to establish what name the ethnic group used to call itself. Unless new evidence comes up, there will always be a controversy surrounding this question. The matter is complicated by the common practice, among scholars in ancient South Asia, of translating proper names from one language into the language in which they were writing. What is worse, where translation from the local name into Sanskrit or Prakrit was not possible (as, for instance, in the case of names where the meaning in the local language was not known or the origin was obscure), the name was Sanskritised or Prakritised (just as South Asian names were Anglicised under English influence in colonial times).[4] Following this practice, the Sanskrit form or translation of the name of the ethnic group under discussion, as we know from the earliest sources, was *Siṃhaḷa/Saiṃhaḷa.*[5] The Pali form, as given in the earliest chronicles of Sri Lanka, was *Sīhaḷa.*[6] In Old Sinhalese, *Heḷa* and *Eḷu* are the forms met with in inscriptions and literature.[7] In Tamil, the form seems to be *Īḻa*, if one is to go by the name *Īḻam* given in the earliest Tamil literary sources to the land where this ethnic community lived.[8] In the Greek sources, the name *Salai* or *Salae* is given to the people, while *Salike*, *Selediba* and *Sielediba* are given to the country.[9]

That the names *Sīhaḷa/Siṃhaḷa/Iḷa/Salai/Siele/Sele* are all related to the name applied to the dominant ethnic group in Sri Lanka in the EHP is hard to dispute. What is difficult to establish is the actual name that this ethnic group used to call itself. Even more difficult to determine is the period when that name came to be first used. There is, however, some evidence that points to the strong possibility that the form *Iḷa* was in use, at least in Prakrit and Tamil, at about the beginning of the Common Era. This evidence comes from three different sources.

The first is the evidence of some early epigraphic records from south India. Among the Early Brāhmī inscriptions of Tamil Nadu, a few have been identified as having references to persons from Sri Lanka. The latest and most reliable readings of these inscriptions confirm only two of them as references to persons from Sri Lanka.[10] One of them mentions a person described as *Iḷa kuṭumpikaṉ,* which may be translated as 'the Iḻa householder', comparable to the '*Dameḍa gahapati'* (Tamil householder) occurring in the Brāhmī inscriptions of Sri Lanka. In his most recent and authoritative edition of the Tamil Brāhmī inscriptions, Mahadevan is inclined to take the name Iḻa as a caste name, that of Īḻavar occurring in the later centuries.[11] But here it is to be interpreted as a group name, comparable to the group name Dameḍa in the Sri Lankan inscriptions. Besides this information about an Iḻa person, the Tamil Brāhmī epigraphs contain evidence about a group named Iḷayar (the Iḷa people) who may well be the same as the Iḷa of Sri Lanka. But at this stage there is no way of establishing this.[12] It is only to be expected that, just as there were Dameḍa persons in Sri Lanka, there were Iḷa persons in Tamil Nadu.

The second source is to be found in Sri Lanka. Though there are a few occurrences of the group name Dameḍa in the early Brāhmī inscriptions of Sri Lanka, epigraphists who have studied these records have not so far identified in them any name that could be considered as the equivalent or variant of the group name Sīhaḷa or Iḷa. There is, however, a solitary occurrence of the name Iḷa, which has not been associated with an ethnic group by scholars.[13] This occurrence is in the name Iḷabarata in an inscription from Anuradhapura. Seneviratne interprets this name as a place-name. Considering the fact that *barata* occurs in a number of Sri Lankan Brāhmī inscriptions as a title or lineage group name, the proper reading would be to separate *iḷa* and *barata* and read them as two descriptive names/titles of the person mentioned, in the same way as *Dameḍa gahapati* or *Dameḍa samana* is read in the same inscription. It has been argued that the ethnic name of the dominant group 'does not occur in these records, for the very good reason that there was no need to distinguish any person by referring to him as such, when the people as a whole were entitled to that name'.[14] However, the group name Iḷa in this inscription occurs in a different context. The names recorded in this inscription, with the exception of one, were those of Dameḍas. The exception was the name of an Iḷa and was, therefore, identified as such. If all the persons whose names are recorded were from the Dameḍa group, one would expect the group name Dameḍa not to be used at all or to be used for everyone. There is, however, the problem of the locative case *hi* being used with Iḷabarata. For this reason, Iḷabarata has been interpreted as a place-name indicating the place from where Samana hailed. It is not common for place-names to be tagged on to personal names in this period. Where place-names were mentioned, it was done in a more explicit manner – like *Upalavi vasika* (resident of Upalavi).[15] It may well be that there is some error here (*hi* may be the first syllable of a personal name which was not completed by the scribe inadvertently). On account of this problem, however, the evidence of this record in respect of the word *Iḷa* will remain a weak one.

The third source is literary, namely the Pali chronicle *Mahāvaṃsa* (and the earlier *Dīpavaṃsa*). A king who ruled from Anuradhapura in the early decades of the first century is referred to in the chronicle as Iḷa Nāga (Nāga the Iḷa).[16] That Iḷa was clearly the group name equivalent to Sīhaḷa or Siṃhaḷa is established by the use of Eḷu as the Sinhala form of this name in the Sinhala chronicles, where Iḷa Nāga is referred to as Eḷun-Nā.[17] Though the Pali chronicles themselves are later than the Brāhmī inscriptions discussed here, they are, as is well established, based on earlier chronicles. Besides, the name Iḷa is unlikely to have been attached to the king's name at a much later date. It was obviously in use in the time of the ruler concerned or very close to his time. It is not hard to explain the use of this epithet, if one considers the circumstances under which this particular king alone had come to be given this name denoting his ethnic identity. Iḷa Nāga spent some years as an exile in one of the Tamil kingdoms in south India, presumably in the royal house of a ruler there, biding his time to regain his throne at Anuradhapura. Being a non-Tamil prince living among Tamils, he was evidently known as Nāga the Iḷa (Iḷa Nāga), just as the Tamil lady whom his son married, presumably during Nāga's sojourn in the Tamil kingdom, was known in Anuradhapura , on the return of the family, as Devī the Tamil or the Tamil Lady (Damiḷā Devī), as she was a Tamil consort to a prince in the Sinhalese (Iḷa) royal family.[18] While it may be debated as to why this epithet was stuck to the king's name in the Sinhalese traditions, there is absolutely no doubt that the name Iḷa means what we now call Sinhala, because of the term Eḷu being used as its equivalent in the Sinhala chronicles.[19]

Though the above discussion leads one to the conclusion that Iḷa was the name of one of the dominant ethnic groups, if not the most dominant ethnic group, in the Anuradhapura kingdom in the centuries immediately preceding the present era, it does not help to answer the question as to what name this group used to call itself in the local language. The occurrences of Iḷa, cited above, are in Tamil, Prakrit or Pali sources. Although Eḷu is used as the equivalent of Iḷa in the later Sinhalese chronicles, one cannot be certain that this was the name in vogue in the Early Historic Period. The Greek sources appear to be of some help in the search for the name that was in vogue at that time.

Salai

The Graeco-Roman writers of the early centuries of this era have left valuable information about Sri Lanka and its people. In their characteristic manner, they have provided interesting details of the geography of Sri Lanka and information about the people living there. While the earlier Greek sources refer to Sri Lanka as Taprobane (derived from Tambapaṇṇi/Tāmraparṇī), the later sources give a new name for the island. Writing in the second century CE, Ptolemy mentions this new name. The comments of Weerakkody on this name are relevant here:

> By Ptolemy's time, or at least by the time of his sources, a new name for the island had come into use, namely, Salike…Salike is the place name derived from Salai, the name given to the inhabitants. This derivation follows regular Greek practice: thus *Salike (nesos)* is 'the island of the Salai'. Thus it is the derivation of Salai, not of Salike, that must be explained; and I believe that it is most probably derived from *Sīhaḷa* (i.e. *Siṃhaḷa*) and may perhaps be compared with our terms Eḷu and Heḷa.[20]

By the time of another well-known Greek writer, Cosmas Indicopleustes (sixth century), a more familiar name of the island begins to find mention in the Graeco-Roman sources. In one place, Cosmas refers to 'the island called by the Indians Selediba, by the Greeks Taprobane',[21] and in another place he describes the same island as 'the great island in the Ocean, lying in the Indian sea, called Sielediba by the Indians and Taprobane by the Greeks'.[22] The two forms given for the name of the island, namely Sielediba and Selediba are of significance for the discussion here. With regard to the form Sielediba, Weerakkody has commented, 'There can be no doubt that this is a transliteration of *Sīhaḷa-dīpa* (*Siṃhaḷadvīpa*).'[23] The Graeco-Roman traders were more likely to have derived this name from the language spoken by the inhabitants with whom they came into contact rather than from the literary Pali. It is, therefore, probable that the name Sielediba in the Greek text is derived from *Siḷa*, a form that can be presumed to be the origin of *Iḷa.* But the other form Selediba, it appears, is derived from what could be conjectured as the original form of Heḷadiva, namely *Seḷadiva.*[24]

It is reasonable to assume that the Graeco-Roman traders, who no doubt provided the information about the people of Sri Lanka to Ptolemy and other Greek writers, had obtained their information from the local traders in the island. This would mean that the names they found out were those that were used by the local population. Even making some allowance for the Helenisation of these names in the hands of the Greek writers, it is likely that the name Salae and the prefixes Sele- and Siele- were close to the local form of the name for the dominant ethnic group. The initial '*s*' was obviously there in the local name and was not introduced by the Graeco-Romans. This is significant in the quest for the original form of the name, as used by the local population. The occurrence of Heḷa as the earliest known form in the Old Sinhalese inscriptions and literature also points to the possibility of the original name having an initial '*s*'(which often interchanges with *h*). The local traders or other local persons from whom the Graeco-Roman traders found out the name of the island and of its inhabitants are unlikely to have used the Pali names Sīhaḷa-dīpa and Sīhaḷa. These forms would have occurred only in literary usage, for Pali was already a dead language. What the Graeco-Roman traders rendered as Salai, Sielediba and Selediba would have been closer to the names in common parlance among the local people. It is likely that these names were Siḷa (from which the form Iḷa could be derived) and Seḷadiva (from which the form Heḷadiva could be derived).

If this argument is acceptable, it raises the possibility of Iḷa being a derivative of the form Siḷa and the latter becoming the basis for the transformation into the Pali Sīhaḷa and for the creation of the origin myth of the lion. On the other hand, the possibility of Iḷa being Prakritised as Siḷa or Sīḷa (in the same way as the south Indian lineage name Atiya-mān was Prakritised as Satiya-puta) cannot be ruled out. It may well be, though it is less likely, that Iḷa and Sīhaḷa are unrelated. Leslie Gunawardana argues in favour of the possibility that the name Siṃhaḷa was first applied to the ruling dynasty, then to the kingdom and finally to the people of the kingdom.[25] If this were the case, we have to either take that Iḷa (Siḷa) is derived from Siṃhaḷa (Sīhaḷa) or assume that the names Iḷa and Siṃhaḷa were originally unrelated, becoming associated with each other at a later date. If Iḷa were derived from Siṃhaḷa/Sīhaḷa, why was it that the Pali chroniclers used the name Iḷa Nāga instead of Sīhaḷa Nāga when in Eḷu the chroniclers used the form EḷunNā? Would this mean that originally Iḷa and Sīhaḷa were unrelated or that the Sīhaḷa myth emerged only after the time of Iḷa Nāga? As long as reliable dates are lacking for the earliest occurrence of these names, it is difficult to argue in favour of one or the other possibility. However, it appears that the use of the name Iḷa is older than that of the name Sīhaḷa.

These are matters that cannot be settled easily with the evidence currently available. Until new evidence comes up, the real name used in the centuries before the present era by those who later called themselves Heḷa cannot be established with certainty. However, it could be claimed that they were known as Iḷa in Prakrit and Īḷa (with the addition of a personal suffix) in Tamil as early as the second century BCE. That the name Iḷa was not transformed into the Pali Sīhaḷa (and the Sanskrit Siṃhaḷa) even in the first century CE may explain why the form Iḷa was used in the Pali chronicles in the name Iḷa Nāga, rather than the form Sīhaḷa Nāga. Since there was no equation of Iḷa with Sīhaḷa in the time of this king, his name continued to be recorded as Iḷa Nāga in the Pali historical tradition, while the Sinhalese historical tradition had the Heḷa equivalent Eḷu, giving him the name EḷunNā. This seems to strengthen the view that Iḷa is not derived from Sīhaḷa.

In the light of the foregoing discussion, it could be concluded that the dominant ethnic group in the kingdom ruled by the Anuradhapura kings was that known as Iḷa in the earliest records (second century BCE – second century CE) and Heḷa in the later records (eighth to tenth centuries). By the third century, the Pali form Sīhaḷa had come into use. About the same time, the Sanskrit form Siṃhaḷa was no doubt also in vogue. References to Siṃhaḷa are to be found in various notable Sanskrit works, such as the *Mahābhārata*, *Kathāsaritsāgara* and the Commentary to the *Arthaśāstra*.[26] It is hard to determine the earliest reference to Siṃhaḷa in Sanskrit literature, as the dates of the Sanskrit works are not easy to establish. The transformation of the ethnic name to Sīhaḷa/Siṃhaḷa and the adoption of the origin myth of the lion marked the beginning of another important stage in the evolution of the Sinhalese ethnic group.[27]

Origin myths

Origin myths are not new in any way nor are they peculiar to Sri Lanka. In various parts of the world, lineage groups have tried to legitimize their position as ruling classes through the creation of myths. In South Asia, and later in Southeast Asia, as the process of Sanskritisation proceeded, local lineage groups embraced the new culture with eagerness and made their Brāhmaṇa or Buddhist court advisers to work hard on creating mythical origins for their lineages. As the local chieftaincies and kingdoms of south India and Sri Lanka came under the influence of the north Indian culture in the first millennium BCE, the lineage groups ruling in those regions appear to have begun to link their origins to events and personalities or lineages already famous in the north Indian tradition. Often, it appears, lineage names were Sanskritised (as part of the Sanskritisation process) and links created with north Indian personalities. Thus, we find one of the Tamil lineage groups having a Sanskritised name, Pāṇḍya, and myths being created about its connection with the Paṇḍus of the *Mahābhārata* epic. We do not know its original name. The name Pāḍā given in Asoka's edicts appears to be closer to the original. The Hathigumpha inscription (second century BCE) refers to Paṇḍarāja, which may also give a clue to the original name.[28] An ancestor of another south Indian lineage group, the Cēras, is associated with the Mahābhārata war. Later, the Cōḷas who ruled over a powerful Tamil kingdom, claimed a solar origin and created long mythical genealogies to establish this.[29] The creation of such genealogies was a familiar phenomenon all over India. As Ludden has pointed out, 'At least forty new dynastic lineages were proclaimed during and soon after the sixth century, and from the seventh century on, they typically construct elaborate genealogies for themselves to trace their origins to mythical progenitors'. [30]

In Sri Lanka, the emergence of a dominant ethnic group appears to have paved the way for the ruling lineage group to create an origin myth in order to establish its legitimacy as the rightful rulers of the island. Gunawardana argues the case for Siṃhaḷa as a name adopted by a ruling lineage group for whose origin the lion myth had been created. He is inclined to think that 'the lion was the emblem of the ruling house of Sri Lanka and that the dynasty got its name from the emblem.'[31] The story of Siṃhabāhu, in his view, was a myth that sought to explain the emblem. As already mentioned, Gunawardana is of the view that the name Siṃhaḷa was first applied to the dynasty, then to the kingdom and later to the people of the kingdom. He argues that, in the early stage of the Sinhala identity, language was not the criterion for inclusion in the group and that this identity 'denoted only a group located geographically in the core regions of the kingdom and limited in terms of status to the upper rungs of the social hierarchy prevailing at the time'.[32] Gunawardana's contention is that

> contrary to popular belief, in ancient times the Sinhala identity was associated primarily with the dynasty which ruled Anuradhapura. Thus the term Sinhala would bear comparison with other South Asian dynastic names like Moriya, Gupta, Pallava and Cōḻa. In a secondary sense this identity denoted the leading families in the kingdom politically linked to the dynasty…at that early stage, the term represented a political identity which excluded lower rungs of society such as craft groups. Evidence on this identity being given a wide definition in order to accommodate a broader cross-section of society, constituted earlier under a multitude of groupings, is to be found by about the twelfth century.[33]

If the name Siṃhaḷa was applied to the people only in the final stage, it may be that originally the same people had a different name. This may lend support to the view that Siḷa/Iḷa was the name by which the dominant group was known at the beginning of the EHP and that it was not related to the name Siṃhaḷa.

Thus, it appears that among the different ethnic groups in the island in the third century BCE, when Buddhism was established at Anuradhapura with royal patronage, there was one that was dominant politically and numerically in the kingdom ruled by the Anuradhapura kings. That group is the one that we know as Heḷa in later times. The rulers of the kingdom, on most occasions, came from this group. It is also possible that members of this group spoke the same language and that this language formed the basis of the language that is later known as Heḷa and Siṃhaḷa. As a result of the continued dominance of this group, other ethnic groups were assimilated into its fold and accommodated, in at least some cases, as distinct service castes. The adoption of Buddhism as the religion of the elite and, before long, of the majority of this group, bringing with it the use of Prakrit (which was no doubt familiar to the elite even before the spread of Buddhism), soon helped them to evolve into a strong and distinct ethnic group with its own linguistic, religious and cultural identity.

The members of this group, though concentrated in Sri Lanka, were also found on the other side of the Palk Strait, just as the Dameḍas who were concentrated in the southeastern part of peninsular India were also found in Sri Lanka. In later times, as the evolution of the larger ethnic groups progressed, the Iḷa group in south India was accommodated within those ethnic groups as a separate caste or completely assimilated, just as Damedas were accommodated within the growing Sinhala ethnic group. The presence of an Iḷa person and an Iḷayar clan in Tamilnadu about the second century BCE has already been noticed.[34] In the later centuries, at least from the ninth century, there are references to a caste of Īḷavar (the Īḷas) in Tamil inscriptions.[35] This caste has survived in Tamilnadu till modern times. However, it is in Kerala that the Īḻavar are found in larger numbers, with their own traditions about their ancestors having migrated from Sri Lanka.[36] In the Tamil inscriptions of the later centuries in Tamilnadu, the Īḻavar were persons associated with climbing coconut palms and tapping toddy (as they are indeed even to this day in Kerala and Tamilnadu).[37]

Archaeological Evidence: Anuradhapura

Archaeological excavations in Anuradhapura in the last two decades have thrown fresh light on questions relating to the spread of a Prakrit language and the origin of the Sinhala language as well as the origins of the Sinhalese ethnic group. Following the important discovery of potsherds with Brāhmī writing dating back to the sixth century BCE by Siran Deraniyagala, a Sri Lankan-British team of archaeologists conducted excavations in Anuradhapura from 1989 and discovered a very large number of inscribed potsherds with Brāhmī writing going back to the fourth century BCE.[38] The language of all the readable inscriptions has been identified as Prakrit.[39] But the cultural context in which these inscriptions occur is not associated with north India, the home of Prakrit. In the trench named ASW2 (Anuradhapura Salgaha Watta 2), the excavators identified five periods covering the time from ninth century BCE to the mid-second century CE. Commenting on the artefacts associated with the first period (840-460 BCE), which included Black and Red Ware with graffiti symbols similar to those found in south Indian megalithic burials, the excavators have pointed out that 'It was evident from the associated culture complex that this period belongs firmly within the Iron Age of peninsular India'.[40] Their comment on the artefacts of the second period (510-340 BCE) is similar:

> The artefactual record continued relatively unchanged from Period K [the first period]. Black and red burnished ware continued to dominate the ceramics...It is notable that the first examples of horse bones were found in the faunal record during this phase. The Iron Age affinities of the period appeared to be reiterated by the identification of a circular pit...The pit, with a diameter of 1.25 m, was filled with ash

and contained an iron arrowhead, a small copper alloy object, a polished rubbing or sharpening stone, three black and red ware burnished cups with holes drilled in their bases and three other vessels with non-scriptural graffiti. Although no bones were found in the pit, it appears to be very similar in form and content to the peninsular Iron Age pit burials.[41]

The evidence of these recent excavations clearly indicates that the most famous urban centre in Sri Lanka in the EHP, namely Anuradhapura, was settled by people who had adopted the south Indian Megalithic-BRW culture from the ninth century BCE. It would then be reasonable to assume that this culture had reached the northwestern coast of Sri Lanka some time before the ninth century. The influence of the Prakrit languages from north India appears to have entered Sri Lanka, as it did into south India, about the fifth century BCE as a consequence of the development of long distance trade.

Early Settlers at Anuradhapura

Nothing is known at present about the ethnic composition of these people at Anuradhapura. It would appear that most of them were descendants of the people of the Mesolithic Age. There also would have been, possibly among the elite, those belonging to the group or groups that were responsible for the introduction of the south Indian Megalithic-BRW culture. As discussed elsewhere, economic motives would have dominated in their movement from south India. It was among these people that another dominant cultural influence spread in the middle of the first millennium BCE, and this time it came from the north and possibly also from the east of India. It was an influence that was spreading all over peninsular India as well.

Arrival of Prakrit

One of the most significant areas in which the north Indian influence made a lasting impact was language. Different areas responded differently to this influence. It would appear that in an area where a local language had already reached a level of development that made it strong enough to withstand the impact of Prakrit, it was not possible to displace that language. But in areas where there was no such strong language, Prakrit exerted a greater degree of influence and in some places even displaced local languages. In most areas of peninsular India, the local rulers used Prakrit as their court language and had their inscriptions written in that language for a long time.[42] In Tamil Nadu, the influence of Prakrit was strong in the protohistoric period and, in some kingdoms, continued well into the EHP, but in the end Tamil was able to emerge without much Indo-Aryan influence. In Andhra, the Prakrit influence was very strong and persisted for a long time. In the end, when the Dravidian language Telugu emerged as the most dominant language of that area, it had acquired many Indo-Aryan features that Tamil had avoided. But in Sri Lanka it was a different situation.

There were in all probability many languages prevalent among the people of Sri Lanka in the Mesolithic Age. It is surmised that Munda, an Austroasiatic language, may have been one of them. It is not known whether there were Dravidian languages, too. With the advent of the Iron Age and the flow of the new Megalithic-BRW cultural influences, particularly from the southern tip of the Indian peninsula, speakers of the Tamil language would have crossed over to the island. As will be seen later, the influence of this language spread in the northern parts of the island. But in the central and southern parts, the earlier languages seem to have persisted. The conditions were ideal for a superior language to establish itself through elite dominance. With the development of long distance trade and the emergence of the earliest polities, there was the need for a developed language for economic transactions and administrative purposes. Prakrit supplied this need and soon the spread of Buddhism, with Pali as its scriptural language, was able to help consolidate the dominance of Prakrit. The result was the evolution of a new language in Sri Lanka, as already discussed.[43]

The speakers of this new language were the Iḷa, descendants of the Mesolithic people and the most dominant ethnic group in the Anuradhapura chiefdom. New migrants from the mainland, particularly Prakrit-speakers but also some from south India, would have mingled with the Iḷa and maintained an elitist position. Long-distance trade and other economic interests continued to bring more Prakrit-speakers in the EHP. The rise of south Indian ports as important centres of trade as well as the development of urbanism in Anuradhapura were factors that aided the arrival of more people belonging to south Indian ethnic groups, particularly the Dameḍa.

Dameḍa

Origin and Early Occurrences

A section of the population of Sri Lanka in the historical period has been designated *Demaḷa* and *Damiḷa* in the major Sinhala and Pali chronicles respectively. In the Sinhala inscriptions of the ninth and tenth centuries the related term *Demeḷ* occurs. There cannot be any dispute about the relationship of these terms to the words *Tamiḻ* and *Tamiḻar* in the Tamil language, denoting that language and the people associated with that language respectively. That the terms *Damiḷa* and *Demeḷa* are the forerunners of the modern Sinhala term *Demaḷa* (often Sanskritised as *Draviḍa* in literary or formal usage) and that they refer to the same ethnic group are also hard to contest.

As in the case of most early societies, in South Asian pre-state societies, too, tribal affiliations would have been more important than attachment to other broader ethnic groupings based on language or other characteristics. Often, names given to broad groups, such as 'Germans' and 'Celts', were those given by outsiders and not by the groups themselves. The Germanic tribes in Europe, for instance, considered themselves as members of their individual tribes and did not possess a collective consciousness of themselves as a Germanic ethnic group. We do not know whether the term *Tamiḻar/Dameḍa* was a name given to the speakers of the Tamil (or its ancestor) language or whether it originated as the name of a group and later came to be applied for their language as well. We will never be able to know, with the evidence that we have, whether the name was given to the group by outsiders or not.

Clearly, one of the ethnic groups whose presence in Sri Lanka in the second century BCE is attested by the early Brāhmī inscriptions is the Dameḍa. Dameḍa has been equated by scholars with the name Damiḷa occurring in the Pali chronicles and is, without dispute, accepted as the equivalent of the name Tamil.[44] Interestingly, it is in these Sri Lankan inscriptions that we find the earliest datable reference to the ethnic name of the Tamils. Although Dameḍa, Damiḷa or Tamiḻ does not occur in the Brāhmī inscriptions of Tamil Nadu, the term Dhamiḷa is found in some inscriptions outside Tamil Nadu. In one of the inscriptions from Amaravati, in Andhra Pradesh, there is a reference to a Dhamiḷa-vāṇiya (Dhamiḷa trader).[45] This is datable to the third century CE. Another inscription of about the same time from Nagarjunakonda (Andhra Pradesh) seems to refer to Damiḷa. A third inscription from Kanheri refers to a Dhamiḷa-gharini.[46] The well-known Hathigumpha inscription of the Kaliṅga ruler Khāravela (first century BCE) refers to the defeat of the *Tramira saṃghāta*, which has been interpreted as a confederacy of Tamil rulers.[47] In one of the *Jātaka* stories, the *Akitti Jātaka*, there is a reference to Damiḷa-raṭṭha (the Tamil country).[48] As mentioned earlier, it would appear that the name Tamiḻ was the origin of the forms Damiḷa, Dameḍa, Dhamiḷa and ultimately Draviḍa but it would be hard to establish when it came into use.[49]

The earliest references to the name *Tamiḻ* in the Tamil language texts are in the oldest extant Tamil grammatical work, *Tolkāppiyam*, and the Sangam poems.[50] There is no possibility of determining the exact date of these texts, except to assign them to the centuries immediately preceding and immediately after the beginning of the Common Era. That would mean that these Tamil references belong to about the same time as the references to *Damiḷa* and *Dameḍa* in the Pali and Prakrit sources. But they are useful in confirming that, even at this early stage, the term was used to refer to the language, the people and the land where they lived. The term *Dameḍa*, too, would have had similar applications.

The occurrence of the name Dameḍa in the earliest Brāhmī inscriptions of Sri Lanka has been reported by epigraphists ever

PLATE 10.

Ruins of Vijayaraja-isvaram (Siva temple named after Vijayabahu I) at Kantalay. This slab inscription in Tamil is dated in the reign of a Cola-Lankesvara, one of the Cola viceroys, and belongs to a period before the reign of Vijayabahu I, when the temple presumably had a different name. See pp.215, 235.

***Photo:** March 2005, by the author.*

PLATE 11.
Ruins of Vijayaraja-isvaram. This inscription in Tamil is dated in the reign of Vijayabahu I. See pp. 252-253.

Photo: March 2005, by the author.

since the discovery and decipherment of the much-publicised Tamil Householders' Terrace Inscription at Anuradhapura.[51] Subsequently, other inscriptions with this word have also been brought to light.[52] The advances made in the study of Sinhalese and Tamil palaeography in the last three decades have called into question the reading of this word in the Sri Lankan inscriptions. Although this does not affect the meaning given to this word, the new views help to confirm the meaning already given. For this reason, a discussion of these developments may not be out of place here.

W.S. Karunaratne identified in some of the Sri Lankan inscriptions a special letter used to represent the Tamil *ḻa* and this enabled him to read the name Dameḻa in an inscription from Periyapuliyankulam.[53] He correctly identified this name as a variant of Dameḍa. In the Brāhmī inscriptions of Tamil Nadu, it appears that the Brāhmī *ḍa* was sometimes used to represent the Tamil letter/sound *ḻa.* In the light of these new findings, one wonders whether the word Dameḍa in the Sri Lankan inscriptions, since it occurs only in inscriptions presumably set up or caused to be inscribed by Tamils, has to be read as Dameḻa and not Dameḍa.

The answer to this may have to await future research. It is, however, now clear that the word Dameḍa is a variant of Dameḷa which is the form closest to the name Tamiḻ. The Pali form Damiḷa is another variant. It is not difficult to see that the Heḷa (or Early Sinhala) form Demeḷa is derived from the inscriptional Prakrit form Dameḻa. The modern Sinhala form Demaḷa is only slightly different from the Heḷa form. With such epigraphic evidence in hand to establish the sound-pedigree of the modern ethnic term Demaḷa, there can be no doubt as to the ethnic community represented by the name Dameḍa in the inscriptions of the EHP.

What distinguished the Dameḍa from the other ethnic groups? This will be hard to discover. Just as the Iḷa ethnic group was the dominant one among many ethnic groups in Sri Lanka in the EIA, the Tamil ethnic group was doubtless the most dominant group in Tamil Nadu. As Gunawardana has argued, it took a long time before all speakers of the Sinhala language were considered as belonging to the Sinhalese ethnic group. In a similar manner, it must have taken several centuries before all Tamil-speakers were accepted as members of the Tamil ethnic community. In the EHP, therefore, the name Dameḍa was possibly applied to a group that called itself Tamiḷ. But it may not have included all those who spoke Tamil. We do not know whether groups like the Barata (Tamil *Paratar*) were considered as a different ethnic group, although many of them may have spoken Tamil.

Viewing from the perspective of the later Tamil and Sinhalese kingdoms as well as from that of the modern political borders, scholars have tended to look at the Dameḍas as outsiders to Sri Lanka. As discussed earlier, the present-day territories of Sri Lanka and south India comprised a single region in which the prehistoric ancestors of the modern Sri Lankans and south Indians freely roamed, with the sea dividing south India and Sri Lanka as a unifier. In such a situation, before the formation of states (and even afterwards), people belonging to the same ethnic group would have lived on both sides of the Palk Strait. The Iḷa (Heḷa) and the Dameḍa, in such a context, would have been freely moving between south India and Sri Lanka at the time we begin to get written records. In this background, there were no doubt invasions from the emerging south Indian chiefdoms directed against the Anuradhapura chiefdom, just as there were invasions of one Tamil chiefdom from another or invasions of Anuradhapura from Rohaṇa or other Sri Lankan chiefdoms. Possibly there were also invasions of south Indian chiefdoms from the Sri Lankan side. In short, to borrow Norman Davies' construction, Heḷa fought Heḷa and Dameḍa fought Dameḍa; Heḷa also fought Dameḍa and on other occasions Heḷa leaders called Dameḍa for assistance against other Heḷa rivals.[54] In fact, in this climate of contest for power and territory, brother fought brother.[55] The idea that the Dameḍa were foreign intruders and that the Heḷa fought to 'liberate' their people is as nonsensical as the idea that the Celts of Britain were 'noble and peace-loving' while the Germanics were 'mean and murderous'. We know more about the invasions that affected Anuradhapura because of the chronicles that have been fortunately preserved in the island. Similar chronicles are sadly unavailable for the history of the south Indian kingdoms.

Dameḍas not outsiders

The Dameḍas in Sri Lanka in the centuries before CE need not, therefore, be considered as outsiders. Unfortunately, even some objective and scientific scholars have tended to make the mistake of considering the Dameḍas/Damiḷas as foreign to the island.[56] The idea of looking upon the Dameḍas as aliens was surely not prevalent in the EHP. The earliest extant chronicle of the island, namely the *Dīpavaṃsa*, does not refer to the first Damiḷa rulers of Anuradhapura in its list (Sena and Guttaka) as invaders.[57] Nor does the *Mahāvaṃsa*. The latter describes them as 'sons of a horse-freighter' (*assa-nāvikaputtā*).[58] In the original Pali version edited by Geiger, it is stated as follows: *Assanāvikaputtā dve Damiḷā Sena-Guttakā Sūratissamahīpālaṃ taṃ gahetvā mahabbalā dve dvāvīsavassāni rajjaṃ dhammena kārayuṃ*. In the English translation, however, this was rendered as: 'Two Damiḷas, Sena and Guttaka, sons of a freighter who brought horses hither, conquered the king Sūratissa at the head of a great army and reigned both (together) twenty-two years justly'.[59] Unfortunately, '*assanāvika*', literally meaning 'horse-sailor', has been translated as 'a freighter who brought horses hither', allowing room for one to imply that he was a trader from overseas. But '*assanāvika*' refers to a freighter (in the sense of a ship or cargo owner) who dealt in horses. And yet present-day historians have assumed that the two rulers were invaders from south India. This is an example of prejudice.

The archaeological discoveries and the re-interpretations of historical evidence in the last three decades, particularly the researches of Sudharshan Seneviratne and Leslie Gunawardana, have contributed significantly to a better understanding of Sri Lankan protohistory and early history. In the light of these, it is now possible to get a clearer picture of the people and events in Sri Lanka at the dawn of history and to understand the processes that eventually led to the evolution of the major ethnic groups and their cultures in the historical period.

The sources that refer to the Dameḍas date back to the earliest lithic records in the island, the Brāhmī inscriptions of the second century BCE. But other archaeological evidence showing links with the culture that was prevalent in Tamil Nadu would indicate the presence of the Dameḍas before the time of the Brāhmī lithic records. As discussed earlier, (chapter on Aryans and Dravidians), the Tamils or Tamil-speakers were already widely spread in the region now known as the State of Tamil Nadu, and possibly in the peripheral areas in the states of Kerala, Karnataka and Andhra Pradesh well before the third century BCE. It is possible that not only Tamil but also other Dravidian languages were among those spoken by various groups in this region. The Malayalam language of Kerala possibly evolved from one such language (which, according to historical linguists, is termed Proto-Tamil-Malayalam). It would appear that the Dameḍas were in Sri Lanka, too, before the third century BCE. Possibly there were also speakers of other Dravidian languages.

New Identities in South India and Sri Lanka

Thus, the story of the evolution of the major ethnic communities now found in south India and Sri Lanka may be said to begin just after 1000 BCE, with the commencement of the EIA. The arrival of the Iron Age culture, followed by the spread of Sanskritisation, in the first millennium BCE created the conditions for the emergence of new identities. Long distance trade, particularly with West Asia, seems to have provided an added stimulus to urbanization and the growth of a literate culture.

The convergence of the EIA culture, Sanskritisation and long distance trade had the powerful effect of paving the way for the rise of new ethnic identities and the emergence of the first states in the SISL region. Various factors seem to have played their part in shaping the final outcome, namely the formation of language-based identities in the EHP. Perhaps the first clear-cut language-based identity to emerge was in the far south of the peninsula. Here, in the southeastern part of south India, the Tamil language developed into a literary medium earlier than any other in SISL. It won the patronage of rising political lineages and proved to be capable of being a court language, defying the intrusion of Sanskrit and Prakrit. But elsewhere, in the regions now known as Karnataka and Andhra Pradesh, Prakrit was able to dominate. It took several centuries, indeed nearly a millennium after the rise of Tamil, before the local languages, Kannada and Telugu, could raise their heads and assert their dominance. But by then, unlike Tamil, they were heavily influenced and enriched by Sanskrit and Prakrit. In Kerala, in the southwest corner, the struggle of a local language to assert its dominance took even longer to succeed. Here, the Tamil language appears to have maintained its hold as a language patronized by the ruling lineages and the elite in the early stages, although there was a strong push by the forces of Sanskritisation that favoured Sanskrit and the Prakrits. In the end, a local language, Malayalam, emerged, maintaining a very close affintity with Tamil, but enriched lexically by Sanskrit.

In Sri Lanka, the situation presented a slightly different picture. Here, too, the EIA culture, Sanskritisation and long distance trade arrived in the first millennium BCE, possibly a little later than in south India. The Prakrit and Dravidian languages accompanied these forces to the island. These superior languages soon gained dominance and began to replace the languages of the Mesolithic people. In the greater part of the island, a new Prakrit with features from the Prakrits of western India and eastern India and displaying its own special local features successfully replaced the earlier languages. But in the north and the northeast, it had to contend with the dominant Dravidian language, Tamil. In this competition, geopolitical factors favoured the Tamil language but not to the extent of ousting the other language. The result was the emergence of two language-based identities.

CHAPTER 5

THE EARLY HISTORIC PERIOD

C. 250 BCE – 300 CE

Growing Up

"One of the commonest oversimplifications [in post-Roman British history] is to reduce the complex interplay of peoples to a straightforward confrontation between 'Celts and Saxons'. This pseudo-racial stereotype simply does not fit the facts, beloved though it may be both by the Celtophiles of recent times and by the older advocates of Anglo-Saxon superiority. The fact is that Celts fought Celts over power and territory just as Germanics fought Germanics. In the shifting kaleidoscope of alliances, Celtic warlords could call in their Saxon counterparts for assistance as readily as, on other occasions, they engaged them in battle. Angles battled Saxons; and Saxons battled Saxons no less frequently than at a later stage they all waged war against the Danes. The idea that Celtic society was somehow noble and peace-loving whilst Germanic society was mean and murderous leads to nonsensical assertions about Celtic warriors being 'enthusiastic' and Saxon raiders 'genocidal'." Prof. Norman Davies, *The Isles: A History*, London 2000: 149.

Periodisation and Sources

Although there is now evidence that writing was known in Sri Lanka as early as the middle of the first millennium BCE, it is not until the spread of Buddhism in the third century that written records or historical traditions become available. The earliest written material so far brought to light in the island is confined to a few potsherds with writing in Brāhmī. The texts yield only a few personal names. Siran Deraniyagala has found them good enough to mark the beginning of written records in the island and has worked out a 'periodisation of Sri Lanka's proto- and Early Historic episodes, based on the calibrated dates secured on charcoal' from his excavations at Anuradhapura. In this periodisation, after the Mesolithic Age, the Protohistoric Iron Age or Early Iron Age begins about 900 BCE and lasts till 600 BCE. The Early Historic Age begins about 600 BCE and ends about 300 CE. This age is, however, split into three periods: Basal Early Historic – c. 600 – c.500 BCE, Lower Early Historic: c.500 - c.250 BCE, Mid-Early Historic: c. 250 BCE – c.100 CE, and Upper Early Historic: c. 100 – c.300 CE.[1] It is yet to be seen whether Sri Lankan historians would accept this fully and push the traditionally accepted date of the third century BCE back to the sixth century BCE for the beginning of the Early Historic Period.

The period from about the third century BCE to the third century CE is relatively well documented. A variety of source material is available for a study of this period. Literary sources, in the form of the well-known Pali chronicles, as well as hundreds of stone inscriptions, provide valuable historical information for a reconstruction of the history of this period. In addition to these, there are also coins and, more importantly, the artefacts unearthed by archaeology. The language of the early inscriptions itself has the potential to yield valuable information. While all these sources can be of great use for understanding the economic, political, social and cultural conditions that prevailed in this period, not much can be gathered about ethnic groups. Though various claims have been made on behalf of one or another ethnic group on the basis of archaeological finds, it must be admitted that the archaeological material cannot be easily used to identify the ethnic group responsible for it. In the last few decades, archaeologists have been questioning some of the concepts traditionally used to link archaeological material with ethnic groups.

Pali chronicles

In view of these limitations, one is made to depend primarily on literary and epigraphic sources for evidence about the Tamils in Sri Lanka in this period, even though there may be significant archaeological material left behind by this ethnic group. The literary sources that have direct references to the Tamils in this period are the Pali chronicles, particularly the *Dīpavaṃsa* and the *Mahāvaṃsa*. The Tamil literary works of this period relate exclusively to south India and have no references to the Tamils in Sri Lanka. But their evidence is indirectly useful, especially in the interpretation of the evidence of the Prakrit inscriptions in the island. These inscriptions are of great value for a study of the presence and influence of the Tamils in this period.

The information in the Pali chronicles is limited to the Tamils who succeeded in capturing power at Anuradhapura. The only information about Tamils outside Anuradhapura is to be found in the Duṭṭhagāmaṇī epic section of the *Mahāvaṃsa*, the reliability of which section as historical evidence is questionable.[2] In this section, the author narrates the defeat of several Damiḷa chiefs along the Mahaväli river by Duṭṭhagāmaṇī. The main chronicle section records the names as well as the period of the reigns of the Tamil rulers at Anuradhapura. Of the twenty-nine rulers of Anuradhapura listed in the chronicles for the period c. 250 BCE to the beginning of the first century CE, nine are described as Tamils.[3]

Epigraphic records

The epigraphic records of this period, though numerous, are brief and largely religious in nature, as they are mainly records of donations to the Buddhist clergy. All the donative records so far discovered are in Prakrit, a fact that clearly indicates the dominance of Prakrit as the elite language. Tamil Buddhists were among the donors. The language of these records is no indicator of the ethnicity of those who had the records inscribed. The Tamils used Prakrit in their records. So did others. Although there were Tamil Buddhists among the donors, they are not identifiable as Tamils by their names as the names are also in Prakrit. They can only be identified as Tamils if they had used the ethnic description Dameḍa. A few had done this but there is no way of finding out whether there were Tamils who had recorded their donations without giving the description Dameḍa. There would have been some who did not feel the need to use the ethnic description.

Evidence of Dravidian Linguistic Influence

Even without the reference to Dameḍas, the Brāhmī inscriptions may still provide some evidence for the presence of Tamil-speakers (or speakers of other Dravidian languages). These early inscriptions, though written in Prakrit, appear to contain indirect information about other languages spoken in the island in the centuries immediately before the present era. Just as the occurrence of Dravidian and Munda words in the *Rigveda* is taken to indicate the presence of speakers of Dravidian and Munda languages when Vedic Sanskrit spread into north India, the incidence of non-Indo-Aryan words in the language of the Sri Lankan Brāhmī inscriptions may help to identify other languages spoken in the island. Such words, of course, need to be those not already borrowed into the Indian Prakrits at an earlier period.

Scholars who studied these inscriptions have indicated that some words in the Brāhmī records are not traceable to Indo-Aryan roots. A few have been identified as of Dravidian origin. It cannot be said that these epigraphs have been thoroughly researched by historical linguists with a good knowledge of Indo-Aryan and Dravidian languages. In the case of many words whose meaning is obscure, the tendency has been to look for an Indo-Aryan root. Under the circumstances, only those words which are easily identifiable as Dravidian have been noted. 'Though it may be correct to assume that the greater majority of vocables in the ancient inscriptions of Sri Lanka have parallels in Sanskrit and the Prakrit languages,' Leslie Gunawardana argues, 'it is quite likely that some others may have a Tamil origin'.[4] Perhaps the best known example is the kinship term *marumakan̲* (usually read as *marumakana*). This is one word, occurring several times in the earliest inscriptions (and changing into *marumanaka* by the first century CE), over the origin of which epigraphists have had no disagreement.[5]

Among other words for which Dravidian origins have been suggested, though not without controversy, are *parumaka*, *aya* and *veḷa*. *Parumaka* occurs in a large number of records as the title of elite donors. Attempts have been made to derive this from the Sanskrit '*pramukha*' (chief).[6] As early as 1892, H.C.P. Bell drew attention to its similarity to the Tamil '*perumakaṉ*' (chief, lord).[7] In recent years, leading Sri Lankan scholars have accepted the possibility of this word being of Dravidian origin. 'On linguistic and etymological grounds', argues Sudharshan Seneviratne, 'it is more correct to derive *parumaka* from (the Dravidian) *perumakan* as originally suggested by Bell (1892: 69, note 3), rather than derive it from (Sanskrit) *pramukha*'.[8] The occurrence of the feminine form '*parumakaḷ*' (which has the Dravidian feminine suffix) weighs in favour of treating *parumaka* as a Dravidian word.[9] In the Tamil poems of the Sangam anthology and in later Tamil usage up to modern times the word is used for a chief, lord or god.[10] 'It is quite likely', according to Seneviratne, 'that some segments of the *parumaka* group, who perhaps represent the earliest political elite during the Early Iron Age, had their origins in the Megalithic BRW complex emanating from Peninsular India'.[11]

Leslie Gunawardana is inclined to take the term '*aya*', the occurrence of which is very widespread in the Brāhmī inscriptions, as 'a word of Tamil derivation which had the same meaning as Rajha and Gamani'. In his view, 'it is possible to suggest that originally it denoted the political leaders of settlements which had been founded in different parts of the island'.[12]

South Indian group names

Another word identified by some as of Dravidian origin is the name Veḷ/Veḷa.[13] Sudharshan Seneviratne identifies this with the clan name Vēḷ / Vēḷir occurring in the Tamil poems of the Sangam anthology.[14]

Barata is another proper noun with a south Indian connection met with in a number of Sri Lankan Brāhmī inscriptions.[15] Seneviratne demonstrates the links between the epigraphic evidence on the one hand and the non-Brāhmī symbols associated with the Baratas and the Iron Age burial sites located near the provenance of the Barata inscriptions.[16] Through this study he shows how the 'Early Brāhmī inscriptions in fact shed a great deal of light on the commercial connection of the Baratas'[17] and how, 'in spite of undergoing a process of acculturation to the Indo-Aryan culture, the Baratas continued to use Dravidian kinship terms and the cross-cousin marriage system, which is clearly alien to the Indo-Aryan kinship structure'.[18]

Kinship terms

Internal evidence of the inscriptions in the form of kinship terms provides interesting information about the presence of groups of south Indian origin. The occurrence of the Dravidian language term *marumakan/na* is of particular relevance here. Differing with Paranavitana on the interpretation given to this term, Seneviratne argues that this term, for which he accepts the meaning nephew or son-in-law, indicates the prevalence of Dravidian kinship and cross-cousin marriage system among some groups like the Baratas.[19] He also draws attention to the evidence relating to another element of Dravidian kinship. Analysing the names adopted by persons with the title Parumaka, Seneviratne shows that 'there is a strict adherence to a practice found in the Dravidian kinship structure, known as *peyaran*, where the grandson takes up the name of his grandfather'.[20]

The occurrence of words of Dravidian origin in areas such as kinship, political structure and personal or clan names in the earliest records of the island point to close contact between the users of Prakrit and local speakers of Dravidian languages. Anyone using these sources for the reconstruction of the early history of the island cannot fail to see the significance of these Dravidian-language terms. 'Since the terms relate to such critical areas as kinship and political organization', Leslie Gunawardana concludes, 'it is likely that the Tamil influences on the island were considerable.'[21]

The views of leading Sinhalese linguists lend support to such a conclusion. In fact, these linguists point out that the Dravidian influence was not confined to mere lexical borrowing but extended to significant linguistic features. M.W.S. de Silva states that 'the early Sinhalese inscriptions show some features which are linguistically Dravidian' and points out that Wilhelm Geiger 'did not fail to observe that the loss in Sinhalese of the old aspirates is perhaps due to Tamil influence'.[22] This loss is already seen in the earliest inscriptions.[23]

Just as the occurrence of Dravidian and Munda words in the Sanskrit of the Vedas in north India points to the presence of speakers of Dravidian and Austroasiatic languages in that region when Vedic Sanskrit spread there, the occurrence of Dravidian words (and possibly Munda words which are as yet unrecognized) in the Prakrit of the Sri Lankan inscriptions would indicate the presence of Dravidian-speakers (and possibly Munda-speakers). If one may borrow the argument used by Romila Thapar (in regard to Vedic Sanskrit and the non-Indo-Aryan languages of north India) that the 'Vedic corpus is the statement of the dominant group, but this does not preclude the presence of others',[24] it could be argued that the Brāhmī corpus in Sri Lanka is no doubt the statement of the dominant group but it does not mean that other language speakers were not present.[25]

In recent years interesting numismatic evidence relating to the activities of Tamil traders in the island has been brought to light. Notable among the newly discovered coins are those with Brāhmī legends in Tamil to which Osmund Bopearachchi has drawn the attention of scholars.[26] Similar discoveries have been reported by P. Pushparatnam.[27] While these numismatic sources may not add anything not known from other sources, they are important for the confirmation they provide for the activities of Tamil traders in the EHP, not only in the north but in the southern ports as well.

The cumulative evidence of the Brāhmī inscriptions, numismatic sources and the archaeological material points to the presence of Tamil traders, Tamil political leaders and Tamil clans associated with the south Indian Iron Age burial culture in the third/second century BCE. The traditions preserved in the Pali chronicles confirm this with references to Tamil political aspirants, Tamil traders and Tamil soldiers. We do not know whether all these people were referred to as Dameḍas at that time. But it is certain that there were traders who were Dameḍas as well as political leaders and presumably their armies. Some of them, if not most of them, were without doubt responsible for several of the Iron Age burials and for the spread of this burial culture among other people in the island. Seneviratne argues that the Vēḷir of south India were among those who 'introduced the Megallithic-BRW techno-cultural complex to Sri Lanka around the 7/6 century B.C.'[28] Whether they were known as Dameḍas or by other clan names, Tamil-speakers seem to have been in Sri Lanka a few centuries before the time of the earliest Brāhmī inscriptions.

If we consider the Dameḍa as a linguistic identity, as suggested by Seneviratne,[29] then many of those who arrived from the Tamil-speaking areas of south India in the EIA could be said to belong to the Dameḍa group in its broadest sense. It is not suggested that from this very early date the group remained completely distinct from the other groups. On the contrary, some members of the Dameḍa group no doubt were assimilated into other groups, especially into the major Iḷa group. It was a time when acculturation and social integration were the norms as the adoption of Prakrit and the acceptance of Buddhism facilitated absorption of members of minor groups into the major group that was evolving, particularly in the domain that had Anuradhapura as the power centre. Elsewhere, in areas where the Dameḍa group was already growing dominant, a process of assimilation into the Dameḍa group would have been the pattern. There were no doubt at that time many areas where neither the Dameḍa nor the Iḷa was in a controlling position.

Though the beginnings of the evolution of the two major ethnic identities of ancient Sri Lanka date back to the EIA, it is with the widespread use of the Brāhmī script and the Prakrit language and the spread of Buddhism that one is able to trace this evolution. There are, however, some difficulties in tracing this development. The ethnicity of persons mentioned in the sources is not always easy to identify as the EHP was a time when names were Sanskritised (or rendered in a Prakrit form, depending on the language of the source). Since Prakrit was the *lingua franca* and presumably the language of the elite, records left by members of different ethnic groups, including the Dameḍas, are in this common language. Archaeological material, too, cannot be easily associated with particular ethnic groups. The urn burial artefacts of Pomparippu, for instance, are closely linked to similar burial artefacts in Adichchnallur and other sites in Tamil Nadu. While the spread of this urn burial culture from Tamil Nadu to Sri Lanka can be established with such evidence, it is not easy to associate any site with a particular ethnic group without other incontrovertible evidence such as written records. This culture, no doubt, was spreading among different groups at that time.

Anuradhapura kingdom:

Early Tamil Rulers – Sena and Guttaka

In this period, for the first time, the Pali chronicles and the inscriptions as well as coins provide names of Tamils and information relating to their political, economic and cultural activities. By the third century BCE, state formation was fairly advanced and there were a few kingdoms and many chiefdoms. The main power centre at Anuradhapura was multi-ethnic. The rulers at this place, though taking on the title of Maharaja (the Great King), were not in control of a large territory until the second century BCE.

Sena and Guttaka, two brothers, are the first Tamil rulers that we know about from the chronicles. Possibly there were others before them. That the ethnicity of the rulers at this power centre was not of great significance is seen from the fact that the earlier chronicle (*Dīpavaṃsa*) does not even describe an important Tamil king, Eḷāra, as a Damiḷa. The two brothers, Sena and Guttaka, we are told, were sons of a horse freighter. They obviously had some economic power that helped them to seize control of the kingdom. The statement in the *Mahāvaṃsa* that these two kings ruled for twenty-two years in a righteous manner indicates that in the historical tradition of the Anuradhapura kingdom their rule was not considered as one marked by resistance or opposition.

Very little is known about these two early Tamil rulers. One edition of the *Mahāvaṃsa* has the interesting information that these two kings had the river Kadamba-nadī (Malvatu Oya) diverted to flow closer to the city of Anuradhapura, their centre of power, to enable them to perform certain sacred rituals associated with water.[30] Seneviratne has suggested that this may indicate that they followed Brahmanic rituals.[31]

Eḷāra

The reign of Sena and Guttaka was not an isolated instance of Tamil rule at Anuradhapura. It was soon followed by the rule of Eḷāra who is described in the chronicles as a person 'of noble birth from the Coḷa country'.[32] This has been interpreted to mean that he was a prince of the Coḷa lineage. It is not necessary to give this interpretation. It is quite possible that he belonged to some other Tamil lineage. The reign of this Tamil king has gained great significance in Sri Lankan history and folk memory as well as in contemporary politics. No other Tamil ruler of a kingdom in Sri Lanka is better remembered or more talked about. The Pali chronicles have more information about Eḷāra than about any other Tamil ruler of Sri Lanka in the EHP. He is unquestionably the only Tamil ruler in the island to be remembered up to the present day by the people of Sri Lanka, particularly the Sinhalese. This is partly due to what the chronicles describe as his rule of 'even justice toward friend and foe'.[33] Not many other ancient rulers of Sri Lanka have found a place in folk memory for so long, a period of more than two thousand years. Another reason for his name being remembered is the well-known conflict he had with Duṭṭhagāmaṇī, the Sinhalese prince of ancient times held up in Sri Lankan historical tradition as a great Sinhalese hero.

The chronicles record four folk tales relating to the just rule of Eḷāra.[34] While there is no need to look for any historical truth in the details of these tales, the underlying purpose that gave rise to these legendary stories is clear, namely to illustrate the fairness and justice with which the king ruled his kingdom. It is indeed admirable that a Buddhist monk living in Anuradhapura almost seven centuries after the rule of Eḷāra considered it important to include these four stories in his account of this ruler's reign. On the one hand, it shows the strength of the folk tradition in respect of Eḷāra's reign and, on the other, it is a measure of the fair-mindedness and lack of prejudice on the part of the author, Mahānāma, in writing about the rule of a non-Buddhist and non-Sinhalese ruler. What is more noteworthy is that one of these tales actually credits Eḷāra with upholding or protecting tradition (*cāritaṃ anupālayaṃ*) and continuing to provide patronage to the Buddhist clergy, even though he himself was not a Buddhist.[35] If, as some believe, Mahānāma wanted to portray Eḷāra as an enemy of Buddhism, it would be hard to explain why he had included this tale in his chronicle.

Some of the above legends may not have been originally associated with Eḷāra, for at least one of them is found in later south Indian sources in connection with another Tamil ruler of the Cōḷa line.[36] A different version of this story seems to have been carried by traders to Europe and it has survived among the tales associated with the famous eighth century French king Charlemagne.[37] It is hard to establish whether this story originated in Sri Lanka and later spread to south India, but its earliest occurrence is in the Sri Lankan sources. What is important is that this legend occurs as an illustration of the high level of justice adopted by the three rulers with whom it is associated.

The period of Eḷāra's rule occupies an important place in ancient Sri Lankan history. This was the time when the ruler of a chiefdom in the southern part of the island was able to launch a campaign of territorial expansion, annex most of the chiefdoms north of it, and successfully challenge the authority of the main kingdom whose power-centre was at Anuradhapura. Duṭṭhagāmaṇī was the southern ruler and Mahāgāma was the centre from where he began to extend his power. Eḷāra, the ruler at Anuradhapura, was defeated and for the first time there emerged a kingdom that wielded authority over a good part of the north and south of the island, paving the way for the evolution of the concept of a Sri Lankan state.

The victory of Duṭṭhagāmaṇī and his subsequent achievements as a great patron of Buddhism and builder of one of the most hallowed Buddhist monuments and, at that time, the biggest, in the island (and indeed in the Buddhist world) stirred the imagination of commoner and chronicler alike. For generations he has been given a special place, not accorded to any other ruler, in folk tradition and monastic history. However, the nobility that he displayed towards the king he defeated tends to be obscured in modern times by contemporary politics. Duṭṭhagāmaṇī showed the highest respect for Eḷāra by having a *cetiya* built at the place where the latter died and, what is more, decreeing that his subjects conduct worship there. This is how the *Mahāvaṃsa* describes this:

> In the city he [Duṭṭhagāmaṇī] caused the drum to be beaten, and when he had summoned the people from a *yojana* around he celebrated the funeral rites for king Eḷāra. On the spot where his body had fallen he burned it with the catafalque, and there did he build a monument [*cetiya*] and ordain worship. And even to this day the princes of Lanka, when they draw near to this place, are wont to silence their music because of this worship.[38]

As has been pointed out several times, this is one instance in the whole chronicle when the chronicler deviates from his narration of historical events and includes a comment relating to what was happening in his own time, more than seven centuries after the event he is narrating. His example was followed by later chroniclers, too, who, even as late as the fourteenth century, mention that in their time, too, Duṭṭhagāmaṇī's decree was being obeyed.[39] This is not surprising since we have evidence from early nineteenth century British writings that, even as Anuradhapura lay in ruins and jungle-covered, people passing through the ruined city remembered to observe Duṭṭhagāmaṇi's injunctions.[40]

It appears that the *cetiya* built by Duṭṭhagāmaṇi at the spot where Eḷāra was cremated became the centre of a separate establishment that continued to exist for several centuries. In addition to the *cetiya*, there was also an image-house or a shrine with an image of Eḷāra, referred to as the Eḷāra-paṭhimā-ghara (Eḷāra Image-house). This structure and the whole establishment appear to have been at Anuradhapura until the city's decline at the end of the first millennium CE.[41]

The *Mahāvaṃsa* has more information about the period of Eḷāra's reign than that of any other Tamil ruler. But much of it is in the Duṭṭhagāmaṇī epic section that cannot be given the same degree of credibility as the chronicle section. In this epic section, there are references to a number of chiefdoms ruled by Tamils, most of which were along the Mahaväli River. Duṭṭhagāmaṇī is said to have defeated thirty-one Tamil kings before he finally confronted Eḷāra.[42] When he realized that he had to fight a powerful enemy, Eḷāra is said to have called for help from south India. In response to his call, Bhalluka, his nephew, arrived with troops but it was too late.[43]

While it would not be surprising if there were several chiefdoms ruled by Tamils in northern Sri Lanka in the second century BCE, it would be hard to establish that the author of the *Mahāvaṃsa* was using historical sources or relying on oral traditions when he composed the epic section some seven centuries after the reign of

Eḷāra. At best, what can be gleaned from this is that there were several Tamil chiefdoms among the many that covered much of the northern part of the island in the second century BCE and that Duṭṭhagāmaṇī had to subjugate a number of these, just as he had conquered the chiefdoms in the southern regions, before successfully launching his campaign against the power-centre at Anuradhapura. The chiefdoms in the south, the chronicles say, were not ruled by Tamils while many in the north were controlled by Tamil chiefs. It is quite possible that the northward expansion of Duṭṭhgāmaṇi's kingdom also resulted in the subjugation of chiefdoms belonging to other ethnic groups about whom we know next to nothing. Since the epic section of the *Mahāvaṃsa* treats the political campaigns of Duṭṭhagāmaṇī as a conflict between a Buddhist Sinhalese hero and non-Buddhist Tamil rulers, there is no room in it for the battles that Duṭṭhagāmaṇī might have waged against other ethnic chiefdoms that were in his path.

Given the very close relations that existed between Sri Lanka and south India, Eḷāra's call for help and the arrival of Bhalluka's troops seem plausible, for the chronicles record many instances of Anuradhapura rulers going over to south India to get assistance in similar circumstances in the centuries that follow.

After Eḷāra

Although Duṭṭhagāmaṇī had succeeded in subjugating a large number of chiefdoms and bringing a good part of the island under the control of the power-centre at Anuradhapura, it cannot be said that at last a strong and stable dynasty had emerged at this capital. Not long after the demise of Duṭṭhagāmaṇī, instability set in and the members of his lineage were ousted from the throne. Looking at the events, as recorded in the chronicles, in the next two centuries following the reign of Duṭṭhagāmaṇī, it is not possible to claim, as has often been done, that the 'triumph of Duṭṭhagāmaṇī marks the first unification of the island'.[44] It was no doubt another stage in the emergence of Anuradhapura as the dominant kingdom in the island. But it is too far-fetched to claim that the whole island was unified.

The emergence of a dominant ethnic identity, which later comes to be known as the Sinhalese, is seen in this period. However, the southern tip of the Indian subcontinent and the northern part of Sri Lanka continue to be a single region within which one could see close interaction among different ethnic groups. The chronicles record the names of as many as seven members of the Damiḷa or Tamil group occupying the throne of Anuradhapura in the two centuries after Duṭṭhagāmaṇī. The tendency has been to see them as adventurers from south India.

Just as it was seen that all the Tamils who sat on the throne at Anuradhapura were invaders from south India, it was assumed that all others who ruled at this power-centre were Sinhalese. It is quite possible that some of them did not belong to the dominant ethnic group which at that time seems to have had the name Iḷa and later came to be known as Siṃhaḷa. It is interesting to note that a number of rulers at Anuradhapura had the name Nāga, even though the chronicles describe them as members of the dynasty begun by Vijaya. The occurrence of this name as that of some members of the main royal lineage at Anuradhapura raises some important questions. If, according to the chronicles, the Nāgas were a distinct ethnic or tribal group who were not connected with the royal lineage at Anuradhapura, how could one explain the use of this ethnic name by some members of the Anuradhapura lineage? At a time when ethnic names like Nāga had special connotations, how could one expect anyone outside the Nāga group to adopt that name? It would appear that this name was taken by only those who had Nāga connections. Just as there were Damiḷas on the throne of Anuradhapura, there were also Nāgas. In course of time, the Nāgas, like many other ethnic groups in Sri Lanka, came to be assimilated into one or the other of the two main ethnic identities that evolved in ancient times, namely the Sinhalese and the Tamils. The Nāgas in south India, too, were assimilated into the major groups there.

It would appear that the traditions relating to the reigns of non-Buddhist kings at Anuradhapura were not preserved in great detail or with care. This may be the reason why the information about these reigns is not merely scanty but also somewhat confused. The *Mahāvaṃsa* records that seven Tamils arrived with an army from south India three decades after the reign of Duṭṭhagāmaṇī, defeated the king of Anuradhapura and took over the kingdom. Of the seven, five sat on the throne, one after the other, and ruled for fourteen years. The Pali commentaries, which are considered to be earlier than the *Mahāvaṃsa*, do not refer to this period of fourteen years as a time when Tamils ruled. Instead, it is referred to as a period when the Brāhmaṇa Tīya ruled.[45] The account of the five Tamil rulers, that they came together and ruled one after the other, seems to be the result of an attempt to fill in the period of Tamil rule with the names of the rulers that were available in the scantily preserved traditions. It is possible that they did not all rule together or one after the other. The best that can be deduced from this account is that, in the period after the death of the strong ruler Duṭṭhagāmaṇī, there were several Tamil kings on the throne of Anuradhapura. There were also possibly kings who belonged to other ethnic groups, particularly the Nāgas.

In the period up to the middle of the third century CE, as many as ten (possibly eleven) Nāgas are listed in the chronicles as rulers of Anuradhapura. It is also possible that the adoption of this name in the case of some was the result of marriage connections with Nāgas. Evidently the ruling elite families of Anuradhapura were not confined to one ethnic group. There is evidence of inter-ethnic marriage in these families. At least two of the rulers from the main lineage family had queens named Damiḷādevī (Tamil princess).[46] The occurrence of the name Nāga as the name of some of the rulers of this period seems to indicate marriage between members of the main lineage and Nāgas. Possibly there were matrimonial relations with other ethnic groups, too.

The cumulative evidence of the chronicles indicates that, although Duṭṭhagāmaṇī succeeded in defeating a number of chiefdoms and creating a large kingdom with its power base at Anuradhapura, he did not establish a stable and powerful dynasty to control the affairs of the kingdom in the decades that followed his reign. Contenders from different ethnic groups were able to seize power for short periods during the next two centuries. When the political events of these early centuries came to be recounted in the chronicles at a later date, a neat division between the main lineage rulers (conveniently labelled as Sinhalese rulers by later writers though not by the chroniclers themselves) and Tamil rulers was established. For, by the time the chronicles came to be written, the evolution of the Sinhalese and Tamil ethnic groups through the assimilation of many other local groups was well under way.

Beyond the Anuradhapura Kingdom

While the evidence of the literary sources (being confined mainly to the affairs of the Anuradhapura rulers) is extremely limited with regard to the Tamils in the island, the epigraphic and archaeological sources provide very reliable and extensive information on this subject. The epigraphic sources in particular help to confirm some of the conclusions drawn from the literary sources and go further to present a better insight into the political and social conditions in most parts of the island than that provided by the chronicles. Unlike the chronicles, the Brāhmī records provide a wealth of information about the elites in different parts of the island. Much work has been done on them in recent decades, especially after the bulk of these records were made easily accessible to scholars with the publication of the first volume of the *Inscriptions of Ceylon* in 1970.[47] This has helped to revise many of the old views about ancient Sri Lanka. The most significant contribution in this respect is that of Seneviratne.[48] Gunawardana, too, has made very valuable contributions to the understanding of these early epigraphic records.

Pre-state polities

The chronicles deal with the history of the island as if there was a single political entity, with a single power centre and a single ruling lineage, from the very beginning of the historic period. This linear treatment has formed the basis of the underlying assumption in modern history books, namely, that the history of Sri Lanka is the history of a single kingdom and its rulers. As Gunawardana has noted, 'the ideological framework inherited from the chroniclers has continued to wield a deep influence on historical writings on the ancient period'.[49] The epigraphic records present a very different picture of the political conditions in the island in the centuries immediately before the Common Era.

In his analysis of the political conditions reflected by the early Brāhmī records of the island, Gunawardana has identified records of rulers of chiefdoms in twenty-eight of the 269 sites of early Brāhmī inscriptions. These are distributed in various parts of the island, but chiefly in the north, central and southeastern parts. The northernmost of the twenty-eight sites is at Periya-puliyankulam in the Vavuniya District. East of this site, in the northeast, is another site, Nacciyarmalai. As Gunawardana has clarified, 'the absence of sites further north has to be perhaps explained more in terms of the geological features of the land than as an indication of political conditions prevalent in ancient times.'[50] In fact, from other evidence it is known that there was a chiefdom named Nāgadīpa in the northernmost part of the island. Its ruler appears to have been known as Dīparāja and there is a Brāhmī cave record of a Dīparajha. Although this record is from Mihintale, Paranavitana suggests that the Dīparajha mentioned here was the ruler of Nāgadīpa. Apart from these references to Dīparaja, there is at least one early Brāhmī record from the Jaffna peninsula itself providing evidence about a chief with the title Kō (the equivalent of the Prakrit *raja* in Dravidian languages).[51]

Cultural diversity

While the use of Prakrit and the stereotyped recording of donations to the Buddhist Sangha provide a veneer of homogeneity to the culture of the persons whom we meet in these records, there is beneath that veneer an element of cultural diversity that is unmistakable. Among those who contributed to this diversity were groups that had moved in from Tamil Nadu. While Gunawardana draws attention to some of the indications of cultural diversity in the inscriptions,[52] it is Seneviratne who cogently relates the evidence of the Brāhmī inscriptions and the archaeological remains from the EIA burial sites to specifically identify the various cultural elements.

Seneviratne uses the evidence of not only the Prakrit texts but also the non-Brāhmī symbols in the cave records and on pottery, together with the provenance of EIA sites in proximity to the cave inscriptions, to locate areas where such groups as the Barata and Vēḷir were established. Bringing together the evidence of the Tamil Sangam poems, the Sri Lankan Brāhmī cave records, the non-Brāhmī symbols associated with these records and the EIA burial sites, Seneviratne throws interesting light on the activities of the Barata group (which he equates with the Bata group) in the Early Historic Period. 'The case of the Baratas and the Batas', in his view, 'can be considered as a useful example to understand the dynamics related to the peopling of Sri Lanka and the process of social formation during the Early Historic period.'[53]

Accepting Maloney's identification of the Barata group with the coastal community of Paratar of Tamil Nadu mentioned in the Tamil Sangam poems, Seneviratne shows that the Barata/Bata groups, like the Paratar, were primarily engaged in trade, dealing in chanks and pearls, gems and horses. In their inscriptions, there is a reference to the Bata-kumara, comparable to the Parata-kumārar of the Tamil literary sources. Their records have symbols associated with maritime trade. The internal evidence of these records reveals the prevalence of Dravidian kinship terms and cross-cousin marriage system among them. Like many other groups in south India and Sri Lanka at that time, the Baratas were coming under the influence of Sanskritisation, as seen in their personal names and in the Sanskrit form of their group name. Seneviratne concludes that the Barata/Bata groups were 'successful in integrating themselves with the Early Historic political, social, economic and religio-cultural structure in total terms.'[54]

Like the Barata group, another group originating from Tamil Nadu is the Veḷ or Veḷa.[55] Seneviratne identifies this with the Vēḷir of Tamil Nadu. He associates certain non-Brāhmī symbols, such as the jar and lance-bearer, found with Veḷ inscriptions and on pottery from burial sites, with the Vēḷir. Many of the *parumaka* chieftains have the name Vēḷ. On the basis of the association of the title *parumaka* with those carrying the name Vēḷ and their connection with the EIA burials, Seneviratne concludes:

> In our view, the introduction of the epithet *parumaka* was from south India, and community movement from Peninsular India did take place at an early date to Sri Lanka. Some of those who arrived belonged to clan groups under the leadership of the Vēḷir chieftains, and introduced the Megalithic-BRW techno-cultural complex to Sri Lanka around the 7/6 century B.C.[56]

Among the sites that Seneviratne associates with the Vēḷir is the well-known megalithic-BRW burial complex at Pomparippu in northwest Sri Lanka. Not far from this place, at Mullegama, Tonigala and Paramakanda, are Brāhmī records with the jar and lance-bearer symbols associated with the Vēḷir. Pointing to the occurrence of these symbols on pottery at the Pomparippu urn-burials, Seneviratne presents the view that the Vēḷir had moved to this part of the island at an early date. 'It is not altogether impossible', he concludes, 'that some of the Veḷ/a found in north Sri Lanka were the decendants of the Vēḷir who arrived with their clans (bringing with them traditions about the jar and Dvārakā) under pressure from the Pāṇḍya, who apparently consolidated their proto-state in the Vaigai-Tambapaṇṇi region at a relatively early date.'[57]

Seneviratne also uses other implicit evidence in the Brāhmī records to draw conclusions about the cultural diversity that prevailed in the EHP. While most personal names in these earliest inscriptions are Prakrit or Prakritised names, there is quite a number that betrays other language affinity. Seneviratne gives several examples of such names and asserts that 'The personal names taken up especially by the *parumakas* north and west of the river Mahaweli have a Dravidian (and possibly a Mundari) origin than Indo-Aryan one, which points to a Deccan and south Indian connection.'.[58] As mentioned earlier, he also extracts from the Brāhmī inscriptions information about the prevalence of Dravidian kinship, cross-cousin marriage and the *peyaraṉ* naming custom.[59]

One may add to these diverse strands of evidence relating to the Tamil element the occurrence of a place-name with the suffix –*paṭṭana* in the northern peninsula. The fact that the leading port of the northernmost region in the island had a name, according to the early Pali sources, with the suffix *paṭṭana* is not without significance. Jambukolapaṭṭana, sometimes referred to as just Kolapaṭṭana, finds mention in the *Mahāvaṃsa*, as well as in other Pali texts, as the premier entrepot in the northern peninsula and the chief port for sailings to the east coast of India.[60] The suffix *paṭṭana* has its origin in the Dravidian *paṭṭiṉam* (coastal town, port, etc.) and is found in the names of some of the well-known ancient ports of south India.[61] It is not known to occur in the names of ports in southern Sri Lanka. The only other Sri Lankan ports with names having this suffix were Mātoṭa (Mahapaṭana) in the northwest and Gokarṇa (Goṇagāmaka-paṭṭana) in the northeast, both known to be areas with a strong Tamil element in the historical period.[62] The name Jambukolapaṭṭana may, therefore, indicate the presence of a strong Tamil element or other Dravidian element in the northernmost port very early in the EHP. The northern part of the island in general seems to have had a stronger Tamil cultural element compared with the southeast.

Earliest Phase: Presence of a Strong Tamil Element

The period c. 250 BCE – c. 300 CE was, without doubt, an important phase in the formative period of the island's history. The varied cultural elements of the EIA came under new influences that had the potential to forge them together into a single homogeneous group. The Mauryan influence, particularly through the establishment of a strong Theravada Buddhist Sangha at Anuradhapura, Mihintale and elsewhere, provided the overarching framework to bring together the diverse elements. But more importantly, the Prakrit language, which clearly had begun to unite the various elements in the centuries before the establishment of the

Buddhist Sangha, continued to bring all the elements closer together and to replace the earlier Mesolithic languages. In this cultural milieu, there was also what may be termed a strong Tamil element. This element manifested itself in various ways. The Damiḷa political leaders of the chronicles, the Dameḍa traders (*vaṇijha*) and sailors (*navika*) of the inscriptions, the Dameḍa *gahapatis*, the Aya chiefs, the Veḷ chiefs, the Damiḷa princesses (Damiḷādevī) and their retinues from south Indian Tamil chiefdoms, the Tamil warriors brought by Anuradhapura leaders and possibly by leaders of other chiefdoms, and, finally, the many anonymous persons buried in several burial sites as well as those who practised the cross-cousin marriage system and the *peyaraṉ* naming system were among those who represented the Tamil element. The various cultural elements that flowed from the Tamil-speaking southern tip of the Indian peninsula would constitute the broad Tamil element. There was also a noticeable cultural element flowing from the east coast of Andhra. The dominant Prakrit element , however, was clearly unshakable. Many of the other elements were already in the process of being assimilated into the dominant culture in this period. However, the Tamil element appears to have been strong enough to survive in the remote north, northeast and northwest and beome reinforced in the next few centuries when strong Tamil kingdoms emerged in south India.

CHAPTER

6 HEḶA AND DEMEḶA

C 300 – 900 CE

Emerging Personalities

The period from about the beginning of the fourth century to about the end of the ninth century is a dark period as far as the northern and eastern regions (the present-day areas predominantly settled by Tamils) are concerned. The Pali and Sinhalese chronicles have no information of any significance about either the rulers or the people of these regions. While a few inscriptions have been found in the eastern region, so far no inscription of this period has come to light in the northern region, with the exception of an inscribed carnelian seal. Archaeological remains of this period, however, have been identified but no proper study of these artefacts has been undertaken. The references to this region in the south Indian Tamil literary sources are also few and far between.

Although the paucity of historical sources makes this a dark period, it is the most significant in the evolution of the separate Tamil ethnic group of ancient Sri Lanka. It is the phase in which various early historic communities in the northern third of the island came under the dominant influence of Tamil-speakers and the Saiva religion. Clearly, the two chief unifying factors in the evolution of a single Tamil ethnic identity were the Tamil language and the Saiva religion, which are seen as the distinctive features of the Sri Lankan Tamils at the beginning of the tenth century.

All the available evidence at the end of the third century points to the presence of various ethnic groups in the island. As seen earlier, from about 300 BCE, the people of the island, the descendants of the Mesolithic inhabitants as well as others who had arrived later, were coming under the influence of very strong forces that were clearly leading to the emergence of a homogeneous group in the areas ruled by the Anuradhapura kings as well as in the southern parts of the island. In these areas, the Heḷa language and the Buddhist religion continued to be the chief unifying factors, although here too the Heḷa language appears to have been under notable pressure from Tamil.[1] In the extreme north of the island a different process, culminating in the emergence of a Tamil-speaking group, was taking place at this time. The successive steps in this long process cannot be easily observed with the evidence that is available but the end result is clearly seen at the close of this period when the Tamil-speaking group is dominant in the northern parts of the island.

The evolution of the Tamil group during this period proceeded through the interaction of various peoples. Among them were the Nāgas, one of the most mysterious peoples in the island. There were the Tamils whose dominating influence in spreading not only the Tamil language but also the Saiva religion is the most significant aspect of this evolution. There were also the Andhras or Telugus, whose influence in the Buddhism of the north and east is attested by archaeology. Possibly the Keralas, too, were there, if one is to go by the survival of Kerala laws and customs in the north and east. The Heḷas, who themselves were evolving as the dominant ethnic group in the south through the interaction of various groups, were also among those who contributed to the formation of the Tamil ethnic identity at this time.

A number of factors were responsible for the strengthening of the Tamil element in northern Sri Lanka in this period. These worked against the northward extension of the process of acculturation that went on in the areas under the direct control of Anuradhapura. These could be grouped under three main headings: political, economic and religious. Aspirants and claimants to the kingship at Anuradhapura, both Sri Lankan and south Indian, brought to the island armies recruited in the Tamil kingdoms on several occasions with consequences in many ways similar to those experienced in Britain in the fifth century when Germanic elements gained ascendancy in that country. The expansion of south Indian maritime trade under the Pallava rulers led to an increase in the activities of Tamil mercantile communities. This was accompanied by the arrival of skilled craftsmen from south India to create works of art and build monuments for the patrons of Mahayana Buddhism. There was also another important area of economic activity that seems to have attracted or provided the impetus for the arrival of unskilled and possibly skilled workers. This was the building of hydraulic works. And then there was the religious factor. Buddhist monks had always been coming to institutions in Sri Lanka from the Tamil kingdoms, just as monks from Sri Lanka went over to south India not only for religious purposes but also to escape from political and economic distresses. But after the fifth century, when Buddhism began to decline in the Tamil kingdoms and to face hostility, it is possible that not only monks but also lay Buddhists moved to Sri Lanka and found sanctuary there.

The Nāgas

About 300 CE, the area roughly covered by the Jaffna District, particularly the Jaffna peninsula, continued to be known as the land of the Nāgas. The only epigraphic reference to the name Nāgadīpa (Nakadiva – the Island of the Nāgas) is datable to the early centuries of this era.[2] The Pali chronicles and commentaries of about the fifth century also refer to Nāgadīpa. One of these refers to a chiefdom in this region whose ruler was known as or had the title of Dīparāja (King of the Island, connoting presumably 'King of the Nāga Island').[3] In the Tamil literature of about this time, there are references to a Nākanāṭu (Land of the Nāgas), across the sea from south India, identifiable with Nāgadīpa.[4] A city named Nākapuram (City of the Nāgas) also finds mention as the seat of kings who had Sanskritised names.[5] These references seem to relate to earlier traditions. In the second century, the Graeco-Roman traders had gathered information about Nāgadīpa and we find Claudius Ptolemy, in his celebrated *Geographia*, referring to Nagadiba as one of the thirteen major coastal towns in Taprobane (Sri Lanka).[6] On the strength of all this literary and epigraphic evidence, the historicity of Nāgadīpa is beyond doubt. That Nāgadīpa referred to a region in the far north of the island and that it derived its name from a people called Nāga who lived there are acceptable. As mentioned earlier, Siran Deraniyagala has speculated that 'the term "Nāgas" refers to the protohistoric Early Iron Age peoples of Sri Lanka'[7] and that they displaced the earlier Mesolithic hunter-gatherers from the northern and western parts of the island from about 1000 BCE.[8]

In the traditions preserved in the early Sri Lankan chronicles as well as in the early Tamil literary works the Nāgas appear as a distinct group. The evidence of the Pali and Tamil literary sources indicates that the process of acculturation of the Nāgas with the dominant groups of South Asia was well under way by the end of the third century. In the cultural milieu of the EHP, when personal names had special significance and were not adopted indiscriminately, the use of the name Nāga along with personal names must have had some significance. A notable number of persons mentioned in the early Brāhmī inscriptions of Sri Lanka bear the name Nāga. Some of them are chiefs with the title *raja*. In the Pali chronicles, too, several persons including rulers of Anuradhapura have the name Nāga. At a time when Nāgas were known to constitute a distinct group, persons outside the group or having no connection with that group could not have adopted that name without a reason. It would appear that in the EHP the Nāgas had begun to lose their separate identity and to be affected by the process of acculturation that was going on in the island. In the kingdom of Anuradhapura and in the areas around it, the adoption of Prakrit, the acceptance of Buddhism and intermarriage may be included among the chief features of the process of acculturation involving several ethnic groups. The Nāga connection is reflected in personal names.

A similar process took place in south India, too. The earliest Tamil poems, namely those in the Sangam anthology, provide the names of several persons with the name Nāga. Many of them were Tamil poets. This would mean that the adoption of the Tamil language was helping the Nāgas in the Tamil chiefdoms to be assimilated into the major ethnic group there.[9] The survival of place-names such as Nāgar-kovil and Nāga-paṭṭiṉam in Tamil Nadu indicates association with Nāgas at an earlier date.

By the end of the ninth century, there is no evidence relating to the Nāgas. Clearly by that time, or very probably long before that time, the Nāgas were assimilated into the two major ethnic groups in the island. These two groups are now referred to as Heḷa and Demeḷa in the inscriptions of the ninth century. The personal name Nāga occurs in royal names until the sixth century. The bearers of this name are, without doubt, members of the Heḷa group. In the north, no record mentioning the Nāgas has come to light. But in the Tamil literary sources of south India the personal name Nāga occurs as a name of persons who belong to the Tamil group. The assimilation of the Nāgas of Sri Lanka and south India into the main ethnic groups of the region was complete before the ninth century. One of the major developments in this period, therefore, was the transformation of the dominant Nāga group of the northern region into a Tamil-speaking group.

What do we know about the Tamils in Sri Lanka in the six centuries between 300 and 900 CE? Although not much is known at present, the little that is available throws light on the process of transformation that went on in the northern parts of Sri Lanka culminating in the emergence of the Sri Lankan Tamil ethnic group in that region. In the first place, the interaction between south Indian and Sri Lankan communities that was seen in the protohistoric and early historic periods continued unabated in this period. It took place in the political, social, economic and cultural spheres. On the south Indian side, it involved not only the Tamils but also the Telugus, Kannadas and the Keralas. In the end, it resulted in the emergence of the two major groups, the Heḷa and the Demeḷa of the ninth century inscriptions.

PLATE 12.
Ruins of Vijayaraja-isvaram. This inscription in Tamil is dated in the reign of Jayabahu I (after Vijayabahu I).

***Photo**: March 2005, by the author.*

PLATE 13.

Vanavan-madevi-isvaram (named after the mother of Cola Rajendra I), now known as Siva Devale No.2, Polonnaruva (known under the Colas as Jananathapuram, after Rajaraja I). 11th century. This temple 'is worthy of the great architectural traditions to which they [the Colas] were heirs and must be reckoned among the notable historical monuments of the Island' (S. Paranavitana).

Photo: *March 2005, by the author.* ***Courtesy:*** *Department of Archaeology.*

The South Indian Scene

The period from the third century to about the sixth century is considered to be a dark age in the history of the Tamil regions in south India. Very little is known about the political developments there. Although historians treat this period as one of much political confusion, it appears that what really happened was the supplanting of the old royal lineages of the Cōḻas and the Pāṇḍyas by a new lineage whose origins and activities have gone unrecorded. The name Kalabhra is given to this lineage, on the basis of a few references in Buddhist literature and some inscriptions.[10]

That there was a disruption of the rule of the traditional Cōḻa and Pāṇḍya dynasties by newcomers cannot be disputed. But it is doubtful that there was any more political instability at this time than there was in the centuries before 300 CE. Seen from the point of view of dynastic history and based on the popular belief that there was peace and prosperity under the three crowned kings (*mūvēntar*) of the Tamil land in the so-called Sangam period, the fall of the traditional lineages would appear to signal political disaster. The information we have about the political conditions in the Sangam period comes from Tamil poets who were patronized by the Coḷa, Cēra and Pāṇḍya rulers and inevitably the picture painted by these poets is generally one of prosperity. There is, however, evidence, that these rulers were often engaged in wars with one another as well as with minor chiefs, a situation not different from that which obtained in the centuries after 300 CE.

Those who overran the Tamil kingdoms in or about the fourth century have not been clearly identified. They may not have all belonged to the same lineage or ethnic group. The Kalabhras were possibly one of the groups that supplanted the established dynasties. Whatever the identity of the newcomers, the political conflicts of this time appear to have led to the fall of the traditional ruling families and the dispersal of some members of these families to areas north of the Tamil land and to Sri Lanka. In all probability, neither the Coḷas nor the Pāṇḍyas lost their hold completely on their traditional power centres. Their re-emergence to power in the later centuries takes place in their respective centres, namely Uṟaiyūr and Madurai. The dispersal of some members of these families is attested by evidence in the Telugu regions and Sri Lanka. While a few lineages claiming descent from the Cōḷas are known from the Telugu sources,[11] some members of the Pāṇḍya family may be among those who seized power at Anuradhapura in the fifth century, as the first of them bears the lineage name Paṇḍu. Clearly in the fourth and fifth centuries, none of the kingdoms in the Tamil land was politically powerful enough to either annex neighbouring kingdoms or even to withstand invasions from outside.

Rise of Non-Brahmanical Religions

The religious scene in this period in south India is of great significance for the understanding of some of the developments in the island. The first half of this period, from about 300 to 600 CE, saw the dominance of Buddhism and Jainism in the south Indian peninsula. Andhra, which was already a major Buddhist region in the centuries before 300, continued to have important centres of Theravada Buddhism. But what is more important is that Buddhism had spread widely in the Tamil regions and won the patronage of rulers there. The major urban centres of Kanchi, Kāvēripaṭṭiṉam, Uṟaiyūr and Madurai were centres of Buddhism and Jainism. These were also important centres of Pali learning. It was at this time that Tamil Nadu gave some of its greatest scholars to the Buddhist world. And it was in this period that the well-known Tamil Buddhist epics, *Maṇimēkalai* and *Kuṇṭalakēci* (*Kuṇḍalakeśi*) as well as the Tamil Jaina epic *Cīvaka-cintāmaṇi* (*Jīvaka-chintāmaṇi*), were produced. In Andhra, Buddhist art and architecture developed along distinctive lines and the influence of Andhra art spread to Sri Lanka and Southeast Asia.

Theravada scholars

The rise of Theravada Buddhism in the Tamil land coincided, quite naturally, with the emergence of Pali learning. This resulted in the production of many Pali works there. Three of the greatest Pali scholars of this period were Buddhaghosa, Buddhadatta and Dhammapāla and all three of them were associated with Buddhist establishments in the Tamil kingdoms. Two of them, Buddhadatta and Dhammapāla, were Tamil Buddhists. The third and the most celebrated, Buddhaghosa, is one about whom we do not have many reliable biographical details because of the many legends that shroud his name.[12]

Two of the commentaries attributed to Buddhaghosa are those on the *Anguttara-nikāya* and the *Majjhima-nikāya.* The former was written when the author was residing at a monastery in Kanchi, while the latter was written at a monastery at Mayūra-rūpa-paṭṭana (identified by some as Mylapore, in Chennai). Since a large number of Pali works are attributed to Buddhaghosa, some scholars doubt whether he was the author of all of them.[13] Buddhadatta was a senior contemporary of Buddhaghosa. Thanks to his works preserved in Sri Lanka, some biographical details about him are available. He was born in the Cōḷa kingdom and lived in the fifth century. He held positions of importance in some of the leading monasteries of the time in Kaveripattinam, Uraiyur, Bhūtamaṅgalam, Kanchi and Anuradhapura. Among his best known Pali writings are the *Vinaya-vinicchaya*, the *Uttara-vinicchaya* and the *Jinālaṅkāra-kāvya.* It is as a commentator that Buddhadatta has gained much reputation in the Buddhist world. Among the commentaries written by him are the *Madhurattha-vilāsinī* and the *Abhidhammāvatāra.* Information about the other renowned Tamil Buddhist scholar, Dhammapāla, is not easy to obtain, as there were several Buddhist scholars in this period bearing the name Dhammapāla. One of them, 'whose reputation is only second to that of Buddhaghosa as the exegetist of Sinhalese Buddhism'[14], was a resident of a Tamil monastery in Badaratittha (identified as Kadalur in Tamil Nadu). His best known work is the *Paramattha-dīpanī,* the commentary on several texts of the *Khuddaka-nikāya..* The author of the commentary on the *Nettipakaraṇa* is considered to be a different Dhammapāla who was a resident of a monastery at Nāgapaṭṭiṉam, which remained a centre of Buddhism in the Tamil land till about the fifteenth century.[15]

Mahayana scholars

The above commentators were all Theravada Buddhist scholars. Their high reputation leaves one with the impression that Theravada was the dominant Buddhist sect in the Tamil land in this period. There were, however, several non-Theravada sects, especially Mahayana, flourishing in Kanchi and other centres but not much is known about them. Again, it is through the work of Mahayana Buddhist philosophers and scholars that we get to know about the strength of the Mahayana sect in the Tamil kingdoms.

Of the great Tamil Mahayana Buddhist philosophers of this time, perhaps the best known is Diṇṇāga (Skt. Dignāga), a native of Siyamaṅgalam (a village to the south of Kanchi). He went to north India and became a Mahayanist under the influence of Vasubandhu and later won recognition as a philosopher and debater at the well-known ancient Buddhist centre of learning, popularly referred to as the Nalanda University. Returning to Kanchi, he spent his later years there. Considered as the founder of the Viññānavāda school of Buddhist philosophy, he wrote two great Sanskrit works on logic, namely the *Nyāya-praveśa* (Introduction to Logic) and the *Nyāya-samuchchaya* (Compendium of Logic).

One of the most interesting aspects of Tamil Buddhism in this period is the missionary activity carried on by Tamil monks in the kingdoms of Southeast Asia and beyond. In the wake of the expansion of south Indian trade under the Pallavas from the ports of the eastern coast of south India, particularly Māmallapuram, Kāvēripaṭṭiṉam and Nāgapaṭṭiṉam, Buddhist missionaries as well as Brahmanical religious leaders went over to the eastern kingdoms ruled by Hindu and Buddhist monarchs. Since all the Buddhist monks who went from India had Sanskrit or Pali names, it is not always easy to identify those from the Tamil kingdoms.[16] It is only from the scanty biographical details supplied by the Chinese sources that some of them could be identified.

Undoubtedly the most famous of the Buddhist monks who went forth to the eastern lands from south India was Bodhidharma (Chinese Tamo, Japanese Daruma). Popularly considered to be the founder of Zen Buddhism (Chinese *Ch'an*, Sanskrit *Dhyāna-mārga*), he lived in the sixth century.[17] According to some of the more popular traditions, he was a son of a king of Kanchi. While the Chinese sources have many accounts of his activities in China, very little is available about his place of origin or early life. As a well-known centre of Mahayana Buddhism, Kanchi was a place of visit for Chinese monks at this time. It is possible that Bodhidharma hailed from a monastery in Kanchi and was influenced by visiting Chinese monks and traders to become a missionary in China.[18]

Rise of Brahmanical sects

The fifth and sixth centuries appear to have seen the peak of Buddhist influence, both Theravada and Mahayana, in the Tamil kingdoms. The situation, however, began to change towards the end of the sixth century when the rise of Vaishnavism and Saivism posed a serious challenge to Buddhism and Jainism. At the beginning of the seventh century, the two major Tamil kingdoms, one ruled by the Pallavas and the other by the Pāṇḍyas, became the scene of an aggressive conflict between the Jainas and the Buddhists on the one hand and the Vaishnavas and the Saivas on the other. Though the two kingdoms were ruled by Jaina kings, there was a significant increase in Brahmanical influences at this time. Soon the worship of Śiva and Viṣṇu began to gain prominence.

Dates are not easy to assign for the stages by which Brahmanical Vedic religion sent its firm roots in the Tamil region. Nevertheless, it is clear that for nearly seven or eight centuries before the rise of the Saiva movement of the Nāyaṉārs in the sixth century the patronage given by local rulers to Brāhmaṇas from the north and the popular appeal of the Vedic rituals led to a silent penetration of the Vedic religion. This religion, unlike Buddhism and Jainism, was not in conflict, at least to the ordinary person, with the local religious beliefs and practices. The result was a process of successful religious eclecticism that led to the evolution of the Hindu religion as practised in south India.

In this religion, there was at the top a profound philosophy as expounded by Kumarila and Śankara in the eighth and ninth centuries. At the other end, there was the folk religion with its ancient rituals and practices. The ability to accommodate the two in the same religion ensured the success of the new Saivism that was evolving in this period. The Nāyaṉārs, with their popular hymns to Śiva and other deities in the local Tamil language, were able to provide the vital link between the higher philosophy of Śankara and Kumarila who wrote in Sanskrit and the religion of the ordinary people who understood only Tamil. These religious leaders, as Nilakanta Sastri describes, 'traversed the whole of the Tamil land several times over, singing, preaching and organising'[19] and brought about a strong awareness of and a deep devotion to the Saiva movement.

The Buddhist and Jaina religions, with their high moral philosophy, emphasis on non-violence and absence of theistic worship with its attendant rituals were not candidates for popular appeal and were supported largely by the elites. Even in their heyday in the Tamil land, it is doubtful that these religions enjoyed much support among the ordinary people. When these religions spread to the south, as Sudharshan Seneviratne has summed it, 'they were in the main urban-based or situated near production-distribution centres, resource areas or along trade routes' and their 'philosophical and ethical pronouncements were far more relevant to the newly evolving urban centres than the pastoral cum subsistence farmers and hunter-gatherers of the hill tracts and arid plains'.[20] The situation does not seem to have been very different even at the height of their power. It is no wonder that when the Nāyaṉārs used the weapon of public disputations, the Jaina and Buddhist leaders became the losers in the eyes of the ordinary people.

The Saiva movement

The ordinary people, however, were not the focus of their attention when the Nāyaṉārs began their movement. They launched their campaign with a strategy that, when it succeeded, was bound to ensure ultimate victory, as such strategies had in the case of other religions in other lands.[21] They started at the very top with the conversion of the rulers. Tirunāvukkaracar, popularly known as Appar (Father) and himself a convert from Jainism, succeeded in converting the mighty Pallava Mahendravarman I from Jainism to Saivism. This marked the beginning of the triumphant march of Saivism throughout the Tamil land. In the Pāṇḍya kingdom, Ñāṉa-campantar, a junior contemporary of Appar, first won over the queen, Maṅkayarkkaraci, and had no difficulty bringing the Pāṇḍya monarch into the Saiva fold. Soon others among the elites followed.[22]

From then on clashes occurred between the two sides in many parts of the Tamil land. Public debates between leaders of the two sides became a notable feature of this conflict. Religious intolerance and persecution followed.[23] By the end of the eighth century, Jainism and Buddhism were completely subdued and Saivism attained dominance among the Tamils.

Rise of maritime commerce

The economic developments, particularly the expansion of overseas trade and the rise of mercantile guilds, give this period an importance that has been often underestimated. Maritime traders from both the eastern and western coasts of south India ventured out as far as the Southeast Asian islands in the east and the Red Sea ports in the west. It is in this period that organized mercantile communities like the Maṇigrāmam and the Aiññūṟṟuvar began their trading activities across the Bay of Bengal. The ports of Sri Lanka played a significant role in this trade.

South India and Sri Lanka

Politics

The Sri Lankan kingdoms, whatever the nature of the political conflicts in the south Indian kingdoms, were not seriously affected by the events on the mainland until the rise of the Pallavas and the Pāṇḍyas in the seventh century. As on earlier occasions, Tamil princes came over to Anuradhapura and seized power for brief periods. Princes from Anuradhapura went across to south India on several occasions to enlist support in order to oust the rulers of Anuradhapura. The Pali chronicle records at least nine occasions between 300 and 900 CE when this happened. Similarly, there is also evidence of Sinhalese rulers taking Tamil brides, presumably from the established royal lineages of the Tamil kingdoms, as on earlier occasions. The Tamil element continued to be strong in the Anuradhapura kingdom in this period.

The events of the first half of the fifth century demonstrate the extent to which Tamil influence was strong at the court of Anuradhapura. Mahānāma, the Sinhalese ruler who ascended the throne in 406, had a Tamil as one of his queens and it was the son born to this queen, Sotthisena by name, who succeeded to the throne when the king died. He did not, however, rule long as he was ousted by his half-sister and her husband. But within two years, a member of the Pāṇḍya lineage from south India seized the throne and inauguarated a period of Tamil rule from 429 to 455. His name is given in the chronicles as Paṇḍu, indicating that he belonged to the Pāṇḍya lineage. It has been surmised that his arrival in the island may have been connected with the defeat of the Pāṇḍyas by the Kalabhras.[24] It may well be that the seizure of power at Anuradhapura by Tamil leaders from time to time flowed from the close relations that the Sinhalese rulers had with the south Indian ruling families. In this instance, the fact that the Sinhalese king Mahānāma was married to a Tamil lady and that the son born to her was ousted from the throne may be connected to the arrival of the Pāṇḍya prince who was possibly related to the ousted Sotthisena through his mother. The fact that Sinhalese princes fled to south

India on many occasions when they were denied the throne of Anuradhapura, or ousted from the throne, or when they plotted to seize the throne, seems to suggest that the Sinhalese ruling families had closer connections with the Tamil ruling families of south India than are discernible from the available sources. As more evidence comes to light from south Indian inscriptions from the seventh century, one finds confirmation of the mutual help that the Pallava, Pāṇḍya and Sinhalese ruling families offered to one another in times of crisis. The success of the Tamil rulers in holding power in the Sinhalese kingdom for more than a quarter of a century would not have been possible as complete outsiders.

Tamil rule in Anuradhapura

By the fifth century, the Heḷa language and the Buddhist religion had helped to unite the majority of the people in the Anuradhapura kingdom into a single ethnic group and the Tamil rulers governed the kingdom like Sinhalese rulers. That they were Buddhists themselves, patronized Buddhism and recorded their donations to Buddhist institutions in the Heḷa language and took over titles used by the Sinhalese rulers is evidenced by the inscriptions left by them. No epigraphic records in the name of Paṇḍu have been found yet but inscriptions of one of his sons as well as of some of his other successors throw interesting light on the rule of these Tamil monarchs.

Paṇḍu, according to the chronicles, ruled for five years. He was succeeded by his son whose name in Pali is given as Pārinda. In a Sinhalese inscription of this ruler, his name is given as Paridadeva (the Tamil form of which may be Pārintira Tēvaṉ, Sanskrit Pārindra Deva?).[25] This inscription records the donations made by this monarch to a Buddhist institution, thereby indicating that he was a patron of Buddhism and possibly a Buddhist himself. His brother, who succeeded him after three years, is called Khudda Pārinda (the Younger Pārinda) in the chronicle. That this Tamil king was a Buddhist is supported by inscriptional evidence. His queen made some benefactions to a Buddhist monastery and in the record of these gifts the king is given the name Ḷa Pari Deva (the Younger Pari Deva) and the title Budadasa (Servant of the Buddha).[26] The title 'Budadasa' was borne by some of the kings of Anuradhapura from the fourth century[27] and the adoption of this title by the Tamil ruler indicates that he wanted to be like the other rulers of this kingdom.[28] (There is a parallel in the eleventh century when Cōḻa princes took over the Sinhalese consecration name as rulers at Polonnaruva.) It also shows that he was an adherent of Buddhism, otherwise it is unlikely that he preferred a title indicating devotion to the Buddha. His successor, however, had a Vaishnava name (Tirītara in the Pali chronicle = Sanskrit Śrīdhara, Tamil Tirutaraṉ) and it is not known whether he was also a Buddhist, although this ruler's son was a patron of a Buddhist monastery. In a Sinhalese inscription of his son, Tirītara is named Sarataraya, a corruption of Śrīdhara.[29] Soon after he ascended the throne, the Sinhalese prince Dhātusena made an attempt to capture the throne. According to the Pali chronicle, Tirītara lost the throne after two months of rule and was succeeded by his son whose name is given as Dāṭhiya (the Bearded One). In the Sinhalese epigraph of Dāṭhiya, recording his benefactions to a Buddhist institution, the king's name is given as Mahadali Mahana (Mahānāga the Big-Bearded One). The name Mahānāga is noteworthy, for it shows that this Tamil prince was given a name that was common among the Sinhalese princes of this time. Whether he was related to the first Tamil ruler Paṇḍu or was from a different line connected with a Nāga family is hard to establish. Dāṭhiya ruled for three years, according to the Pali chronicle, and was succeeded by Pīṭhiya. This last ruler reigned only for seven months and faced defeat at the hands of Dhātusena.

The information that we have about the quarter century of Tamil rule at Anuradhapura is of special interest in demonstrating how the twin forces of the Heḷa language and the Buddhist religion operated to accommodate the Tamil conquerors and soon assimilate them into the local system. This is a process that we see continuing in the later centuries until the time of the last rulers of the last Sinhalese kingdom. If the chronicles did not tell us that they were Tamils and if we were to depend only on the Sinhalese inscriptions, we would not have known that these fifth century kings of Anuradhapura were of Tamil origin. While it is true that there were Sinhalese aspirants to the throne who wanted to oust them, just as there were similar aspirants in the time of Sinhalese kings, any interpretation that the Tamil rulers 'imposed foreign rule' and any suggestion that 'even though they themselves were not adherents of the Buddhist faith, they supported the religion as a matter of political expediency in order to win the favour of the people' is not a reasonable one.[30] This interpretation is another instance of the prejudice with which some historians have viewed the role of Tamils in Sri Lankan history. Clearly such an interpretation does not take into account the fact that in the Tamil land itself Buddhism was patronized by Tamil kings in the fifth century and that the ordinary people in these early times did not behave in the same way as people did in modern times, after the rise of nationalism, when they resented the rule of persons whose faith or language was different from theirs. In fact, the Pali chronicle states that there were Sinhalese nobles who had given support to the Tamil rulers, for which support they were later punished by Dhātusena. These Tamil rulers after all were not ruling the Sinhalese kingdom on behalf of an overlord or emperor in south India. That there was no racial animosity in the conflict between Dhātusena and the Tamil rulers is suggested by the fact that Dhātusena's own son, Moggallāna, fled to India, presumably to the court of a Tamil king, when he was denied his right to the throne and returned eighteen years later with an army to claim his right.

Tamil bodyguards and soldiers

Moggallāna was following a practice established by disinherited or ambitious Sinhalese princes as early as the first century. It is not known how many of the politically ambitious persons went over to south India and returned with troops to achieve their goals. What we know are only those who are recorded in the chronicles. Even in the time of Moggallāna, bringing troops from south India to oust the ruling monarch must have posed a serious problem, for the king is said to have instituted a coastal guard to prevent invasions.[31] After the time of Moggallāna, fleeing to south India to obtain help occurred all too frequently.

In this period of palace intrigues, political machinations and mistrust, the Anuradhapura rulers came to depend more and more on Tamil bodyguards for their personal security and protection of their assets. The inscriptions of this period have numerous references to these bodyguards (*meykāppar*, Tamil *meykāppar*).[32] Just as the Sinhalese rulers employed Tamil bodyguards, from whom they could expect more loyalty, Tamil rulers in south India also appear to have kept Sinhalese bodyguards (*Ciṅkaḷa meykāppar*) in their service.[33] The recruitment of bodyguards and troops from south India was no doubt a common practice at this time. Indeed, relying on bodyguards from outside the kingdom had been a practice in Tamil and Sinhalese courts from the early centuries of the Common Era. The Tamil Sangam poems have references to Graeco-Roman (*Yavana*) bodyguards in the courts of Tamil rulers. Possibly Graeco-Romans were also employed in the Sinhalese courts.

The landing of troops from south India reached its peak in the seventh century. Within a period of nearly fifty-five years, beginning from 628, Sinhalese aspirants to the throne of Anuradhapura are recorded to have brought south Indian troops on as many as eight occasions. These troops whose number kept increasing, according to the Pali chronicle, grew uncontrollable and the Tamil soldiers caused many problems. In the court, too, the Tamil element was strong. In the reign of Aggabodhi IV (667-683), several Tamils are named in the chronicle as holding high office. Some of them, such as Potthakuṭṭha, Potthasāta and Mahākanda, are described as benefactors of Buddhist institutions. It is possible that some influential Tamil Buddhist families moved to Sri Lanka at this time as a result of the religious conflict in the Tamil kingdoms. One of the benefactors of Buddhist institutions, Potthakuṭṭha, was so influential that he eventually became a kingmaker.[34]

When Potthakuṭṭha was at the height of his power, a new development drew the Sinhalese kingdom into the politics of the

Tamil land. This was the arrival of Mānavamma (Mānavarma), a Sinhalese prince who had sojourned at the capital of the powerful Pallava ruler, with an army that defeated Potthakuṭṭha and helped the prince to seize the throne. Mānavamma had found refuge in the Pallava court at Kanchi in the time of the powerful Narasiṃhavarman I (630-668), helped the Pallava ruler in his wars against the Chālukyas and received as a reward an army to make a bid for the throne of Anuradhapura. Mānavamma landed with this army and successfully marched towards Anuradhapura. But, we are told, the victorious army had to abruptly end its campaign and hurriedly return to Kanchi as news was received of the serious illness of the Pallava ruler. Mānavamma made a second attempt with the help of the Pallavas in the time of Narasimhavarman II (680-720), defeated Potthakuṭṭha and became king at Anuradhapura.

Pallava forces in Sri Lanka

The assistance provided by Narasiṃhavarman I is the first recorded instance of a major Tamil king sending his troops to Sri Lanka to enable a Sinhalese prince to wrest power in the Sinhalese kingdom. Although several Sinhalese princes had been fleeing to south India before this and bringing troops from there, it is not known whether they obtained military aid from the major kings or from local chieftains. The grandfather of Narasiṃhavarman I, namely Pallava Siṃhaviṣṇu, claimed to have vanquished, among other kings, the Sinhalese ruler but in the Sri Lankan sources there is no evidence of any south Indian invasion that could be dated in the reign of this Pallava ruler. Siṃhaviṣṇu's claim cannot be dismissed easily just because it is not corroborated by Sri Lankan sources. It would appear that Simhavisnu had invaded the island and gained a foothold in that part of Sri Lanka where significant evidence of Pallava influence is found. It is possible, however, that the new line of powerful Pallava rulers beginning with Siṃhaviṣṇu had close relations with some of the rulers of Anuradhapura. This would explain the circumstances under which a Sinhalese prince, Mānavamma, lived for a long time in the Pallava capital, enjoying the hospitality of the Pallava rulers and rendering services to them in their wars.

The alliance between the Pallava rulers and the Sinhalese kings that Mānavamma succeeded in establishing in the seventh century lasted for two hundred years, until almost the end of the Pallava dynasty. Since the Pāṇḍyas were the enemies of the Pallavas in the Tamil land, the Sinhalese alliance also led to hostilities between the Pāṇḍyas and the Sinhalese kings, resulting in at least one major invasion of the island by the Pāṇḍyas and a counter-invasion of the Pāṇḍya kingdom by Sinhalese armies. These invasions took place in the ninth century when the Pāṇḍyas were on the ascendant and the Pallava power was declining.

Pāṇḍya invasion

The invasion of the Sinhalese kingdom by the Pāṇḍyas took place in the reign of Sena I (833-853). It was led by the powerful Pāṇḍya ruler Śrī Māra Śrī Vallabha (815-862). This is the first recorded instance of an invasion of Sri Lanka by a Pāṇḍya king. Some time in the early part of Sena I's reign, the Pāṇḍya ruler landed with an army in the north of the island and made a successful march to Anuradhapura. Sena fled to Malaya in the south, leaving the capital open to the attack of the Pāṇḍya army. Having taken the royal treasures, the Pāṇḍya king sent messengers to Sena, imposed a treaty and left the island.

In the reign of Sena I's successor, Sena II (853-887), events took a different turn. The Pāṇḍya ruler's son, Varaguṇa by name, became estranged with his father and sought refuge in the Sinhalese court. This seems to have provided an opportunity for the Sinhalese monarch and the Pallava ruler to keep the aggressive Pāṇḍya under check. While the Pallava Nrpatuṅgavarman attacked the Pāṇḍya territories from the north, provoking Śrī Māra Śrī Vallabha to march against him, the Sinhalese ruler sent his army to the Pāṇḍya capital from the south. The Pāṇḍya army was defeated by the Pallavas at the Battle of Arisil. The Sinhalese army succeeded in overrunning the defences of the Pāṇḍya capital, Madurai, and defeating the depleted Pāṇḍya army that rushed back from the Battle of Arisil to save the capital city. What turned out to be more disastrous to the Pāṇḍyas in this encounter was the death of Śrī Māra Śrī Vallabha himself. This event cleared the way for the Sinhalese army to place the Pāṇḍya prince Varaguṇa on the throne at Madurai. These events took place in 862.

These developments demonstrated the inevitability of Sri Lanka being affected by the rise and fall of empires in south India. What began as a friendly alliance between the Pallavas and the Sinhalese rulers in the seventh century brought the latter into the conflict between the two major powers contending for the overlordship of the Tamil land. At first the contest was between the Pallavas and the Pāṇḍyas, in which the Sinhalese were on the side of the Pallavas. But with the fall of the Pallavas and the rise of the Cōḷas, it was with the Pāṇḍyas that the Sinhalese allied and this alliance continued for another three centuries until the emergence of the second Pāṇḍya empire in the thirteenth century.

Religion: Buddhism

In the sphere of religious activities, there is considerable evidence of close relations and interactions between south India and Sri Lanka in this period. As Buddhism was one of the dominant religions in south India, naturally there were very close relations between the two regions. Much of the information about this comes from the Pali Buddhist sources.

As mentioned earlier, there was a great interest in the Buddhist commentaries preserved in Sri Lanka and some of the eminent scholar monks from the Tamil Buddhist centres of south India came over to Sri Lanka to translate the commentaries into Pali. These monks resided in the leading monasteries of Anuradhapura, especially the Mahāvihāra and the Abhayagirivihāra and engaged themselves in the translation of the commentaries. Monks from Sri Lanka, too, went across to the Tamil kingdoms and stayed in the monasteries at Kanchi, Kaveripattinam and Madurai. It was a period of much interaction between the Theravada centres of the Tamil land and those of Sri Lanka.

Although Mahayana scholars also came to Sri Lanka from south India at this time and spread the influence of Mahayana sects, evidence relating to their activities has not survived. From the archaeological remains of Mahayana institutions in the island, clearly revealing influences from the Tamil kingdoms, it would appear that the interaction between south India and Sri Lanka in the centuries after 600 were more among the Mahayanists than among the Theravadins. These relations have, for obvious reasons, gone unrecorded in the Pali chronicle or other literary texts written by the Sinhalese Theravada monks. However, there is archaeological and epigraphical evidence that throws interesting light on the flow of Mahayana influences from the Tamil land, particularly from the Pallava kingdom.

Epigraphic records, the contents of which relate to the Mahayana sect, have been found in Sri Lanka revealing distinct influences from the Pallava kingdom. These are not only in the Sanskrit language but are also written in the Pallava-Grantha script, which was used in south India at this time by Mahayana Buddhists and Hindus to write their Sanskrit works. As Paranavitana opines, these Mahayana inscriptions were probably the result of the activities of the Mahayana teachers who went to Sri Lanka from the Pallava kingdom.[35] The movement of Buddhist scholars between Sri Lanka and south India, which seems to have been very intensive in the sixth and seventh centuries, was first due to the increasing interest in Pali learning and the activities of the Mahayanists. But later it was one of the consequences of the conflict with Saivism and Vaisnavism. The impact of this movement is most visible in the art of writing in Sri Lanka.

The Brāhmī script of the ancient Prakrit inscriptions in the island had, in the early centuries of the Common Era, begun to develop along independent lines as the script of the Heḷa language. A similar development took place in the Tamil land leading to the evolution of the Tamil script. In the Pallava kingdom, where the Sanskrit language was also extensively used by the rulers along with Tamil and where the Brāhmaṇa priests as well as Mahayana Buddhist monks used Sanskrit as the language of their religious writings, the Brāhmī script developed into what came to be known as the Pallava-Grantha script. This script was soon introduced to Sri Lanka. Consequently, the separate development of the Heḷa script was suddenly interrupted by the innovation of the Pallava-Grantha script. The inscriptions of the seventh and eighth centuries in the island bear testimony to this. Some of the inscribed Sanskrit records of this period, like the one from Tiriyay, were written in the Pallava-Grantha script as used in south India, while some others, like those from Kuccaveli and Mihintale, were written in a script closely resembling Pallava-Grantha. Several of the Heḷa records of this time also reveal distinct influences of this script. For the Pallava-Grantha script to have had such a pervasive influence over the local script so as to change its course of independent development, the Mahayanists from the Pallava kingdom must have had far more influence in the island than is generally conceded.

Pallava artisans

The activities of the Mahayanists also led to the arrival of artisans from the Pallava kingdom for the erection of Mahayana structures and production of sculptures, particularly Buddha and Bodhisattva images. The result was the flow of fresh artistic influences from south India. It is well known to students of Sri Lankan art history that the relief sculpture of a seated man, with a horse's head behind him, at Isurumuniya (in Anuradhapura), is one of the best specimens of the Pallava style in the island.[36] Among the other Mahayana sculptures of about the same age (seventh century), showing Pallava artistic influence, are the Bodhisattva figure from Situlpavu and a similar figure at Kurukkalmadam, in the Eastern Province.[37] The *dvārapāla* (gatekeeper) figures at the circular shrine at Tiriyay, also in the Eastern Province, exhibit Pallava influences of the eighth century.[38] The Kuvēra figure at Nalanda is another good example of this style. There is also a half-finished rock relief in the Pallava style at Andiyagala.[39]

Pallava artisans introduced the Tamil style of architecture to build Mahayana edifices. Under the patronage of the Pallava rulers, a tradition of stone architecture, replacing the previous wooden architecture, was begun in the Pallava kingdom in the sixth century. As is well known, this developed into the distinctive temple architecture of the Tamil land, commonly referred to as Dravidian architecture. This new tradition soon found its way to Sri Lanka. The earliest surviving structure in this style is the Mahayana shrine at Nalanda (Geḍigē), which appears to be of the eighth century.[40] Another shrine of about this period at Devundara also shows influences of the Pallava style.[41]

Religious unrest

As seen earlier, there was also another side to the religious developments of this period in south India. By the end of the sixth century, the period of glory was over for both Buddhism and Jainism. At the beginning of the seventh century, when they began to lose the patronage of the major rulers, they also faced a violent opposition from the two main Hindu sects, Saivism and Vaisnavism. Buddhist and Jaina institutions were under attack and popular support was lost. One result of this was the migration of Buddhist and Jaina monks, and possibly some lay members who were devoted to their religions, to kingdoms where they could find refuge. While the Jainas were able to go to the Kannada and Telugu regions, the Buddhists turned to Sri Lanka.

Although the Kalabhras, and possibly some of the minor rulers in the Tamil land, were patrons of Buddhism, the Pāṇḍyas and the Pallavas who supplanted the Kalabhras were supporters of Jainism. However, there is no evidence that they were opposed to the Buddhists. But at the beginning of the seventh century the tide turned against the Jainas and the Buddhists. As discussed earlier, two Saiva hymnodists (better known as Nāyaṉārs), Appar and Ñāṉacampantar, began a relentless campaign to revive Saivism and tirelessly journeyed to different sacred places of Saivism and rallied support for their religion.

One of the notable features of the Saiva campaign was the conduct of public disputations between the Saiva Nāyaṉārs and their opponents. Often harsh punishments seem to have been meted out to those who were defeated. Saiva traditions refer to opponents being impaled on stakes. Other traditions mention banishments. According to Saiva traditions, Buddhist monks from Sri Lanka were among those who entered into disputations with Saiva leaders in the Tamil land. An interesting case is that of the Saiva hymnodist, Māṇikkavācakar, who is said to have defeated Sri Lankan Buddhist monks in a public disputation. Some Telugu and Kannada sources also refer to disputations between Jainas and Buddhists in Kanchi. Late Telugu works such as the *Rājāvali-kathe*, the *Akalāṅka-carita* and the *Akalāṅka-stotra* refer to an eighth-century Jaina teacher, Akalāṅka by name, from Sravana Belgola in Karnataka, as having disputed with the Buddhists of Kanchi and defeated them.[42] These Buddhists, we are told, were in consequence banished to Sri Lanka. The substance of these accounts seems credible, for, two Kannada inscriptions of earlier dates also refer to the same incident.[43]

The incidental information in the Saiva and Vaisnava hymns, not to mention their aggressive and sometimes abusive tone, leads one to the conclusion that the religious conflicts of this time were not entirely non-violent. If there were instances of banishment and impaling of Buddhists and Jainas, one cannot rule out the possibility of some of the oppressed moving out to safer kingdoms. Just as Sinhalese monks from Anuradhapura went over to the Tamil kingdoms in times of famine and political pressures, Tamil Buddhist monks probably sought refuge in Sri Lanka at this time. It is possible that lay Buddhist families also migrated to the island. Analysing the Sinhalese folk traditions embodied in the ritual dramas as an anthropologist, Obeyesekere makes 'a strong case for Buddhist migrations from South India' as a consequence of the Saiva-Vaishnava movement.[44]

Tamil traders

The commercial activities of the Pallava kingdom led to the growth of mercantile organizations that played an important role in the Indian Ocean trade. The international trade that began to grow between India and the Southeast Asian kingdoms, particularly Funan, about the first century CE involved traders from the Tamil kingdoms as well. No doubt, Southeast Asian traders played a major role in this trade that resulted in a long-lasting dialogue with Indian culture. In the time of the Pallava rulers, after about 500 CE, there was a significant growth in this trade and in the cultural dialogue between India and Southeast Asia. Using the evidence of Chinese sources, Gunawardana argues that 'between the third and fifth centuries A.D., a change of fundamental importance in navigational technology appears to have taken place, ushering in a transformation in the patterns of navigation which helped to elevate Sri Lanka, with its strategic location in the Indian Ocean, and the southeastern coastal belt of the subcontinent to positions of important intermediaries in the trade between east and west.'[45] It is in this background that one has to understand the activities of Tamil traders in Sri Lanka.

The growth of mercantile communities is one of the notable developments in the overseas trade of south India from about the sixth century. The rise of the first powerful kingdom in the Tamil region of south India, namely the Pallava kingdom, at the beginning of the sixth century clearly gave an impetus to the overseas trade of the south Indian mercantile communities. Archaeological evidence relating to the period between the sixth and the ninth centuries, but mainly to the seventh century, from the east coast of south India, the eastern region of Sri Lanka and the southern coastal regions of Thailand and Vietnam bear testimony to the varied activities of the south Indian traders, with whom were associated Brāhmaṇas, Buddhist monks and artisans. The ports of Māmallapuram and Nāgapaṭṭiṉam on the east coast of south India were linked by a network of trade routes across the Bay of Bengal with the ports of Tirukōṇamalai (Gokarṇa/Trincomalee) and Pallavavaṅka (north of

Kuccaveli) on the east coast of Sri Lanka, the port of Takua-pa on the west coast of Thailand and the port of OcEo in southern Viet Nam.

On the Indian side, unfortunately, much of the evidence for the period up to 900 CE is lost. Neither inscriptions nor literature provides any valuable information relating to this important maritime activity. Apart from the few references in the Tamil epic *Maṇimēkalai* to ships departing to Cāvakam (Jāvaka), it is hard to find any reference to the Southeast Asian trade in the rich body of Tamil literature of this period. As for epigraphy, the earliest references in south Indian inscriptions to merchants or organizations associated with the maritime trade, such as the Maṇigrāmam and the Añjuvaṇṇam, do not occur before the ninth century.

One of the earliest of these communities was the Maṇigrāmam.[46] Records of the ninth and tenth centuries show that they were active in several places in south India, Sri Lanka and Thailand. In Sri Lanka, there is evidence of their activities in the interior market-town of Hopitigamu, near Mahiyangana, in the middle of the tenth century.[47] It is not known from which date they began their operations in the island. If, in the tenth century, they were active in an interior market-town in the Badulla region, it is reasonable to surmise that they had establishments in the main ports before that. In Tiriyay, Trincomalee District, there is evidence of the activities of other merchant communities with Pallava associations in the seventh century. Given the prominent role played by the Maṇigrāmam in the overseas trade of the Pallava empire, this community may well have established its position in the ports of the Trincomalee District which were participating in the trade across the Bay of Bengal.

In Sri Lanka and Southeast Asia there is interesting archaeological evidence connected with the activities of Tamil traders and the artisans and religious personalities who went with them. At least one inscription, in Tamil, discovered in the ancient Thai port of Takua-pa refers to the Maṇigrāmam, Cē<u>n</u>āmukam and another organization (the name of which is illegible). The record is datable to the ninth century.[48] It is reported to have been discovered along with a stone Viṣṇu image and other statues in the south Indian Pallava style. Undoubtedly, this is the clearest evidence we have for the activities of Tamil trading organizations in Southeast Asian ports at this time. As usual, extended commercial activities were accompanied by the erection of religious edifices. It was about this time that the Maṇigrāmam was active in Sri Lanka. Another south Indian mercantile community that was trading in the island in the ninth century was the Nāṉku-nāṭu.[49] In the same century, members of the trading community called Ceṭṭis were also active.[50]

But earlier evidence, though indirect, relating to the south Indian overseas trade of this time and its cultural influences comes in the form of several Sanskrit inscriptions in the Southern Indian Brāhmī and Pallava-Grantha script as well as Saiva-Vaisnava and Buddhist sculptures. One of the earliest records is found in Laos, in the town of Champassak. It is a long pillar inscription in Sanskrit, written in the late Southern Indian Brāhmī of about the 5th-6th century.[51] The record is associated with a pilgrimage centre dedicated principally to Brahma, Viṣṇu and Śiva. Two other Sanskrit inscriptions in Pallava-Grantha characters of about the seventh century have been found close to Champassak.[52] Another comes from the well-known archaeological site Oc-eo, in southern Vietnam (ancient Fu-nan). Oc-eo was an entrepot from the second to the sixth century. The Sanskrit inscription found here is in the late Southern Indian Brāhmī characters of about the 6th-7th century and records the construction of a brick temple for the god Varddhamāna.[53] More Sanskrit inscriptions in Pallava-Grantha characters have been discovered in Malaysia and Thailand.[54]

In Sri Lanka, too, a number of Sanskrit inscriptions in the Pallava-Grantha script of about the seventh and eighth centures have been discovered. They are mostly in the northeastern part of the island where Tamil influence from the Pallava kingdom seems to have been very strong. A record that gives a clear indication of the involvement of traders in the spread of Pallava influences is the Sanskrit inscription from Tiriyay, datable to about the seventh century.[55] It refers to organizations of merchants (*vaṇig-gaṇa*) who were associated with the Buddhist shrine at Tiriyay. Other Sanskrit inscriptions in Pallava-Grantha have been found in Mihintale and Kuccaveli.[56]

Hydraulic technology

Exchange of ideas

Irrigation technology was another area in which there was significant interaction between south India and Sri Lanka in this period. The mutual exchange of technology that appears to have taken place between the two regions, as revealed by the researches of Gunawardana, would have also led to movement of skilled persons to both regions. The beginnings of irrigation technology in Sri Lanka, it is now believed by leading historians, was introduced by those who brought the Megalithic-BRW culture from south India. 'Megalithic folk', in the words of Gunawardana, 'appear to have been among the earliest migrants from India to Sri Lanka and it seems likely that they brought with them several cultural traits including the use of iron, the domestication of the rice plant and, if we are to accept the implications of the observations made by Srinivasan and Banerjee, a rudimentary irrigation technology including the art of constructing small-scale reservoirs.'[57]

As village settlements expanded and agricultural activity assumed importance, the need to secure an adequate water supply was recognized very early in the kingdoms of south India and Sri Lanka. While the chronicles in Sri Lanka provide information about the reservoirs constructed under the direction of the Anuradhapura rulers, the earliest Tamil poems of south India give praise to those rulers who paid attention to constructing reservoirs and increasing fertility.[58] Clearly one of the main ideals of the early rulers was to ensure an adequate supply of water for cultivation through the construction of reservoirs and dams. This was as important as the ideal of erecting religious edifices. It is no surprise, therefore, that the brief annals of the Anuradhapura rulers, as given in the chronicles, do not fail to record the religious buildings and the irrigation tanks constructed by every monarch. In the south Indian kingdoms, too, the available evidence suggests that the rulers paid much attention to the provision of irrigation facilities, although the details are not available as in Sri Lanka owing to the absence of chronicles. When stone inscriptions came to be set up widely from the sixth century onwards, information about irrigation works becomes available in south India.

Karikālaṉ legends

Some of these inscriptions preserve traditions relating to builders of reservoirs of earlier times. An early Tamil ruler who is famed in literature and legend as a great builder of dams and reservoirs is the Cōḻa king Karikālaṉ. He lived very probably in the first or second century of the Common Era. While a poem in the Sangam anthology praises this monarch for his contribution to the prosperity of the land through his achievements in 'clearing forests to extend settlements and constructing reservoirs to increase fertility',[59] inscriptions of the Telugu-Coḍa (who claimed descent from the Cōḻas) refer to Karikālaṉ's success in raising the flood-banks of the mighty Kaveri river by employing his subordinate kings to accomplish this task.[60] The legends of Karikālaṉ have also been preserved in Sri Lankan folk traditions relating to Sinhalese ritual dramas While the information in these legends is historically unreliable, the legends themselves indicate the special interest taken by rulers in the building of dams and reservoirs and the use of prisoners of war in these constructions.

Considering the many occasions on which south Indian armies were brought to Sri Lanka by aspirants to the kingship of Anuradhapura between 300 and 900, it is possible that many of the soldiers in these armies were eventually used as labour in the construction of irrigation works. This would have formed the basis of the Karikālaṉ and Gajabāhu myths, according to which Karikālaṉ had taken 12,000 captives from Sri Lanka to build the flood-banks of the Kaveri river in the Cōḻa kingdom and Gajabāhu brought back these 12,000 men and an additional 12,000 captives from the Cōḻa kingdom to be employed in irrigation works in the Anuradhapura kingdom.[61] As Gananath Obeyesekere has shown through his anthropological analysis, the Karikālan̲ and Gajabāhu myths cannot be considered as based on historical events.[62] However, they indicate that the ancient rulers who were responsible for the construction of major irrigation works made use of prisoners of war and other captives in these public works.

Role of mercantile communities in irrigation works

Kings were not the only persons responsible for the construction of reservoirs and canals. In this period, it would appear that the influential mercantile communities were also associated with the building of irrigation facilities and their maintenance. The Maṇigrāmam, which was engaged in trading activities in south India, Sri Lanka and Southeast Asia, is known to have been associated with the maintenance of a reservoir, which bears the name of a Pallava ruler, in the ninth century in Takua Pa, Southern Thailand. Along with the Maṇigrāmam is mentioned another community, the Cēn̲ā-mukam, which, judging from its name (Skt. Senā-mukha), appears to have been a body of soldiers.[63] A study of the activities of the south Indian mercantile communities shows that they took with them soldiers and artisans to be employed in their non-mercantile pursuits.

The construction of reservoirs and religious edifices were undoubtedly among the major non-mercantile pursuits of the wealthy mercantile communities. The period 600-900, when the earliest mercantile communities of south India became active with the expansion of overseas trade under the Pallavas, was also a time of significant developments in irrigation engineering in Sri Lanka as well as south India. That these developments took place in Sri Lanka in a climate of political instability is indeed surprising. In the south Indian Tamil kingdoms, on the other hand, the Pallavas and the Pāṇḍyas were in a powerful position to undertake major irrigation works. Unfortunately, neither the inscriptions nor the literary sources tell us much about these constructions. However, it cannot be doubted that the parallel developments in this area of economic activity in Sri Lanka and south India were closely connected. There would have been transfer of technology and movement of labour between the two regions. In this respect, it is the mercantile communities who would have played a major role.

Tamil population in Anuradhapura

The cumulative effect of the foregoing developments in the political, religious and economic spheres was the strengthening of the Tamil element in the demography of the Anuradhapura kingdom. The evidence of the Pali chronicle and Sinhalese inscriptions supports this conclusion. The south Indian troops brought to Anuradhapura on several occasions by Sinhalese aspirants to the throne were, according to the chronicle, a source of instability to the Anuradhapura rulers in the seventh, eighth and ninth centuries. Many of the rulers had difficulty controlling these soldiers whom the chronicle almost always refers to as Damiḷas. They showed no desire of returning to their homelands, resisted being expelled by the rulers, created trouble over payments and at times took over power at the capital. For instance, the Pali chronicle says, immediately after the death of Kassapa II (650-659), his nephew Mana 'had the Damiḷas expelled'. But they resisted this and 'banded themselves with the resolve: we will drive him out'. With that resolve, 'they seized the town' and it was only by making a mock treaty with them that Mana was able to regain power.[64] This uneasy truce did not last long. Not long after this, a Sinhalese aspirant to the throne, Hatthadāṭha, returned to the island with a Tamil force and the Tamil forces that were already in the kingdom 'arose and joined him on the way as he approached'. 'Hatthadāṭha, who had won over the party of the Damiḷas for himself, occupied the royal city' and ruled for some time.[65] The chronicle refers to many more incidents like this taking place well into the tenth century.

That the Tamils formed a section of the population at least in the northern parts of the Anuradhapura kingdom becomes clear from various incidental references in the Pali chronicle. The areas between the major northern ports and Anuradhapura in particular were prominent among the Tamil settlements. The earliest reference to this occurs in the seventh century. As mentioned before, in the account of Hatthadāṭha's usurpation of the throne in 684, the Pali chronicle states that 'all the Damiḷas who dwelt here arose and joined him on the way' (*Cv* 45: 19). Evidently this is a reference to the Tamils who lived in the areas between one of the ports and the capital. Two of the major ports used for voyages to south Indian marts at this time were Mātoṭa, on the northwestern coast, and Gokarṇa (modern Trincomalee) on the northeastern coast. Both were renowned in the Tamil kingdoms at this time as places with hallowed Śiva temples. The areas referred to by the Pali chronicle may be those between Mātoṭa and the capital or those between Gokarṇa and the capital, both of which were Tamil regions in the later centuries.

The conclusions drawn from the scattered references in the Pali chronicle are further strengthened by incidental information in Sinhalese inscriptions. By the time of Kassapa IV (898-914), there are definite references in these epigraphs to Tamil villages and lands. Three significant terms are met with in these records in this connection. They are *Demeḷ-käbälla*, *Demeḷat-välademin* and *Demeḷ-gam-bim*, which have been translated as 'Tamil allotment', 'Tamil lands' and 'Tamil villages and lands' respectively. Tamil lands. The interpretation of these terms and the provenance of the inscriptions referring to these terms are of great significance for the study of the Tamil population in the Anuradhapura kingdom in the period under discussion.

The term '*Demeḷ-käbälla*' has been interpreted by Paranavitana to mean 'an allotment of land in a village set apart for the Tamils'. In his opinion, such allotments seem 'to have been set apart for the maintenance of Tamil soldiers in the king's service and must have been administered by royal officers'.[66] On an examination of the different occurrences of this term in the published inscriptions, it appears that the above interpretation does not always yield a satisfactory meaning. Though it is difficult to arrive at the exact meaning of this term, it appears to refer to lands enjoying privileges different from those associated with lands classified as '*pamuṇu*'.[67] But certainly it is not always an allotment from the royal household. In one of the records, a *Demeḷ-käbälla* is found to be the private property of an individual.[68] In this epigraphic record, the allotment was granted immunities as a *pamuṇu* on condition of paying annually an amount of dried ginger to a hospital. There is no reference here, or for that matter in any of the records where the term *Demeḷ-käbälla* occurs, to any share of the revenue being allocated for the maintenance of Tamil soldiers. It is, therefore, evident that a *Demeḷ-käbälla* did not always denote an allotment from the royal household nor was it necessarily set apart for the maintenance of Tamil soldiers. It could only mean an allotment or portion of a village where Tamils lived, presumably separated from the others. Some other references in the Sinhalese inscriptions lend support to this interpretation. In one of the records of Mahinda IV (956-972), it is stated that certain immunities were granted to the village of Kiṇigama.[69] The *piraläkkam*, who appear to have been a class of officials, were granted certain privileges in a place called Demeḷ-Kiṇigam (Tamil Kiṇigama) but not in Kiṇigama. From the context it is clear that Demeḷ-Kiṇigam was not far from Kiṇigama. Indeed, Demeḷ-Kiṇigam appears to have been a Tamil sector that was originally a part of the village of Kiṇigama. This probably is an example of a *Demeḷ-käbälla*.

The term *Demeḷat-välademin*, which can be rendered as 'lands enjoyed by Tamils', appears to refer to lands owned by Tamils and occurs in the tenth century. In the same century, another term, *Demeḷ-gam-bim*, refers to such lands and Tamil villages. An inscription of Mahinda IV (956-972) lays down that '(the produce) of trees and shrubs which exist … in the Tamil villages and lands (situated) in the four directions shall be appropriated in accordance with former custom'.[70] The implication that there were several Tamil villages is echoed in the Pali chronicle which refers to 'the many Tamils who dwelt here and there' when a Pāṇḍya invasion took place in the reign of Sena I (833-853).[71] The occurrence of place names such as Demeḷ-Kiṇigam (Tamil Kiṇigam) and Demeḷinheṭihaya, with the prefix Demeḷ (Tamil) also point to the existence of villages that were exclusively or predominantly settled by Tamils.[72]

More evidence about the Tamils living in the northern part of the Anuradhapura kingdom can be gleaned from certain other terms occurring in the Sinhalese inscriptions. The term *kuḷī* occurs as a type of impost levied at this time. In some records, the ethnic qualifiers *Demeḷe* (Tamil) and *Heḷe* (Sinhalese) are used as prefixes (*Demeḷe-kuḷī* and *Heḷe-kuḷī*). An examination of the occurrence of these terms suggests that the term *kuḷī*, without the ethnic qualifier, was used in respect of villages where there were no mixed populations. The terms *Demeḷe-kuḷī* and *Heḷe-kuḷī*, which always occur together, were used in the immunity grants only in regard to villages where both Tamils and Sinhalese lived.[73] These were probably villages where the Anuradhapura rulers had settled the Tamil soldiers brought from south India. These soldiers presumably had to pay imposts different from those paid by the Sinhalese subjects.

In the time of these records, it appears that there was a special officer to look after the affairs of the Tamil soldiers settled in the kingdom. This officer had the title of Demeḷa-adhikāra (literally, Tamil Officer or Officer for the Tamils). It would be far-fetched to consider him as some kind of minister in charge of Tamil affairs. More probably, he was an officer in charge of matters relating to the large number of Tamil soldiers in the kingdom at this time. As Paranavitana has remarked, it is when the edicts are concerned with Tamil allotments that this official takes a part in the promulgation of the edicts.[74]

The provenance of the Sinhalese records referring to Tamil lands and Tamil villages is also of significance. These records were found in the northeastern region and close to Polonnaruva. This is the area close to the major ports of the eastern coast that were used not only for commercial activities but also for bringing south Indian troops into the island. This is also the area where considerable evidence of Mahayana Buddhist activities and Pallava influences is found. But what is even more interesting is the fact that some of the earliest

Tamil inscriptions and archaeological remains, especially ruins of Saiva temples, of the eleventh century have been found in this region. It is in the same area that Tamil inscriptions later reveal that some of the more influential Tamil merchant guilds were very active in the eleventh and twelfth centuries. When the Cōḻas conquered the northern part of the island at the end of the tenth century, this was the area that became their stronghold. Clearly all the evidence points to the dominant presence of a Tamil population in the areas extending from the modern Trincomalee District in the east to the Mannar District in the west.

The Extreme North and Northeast

Outside Anuradhapura's control

But it is in the extreme north, the area now covered by the Jaffna District and parts of the Vavuniya District that the developments of this period are not known from the existing sources. As the Pali chronicle is only recording the annals of the Anuradhapura rulers, it has very little information about the events that happened outside the realm of the Anuradhapura monarchs. On the occasions these rulers faced problems in their capital and fled to the hill country (Malaya) or the southern kingdom (Rohaṇa), some information about these areas is included. Until the seventh century, there is absolutely no valuable information in the Pali chronicle about the northernmost part of the island.

From about the seventh century, there are references in the Pali chronicle to three territories in the island, in addition to the ancient regions of Rohaṇa and Malaya. These are the Uttara-desa (the Northern Territory), Pacina-desa (the Eastern Territory) and the Dakkhiṇa-desa (the Southern Territory). There is, of course, no way of definitely identifying the geographical extent or boundaries of these territories. They were no doubt vaguely designated areas to the north, east and south of the core of the Anuradhapura kingdom over which the Anuradhapura ruler claimed overlordship. The king appointed members of his family, usually his sons, to administer these territories. Appointing the heir to the throne to be in charge of the Southern Territory seems to have been the general practice. Although there are some references to the appointment of a prince to administer the Eastern Territory, the dispatch of princes to the Northern Territory is hard to find.

An analysis of the few notices of the Northern Territory in the Pali chronicle indicates that it was an area different from the other territories. Often it is found to be a rebellious area that the Anuradhapura rulers found hard to control. It was a place where rebel princes or aspirants to the throne found ready support. Unlike in the previous centuries, in the period after the sixth century invading armies from south India landed here, consolidated their position in that region and then marched towards Anuradhapura. Clearly conditions were unfavourable here for the Anuradhapura rulers.

Pallava connection

Early in the seventh century, in the reign of Silāmeghavaṇṇa (619-628), a military leader named Sirināga made an attempt to overthrow the king with the help of a Tamil army. He invaded Anuradhapura from the Northern Territory. It is significant that the invasion led by this rebel came from the north. From now on, the Pali chronicle records more such invasions. Perhaps the most notable of these is that of the Sinhalese prince Mānavamma who had gained the support of the powerful Pallava emperors. The case of Mānavamma is extremely useful in an assessment of the role of the Northern Territory in the political turmoils of this period. The details of his early life are not known. What is known from the Pali chronicle is that he was the son of Kassapa, identified as the second of that name, who ruled at Anuradhapura from 650 to 659. In the political confusion that ensued the death of his father, Mānavamma seems to have fled the capital and found refuge in the Northern Territory. As a potential claimant of the throne, he seems to have been pursued by the successors of his father and he had found it safe to live in the Northern Territory. He was, however, discovered by

Hatthadāṭha, the ruler at Anuradhapura. Mānavamma was, therefore, forced to flee from there to the court of the Pallava king in Kanchi.

The flight of Mānavamma from the north of Sri Lanka to the Pallava capital may suggest that this prince was in contact with the Pallavas even before he left for Kanchi. That the Pallavas already had a foothold in northern or northeastern Sri Lanka or that conditions in that part of the island were favourable to the Pallavas is to be suspected from this and other events of this period. It is in this context that the claim of Pallava Siṃhaviṣṇu (c. 575-600) regarding his victory over the Siṃhaḷa ruler comes into significance. As already suggested, Siṃhaviṣṇu's claim cannot be dismissed lightly. From the time of Siṃhaviṣṇu, Pallava political influence appears to have been present in the north or northeast. It was in such favourable circumstances that Mahayana Buddhism, Pallava art and architecture and south Indian mercantile communities were able to flourish in the region on the northeast, between Pallavavaṅka and Gokarṇa.

The sojourn of the Sinhalese prince in the Pallava capital lasted several years. In this period, he participated in the Pallava wars against other south Indian rulers. Eventually, Pallava Narasiṃhavarman I (630-668) provided Mānavamma with troops for an invasion of Sri Lanka. Although his army was able to march towards Anuradhapura successfully, he failed to complete the conquest as the Pallava army had to leave suddenly. Mānavamma returned to Kanchi and had to wait for several years before a second invasion was undertaken. On this occasion, the Pallava army landed in the Northern Territory and first consolidated its position there. Anuradhapura was at this time under the control of the Tamil kingmaker, Potthakuṭṭha, and his puppet king Hatthadāṭha. They marched against Mānavamma but were defeated and the latter finally became king at Anuradhapura in 684.

Mānavamma's invasion and ultimate success raise certain interesting questions about the Northern Territory. Why did Mānavamma seek refuge in this region when he was first deprived of his rights to a position in Anuradhapura? Was not the normal

PLATE 14.
Siva temple (name unknown – referred to now as Siva Devale No.1), Polonnaruva. 11th century.

Photo: March 2005, by the author.

PLATE 15.
Ruins of the Rajaraja-perumpalli (the Great Rajaraja Monastery) – Tamil Buddhist monastery named after Cola Rajaraja I, near Trincomalee. This monastery, the impressive ruins of which cover an extensive area, is 'interesting as the only known example of a Tamil Buddhist *palli* preserved even in ruins up to our day' (Prof. S. Paranavitana). See pp. 233, 238.
Photo: *March 2005, by the author. Courtesy: Department of Archaeology.*

practice for Sinhalese princes in similar circumstances to flee to Malaya or Rohaṇa? What were the conditions that favoured him there? When discovered by his enemies, how was it possible for him to go to the court of the most powerful ruler in the Tamil land and enjoy his hospitality for a long period? When the time was ripe for him to invade the Sinhalese kingdom, why did he choose to land in the north and then march to Anuradhapura? Were not the ports of the east coast in greater use at this time for relations with south India? The paucity of information about this part of the island does not help to find the answers to these questions. But it is clear that for a prince marching with an army from the Tamil land the conditions in the north were more favourable than elsewhere. As the Pali chronicle says, Mānavamma was able to consolidate his position there, presumably without any difficulty, and then march to Anuradhapura.

It would appear that in this period the Northern Territory had come under greater Tamil influence than the southern parts of the island. With the rise of the first Tamil empires in the seventh century, namely the Pāṇḍya and the Pallava, the north of Sri Lanka, as the area closest to these empires, was at the receiving end of significant influences from south India. Pallava influences in particular were filtering down the east coast. The Tamil empires had, in a sense, expanded into northern Sri Lanka. Once again the sea separating the island and south India was functioning as a unifier. At first these influences were Buddhist as well as Saiva, Tamil as well as Sanskritic, political as well as religious. But ultimately the Tamil language and the Saiva religion became the dominant factors that helped to forge a single ethnic identity in the northwestern, northern and eastern regions. The melting pot was simmering for over a thousand years and the end product was seen when the lid was lifted with the Cōḻa invasion at the end of the tenth century.

End of the tenth century

What then do we see at the end of the tenth century and early in the eleventh when the Cōḻas occupied a good part of the island, including the whole of the northern region? Two things unmistakably proclaim the transformation that had occurred in this region in the previous centuries. One is the widespread appearance of stone inscriptions in Tamil, most of which were dated in the regnal years of the Cōḻa rulers. The other is the large number of Saiva temples, almost all of which were named or renamed after the Cōḻa emperors. Even the few surviving Tamil Buddhist institutions were renamed after the Saiva Cōḻa monarchs. From Mātoṭa (Mātōṭṭam) in the northwest to Gokarṇa (Kōṇamalai) in the east lay the line that was soon to become the dividing line between the Tamil and the Sinhalese regions.

North of this line, the ancient Nāga and other Mesolithic people, the later Telugu, Kerala and Kannada people as well as the Heḷa came under the dominant influence of the Tamils and their language. With the success of the Saiva movement in south India, Saivism supplanted Buddhism in this region.

All that we know at present about the northern regions of Sri Lanka, roughly corresponding to the modern Northern Province and the Trincomalee District of the Eastern Province, in the period 300-900 CE, is confined to the information extracted from a few inscriptions, some sculptural artefacts, remains of a few Buddhist structures and some incidental references in the Pali, Graeco-Roman and Tamil literary sources. Valuable as they are for the history of this region, hardly any coherent historical reconstruction of the developments there is possible with such meagre evidence.

An irrefutable conclusion that can be drawn from the evidence of these sources is that Buddhism was a religion of considerable significance in the region during this period. It is also evident that the Buddhism of this region displayed traits that were different from the features of Buddhism in contemporary Anuradhapura. While the Jaffna peninsula showed traces of influence from Andhra, there was unmistakable influence of Mahayana Buddhism from the Pallava kingdom in the Trincomalee District. While Theravada Buddhism and the Pali language were influential forces in the Jaffna peninsula,

Mahayana Buddhism and the Sanskrit language exerted much influence in the Trincomalee District.[75]

The Buddhism that was introduced in the northern peninsula in the centuries before the Common Era saw significant growth in the early centuries of this era in the same way as Buddhism did elsewhere in the island. Remains of Buddhist establishments datable to the period under review have been found in several parts of the peninsula, including Kantarodai, Vallipuram, Ponnalai, Makiyapitti, Nilavarai, Uduvil, Nainativu, Punkudutivu and Neduntivu (Delft).[76] Of these, the best known site is Kantarodai where more archaeological remains have been found than anywhere else in the peninsula.

Kantarodai, as well as some of the other sites, has also yielded Buddha images that were once housed in the Buddhist establishments. Perhaps the biggest and the least damaged of these is a standing Buddha image from Vallipuram datable to about the fourth century.[77] Seated Buddha images have also been found at Kantarodai. A broken sedent Buddha image was discovered in the premises of the Viṣṇu temple at Ponnalai while another was found in Makiyapitti. Other Buddha images have come from Uduvil and Nilavarai.[78]

An epigraphic record of exceptional interest relating to Buddhism in the Jaffna peninsula in the early centuries of this era is the Vallipuram gold plate. Datable to the first century CE, this records the construction of a monastery (*vihāra*). It was presumably buried in the foundation of this structure. Since a Buddha image was also discovered in Vallipuram, this place in the northernmost corner of the island was no doubt the site of an ancient Buddhist monastery.[79]

Kantarodai appears to have been an important centre of Buddhism and possibly also a centre of political authority. Remains of Buddhist monuments of this period as well as artefacts indicating foreign commercial relations have been brought to light in this place.[80]

Sinhalese tradition, too, preserves the memory of Buddhist establishments in the northern peninsula. There is no doubt that the Jaffna peninsula was reputed among the Buddhists of the island as a region with many Buddhist places of worship that were worthy of a pilgrimage. Clearly these establishments could not have arisen after the ninth century when we see the decline of Buddhism and its total displacement by Saivism. Sinhalese Buddhists considered it important to include the more famous establishments in the area in the list of Buddhist shrines that a pious Buddhist was expected to know about and to visit in his or her lifetime. And so the shrines of Nāgakōvila (Nākarkōvil), Telipola (Tellippaḷai), Mallāgama (Mallākam), Minuvangomu-vihāraya (Vīmaṉkāmam), Tanni-divayina (Taṉa-tīvu or Kayts), Nāga-divayina (Nayiṉātīvu), Puvaṅgu-divayina (Puṅkuṭutīvu) and Kāra-divayina (Kāraitīvu) in the north (which territory, when this list was composed, was recognized as a Tamil region by the usage of the name Demaḷa-paṭṭanama or Tamil City to describe it) were included in the popular *Nampota* or Book of Names (of Holy Places), memorized and handed down from generation to generation.[81] Of these, Nāga-divayina (modern Nayiṉātīvu or Nāgadīpa) has remained the most hallowed one (and the only surviving shrine) up to the present day for the Sinhalese Buddhists who make the pilgrimage up to the north whenever circumstances permit, in the same manner as Kataragama in the far south has remained a place of pilgrimage for the Saiva Tamils of the north up to the present day. For these northern shrines to be so hallowed, it is obvious that their origins go back to much earlier times.

It is in the Trincomalee District that influences from the Tamil kingdom of the Pallavas were dominant. The inscriptions and archaeological remains in this region provide an interesting insight into the developments here. With the expansion of the overseas trade under the Pallavas, the ports of the Trincomalee District acquired an importance that they did not enjoy in the earlier centuries. The activities of affluent south Indian mercantile communities in these ports led to their patronage of Buddhist and Saiva institutions. While there is no doubt that the Theravada establishments of the earlier period continued to receive the patronage of the elite, it is the emergence of Mahayana institutions showing distinct Pallava influence that draws our attention to this area.

Tiriyay and Kuccaveli are two of the places where Mahayana Buddhism flourished in the seventh century. Of these, Tiriyay still has the remains of one of the structures of the Mahayanists in the form of the *vaṭadāge* (the circular shrine) along with an important Mahayana inscription in Sanskrit, written in the Pallava-Grantha script of south India. As discussed later, the penetration of Mahayana cults was the result of a powerful Mahayana movement originating from the Pallava kingdom and spreading across the Bay of Bengal to the eastern part of Sri Lanka and the kingdoms of Southeast Asia. In the seventh century, Kanchi, the capital of the Pallavas, was a centre of Mahayana Buddhism, visited by Chinese, Southeast Asian and Sri Lankan Mahayana monks. Mahayana monks from Kanchi and other centres in India, in turn, visited Sri Lanka. Some of them proceeded to Southeast Asia and China from there. An eminent Mahayana teacher, Guṇavarman, visited Sri Lanka and stayed there for some time before proceeding to Southeast Asia.[82] Another well-known Mahayana monk, Vajrabodhi, stayed in Kanchi for a considerable time and then went to Sri Lanka where he expounded the Mahayana doctrine before proceeding to China towards the end of the seventh century.[83] Clearly there was local support for Mahayanism. Along with south Indian mercantile communities, local elites would have played a significant role in the growth of Mahayanism in Sri Lanka.

The spread of the Saiva movement

Another important religious development in this period is the impact of the Saiva movement in the northern and eastern regions of Sri Lanka. This popular campaign of the Nāyaṉārs, the tide of which the Jains and Buddhists in south India found hard to stem, spilled over to the island and left a more lasting impact compared with that of the Mahayana movement. As in the Tamil region of south India, in Sri Lanka, too, the main consequence of the success achieved by the Saivaites was the dislodgement of Buddhism, both Mahayana and Theravada, from the northern and eastern parts of the island. Although there were Tamils in this region who continued to be Buddhists even after the end of the Saiva movement, by the end of the twelfth century the Tamils there were completely within the fold of Saivism. Those Tamil Buddhists who were living in the areas outside the north and east were gradually assimilated into the Sinhalese population, just as the Sinhalese Buddhists who lived in the north and east, no doubt, were absorbed into the Tamil-speaking population. Saivism clearly was one of the two main elements in the evolution of the Sri Lankan Tamils, the other being the Tamil language.

The worship of Śiva was prevalent in Sri Lanka from even before the mission of Mahinda in the third century BCE, the mission that resulted in the king of Anuradhapura and many of his subjects being converted to Buddhism. After all, the father of this Anuradhapura ruler was Muṭa Siva, whose name implies association with the worship of Śiva. The evidence of the early Pali chronicles leave us in no doubt that the cult of Śiva was prevalent in Anuradhapura and elsewhere in the island.[84] The numerous occurrences of the personal name Siva in the early Brāhmī records also support this.

The ground was prepared for the success of the Saiva movement by the local rulers and the mercantile communities in another significant development at this time. In a region where local rulers and the elite were favourably inclined to adopt north Indian traditions, the Pallavas went one step further. They were themselves outsiders to the Tamil land and were already steeped in Brahmanical traditions. When they became rulers of a part of the Tamil land, in the territory known as Toṇḍaimaṇḍalam, they practised Brahmanical traditions and rituals in a manner unprecedented in the Tamil kingdoms. While Brāhmaṇas were always patronized by local rulers in south India, they became the recipients of special patronage under the Pallavas. One of the results of this special patronage was the establishment of *brahmadeyas* or Brāhmaṇa settlements in various parts of the kingdom. The Pāṇḍyas, too, followed the example of the Pallavas in their kingdom. It was a trend that was seen all over South Asia at this time. As David Ludden, in his study of the agrarian history of South Asia, has pointed out, 'Gifts of land by kings and their officers to temples and Brahmans…became a hallmark of new dynasties at the end of Gupta hegemony, from the sixth century onward'.[85]

The *brahmadeya* was more than a settlement of Brāhmaṇas. Champakalakshmi has described it 'as an institution integrating pre-existing pastoral and agricultural settlements into a new agrarian order and as the disseminator of brahmanical ideology.'[86] The *brahmadeya* emerged with the temple as its nucleus and pre-existing agricultural and pastoral settlements were appended to it. The *brahmadeya* and the temple 'developed into institutions of substantial political and social power with economic privileges'.[87] Champakalakshmi further elaborates on the significance of these twin forces:

> Two important spheres in which the *brahmadeya* and temple may be seen as harbingers of advanced farming methods were the technology of irrigation and the seasonal regulation of the cultivation process…With each of the *brahmadeya* and temple settlements an irrigation system was invariably established, either in the form of tanks, canals or wells…Many of them were initiated by the rulers but managed by the local bodies. Elaborate arrangements for their upkeep were made by the *sabhās* or assemblies of the *brahmadeyas*, including maintenance, repair, attention to silting and control of water supply through cesses, and specifying committees (*vāriyams*) for their supervision and administration.[88]

Providing patronage to Brāhmaṇas was always considered to be one of the ideals of kingship in India. This was adopted by rulers in Sri Lanka and Southeast Asia, too. One of the results of the cultural inspiration received by the kingdoms in Sri Lanka and Southeast Asia from India, particularly from south India, was the arrival of considerable numbers of Brāhmaṇas. With the earnest patronage of the local elite and the south Indian merchants, they played a significant role in the spread of Siva worship. The introduction of the institution of the *brahmadeya* in Sri Lanka provided the institutional force for strengthening the position of Saivism.

In Sri Lanka, the Buddhist rulers of Anuradhapura unwittingly aided the Saiva movement through their patronage of Brāhmaṇas at a time when Hindu movements in south India were turning against the Buddhists. For centuries their predecessors, like the rulers of the Southeast Asian kingdoms, had extended their patronage to Brāhmaṇas. The reign of Mahāsena in the third century was a notable exception when Brahmanical establishments, according to Pali sources, were destroyed.[89] Until about the sixth century, this patronage did not affect the status of the Buddhist Sangha. Possibly such patronage did not go beyond the circle of Brāhmaṇas who were court officials, such as the *purohitas* and astrologers.[90] From the sixth century, no doubt influenced by the practices in the Pallava court, patronage given to Brāhmaṇas became a more elaborate affair. We hear of a king 'renovating the temples of gods that had fallen into disrepair here and there, and feeding the Brāhmaṇas with food fit for kings'.[91] Another encouraged Brāhmaṇas to lead the lives appropriate to their calling.[92] A third one is said to have made expensive gifts of gold, pearls and gems to a thousand Brāhmaṇas.[93] Though the Buddhist chronicles do not provide any information about the establishment of *brahmadeyas* by the Anuradhapura rulers, it would appear that such settlements were established at least in those areas that had come under strong Pallava influence in the east.

The area in the east where we get the most number of archaeological remains indicating Pallava influence is that between the ancient port of Pallavavaṅka in the north and Gokarṇa (Trincomalee) in the south, and extending interior as far as Padaviya and Kantalay. In this territory, while Tiriyay and Kuccaveli have yielded inscriptions and monuments revealing Mahayana influences, Padaviya and Kantalay have remains showing that these were Saiva centres with Brāhmaṇa settlements.

As Saiva centres, Padaviya and Kantalay rose into prominence with the Cōḻa conquest at the end of the tenth century. Clearly they were two of the prominent *brahmadeyas* in the island. That Padaviya was a Brāhmaṇa settlement with the name Śrīpatīgrāma (village of Viṣṇu) is known from a Sanskrit inscription in Grantha characters.[94] The origin of this settlement, however, is yet to be established. Soon after the invasion of the Cōḻa emperor Rājarāja towards the end of the tenth century, a Śiva temple at Padaviya was named as Ravikula-māṇikka-īśvaram, after the emperor.[95] The ruins of this temple are still there at Padaviya. The ruins of more Saiva temples have also been found, clearly establishing the importance of this place as a centre of Saivism. The origin of the Brāhmaṇa settlement may well go back to a period before the tenth century.

Kantalay was a prominent *brahmadeya* that enjoyed the patronage of both Cōḻa administrators and Sinhalese monarchs. Situated in an area irrigated by the large Gaṅgā-taṭāka (Kantalay) reservoir, it may have originated when this tank was built in the seventh century. In the reign of Rājarāja Cōḻa I, this *brahmadeya* had the name Rājarāja-caturvedimaṅgalam.[96] The Śiva temple there was also, in all probability, given a name after the Cōḻa emperor. For, we find that when Vijayabāhu I succeeded in ousting the Cōḻa rulers from the island, the name of the *brahmadeya* was changed to Vijayarāja-caturvedimaṅgalam, after the Sinhalese monarch, and, interestingly, the Śiva temple was re-named as Vijayarāja-īsvaram, giving room to surmise that the earlier name was associated with Rājarāja.[97] After Vijayabāhu I, one of the notable royal patrons of this *brahmadeya* was his grandson, Gajabāhu II (1132-1153).

With the establishment of Brāhmaṇa settlements in the east and possibly in the north, the ground was prepared for Saivism to be firmly rooted in the north and east. Although Mahayana Buddhism, too, had crossed over from the Pallava kingdom and found favourable conditions for growth in the east, the growth of Saivism is of greater significance. The patrons of Mahayanism were not the kings of Anuradhapura. Without the patronage of these rulers

Mahayanism did flourish in the east. The archaeological remains in Tiriyay and other sites leave us in no doubt about this. This Buddhist sect clearly enjoyed the patronage of the local elite and some of the mercantile communities. But the gradual growth of Saivism from the seventh century seems to have led to the religious conflict of south India being carried across to Sri Lanka.

Information about Saivism in Sri Lanka in the period 600-900 CE comes from limited literary and archaeological evidence relating to Saiva temples. Except for some late traditions that tell about an ancient temple named Nakulesvaram, nothing is known about the Śiva temples of the far north (modern Jaffna District) which today is a stronghold of Saivism. However, there is indisputable evidence about two other ancient Śiva temples at the port of Mātoṭa in the northwest and the port of Gokarṇa in the east.[98] By the time of the commencement of the Saiva movement, in the seventh century, these were counted among the holiest Śiva temples and were the only temples in Sri Lanka in praise of which the Saiva Nāyaṉārs sang hymns.

Ñāṉacampantar, the Saiva stalwart who had converted the Pāṇḍya royal family to Saivism, traversed the Tamil land, making pilgrimages to the holiest Saiva shrines and singing hymns to the deities there. These pilgrimages helped to arouse greater consciousness in favour of Saivism among the ordinary people and to hallow a large number of ancient shrines that were scattered across the land. It is not known whether Ñāṉacampantar visited temples in Sri Lanka, but he did sing a hymn to the deity at the renowned Kētīśvaram temple at Mātoṭa and another to the deity of the equally renowned Kōṇēśvaram temple at Gokarṇa.[99] Ñāṉacampantar composed these hymns in the seventh century. In the ninth century, the deity of Kōṇēśvaram was the subject of another hymn by the Saiva Nāyaṉār Cuntaramūrti.[100]

A third renowned Saiva leader, Māṇikkavācakar, who lived probably in the eighth century, is closely associated with the Saiva movement in Sri Lanka in certain legends. According to Tamil tradition, he was at first a minister in the court of a Pāṇḍya king at Madurai and had responsibility for purchasing horses for his ruler. This often took him to a port named Perunturai. In his most celebrated work called *Tiru-vācakam*, Māṇikkavācakar often sings the praise of the "Śiva who resides at the sacred Perunturai".[101] It is of interest to note that the names 'Perunturai' and 'Mātoṭa' both mean 'the Great Port'. As the identification of Perunturai with any port in south India poses a problem, this place may well be Mātoṭa in Sri Lanka. Māṇikkavācakar's association with Sri Lanka in the Saiva traditions is so strong that the identification of Perunturai with Mātoṭa, with its Śiva temple hallowed by the hymn of Ñāṉa-campantar and its importance in the Arab horse trade, cannot be ruled out. Māṇikkavācakar is the only known Saiva leader who, according to two Tamil Saiva *purāṇas* (religious histories), had participated in public disputations with Buddhists from Sri Lanka and defeated them. The Buddhist king of Sri Lanka who was present at these disputations, it is said, became a convert to Saivism when the Buddhists were defeated. What is of even greater interest is the tradition preserved in two Sinhalese chronicles about the Sinhalese king Sena I (833-853) as having been converted to Saivism by an 'ascetic clad in the robes of a priest'.[102] For Buddhist chronicles to say this of a Buddhist king, there obviously was some basis.

Hallowed by the hymns of the Nāyaṉārs as well as by its antiquity, the temple of Kētīsvaram, it was believed, bestowed a special sanctity to Mātoṭa as a sacred place. This special status was conferred to it not only by the Saivaites but also by others. This is evidenced by Sinhalese inscriptions. An interesting imprecation in the Sinhalese epigraphic records of the tenth century states that those who violate the provisions of those records will "incur the sin of slaughtering cows at Mātoṭa".[103] Slaughtering cows is considered a great sin in Hinduism and when that slaughter is committed in a very holy place, it becomes a heinous crime. In the south Indian inscriptions, a similar imprecation is found. It reads as: 'May the one who violates this incur the sin of slaughtering the holy cow at the banks of the Ganges River'. There is no doubt that Mātoṭa was considered a holy Saiva site in this period.

Besides the temples of Mātoṭa and Gokarṇa, there were no doubt other Siva temples in the island. A Tamil inscription from Nilaveli, on the east coast, refers to the temple of Matsyesvaram (which is another name for Kōṇesvaram but may well refer to a different temple) at Gokarṇa while two Tamil inscriptions from Anuradhapura refer to a Saiva shrine there.[104] The remains of several shrines have been unearthed at Anuradhapura.[105] These belong to the period before the tenth century. Some of the ruins of temples at Padaviya and Kantalay may also go back to the period before the tenth century.

The expansion of overseas trade under the Pallavas had a significant impact on the strengthening of the Tamil element in the north and east of the island. Trade, more than anything else, helped to maintain close relations between this part of Sri Lanka and the east coast of south India, easing the flow of economic, political and cultural influences and aiding the interaction between the elites of the two regions. The arrival of the powerful south Indian trading communities led to the establishment of market-towns. Many of these later became centres of Saivism, patronized by the affluent merchant communities.

Mercantile communities, identifiable as belonging to the Mahayanist faith and connected with the Pallava kingdom, were active on the east coast (present Trincomalee District) in the eighth century. They were responsible for the construction of the Mahayana shrine named Girikanda-caitya at Tiriyay. The ruins of this establishment, including the circular shrine (*vaṭadāgē*) with its beautiful sculptural ornaments, exhibit unmistakable Pallava artisitic influence. The *dvārapāla* (gatekeeper) sculptures at this shrine, in Paranavitana's words, 'exhibit the elongated limbs and the cold severity of expression which distinguish Pallava work'.[106] In this same ancient site is a Mahayana inscription in Sanskrit, written in the Pallava-Grantha script, also showing influences from the Pallava kingdom. Not far from Tiriyay, at Kuccaveli, another Mahayana inscription reveals similar influences. Mahayana Buddhist sculptures found elsewhere in the eastern region, at Situlpavu and Kurukkalmadam, and belonging to the same period, are also in the Pallava style.[107] Further interior, at the capital Anuradhapura, is to be seen the most famous of the sculptures in the Pallava style in Sri Lanka, popularly known as the Man and Horse's Head (Isurumuniya). To quote Paranavitana again, 'This work has earned the highest encomiums from art critics; and, in the studied restraint which characterizes the form of the man, the paucity of jewellery which accentuates the plastic form, and in the elongated slender limbs, the work is reminiscent of the sculptures executed under the patronage of the Pallavas of Kanchi'.[108] The Dutch art historian J.E.van Lohuizen-DeLeeuw has identified this figure as Aiyaṉār, one of the most popular gods in south India.[109] Perhaps the strongest influence of Pallava art is to be seen at the Mahayana structure at Nalanda, often described as the Geḍigē. It is the earliest building in Sri Lanka entirely constructed with stone, like the Pallava monuments at Mamallapuram in Tamil Nadu and is in the late Pallava style of architecture (eighth century). All these archaeological remains bear witness to the presence of considerable numbers of artisans from the Pallava kingdom.

These artefacts revealing Pallava connections need to be interpreted and assessed for their significance in the context of similar artefacts, of about the same period, discovered in Thailand, Malaysia, Indonesia, Vietnam and Laos. The finds in these countries include Hindu and Buddhist sculptures, Sanskrit, Prakrit and Tamil inscriptions written in the script used in the Pallava kingdom, and the remains of shrines. Almost all of them belong to the 6th-9th centuries. The Pallava style archaeological material in Sri Lanka belongs to the same period.

What happened in the kingdoms around the Bay of Bengal and beyond, in Vietnam, Cambodia and Laos, was the dissemination of Buddhist and Hindu influences from and via the Pallava kingdom in the wake of the expansion of south Indian trade. Not only the south Indian traders, those from Sri Lanka and the Southeast Asian kingdoms were also participants in this activity which resulted in a vigorous cultural dialogue between South Asia and Southeast Asia. The rise of a new political power in south India, namely the Pallavas, coincided, firstly, with the emergence of well organized south Indian mercantile communities, which before long came to play a pivotal role in the Indian trade with Southeast Asia and dominated that trade till the end of the twelfth century, and, secondly, with the growth of two vigorous religious movements, each opposed to the other. One was the relentless campaign of the Saiva Nāyaṉārs, directed primarily against the Jainas and the Buddhists, focusing mainly on the Tamil-speaking regions, including northern Sri Lanka. The other was the resolute movement of the Mahayana Buddhists who, though waging a losing battle in the Tamil kingdoms, successfully penetrated into the kingdoms across the Bay of Bengal, including the eastern part of Sri Lanka, with the aid of the influential trading communities.

The result was the establishment of Hindu and Buddhist institutions in these kingdoms, particularly in and around the major ports. Brāhmaṇas and Buddhist monks as well as artisans well versed in sculpture and architecture were taken to these places and, with the patronage of local rulers or elites who had come under the influence of Hinduism and Buddhism, several Buddhist and Hindu institutions were established. The influence of Pallava polity was also seen in the adoption of royal names ending in –varman by almost all the Southeast Asian dynasties of this period. Even in Sri Lanka, at least one of the kings, who ruled in the seventh century after spending a good part of his life in the Pallava capital of Kanchi, had a name ending in –varman. Though Mānavarma (Pali Mānavamma) is the only one in the list of kings in the Pali chronicle who has a name ending in –varma or –varman, there were other Sinhalese rulers, too, who added that suffix to their names, or at least this suffix was added when their names were written in Tamil records, following the practice among the Pallavas.[110]

While in the Southeast Asian kingdoms the rulers and the elite were active participants in this cultural dialogue and were encouraging and patronizing the establishment of Mahayana and

Hindu places of worship, in Sri Lanka the situation was different and, therefore, the results were also different. The Anuradhapura rulers were, with few exceptions, ardent supporters of Theravada Buddhism and the Sinhalese Buddhist Sangha was strongly of the Theravada school and had an enviable reputation in the Buddhist world as a very orthodox organization. There was no way a Sinhalese monarch could encourage Mahayana activities or extend patronage to a Mahayana institution, let alone establish one, without incurring the wrath of the elites and the Sinhalese Sangha in his kingdom.[111]

Considering the fact that most of the remains of Pallava art, architecture and epigraphy are in the eastern region of the island, away from Anuradhapura, the power-centre of the Theravada Buddhist Sinhalese kings, and the fact that these Sinhalese rulers were not patrons of Mahayana Buddhism, those who were responsible for employing the artisans versed in Pallava sculpture and architecture must have been the influential mercantile communities from south India and local overlords. These elite groups would have also played an important role in the construction of irrigation works in the regions where the above archaeological evidence of Pallava influence has been found, namely the eastern part of the island.

The northeastern littoral, between Kokkilai lagoon and the Trincomalee harbour, seems to be the area where the activities of the south Indian mercantile communities were concentrated from about the seventh century. It is in this area that we find two of the largest reservoirs constructed about this time but not identifiable in the chronicles as tanks built by Anuradhapura rulers. These are the Padaviya and Vahalkada tanks. In Paranavitana's words: 'The chronicles and the epigraphs contain no information about the construction of the immense reservoir Padīvāpi (Padavi); it is not in the list of tanks restored by Vijayabāhu I, although Parākramabāhu I restored it. The ancient name of the large, breached Vahalkada tank on the Yan Oya cannot be traced.'[112] (The name of the latter is given as Kāṭṭaṉ-ēri in the Tamil inscription from Vahalkada). Considering the activities of the south Indian mercantile communities in this region, it appears that they had a share in the construction of some of these reservoirs.

The Padaviya tank is one of the largest in the region, some 10,000 acres in extent, and is to be counted among the numerous tanks enlarged in the time of Parākramabāhu I in the twelfth century. In the ancient settlement near the tank are to be found the ruins of several Saiva temples with Tamil inscriptions. One of these temples had the name Iravikulamāṇikka-īśvaram (Skt. Ravikula-māṇikya-īśvaram) and was older than the Saiva temples at Polonnaruva. In fact, it could be considered as the oldest of the Siva temples in a ruined state in Sri Lanka. A member of the Nānādeśi merchant community was among the patrons of this temple early in the eleventh century. Non-mercantile communities like the Vīrakkoṭiyar as well as the powerful mercantile communites continued to flourish at this place in the twelfth century.

The Padaviya and Vahalkada tanks as well as other reservoirs in the northeastern part of the island, where the Pallava influence is seen to be strongest, were probably constructed by local chiefs with the assistance of mercantile communities. After all, it cannot be claimed that the monarchy in Sri Lanka was highly centralized and that the ruler of Anuradhapura was always directly responsible for the construction of irrigation works. The fact that many important irrigation works continued to be constructed in the time of political instability in the 6th-9th centuries seems to indicate that the local elites played a major role in the construction and maintenance of reservoirs. As noticed earlier, the establishment of *brahmadeyas* (Brāhmaṇa settlements) also led to the construction of irrigation facilities.

There is epigraphic evidence pointing to the association of mercantile communities with irrigation facilities in the ninth century. In a Tamil inscription from Thailand, the Maṇigrāmam traders are associated with the Avanināraṇam reservoir at Takua-pa while in another inscription from Munasandal in Tamil Nadu the

Aiññūṟṟuvar community is associated with a reservoir which bore the name Aiññūṟṟuvappērēri (the Great Aiññūṟṟuvar Reservoir), presumably because it was built by them.[113] Although direct evidence is not available about the participation of the south Indian mercantile communities in the construction of reservoirs in Sri Lanka, there is some evidence pointing to connections between the Pallava kingdom and the northeastern part of the island in the field of irrigation works as indeed there is in the sphere of religion. The term used for 'reservoir' in the names of some of the tanks in this region is an interesting piece of evidence in this respect. From the time of the earliest Brāhmī inscriptions, the word *vapi* is used to denote a tank or reservoir. The Sinhalese word *väva* is derived from this. While the cognate word *vāvi* was also used in Tamil in south India, the more common Tamil word was *kuḷam.* However, in the time of the Pallava rulers, especially in the areas ruled by the Pallavas, the word *taṭākam* was also popular (the Vairamēgha-taṭāka of the Pallava inscriptions in Uttaramerur, the Mahēndra-taṭāka and the Paramēśvara-taṭāka in the Pallava kingdom). Another term that was widely used about this time to denote a tank was *ēri*. In some of the places outside south India where Pallava influence was felt, we come across the terms *taṭākam* and *ēri*. In Thailand, a Sanskrit inscription refers to the construction of a tank named Śaṅkara-taḍāka.[114] In Sri Lanka, we come across the name of Gaṅgā-taṭāka for a large tank in a place which is well-known as a prominent Brāhmaṇa sttlement (*brahmadeya* or *caturvēdimaṅgalam*) in the eleventh and twelfth centuries. This tank, according to the Pali chronicle, was built early in the seventh century, the time when Pallava influences spread to lands outside south India. Another tank in Sri Lanka, the name of which also has a suffix derivable from *taṭāka* (Giri-taṭa-vāpi), was also built about the same time. The Vahalkada tank in the northeastern part of the island is given the name of Kattan-eri in a Tamil inscription found near the tank.[115] The terms *taṭāka* and *ēri* are not commonly used for tanks in other parts of the island and may, therefore, indicate some Pallava connection.[116]

The continuous flow of influences from south India gave an edge to the Tamil-speakers over the other ethnic groups in the north and east. In the south and centre the Heḷa-speakers were in a strong position of dominance over the others. With its power-centre in Anuradhapura, the Heḷa group, having survived the challenges from south India in the Early Historic Period, was in a far better position to absorb the groups in the north. For a long period the outcome hung in the balance. The turning point came with the expansion under the Pallavas. Until then an ultimate Heḷa victory in this silent contest between the two major ethnic groups was possible. The critical element in the eventual outcome lay with the Tamil-speakers. The fate of the north and east was decided by the victory of Saivism over Buddhism. As the Saiva religion went hand in hand with the Tamil language, its victory completed the evolution of the ancient Sri Lankan Tamil ethnic community. The Tamils who lived south of Anuradhapura were assimilated into the language, religion and culture of the Sinhalese whereas in the areas north and east of Anuradhapura the Heḷas and others were assimilated into the Tamil population.

CHAPTER 7

THE PERIOD OF CONSOLIDATION: C 900 – 1100 CE

Reaching Adulthood

The outcome of the processes that went on in the northern and northeastern parts of the island from about 300 to 900 CE was beginning to come to light in the tenth century. After a long period of almost total darkness during which the ethnic pot was simmering, the lid is slowly lifted in the tenth century revealing the end product. One thing is clear – the outcome is no more hanging in the balance.

What then do we see in the tenth century? What is the political scene? As far as the northeast region was concerned, the rulers of Anuradhapura had no control over it. As in the previous three centuries, south Indian rulers were sending their armies to this region with the aim of gaining a foothold there. In the tenth century, it was the turn of the Cōḷas to invade the island. Having supplanted the Pallavas and the Pāṇḍyas in south India, they directed their attention towards Sri Lanka.

The South Indian Background

The tenth and eleventh centuries constitute a period dominated by the Cōḷa dynasty. A lineage that had risen to prominence in the eastern part of Tamil Nadu as early as the third century BCE, it disappeared from the political scene in the early centuries of the Common Era. It took another six centuries before someone claiming descent from the ancient Cōḷas re-established the rule of the Cōḷa lineage in the region of Thanjavur. Vijayālaya was the ruler and the date was the middle of the ninth century. He started his career as a vassal of the Pallavas who were dominant in the northern part of Tamil Nadu known as Toṇḍaimaṇḍalam. A quarter of a century later, Vijayālaya's son, Āditya I (c. 871-907), defeated the Pallavas, annexed Toṇḍaimaṇḍalam and inaugurated the period of Cōḻa expansion. With the accession of his son Parāntaka I (907-955), the power of the Cōḻas was well and truly on the ascendant. During his long reign of nearly half a century, the Cōḻa monarch had to confront the might of the Rāṣṭrakūṭas in the north. In the south he had greater success in subjugating the Pāṇḍyas and the Cēras and securing the southern frontier.

Towards the end of Parāntaka's reign, the Raṣṭrakūṭas defeated the Cōḻas and conquered some of the northern regions of the latter's kingdom. For nearly three decades after Parāntaka's death, the Cōḻas struggled with weak successors until the accession of Rājarāja I in 985. Considered as the greatest of the Cōḻa rulers, Rājarāja conducted campaigns in almost every direction and expanded the area under Cōḻa rule. Very early in the reign, he broke the alliance of the three southern kingdoms – that of the Cēra, Pāṇḍya and Siṃhaḷa rulers. Interestingly, even the Maldive Islands to the southwest of Sri Lanka were included in Rājarāja's naval expeditions. It would appear that these southern campaigns had some commercial objectives as well. They may have been aimed at controlling the lucrative trade with West Asia. In the north Rājarāja fought with the Cāḷukyas who had succeeded the Rāṣṭrakūṭas in the Deccan.

The height of Cōḻa power was attained in the reign of Rājarāja's son and successor Rājendra I (1012-1044). A ruler who showed his prowess in successfully conducting major expeditions on land and sea, Rājendra made his influence felt beyond the borders of peninsular India – in the kingdoms up to the Ganges on the eastern seaboard and in the ports around the Bay of Bengal. Following the footsteps of his father, he appears to have been concerned about the overseas trade that brought considerable wealth to the Cōḻa state. In a possible bid to remove obstacles to this trade, especially with China, he sent a naval expedition, the like of which was not undertaken by any other Indian monarch, to some of the major ports of southeast Asia. The campaign appears to have been aimed at the Southeast Asian kingdom of Śrī Vijaya, although there is little evidence to determine the immediate causes. Romila Thapar is inclined to think that Rājendra was motivated by 'a desire to protect Indian commercial interests'. As a result of this campaign, 'Indian shipping and commerce were safe in their passage through Shrivijayan territory'.[1]

In the north, Rājendra's armies succeeded in annexing some of the southern regions of the Cāḷukya dominions. Perhaps the most notable military expedition conducted by Rājendra, unparalleled in the annals of south Indian history, was the march to the Ganges along the eastern seaboard. Bringing water from the Ganges as a symbol of his conquest of the north, he built a new city and named it Gaṅgaikoṇḍacōḻa-puram, the City of the Cōḻa who conquered the Ganges. These northern campaigns, however, did not result in any extension of the Cōḻa empire northwards. In the south the Cēra, Pāṇḍya and Siṃhaḷa kingdoms were subjugated and their rulers replaced by Cōḻa viceroys. Cōḻa power clearly reached its peak early in the eleventh century under Rājendra I.

After Rājendra, the Cōḻas faced opposition from the Cāḷukyas on their northern frontier. There were frequent conflicts between these two powers and by the time Cōḻa Kulōttuṅga I (1070-1120) ascended the throne the empire was shrinking. This provided the opportunity for the southern lineages to reassert themselves.

The developments in the economic, religious and cultural spheres in this period were also remarkable. The expansion of trade, both inland and overseas, led to the growth of powerful mercantile communities whose influence was felt not only everywhere in peninsular India but also in Sri Lanka, Southeast Asia and China. The major ports of the eastern coast, from Viśākapaṭṭiṉam in the north to the Pāṇḍya ports in the south, had well-organized mercantile establishments controlling the overseas trade with Sri Lanka and the east. Of special significance was the trade with China which reached new heights in this period. Across the Arabian Sea, the trade with Persia, Arabia and Egypt was also equally important.[2] The expansion of inland trade led to the growth of several urban centres. These were the exchange centres scattered all over south India, organized and administered as *paṭṭaṇam* or *nagaram* by mercantile communities.

Irrigation works

A major area of economic activity that has not received the importance it deserves is the building of irrigation facilities on an unprecedented scale. Such activity in Sri Lanka has been meticulously recorded in the chronicles, thus aiding to establish dates for the major irrigation works as well as to identify the rulers whose initiative helped to create these enormous reservoirs and canals. While the development of hydraulic technology and the building of huge reservoirs were equally magnificent in south India as in Sri Lanka, there are no chronicles or epigraphic records that document these activities. There is, however, the evidence of archaeology. And, of course, most of the major reservoirs are still in use. The eleventh and twelfth centuries once again saw the peak of this technological development, as in Sri Lanka, resulting in the creation of the largest human-made reservoir in the world until modern times. The second and third largest were in Sri Lanka.[3]

Architecture

This period of the imperial Cōḻas also saw unparalleled activity in temple-building. Not only was there an increase in the number of temples built, some of the new temples had enormous proportions. The most famous and the largest of them all, built by Rājarāja I, was the Rājarājeśvara Temple at Thanjavur. Still standing in the middle of a modern city and still in use for daily worship, this imposing structure has been described as 'the finest monument of a splendid period of South Indian history and the most beautiful specimen of Tamil architecture at its best'.[4] In this period, the temple was more than a place of religious worship and performed a number of functions. It had, in fact, evolved into a complex institution 'related not only to religious requirements but also to fiscal, political and cultural needs'.[5]

As one would expect in times of imperial splendour, this period of Cōḻa power witnessed the efflorescence of some of the fine arts of south India. Among these, sculpture, particularly the art of metal-casting, attained a great height resulting in some of the finest bronzes ever produced in South Asia. 'The Naṭarāja image in its various forms', as judged by Nilakanta Sastri, 'naturally holds the first place among the Cōḻa bronzes'.[6] Dance, music and drama were promoted through special endowments to temples. The Cōḻa temple, as Nilakanta Sastri sums up, 'was the centre of all the institutions of popular culture and amusement...Music and dancing, and theatrical presentations of popular tales and legends, formed part of the ordinary routine of the temple, and received special attention on festive occasions; and *Nāṭakaśālās* were specially constructed for these purposes'.[7] Special endowments were made for the maintenance of dancing masters, musicians and drummers as well as dancing girls (*tēvaraṭiyār*). The period of Cōḻa rule without doubt saw much of the development that led to the evolution of the south Indian music (*Karnāṭaka saṅgīta*) and dance (*Bharatanāṭya*) that have become two of the hallmarks of the civilization of the south.

Cōḻa Expansion into Sri Lanka

All the above developments in south India under the imperial Cōḻas had a direct impact on Sri Lanka and contributed to the strengthening of the Tamil element in the island. Since the northern part was annexed to the Cōḻa empire as one of its provinces (*maṇḍalam*) and kept under direct Cōḻa rule for well over half a century, there were long-term consequences for the Tamil language and the Saiva religion in the island. Some of the trends set in motion during the period of Cōḻa rule became irreversible even after the restoration of Sinhalese rule in the north.

The clash between the Cōḻas and the Anuradhapura rulers began in the reign of Cōḻa Parāntaka I (907-955). From the seventh century, as seen earlier, the rulers of Anuradhapura were drawn into the political conflicts in south India. Often they allied with the dynasties that were opposed to the dominant power there. First they supported the Pallavas against the Pāṇḍyas. Later when the Pāṇḍyas were the underdogs, they allied with them against the rising Cōḻas. When Parāntaka invaded the Pāṇḍya kingdom, the Pāṇḍya king Rājasiṃha was assisted by an army sent by the Anuradhapura ruler Kassapa V (913-923). Parāntaka was victorious in this war and the defeated Pāṇḍya ruler fled to Anuradhapura, taking with him his regalia. Parāntaka's invasion of Sri Lanka (referred to in Cōḻa inscriptions as Īḻam) must have taken place some time later, for we find him adopting the title '*Maturaiyum Īḻamum koṇṭa*' (Conqueror of Madurai and Īḻam) as early as 923.[8]

Parāntaka's claim of a victory in Sri Lanka has not been taken seriously by most Sri Lankan historians. The heavy reliance on the Pali chronicles would explain why anything not confirmed by these sources is not taken seriously. But the Pali chronicle, *Cūḷavaṃsa*, does refer to a Cōḻa invasion in the reign of Udaya IV (945-953) in which the Sinhalese commander was killed, forcing Udaya to seek refuge in Rohaṇa.[9] Although Anuradhapura was not occupied by the Cōḻas, it would appear that there was a Cōḻa presence in the northern or eastern part of the island.

Indeed the Cōḻa conquest of Sri Lanka was done in stages and never completed. The different stages reflected the successive phases in the expansion of Cōḻa power in peninsular India. The first Cōḻa invasion under Parāntaka I, about 923, seems to have resulted in only a small part of the island being brought under Cōḻa control. This part was probably the northeast and the north where conditions already were favourable for Cōḻa rule. The Anuradhapura ruler was not ousted and he continued to rule from his capital, albeit in a shaky position. According to the Pali chronicle, he was still anxious to help his Pāṇḍya ally to regain his kingdom but 'the nobles dwelling on the island for some reason or other stirred up a sorry strife to the undoing of the Paṇḍu king', as a consequence of which the disappointed Pāṇḍya king decided to go to Kerala.[10] The problem created by 'the nobles dwelling on the island' may have something to do with the areas under Cōḻa control.

The second stage of the Cōḻa conquest saw the defeat of the Anuradhapura ruler and his flight to Rohaṇa, in southern Sri Lanka. This was some time in the middle of the tenth century, towards the end of Parāntaka's reign. Although the whole island was not conquered, this invasion brought to an end the kingdom that had Anuradhapura as the power-centre for nearly 1300 years. On this count, it is a very significant event. The Cōḻas, however, were not going to rule from Anuradhapura. They had in all probability already created elsewhere the necessary administrative structure to control that part of the island that really mattered to them, namely the northern and eastern regions giving control of the major ports including Mātoṭa and Gokarṇa.

It is not known whether Polonnaruva was already functioning as the Cōḻa administrative centre in Parāntaka's reign. Possibly the centre was a place further east or north, either Padaviya or Kantalay. The earliest Tamil inscriptions of the Cōḻas have been found at Padaviya, and not at Polonnaruva. Possibly at this stage of Cōḻa rule, Polonnaruva was another Brāhmaṇa settlement for it had the name Jananātha-maṅgalam in the next stage of Cōḻa rule. The suffix –*maṅgalam* denotes a Brāhmaṇa settlement.[11] The Brāhmaṇa settlement and the earliest Saiva temples of this place may date back to a period before the Cōḻa invasion.

The next stage in the conquest of Sri Lanka came four decades later, in the reign of Rājarāja I (985-1014). The internal political problems following the death of Parāntaka I may have turned the attention of the Cōḻas away from Sri Lanka.[12] But at least one invasion was directed against the island a little before 965. The Pāṇḍyas were in alliance with the ruler of Anuradhapura at this time and the Cōḻa army, after a campaign in the Pāṇḍya kingdom, landed in the northern part of the island. The Cōḻa commander, Ciriyavēḷār, who led this expedition, fell fighting there.[13]

Rājarāja ascended the throne in 985 and soon afterwards launched a campaign of expansion that brought not only the whole of the Tamil-speaking regions of south India but also the Malayalam-speaking areas and some Kannada and Telugu territories under Cōḻa rule. But what were even more spectacular were the naval campaigns. In the course of these naval expeditions the Laccadive Islands and the Maldive Islands came under attack. About 992 Rājarāja's navy attacked Sri Lanka and the island was added to the growing list of Rājarāja's conquests.[14]

Even these campaigns of Rājarāja did not result in the entire island coming under Cōḻa control. The last king of Anuradhapura, Mahinda V, who had abandoned his capital in the time of Parāntaka, was still in Rohaṇa. The Cōḻas, for their part, did not show any interest in holding Anuradhapura. Evidently they were controlling the conquered areas, in the north and east, from a place that was more favourable to them. That Cōḻa administrative arrangements were in force in Sri Lanka in the time of Rājarāja is known from inscriptions in south India.[15] It is possible that the existing local administrative structure continued to be in use with a Cōḻa superstructure.

Rājarāja's conquest, though not marking the final stage of the Cōḻa conquest, clearly resulted in the annexation of the conquered part of the island to the Cōḻa empire and the recognition of it as one of the imperial provinces or *maṇḍalam.* Obviously Rājarāja was very proud of his conquest and gave his own name to the province, to some of the sub-divisions and to the new capital. The province was named Mummaḍi-Cōḻa-maṇḍalam. Mummaḍi-Cōḻa was one of his numerous titles. Following the Cōḻa administrative system, the province was divided into sub-divisions called *vaḷanāḍu.* Of the *vaḷanāḍus* in the island, the following are some known from inscriptions: Rājarāja-vaḷanāḍu, Arumoḻideva-vaḷanāḍu, Nikarili-cōḻa-vaḷanāḍu, Rājendra-siṅha-vaḷanāḍu, Vikrama-cōḻa-vaḷanāḍu, Abhayāśraya-vaḷanāḍu and Parakeśari-vaḷanāḍu. Except Parakeśari and Vikrama-Cōḻa, all the others are names or titles of Rājarāja. With Polonnaruva being named Jananātha-maṅgalam (also Jananāthapuram), it is possible that it became the administrative centre of the province. Jananātha was another of the titles of Rājarāja.[16]

As the Cōḻa monarch whose conquest made the greatest impact in the island, Rājarāja's name was everywhere. At least two temples were named after him. One was the Rājarājeśvara temple at Mātoṭa and the other was the Ravikula-māṇikka-īśvaram at Padaviya. A Buddhist establishment was named Rājarāja-perumpaḷḷi. A town was named Nittavinoda-puram. A Brāhmaṇa settlement was named Rājarāja-caturvedimaṅgalam and even a street was named Rājarāja-perunteru.[17]

The final stage of the conquest came in 1017. In that year Rājendra I (1012-1044), the son and successor of Rājarāja I, sent an expedition to the island. It was led by Mūvēnta-vēḷār, who had the very impressive and high sounding titles of 'Adhikāra Daṇḍanāyaka Jayaṅkoṇḍa Cōḻa'.[18] Judging from his title 'Jayaṅkoṇḍa Cōḻa', he seems to have been a member of the Cōḻa imperial family. Even in this final stage, the Cōḻas failed to bring the whole island under their control, although both Rājendra and Mūvēnta-vēḷār claim to have conquered the 'whole of Īḻam' (Sri Lanka).

Mūvēnta-vēḷār defeated the Sinhalese ruler Mahinda, who had taken refuge in Rohaṇa, and took him prisoner. The Cōḻa armies had evidently marched up to the southern extremity of the island. In this final victory, the Cōḻa general also succeeded in recovering the Pāṇḍya regalia which Varaguṇa Pāṇḍya had left in Sri Lanka in the reign of Parāntaka I. Having accomplished the twin purpose of capturing the Anuradhapura ruler and recovering the Pāṇḍya crown, Mūvēnta-vēḷār returned to the Cōḻa capital with his captives, Mahinda and his queens, as well as the Pāṇḍya regalia and other treasures.[19]

When he triumphantly returned to surrender his captives and the treasures to Rājendra, the emperor had new plans for him. A new system of provicial administration had been devised to hold together the rapidly expanding Cōḻa empire. According to this scheme, the emperor hand-picked the viceroys to govern the provinces (*maṇḍalam*), ceremoniously crowned them, conferred on them the respective titles that marked their official appointment and dispatched them to their respective provinces. They were to rule, for all practical purposes, like the local kings whom they replaced. They were given even new dynastic names that reflected this status. These names were the result of a novel idea of combining the dynastic name of the former local ruler and that of the emperor, namely 'Cōḻa'. Thus, the viceroy of the Pāṇḍya realm assumed the dynastic name of Cōḻa-Pāṇḍya while the one who was sent to Kerala received the name Cōḻa-Kēraḷa. These viceroys also had the right to use the consecration names of their local predecessors and to date their records in their own regnal years like independent rulers. Since loyalty to the emperor was of paramount importance for the viceroys, they were chosen from among the able members of the imperial family and not allowed to rule for life. When the emperor died they were recalled and re-appointed by the new emperor or relieved of their positions and others appointed in their places.

Under this new scheme, Sri Lanka, the new province of Mummaḍi-Cōḻa-maṇḍalam, was placed under a viceroy who carried the dynastic name of Cōḻa-Laṅkeśvara. Laṅkeśvara was the title that Sinhalese rulers used at Anuradhapura in the tenth century. Since the last Laṅkeśvara (Lord of Lanka), Mahinda V, bore the consecration name Śrī Saṅghabodhi, the first Cōḻa-Laṅkeśvara had to take the alternate consecration name Abhaya Salāmegha. From the inscriptional evidence that is now available, it is possible to reconstruct the following sequence of events immediately following the final conquest of Sri Lanka in 1017.[20] When Jayaṅkoṇḍa Cōḻa Mūvēnta-vēḷār returned to the Cōḻa capital after his victory in the island, Rājendra appointed him as the viceroy of the new province of Mummaḍicōḻa-maṇḍalam. The viceroy returned to the island, possibly arriving at Mātoṭa and invoking the blessings of the deity at the renowned temple of Kētīśvaram, where he left an inscription. He assumed the dynastic name of Cōḻa-Laṅkeśvara and the consecration name of Salāmegha. Jananātha-maṅgalam (Polonnaruva) became his capital with a slight name change, namely Jananātha-puram (the City of Jananātha) to mark its new status. Perhaps to mark his assumption of duties, a new Brāhmaṇa settlement was established or an old one was renamed Jayaṅkoṇḍa Salāmegha Caturvedimaṅgalam.

It is not known how long this Cōḻa-Laṅkeśvara ruled or how many other Cōḻa-Laṅkeśvaras were sent to govern the Cōḻa territories in Sri Lanka. A Laṅkeśvara was in the Cōḻa capital in 1019 making obeisance to the emperor, Rājendra I.[21] Whether the first Cōḻa-Laṅkeśvara returned to the capital in that year and made way for the appointment of another is not clear. However, it is known that Rājādhirāja I (1018-1054), who ruled jointly with Rājendra I and later succeeded him as the supreme ruler, appointed a prince to rule as Cōḻa-Laṅkeśvara.[22] A Cōḻa-Laṅkeśvara who ruled in Sri Lanka in the time of Rājādhirāja I had the consecration name Śrī Saṅghabodhi. He was probably the second Cōḻa-Laṅkeśvara, as the first one, as seen above, was not entitled to this consecration name. As a record dated in his tenth year has been found, he ruled for ten years or more. There was possibly a third Cōḻa-Laṅkeśvara with the consecration name Salāmegha, for we come across the name Vikrama Salāmegha in a record of the eleventh century.[23] The town named Vikrama-calāmēka-puram, the Siva temple of Vikrama-calāmēka-īśvaram and the community of soldiers who went by the name of Vikrama-calāmēka-terinta Valaṅkai Vēḷaikkārar were named apparently after this Cōḻa viceroy. Possibly, the administrative sub-division of Vikramacōḻa-vaḷanāḍu was also named after him.[24]

Going by the evidence of the Tamil inscriptions in Sri Lanka, the territories under the direct rule of the Cōḻas were confined to the northwestern, northern and eastern regions of the island. The central highlands and the southern part did not come under the administration of the Cōḻa viceroy and played a significant role not only in the campaigns to oust the Cōḻas but also in the survival of

Buddhism and the Sinhalese language in the island. From the time of the first Cōḻa invasion in the tenth century this region of Sri Lanka provided a safe haven for the disinherited rulers of Anuradhapura as well as for other opponents of the Cōḻas. Even the mightiest of the Cōḻa emperors could not subjugate this region. Consequently, it was from here that the Sinhalese leader, Vijayabāhu, was able to organize his campaign against the Cōḻas and capture power at Polonnaruva.

Although there was opposition to Cōḻa rule from the very beginning, resulting in much fighting for over a century, the battle was never taken into the Cōḻa-controlled territory until the final campaign of Vijayabāhu. The fighting was mainly to resist the attempts of the Cōḻas to control the south and flush out their opponents. These opponents were not a united force and were not only the disinherited Sinhalese princes. There were other Sinhalese leaders as well as princes who had fled from India, north and south, and sought refuge in the secure fastnesses of Rohaṇa. They included the Pāṇḍyas, the Keralas and even princes from Ayodhya and Kānyakubja.

In the areas north of Rohaṇa and the central highlands, the Cōḻas provided nearly a century of undisturbed Tamil rule and favourable conditions for the flowering of Saivism. It was a period in which the powerful south Indian mercantile communities and the influential south Indian Brāhmaṇas were able to help consolidate the position of the Tamil language and the Saiva religion, with state patronage, in the northwest, north and east. And when the end came for Cōḻa rule, not even the triumphant Vijayabāhu could reverse the process. We find him in a position in which he continued the patronage given to Saiva institutions and the Saiva Brāhmaṇas as well as to the south Indian mercantile communities and the military communities associated with them. While he no doubt was a great defender of Buddhism and took important steps to re-establish the Buddhist Sangha in the north, his own son and grandson, both of whom were among his successors, were not themselves Buddhists like him. They were clearly on the side of Saivism, revealing the extent to which this religion had become influential in the period of Cōḷa rule.

The strenuous efforts of Vijayabāhu may have successfully ended Cōḷa rule. But they came far too late to stem the tide of Saivism and Tamil, the twin forces that had begun their flow from the north and east with the rise of the Pallavas, about the seventh century. Buddhism could not withstand the impact of Saivism. The Heḷa language was on the retreat.

Significance of Cōḷa Rule

More than a century of Cōḷa influence and administration, from about the middle of the tenth century to 1070, put the final seal on the evolution of a separate ethnic identity with the twin markers of Saivism and Tamil. When Sinhalese rule was re-established in the north in 1070, it was a completely different scenario that presented itself to the new monarch from that which the last king of Anuradhapura had left behind when he fled to Rohaṇa. Buddhism had lost its pre-eminence. Siva temples were adorning every major urban centre and port. The Tamil language was in wide use in administration. South Indian mercantile communities were in full control of foreign trade and economic transactions in the market towns. Tamil, Telugu, Kerala and Kannada martial communities provided security in the capital city and to important religious institutions elsewhere. Tamil artisans and masons were busy in the urban centres. The return of Sinhalese rule only replaced the political superstructure at the apex.

Direct Cōḷa rule was confined to the areas that are covered by the present-day North-Western Province, Northern Province, North-Central Province and Eastern Province. With the centre of power at Jananāthapuram (Polonnaruva), they superimposed a political administration over the village structure that was functioning at the grass-roots level. At the head of this framework was the viceroy (Cōḷa-Laṅkeśvara) who, for all practical purposes, ruled like the former Sinhalese monarchs. His realm, which theoretically embraced the whole of Īlam or Sri Lanka, was one of the provinces (*maṇḍalam*) of the Cōḻa empire.

As in the case of the south Indian *maṇḍalams*, this was divided into *vaḷanāḍus*, *nāḍus* and villages. The nature of local rule, which helped villages to continue without disruption even in times of political conflict and dynastic changes, was strengthened by the Cōḻa system of local government. There is evidence that the efficient system of village government that prevailed in the Cōḻa kingdom was in vogue in Sri Lanka under Cōḻa rule. It was through this village government that the irrigation works were maintained. The end of Cōḻa rule saw only the removal of the superstructure. The system of village government no doubt continued as before.

Cōḻa rule also strengthened the Brāhmaṇa settlements (*caturvedi-maṅgalam*) in the conquered areas and increased their influence significantly. Jananātha-maṅgalam, one of the leading Brāhmaṇa villages at the beginning of Cōḻa rule, was chosen as the capital of the Cōḻa province and soon became an urban centre with the name Jananātha-puram (City of Jananātha). Kantalay was another important Brāhmaṇa village and had the name Rājarāja-caturvedi-maṅgalam. There were other Brāhmaṇa settlements, such as the Jayaṅkoṇṭacōḻa-caturvedi-maṅgalam and Nittavinodapuram, in other parts of the north.[25] These Brāhmaṇa villages were centres of Saivism with important Siva temples. These centres helped the growth of Saivism and the influence of the Tamil language in the period of Cōḻa rule.

The growth of Saivism hastened the decline of Buddhism in the north and east, particularly among the Tamils. There were still some Tamil Buddhist establishments (*paḷḷi*) in the east and possibly in the Jaffna peninsula. The best known establishment was Velgam Vehera, which was renamed Rājarāja-perumpaḷḷi, after the Cōḻa emperor. Another was the Vikkirama-calāmēkaṉ-perumpaḷḷi. Possibly, these were Mahayana Buddhist establishments. There was no proper Theravada Buddhist Sangha to provide leadership to the Buddhists

PLATE 16.

Ruins of the Rajaraja-perumpalli – Image House. 'The base mouldings of this Tamil *vihara*, in their details, differ from those of the Buddhist edifices at Anuradhapura and Polonnaruva. They are similar to the mouldings of the Hindu shrines built by the Cholas at Polonnaruva' (Prof. S. Paranavitana).

***Photo:** March 2005, by the author. Courtesy: Department of Archaeology.*

PLATE 17.
Ruins of the Rajaraja-perumpalli.
Photo: *March 2005, by the author. Courtesy: Department of Archaeology.*

and, when Cōḷa rule ended, Vijayabāhu had to send for Buddhist monks from Rāmañña (Burma) in order to purify the Sinhalese Sangha and set it on a proper footing.

Mercantile communities

The growth of Cōḷa political power in the island was paralleled by the increase in the activities of the south Indian mercantile communities. Recent studies on these communities have thrown much light on their activities. Despite the availability of a large number of comparatively lengthy stone records left by them, these communities continue to be among the most intriguing groups whose origin, composition and multifarious activities pose many questions that are difficult to answer. Unlike the stone inscriptions of kings, village assemblies and religious institutions which constitute the bulk of the epigraphic records of south India and Sri Lanka, the inscriptions of the mercantile communities are rarely dated, hardly mention a local ruler and woefully lack in details about their internal organization. The dating of these records is often based on palaeography and is not always quite satisfactory. There is even a confusion of names, as more than one name seems to have been used by the same organization.

Despite these shortcomings, the records of the mercantile communities are extremely useful sources of information for the historian. As seen earlier, in the time of the Pallavas south India and Sri Lanka participated in an extensive commerce that resulted in close relations with West Asia, Southeast Asia and China. With the rise of the sea-oriented empire of the Cōḷas in the tenth century, this commerce as well as south India's relations with other Asian empires developed further.[26]

Unlike in contemporary China, trade was not a royal monopoly in the Cōḷa empire. It was purely a private enterprise. But the nature and volume of the trade, both internal and foreign, that developed in South Asia in this period demanded co-operation among merchants on a bigger scale than there had been before. And so we find in the tenth century the emergence of very complex organized mercantile communities, often described as guilds after their European counterparts, whose strength grew almost parallel to the expansion of Cōḻa power. Indeed it would appear that the Cōḻa flag followed the merchant fleets of these communities.

Among the more powerful mercantile communities were the Aiññūṟṟuvar (also called the Ayyāvoḷe, Ticai-āyirattu-Aiññūṟṟuvar, Nānādeśi and Vīra-valañciyar). The details relating to their composition and organization are so complex in the various records belonging to them that it is extremely difficult to comprehend the nature of their structure. The most recent attempt to understand the organization of these merchants tentatively concludes that 'the *ainūṟṟuvar*, otherwise known as *padineṇ-vishayam/padineṇ-bhūmi* or *nānādesi*, is a concept of the merchant organization which overarches all the substantial merchant organizations formed in some particular area, locality or town'.[27] Since the name Aiññūṟṟuvar is always associated with a large number of mercantile, military and professional groups, it seems to have been applied to a loose umbrella organization of all those groups in a particular locality.[28]

The Aiññūṟṟuvar and their associates dominated the internal and external trade of the island. They controlled key market towns and established their *eṟivīra-paṭṭiṉam* in the major urban centres. Their records as well as other records mentioning them have been found in Polonnaruva, Anuradhapura, Padaviya, Vahalkada, Viharehinna and Budumuttava which were all major urban centres in the eleventh and twelfth centuries. They brought under their wing various ethnic groups of south Indian origin, such as the Telugus, Keralas and the Kannadas, but used only the Tamil language in their records.[29] A section of the Aiññūṟṟuvar, who were well established in Sri Lanka and whose base was therefore in the island, called themselves Ten-Ilaṅkai Valañciyar (the Valañciyar of Lanka in the South) when they were engaged in activities in south India.[30]

Of the mercantile communities that can be identified as distinct from the Aiññūṟṟuvar are two who had their roots in Kerala, namely the Maṇigrāmam and the Añjuvaṇṇam. It would appear that the activities of these two in the period of Cōḻa rule were completely overshadowed by the Aiññūṟṟuvar. However, in the present state of our knowledge, the Maṇigrāmam were active in Sri Lanka even before Cōḻa rule. Although no record of the Añjuvaṇṇam has come to light anywhere in Sri Lanka, there are records in Andhra that refer to the Añjuvaṇṇam who were established in Mātoṭa.

The Maṇigrāmam, as seen earlier, were active in Sri Lanka possibly as early as the ninth century. While a considerable number of inscriptions relating to the Aiññūṟṟuvar have been discovered, none belonging to the Maṇigrāmam has come to light. As a consequence of the predominant position occupied by the Aiññūṟṟuvar, it would appear that the activities of the other south Indian mercantile communities were not widespread. This would apply to the Añjuvaṇṇam, too.

The Añjuvaṇṇam was a community of merchants of West Asian origin. They seem to have been of Persian and Arab descent and may have included both Muslims and Jews. The settlements of these West Asian seafarers appear to have led to the emergence of the Añjuvaṇṇam, a name apparently derived from the Persian *hanjamana*. By the ninth century Añjuvaṇṇam settlements were found in the ports of the west and east coasts of south India. The expansion of the activities of the Añjuvaṇṇam no doubt included the ports of Sri Lanka and it is possible that there were Añjuvaṇṇam settlements there as early as the ninth century. These may have formed the nuclei of the Tamil-speaking Muslim settlements of the west and east coasts of Sri Lanka. The only evidence we have about their presence in a Sri Lankan port in the eleventh century comes from Andhra in south India. Inscriptions from the port of Visakhapatnam refer to an Añjuvaṇṇam settlement at Mātoṭa.[31]

However, there is evidence to suggest that the Añjuvaṇṇam and the Maṇigrāmam, along with the Aiññūṟṟuvar, were active in South Asia until as late as the end of the thirteenth century. As they are known to have been engaged in various pursuits in the southern parts of the Tamil region of south India, in close proximity to the ports on the western and eastern coats of Sri Lanka, their presence in the island in the same period can be reasonably assumed. Supporting this assumption is the interesting evidence from south India about a joint meeting of the Tennilaṅkai Valañciyar (the Valañciyar of Lanka in the South) with the Añjuvaṇṇam and the Maṇigrāmam to deliberate on a charitable donation.[32] Though the Aiññūṟṟuvar were clearly dominating the scene in Sri Lanka, there was probably no serious rivalry or competition between them and the other mercantile communities.

The exclusive use of Tamil (apart from the Sanskrit preamble) in the records of the Aiññūṟṟuvar in Sri Lanka shows the dominance of the Tamil-speakers in this merchant community and also indicates that their activities were largely among the Tamil-speaking population. The *eṟivīra-paṭṭaṇams* established by them were also in predominantly Tamil-speaking areas. As it is known that there were Telugu, Kannada and Kerala elements associated with the Aiññūṟṟuvar, one can safely assume that these elements also used Tamil. One can see here a clear instance of the manner in which various south Indian elements contributed to the evolution of the Tamil ethnic identity in ancient Sri Lanka. As will be seen later, various elements of the warrior communities also made a similar contribution. Tamil became the major language of foreign trade in the ports of Sri Lanka. In the twelfth century, Parākramabāhu I used Tamil in his edict relating to foreign trade set up in the northern port of Ūṟātturai while the record of Chinese traders in the southern port of Galle, dated 1410, was in Tamil, Chinese and Persian.

Warrior communities

South Indian warrior communities were present in Sri Lanka in notable numbers from about the seventh century. As seen earlier, there are several recorded instances of princes and political aspirants from the island going over to south India and bringing armies to fight for their claims. The growth of commerce and the establishment of new market towns in several parts of the country were other factors that introduced more members of the warrior communities from south India. Further, the political instability of the period after the seventh century seems to have led to the employment of soldiers to protect religious establishments for which mercantile communities accepted custodianship. In the period of Cōḻa rule, there is evidence for the conspicuous presence of south Indian warrior communities in the urban centres.

Indisputably the most important south Indian warrior community in Sri Lanka in the eleventh century was that generally known as the Vēḷaikkārar. Like many other communities given to martial pursuits, they were associated with the powerful mercantile communities, especially the Aiññūṟṟuvar. They enjoyed a very high reputation for their loyalty and were given custody of important religious institutions, including the Temple of the Tooth Relic. There is hardly any evidence of other warrior communities being custodians of institutions.[33]

Among the other warrior communites, the most notable is the Vīrakoṭiyar. This community is sometimes referred to as the Patiṉeṇ-pūmi Vīrakoṭiyar.[34] Another community that is often associated with the protection of urban centres is the Eṟivīrar (sometimes referred to as as the Patiṉeṇ-pūmi Vīrar).[35] Two others referred to in the epigraphic records are the Aṅkakkārar and the Karuṇākara-vīrar. Aṅkakkārar may be only another term for *meykāppar* (bodyguards) rather than the name of another community of warriors.[36]

Another group of warriors of south Indian origin was the Akampaṭiyar (Agampaḍi). These warriors seem to have originated as bodyguards in the inner apartments of the royal palace and later evolved into a military caste. They are referred to in inscriptions as well as in Sinhalese literary sources.[37]

Masons and artisans

A group of Tamil origin whose migration has found no mention in the inscriptions or chronicles is that of the skilled masons and artisans. The building and renovation of the Saiva temples would not have been possible without significant numbers of artisans skilled in the Cōḻa style of architecture in which these temples were constructed. All the Saiva and Vaisnava shrines, as seen from their remains, were built in the architectural style prevailing in Tamil Nadu. Even the Tamil Buddhist monasteries were built in this style, as is evidenced by the remains of the Rājarāja-perumpaḷḷi at Periyakulam. As Paranavitana has remarked, this monastery in ruins is 'interesting as the only known example of a Tamil Buddhist paḷḷi preserved even in ruins up to our day'.[38]

Conclusion

The mercantile communities and the warrior communities contributed in a very significant way to the strengthening of the Tamil element in the northern, northwestern and eastern regions of Sri Lanka. The dominance and the increased activity of the mercantile communities under Cōḻa rule resulted in the arrival of merchants and soldiers as well as artisans from different parts of south India. They included persons from the Telugu, Kannada and Kerala regions, but predominantly from the Tamil region. The different ethnic groups were eventually assimilated into the Tamil or Sinhalese populations. But most of them were active in the areas that were already populated by Tamil-speakers and were consequently absorbed into the Tamil population. Cōḻa rule thus helped to consolidate the results of the process of Tamilisation that had been going on for over a thousand years and make this process irreversible. As a result, when Cōḻa rule ended, the victorious Sinhalese leader Vijayabāhu had to acquiesce with the status quo.

Undeniably the period of Cōḻa rule saw Tamil and Saivism gain complete dominance in the northwest, north and east. The archaeological evidence is clear in this respect. The ruins of a considerable number of Saiva and Vaishnava temples, with Cōḻa architectural features and stone inscriptions in Tamil, have come to light in various places. Most of these sites have not been excavated or subjected to intensive study. But what has been gained from these sites provides sufficient evidence of the dominance achieved by Tamil and Saivism in the northern half of the island in the eleventh century.

CHAPTER 8

THE FINAL PHASE

1070 - 1200

SINHALA AND TAMIL

The Joint Achievers

The resumption of Sinhalese rule in the former kingdom of the Anuradhapura monarchs was no doubt a victory for Vijayabāhu but not for the Heḷa language or Theravada Buddhism. The coronation ceremony that Vijayabāhu held in Anuṛadhapura, the great centre of Theravada Buddhism for over a millennium, was only symbolic. The glory of that ancient city had well and truly ended. The reality was that the new Sinhalese king had to rule from what was a Tamil city for nearly three-quarters of a century, a city where there was no major Theravada institution. For a brief period amounting to a little over a century, this city was to reflect the new reality in the island, and show to the outside world a splendour born out of the union of two great South Asian cultures.

The conditions for a successful, though short-lived, partnership between the two cultures, the Tamil and the Sinhalese, were laid under Cōḷa rule. Vijayabāhu's campaign was clearly against the Cōḷa rulers and not against the Tamils or other ethnic groups. Tamil soldiers fought on his side. After his triumph, he was as good a patron of the Brāhmaṇas, Saivism and Tamil as the Cōḷa viceroys were. Tamil soldiers, clerks and artisans continued to be in royal service under him. Strengthening the Tamil element further in politics, he even contracted matrimonial alliances with Tamil royal families. No action taken by him was directed at weakening the Tamil forces in the heart of the new kingdom which came to be known as the Rajaraṭa (King's Country).

In his wars against the Cōḻas, Vijayabāhu is known to have used at least one division of the army commanded by a Tamil. In a Cōḻa record dated 1067, a personality named Kurukulattaraiyan̲ is mentioned as one of the commanders who fought on the side of Vijayabāhu against Cōḻa Vīrarājendra's forces and fell in battle. What is of even greater interest (reminiscent of the battle between Duṭṭhagāmaṇī and Eḷāra more than a millennium earlier), according to the Pali chronicle, two Sinhalese chiefs, Ravideva and Cala, deserted Vijayabāhu and went over with their men to the side of the Cōḻa forces. Any attempt to make the campaigns of Vijayabāhu appear as a surge of Sinhalese liberation forces against the Tamil Cōḻas would be seen as groundless. The Cōḻas faced as much opposition from Tamil and other south Indian elements in the Tamil land as the forces of Vijayabāhu faced from Sinhalese elements in southern Sri Lanka. In fact, even after defeating the Cōḻas and establishing his authority at Polonnaruva, Vijayabāhu faced several rebellions and revolts led by Sinhalese leaders some of whom went to south India to get support. There was nothing racial in these political conflicts. Vijayabāhu's own sister was given in marriage to a Pāṇḍya prince. What is of greater interest is that the son of this sister, Vijayabāhu's nephew, was later married to a daughter of Cōḻa Kulottuṅga I, the Cōḻa ruler from whom Vijayabāhu wrested the Sri Lankan kingdom.

It is therefore not surprising that the reign of Vijayabāhu ushered in a period of remarkable partnership between the Sinhalese and the Tamils in the island. Beginning with religion, every sphere of activity in which Vijayabāhu was engaged reflected this harmonious relationship. The new Sinhalese ruler was without doubt a champion of Buddhism. That is not to say that he was an opponent of Saivism. By his time, the antagonism between these two religions had died down. With the dominance achieved by Saivism under the Cōḻas, it appears that eclectic tendencies were on the rise. We know that Vijayabāhu devoted much attention to the construction of major Buddhist structures and the renovation of several Buddhist shrines in the capital and elsewhere. It is not known whether he built any Saiva temples. But there is evidence that at least one Saiva shrine was renamed after him. This was the Vijayarāja-īśvaram at Kantalay which presumably was named earlier after a Cōḻa monarch. The Brāhmaṇa settlement of Kantalay, which earlier had the name Rājarāja-caturvedi-maṅgalam (after Rājarāja I), was also renamed Vijayarāja-caturvedi-maṅgalam. This provides testimony to the king's patronage of the Brāhmaṇas. Considering the practices in the courts of the Sinhalese rulers at Polonnaruva, there is room to surmise that Vijayabāhu had Brāhmaṇas at his court to perform various Brahmanical rituals.

End of Cōḻa Rule

It is generally agreed that Cōḻa rule in Sri Lanka came to an end in 1070. Of the Tamil inscriptions in the island dated in the regnal years of Cōḻa monarchs, the latest is dated in the third year of Adhirājendra (1070).[1] Until then the Cōḻas were in firm control of the northern half of the island. But they could never subjugate the south. This region, as mentioned earlier, was not merely a safe haven for Sinhalese leaders to organize their armies for ousting the Cōḻas, but, what is more interesting, it also provided sanctuary to various dispossessed princes from India. The armies of the Cōḻa viceroy fought these princes with little success. Among these princes were two members of the Pāṇḍya family and at least one prince from north India. Any description of these conflicts as wars between the Tamils and the Sinhalese would be seen as groundless. The Cōḻa imperial forces had to contend with Tamil opposition in the Pāṇḍya territory in the same way as they had to fight Pāṇḍya as well as Sinhala rulers who controlled southern Sri Lanka.[2]

Vijayabāhu was the most successful of these rulers in southern Sri Lanka. Eliminating all rivals, he gained control of the southern region in 1055 or 1056 but had to face Cōḻa opposition almost immediately. For nearly a decade he was in no position to fight the Cōḻas. The developments in south India after 1063, the year Cōḻa Rājendra II died, offered an opportunity to Vijayabāhu to attempt an attack on Cōḻa power in the north. Vīrarājendra I who succeeded

Rājendra II had to face serious opposition from the Western Cāḷukyas in the northern frontier of the Cōḷa empire and was in no position to protect the Cōḷa possessions in the south.

As Vijayabāhu kept up the pressure on the Cōḷa forces in the island, Vīrarājendra sent reinforcements to Polonnaruva. In the battles that ensued, two powerful Sinhalese chiefs, Ravideva and Cala, crossed over with their men from Vijayabāhu's side to the Cōḷa commander.[3] Vijayabāhu, however, was able to regroup and take control of Polonnaruva about 1067. But the Cōḷas were not prepared to give up easily. Fresh forces were despatched to the island and Vijayabāhu was compelled to abandon Polonnaruva. One of Vijayabāhu's Tamil commanders, Kurukulattaraiyan̲, fell in battle.[4] But worse still, a Sinhalese chief in the south rose against Vijayabāhu and went over to the Cōḷa-held territory. Such was the plight of Vijayabāhu. In Paranavitana's lamenting words, 'Not only had he to face the military might of a great empire with very little more than his own courage and determination, but also, on more than one occasion, when it appeared that he was on the road to success, his own people proved false to him and he had to start all over again'.[5] Once again, it is seen how there is no room for interpreting the war against the Cōḷas as a Sinhalese-Tamil conflict.

After 1067, Vīrarājendra was too preoccupied with his encounters against the Western Cāḷukyas to send any further reinforcements to aid the Cōḷa viceroy in Sri Lanka. He died in 1070 and was succeeded by Kulottuṅga I whose most pressing task was to defend the Cōḷa territories against the inroads of the Western Cāḷukyas. All this meant that the defence of Sri Lanka was given a low priority enabling Vijayabāhu to seize the opportunity and march against the isolated Cōḷa forces in the north. The result was the conquest of Anuradhapura and Polonnaruva and the end of Cōḷa rule in the island.[6]

Sinhalese Rule at Polonnaruva

The return of Sinhalese rule to the old kingdom of the Anuradhapura monarchs marked an important and interesting stage in the history of Sinhalese-Tamil relations in the island. For the next century and a half Sri Lanka was to witness an unprecedented partnership between the two ethnic groups in practically all areas of activity. In dynastic affairs there never was such close matrimonial alliances between Sinhalese and Tamil royal families as in this period. In administration, military organization, commercial activity, hydraulic works, religion and the arts there was an admirable partnership between the two groups that has often been overlooked. The result was a glorious period of Sri Lankan history, uninspiringly styled the Polonnaruva Period, which saw the flowering of a truly great Sri Lankan civilization.

From the very beginning of Vijayabāhu's reign there was no show of animosity towards the Tamils by the Sinhalese monarch. It was not just a unilateral phenomenon, for his Cōḻa contemporary, Kulottuṅga I, was equally free of any feeling of enmity towards the Sinhalese ruler, although the Pali chronicle would have us believe that he continued hostile activities against Vijayabāhu. In fact, the Cōḻa ruler had asked for Vijayabāhu's sister in marriage. For some reason Vijayabāhu was not keen on establishing such a close matrimonial alliance with the Cōḻa family and, instead, preferred to give his sister in marriage to another Tamil, a Pāṇḍya prince.[7] This Tamil prince was to become the grandfather of Parākramabāhu I, traditionally hailed as the greatest of the Sinhalese kings. Kulottuṅga, however, did not give up his efforts to forge an alliance with the Sinhalese ruling family. We find that at a later date he gave one of his own daughters, Cuttamalli Āḻvār, in marriage to a Sinhalese prince (identified as one of Vijayabāhu's nephews).[8]

Vijayabāhu's policy of having a closer alliance with the Pāṇḍya family than with the Cōḻa family had its own adverse consequences in the politics of the kingdom. The Pāṇḍyas, who were allied to the Sinhalese rulers against the Cōḻas from the tenth century, already enjoyed considerable influence in Sri Lanka in the period of Cōḻa rule. At least two Pāṇḍya princes were accepted as rulers in the territories outside Cōḷa control.[9] The policy of Vijayabāhu, while it may have helped keep the Cōḷas in check, doubtless increased Pāṇḍya influence in the affairs of the kingdom. A strong political group, usually referred to as the Pāṇḍya faction, emerged at Polonnaruva after the death of Vijayabāhu and exerted considerable influence in the affairs of the kingdom. This faction often succeeded in placing its members or Pāṇḍya princes from south India on the throne at Polonnaruva. Its influence continued even after the fall of Polonnaruva.

It would appear that Vijayabāhu retained the administrative structure of the Cōḷas and made significant changes only at the top. There is little information on this point. The reference to a register of Tamil clerks (*Demaḷa lesdaru pota*) in Vijayabāhu's Panakaduva Copper Plate inscription points to his employment of Tamil officers in the adminsistration. Possibly many of them continued in service from the time of Cōḷa rule.[10]

Perhaps the combination of Sinhalese and Tamil (including other south Indian) elements was reflected more in the military organization of the new ruler than in any other area. Indeed it seems that Vijayabāhu depended more on Tamil troops than on Sinhalese soldiers. This is understandable in view of the opposition he faced from some Sinhalese chiefs in the early years of his reign. But he may have made a miscalculation in relying too much on the Tamil forces in his battles against the Cōḷas, if we accept the evidence in the Pali chronicle.[11]

Religion

Vijayabāhu's reign also marked the beginning of a new eclecticism in religion. While eclectic tendencies have always been a feature of Sri Lankan religions, the eleventh and twelfth centuries saw a marked increase in mixed Buddhist, Brahmanical and Saiva practices at the elite level. Emulating the contemporary practice at the Indian, particularly southern, royal courts, Vijayabāhu as well as his successors at Polonnaruva encouraged elaborate Brahmanical rituals. Royal patronage of the Brāhmaṇas was naturally followed by endowments to Brahmanical institutions. The desire to establish matrimonial alliances with non-Buddhist royal families in India resulted in the presence of influential non-Buddhist queens at Polonnaruva. These queens not only encouraged elaborate Brahmanical rituals in the court but also influenced the religious life of young princes who later ascended the throne with less attachment to Buddhism than that of earlier rulers.

This trend is clearly seen from the reign of Vijayabāhu I. Both his queens Līlāvatī (a princess from Oudh) and Trilokasundarī (a princess from Kaliṅga) were from a non-Buddhist background. The latter presumably was the more influential of the two. The author of the Pali chronicle, *Cūḷavaṃsa*, minces no words in accusing her of anti-Buddhist activities. Her son, Vikramabāhu, who later succeeded to the throne, was without doubt influenced by her religious leanings. After a lengthy analysis of the literary and inscriptional evidence relating to this prince, Sirima Kiribamune has concluded that it is fairly clear Vikramabāhu was not a Buddhist.[12] He married a non-Buddhist princess and his son, Gajabāhu, was without doubt, as will be seen later, a follower of Saivism.

Even the rulers of Polonnaruva who are known as better supporters of Buddhism not only patronized Saivism but practised Brahmanical rituals in their private and public lives. The *Cūḷavaṃsa* provides an insight into court Brahmanical practices at Polonnaruva as well as in the regional capitals.[13] The inscriptions give information about elaborate Brahmanical ceremonies performed in public.[14] In the end, we see the last rulers of Polonnaruva openly professing Saivism and adopting an anti-Buddhist policy. They brought to an end a policy that saw both Buddhism and Saivism flourishing harmoniously unlike in any other period.

Vijayabāhu himself is not known to have practised Brahmanical rituals. But with two queens who had come from royal families in India, Brahmanical rites would have been introduced to his palace and court. The fact that one of the leading Brāhmaṇa settlements in the island was renamed after him (Vijayarāja-caturvedi-maṅgalam) and a temple there was also renamed after him (Vijayarāja-īśvaram) would indicate that Vijayabāhu was closely associated with Saiva institutions and patronized Brāhmaṇas.[15] When this king died in 1110, his younger brother Jayabāhu was elevated to the throne through a palace intrigue but he was able to rule in Polonnaruva only for a few months. Nothing is known about his support for Saivism.

Jayabāhu was ousted by Vikramabāhu, the son of Vijayabāhu by his queen from Kalinga. The new ruler was a devoted Śiva worshipper. The extraordinary Sanskrit epithet *Pārvatī-pati dattāsīr-vīra-mahā-vrṣa* (= the heroic great bull who has been given the blessings of the husband of Pārvatī) assumed by him in one of his inscriptions puts this matter beyond doubt.[16] He has no epithets in these inscriptions indicating his association with Buddhism. In fact, the Pali chronicle gives many details of his anti-Buddhist activities saying that he behaved like a heretic.[17]

Vikramabāhu's son Gajabāhu who succeeded his father to the Polonnaruva throne was clearly a devotee of Śiva. We have Pali, Sinhalese and Tamil sources, both literary and epigraphic, that provide evidence to establish this. He performed Brahmanical sacrifices, worshipped at the Saiva shrine of Kōṇēsvaram in Trincomalee and spent his last days in the Brāhmaṇa settlement at Kantalay. But, unlike his father, he patronized Buddhist institutions as well.[18]

Gajabāhu's successor, Parākramabāhu, was unquestionably one of the outstanding patrons of Buddhism in this period. But this does not mean that he was not supportive of the Saiva religion. The fact that Brāhmaṇas played an important role in the court rituals relating to various stages of the life of Parākramabāhu as a prince indicates that he was associated with non-Buddhist religious practices. Although no direct evidence of his patronage of Saiva institutions has come to light, there is no reason to believe that he did not extend support to Saivism.[19]

Sinhalese rule at Polonnaruva may be said to have come to an end with Parākramabāhu. In fact, of all the rulers of Polonnaruva, only the first two, Vijayabāhu I and his brother Jayabāhu (who ruled only for about a year), were descended from Sinhalese families on both the paternal and maternal sides. Parākramabāhu himself was the grandson of a Tamil prince and almost all his successors were from Kalinga. The two exceptions were Līlāvatī, a granddaughter of a Pāṇḍya prince, and Parākrama Pāṇḍya, a Tamil prince. All of them, it appears, patronized both Buddhism and Saivism, except the last one Māgha, who is described in the chronicles as an anti-Buddhist.

Of the successors of Parākramabāhu I, Niśśaṅka Malla (1187-1196) is better known for his patronage of Buddhism than any of the others. Although the Pali chronicle does not devote much attention to his reign, his numerous and elaborate epigraphic records help to gain some knowledge of his benefactions to Buddhist and Saiva institutions. A very colourful and boastful personality in Sri Lankan history, Niśśaṅka Malla issued epigraphic records that in fact constitute 'the largest number of inscriptions credited to any single monarch of the Island.'[20] Most of these records have a lengthy historical introduction (*praśasti*), following the practice of south Indian kings. It is in this introduction that Niśśaṅka Malla details his religious services in a bragging tone.

Like most ambitious political leaders with some element of foreign ancestry and/or a different religious heritage from the one they embraced for political or other reasons, Niśśaṅka Malla took strenuous efforts to present himself as a great defender of the religion he adopted. He went to great lengths to prove himself to be a better king of the Sinhalese than any Sinhạlese ruler and a greater Buddhist patron than other Buddhist rulers before him. Often emphasizing that he belonged to the dynasty of Vijaya, the legendary founder of the Sinhalese ruling family, he declared himself to be the lord of Lanka 'by right of descent' (*parapuren himi*).[21] Though himself a foreigner, he urged his subjects not to choose Cōḷas, Keraḷas or Pāṇḍyas as their rulers because they were non-Buddhists.

Though Niśśaṅka Malla was opposed to non-Buddhist aspirants to the throne, he was by no means an enemy of Saivism. If we are to believe his boasts, his numerous benefactions included lavish gifts to Buddhist monks as well as Brāhmaṇas. Among the many alms-houses he established were the Brāhmaṇa-satra at Polonnaruva and another at the south Indian Saiva temple of Rāmeśvaram.[22] An inscription of Niśśaṅka Malla at this famous Saiva site refers to his activities there. The Brāhmaṇa settlement at Kantalay received his patronage.[23] There he visited the Pārvatī-satra (an alms-house named after the Saiva goddess Pārvatī or, more likely, after Niśśaṅka Malla's mother whose name was Pārvatī Mahādevī), witnessed the distribution of alms and watched dancing and singing. On at least one occasion, he performed a Brahmanical ritual, the *navagraha-śānti* (propitiation of the nine planetary gods). Although we have no information of his building a Saiva temple, an old temple in the Pāṇḍya kingdom was repaired by him (during one of his invasions) and renamed Niśśaṅkeśvara, after his own name.[24] One thing is clear from all these claims – Niśśaṅka Malla was a patron of both Buddhism and Saivism.

By 1200, the partnership in religion, between Saivism and Buddhism, had almost come to an end. With the death of Niśśaṅka Malla, a period of political confusion and instability followed. Almost all the rulers at Polonnaruva for the next few years, until the fall of that great city in 1215, were foreigners but were supporters of Buddhism.[25] After Niśśaṅka Malla, there was a rapid change of rulers and within a few years the glory of Polonnaruva came to an end. Both Buddhism and Saivism suffered in the chaotic conditions of the early decades of the thirteenth century. The eleventh and twelfth centuries thus stand out as a period of very close relations between the two major religions – Buddhism and Saivism.

Relations between Tamil Buddhism and Sinhalese Buddhism

This period constitutes another interesting chapter in the history of the very close relations that had existed between Tamil Buddhism and Sinhalese Buddhism for over a thousand years. After the religious conflicts of the 6th-10th centuries, at the beginning of the eleventh century, when Vaisnavism and Saivism had triumphed over the other religions, south India entered a period of religious peace. The religious policy of the Cōḻa emperors indeed helped Buddhism to recuperate. Both Theravada and Mahayana continued to maintain their hold in some of the earlier centres of Buddhism. Though considerably reduced in numbers, Tamil Buddhists formed a significant community in some parts of Tamil Nadu and in Sri Lanka. The close relations with Sri Lanka and the presence of Tamil Buddhist establishments in the island seem to have been a source of inspiration to the Tamil Buddhists on the mainland. In addition, the very friendly relations of the Cōḻa emperors with the Buddhist Śailendra rulers of Sri Vijaya, in Southeast Asia, undoubtedly helped to foster certain centres of Mahayana Buddhism, like Nāgapaṭṭiṉam, in Tamil Nadu. Unfortunately, not much evidence of this chapter of Buddhism has survived in Tamil Nadu itself.[26]

It is from the historical sources preserved in Burma and Sri Lanka that we get useful information about the Tamil Buddhists of this period and later. The evidence preserved in the Pali chronicles and commentaries in Sri Lanka is worthy of special mention in this respect. If not for this body of Pali literature, one would not have known that Buddhism was very much alive among the Tamils in the period after the tenth century and that the Tamil Buddhist Sangha, particularly of the Cōḻa kingdom, played an active role in the Buddhist world of that time.[27]

The Pali Buddhist writings of the eleventh, twelfth and thirteenth centuries leave one in no doubt that the Buddhist Sangha continued to be active, even after the triumph of Saivism, in the three Tamil territories of south India, namely the Cōḻa, Pāṇḍya and Toṇḍai-maṇḍalam (former Pallava) regions. In the Pāṇḍya kingdom, there were feudatory rulers who patronized Buddhism. Kanchi, in Toṇḍai-maṇḍalam, continued to be a centre of Theravada Buddhism. There were centres of Theravada and Mahayana Buddhism in the Cōḻa kingdom. What is most interesting is that the Theravada Sangha of the Cōḻa kingdom in particular emerged into prominence with renewed vigour and was held in high esteem in the Buddhist world. A 'purification' of this Sangha led to the Cōḻa monks considering themselves to be even more orthodox than the Siṃhaḷa Sangha, which was traditionally looked up to as the most orthodox of the Theravada Sanghas. Cōḻa monks frequently visited Sri Lanka, some for their studies, and probably derived inspiration from leading Buddhist teachers there.

A number of Cōḻa monks are mentioned in the Buddhist writings of Sri Lanka as having gone over to the island for various purposes. A monk named Dīpaṅkara, for instance, went to study under the Sinhalese monk Ānanda Vanaratana. Since he hailed from the Cōḻa kingdom, he was known in the island as Coḷiya Dīpaṅkara.[28] Among the other important Coḷa monks who went to Sri Lanka, we get the names of Kassapa, Buddhamitta, Ānanda and Anuruddha. Possibly Dhammakitti of Tambaraṭṭha also hailed from the Cōḻa kingdom (if we take Tambaraṭṭha as a locality in that kingdom). Undeniably there were very close relations between the Cōḻa monks and those of Sri Lanka. As Leslie Gunawardana has concluded, 'The co-operation between the *sangha* of South India and Sri Lanka produced important results which are evident in the Pali works of this period.'[29]

The Theravada Sanghas of the two kingdoms seem to have been engaged in a friendly rivalry as to which one was more orthodox in its practices and interpretations of the Buddhist scriptures. An instance of this is found in one of the writings of the Cōḻa monk Kassapa. In his Pali work, *Vimatti-vinodanī*, this Tamil monk provides interesting information about the rise of heretical views in the Cōḻa Sangha and the consequent purification that took place there. A major controversy that raged between the heretics and the orthodox monks was over the consumption of liquor without intent or knowledge. In Tamil Nadu, a monk named Nāgasena had propagated the view that only intentional consumption of liquor by a member of the clergy amounted to an offence. But the Coḷa Mahāthera (Chief Monk) Buddhapiya suppressed such a view and 'purified' the *sāsana* (the Buddhist Order). When similar 'heretical' views with regard to the consumption of liquor were put forward in Sri Lanka in the twelfth century, the Cōḻa monk Kassapa criticized the Sinhalese monks for this and claimed that such views had been rejected as unorthodox in the Cōḻa kingdom by the leading monks there.[30] As Leslie Gunawardana says, 'It is also evident from this that the South Indian monks claimed to be more orthodox than their counterparts from Sri Lanka' during this period.[31] There were, however, other instances where the Sinhalese monks felt that their interpretations were more in accordance with the Buddhist scriptures than those of their Cōḻa counterparts. A work on the demarcation of ceremonial boundaries written by a Sinhalese monk claims that the views of the monks of the Cōḻa kingdom were incorrect.[32] Leslie Gunawardana sees the possibility of regional rivalry in the Pali writings of the Tamil and Sinhalese monks.[33] While this may be true, there is certainly no evidence of any hostility towards the Cōḻa monks on the part of the Sinhalese monks.

On the contrary, as Amaradasa Liyanagamage has clearly demonstrated, 'Coḷa *mahātheras* like Dīpaṅkara and Kassapa, were held in high esteem in Ceylon, and nowhere in the record is the slightest insinuation that they hailed from an 'enemy' territory or that they belonged to a different racial group'.[34] Indeed the relations between the Tamil monks and the Sinhalese monks were so close that the latter sought the assistance of the former in times of political turmoils. In the thirteenth century, when the Sinhalese Buddhist Sangha faced one of its worst crises with the fall of Polonnaruva, it was in the monasteries of the Tamil kingdoms that many Sinhalese monks found refuge and patronage. And when the Sinhalese king, Parākramabāhu II (1236-1270) founded a new capital and set about organizing the administration, he found that the Buddhist Order was in need of 'purification'. The Pali chronicle, *Cūḷavaṃsa*, records:

> All the corrupt groups (of bhikkhus) who since the Interregnum lived only for their own desires, following forbidden occupations, with senses ever unbridled, he sought

> out rigorously, dismissed them (from the Order) and thus purified the Order of the perfectly Enlightened One. Then the King sent many gifts to the Coḷa country and caused to be brought over to Tambapaṇṇi (Sri Lanka) many respected Coḷa bhikkhus who had moral discipline and were versed in the three Piṭakas.[35]

This last statement is perhaps the best tribute that a Sinhalese monk had paid to the Tamil monks. The activities of the Tamil Buddhist monks in the eleventh and twelfth centuries (as in the centuries that followed) in Sri Lanka no doubt should be reckoned as the Tamil contribution to the achievements of Buddhism in this period.

Military organization

The mixed character of the population and the close co-operation between the Sinhalese and the Tamils were significantly reflected in the composition and organization of the armies of the Polonnaruva rulers. The Vēḷaikkārar, the Akampaṭiyar (Agampaḍi), the Vīrakkoṭiyar and other military communities continued to play an important role in the wars of this period as in the period of Cōḷa rule. These sections of the army were organized under Tamil officers with the designation Demaḷādhikāra (Pali Damiḷādhikārin), a title that had come into vogue before Cōḷa rule. Without doubt the Polonnaruva monarchs heavily depended on these forces even to fight their south Indian foes.

A powerful section of Vijayabāhu's army was the Vēḷaikkārar division. In all probability these soldiers were recruited locally or from south India through the mercantile organizations. This division, however, caused serious problems for Vijayabāhu when he attempted to launch an invasion of south India. The Vēḷaikkārar revolted against the king and burned down the royal palace, forcing Vijayabāhu to flee the capital and take refuge in a rock fortress. This would show the extent to which the Vēḷaikkārar division was a strong element of Vijayabāhu's army. They were later brought under control and the leaders punished.[36] This incident, in which perhaps only a section of the Vēḷaikkārar was involved, did not seem to have shaken the trust that the Polonnaruva monarchs had in this Tamil military group. When Vijayabāhu died and the security of the Temple of the Tooth Relic was threatened, the institution was entrusted to the care of a Vēḷaikkārar division.[37]

It is known that the Vēḷaikkārar forces continued to be active in the period after Vijayabāhu. In the twelfth century, there is a reference to a unit of the Vēḷaikkārar called the Vikkirama Calāmēkaṉ Nāṟpaṭai.[38] In his wars against Jayabāhu, the Polonnaruva-based Vikramabāhu probably used Vēḷaikkārar units along with others. Gajabāhu did employ Vēḷaikkārar troops and faced some problems from them.[39] Parākramabāhu, too, relied heavily on Vēḷaikkārar troops. Some of the important generals in charge of the Tamil troops are mentioned in the Pali chronicle. Among them are Malayarāyara who led the Tamil troops of Parākramabāhu on the western coast, Damiḷādhikārin Rakkha who led a strong division against Queen Sugalā in the south, and Damiḷādhikārin Ādicca who commanded the expedition to Burma.[40] Clearly, both Tamil and Sinhalese soldiers contributed to the military achievements of the Polonnartuva rulers, particularly in the overseas campaigns of Parākramabāhu I and Niśśaṅka Malla.

Architecture

The splendour of the civilization of the island that marks out the period when Polonnaruva was the main capital rests largely on the achievements in the fields of architecture, sculpture and hydraulic engineering. In the same period, similar achievements took place in the kingdoms of south India. Inspiration and influences no doubt flowed from one area to another in this whole region.

Writers on the architecture of this period have sometimes lamented that the Cōḷa conquest 'spelt doom to the building activities of the Sinhalese Buddhists' and that the 'buildings which did not suffer wilful destruction at the hands of the Coḷa rulers thus suffered through neglect'.[41] Wars always cause destruction and soldiers in times of conflict are not the greatest respecters of artistic creations. As Amaradasa Liyanagamage has pointed out, 'it is very doubtful that the Coḷas or the Pāṇḍyas for that matter destroyed Buddhism with a persecutionist objective'. Referring to certain Sinhalese rulers, he has shown that 'some of these Sinhalese kings were no second to the Coḷas and Pāṇḍyas…when they set out on a spree of plunder of monastic wealth' (of the Buddhists in Sri Lanka).[42] Cōḷa armies are known to have plundered temples in south India, too.[43] It is, therefore, difficult to establish whether the great monuments of Anuradhapura and other urban centres were wilfully destroyed. But once the Cōḷas were in control, a new period of architectural activity began.

The eleventh and twelfth centuries will always be remembered as a period when some of the finest Ṣaiva and Buddhist monuments were erected in the island by Sinhalese and Tamil artisans. A period of such co-operative achievement in architecture was not seen before or after this period. As seen earlier, in the period of Cōḷa rule there was widespread construction of Saiva temples. From the remains of these structures still found in Polonnaruva, Padaviya and elsewhere, it could be said that these were all constructed in the Cōḷa architectural style of that time. This would mean that a considerable number of Tamil artisans were employed to erect these temples. It is very likely that Sinhalese artisans were also used for this construction work.

Admittedly, Sinhalese architectural and sculptural traditions of the pre-Cōḷa period continued well into the post-Cōḷa period. Paranavitana, who has often highlighted the view that Sinhalese artisans were unable to practise their art when the Cōḷas were in Sri Lanka, has himself expressed surprise at the continuation of their traditions after the end of Cōḷa rule. Referring to the Temple of the Tooth (Aṭadāgē) at Polonnaruva, the only monument in that city dating from the time of Vijayabāhu I, he says:

When we study this building we are struck by the fact that, though it was one of the first edifices to be erected after an interval of nearly a century, during which the practice of monumental architecture had been in abeyance among the Sinhalese, it follows the older buildings at Anuradhapura not only in the methods of construction, but also in design and in the details of architectural mouldings.[44]

It is very unlikely that for about a century Sinhalese artisans did not practise their art but that a new generation was able to continue the same tradition when Vijayabāhu came to the throne. There is no reason why these artisans were not employed in the construction of monuments when the Cōḻas were wielding power. The Saiva shrines built in the eleventh and twelfth centuries in the contemporary Tamil architecture, of course, bear ample testimony to the presence of considerable numbers of Tamil and other south Indian artisans in the island. While there is no visible evidence of Sinhalese architectural features in them, both Tamil and Sinhalese artisans may have been employed to erect these structures. Similarly, Tamil and other south Indian artisans would have been employed in the building of Buddhist monuments.

There is, of course, literary as well as archaeological evidence indicating the participation of Tamil artisans in the building of various structures, secular and religious, in Polonnaruva. The Pali chronicle records that Tamil prisoners-of-war were used in the twelfth century to rebuild destroyed Buddhist monuments as well as to erect new ones.[45] The ancient Ratanavāluka-cetiya (Ruvanvälisäya) was one of the monuments where the work of restoration was begun, using Tamil prisoners, in Parākramabāhu's reign. A new ambitious structure at Polonnaruva, according to the chronicle, was named Damiḷa-thūpa (the Tamil stupa) 'because it had been built by the Damiḷas who had been brought hither after the conquest of the Paṇḍu kingdom.'[46] Not only prisoners-of-war but also other skilled artisans brought over to the island by mercantile organizations would have been employed in these building activities.[47] 'When there was a demand for their art', as Paranavitana says, 'it is likely that skilled workers came to Ceylon from the neighbouring continent where they must have been quite numerous at that time.'[48] There were no doubt local Tamil artisans, too, who were employed for erecting religious as well as secular structures.

In support of the view that Tamil skilled workers were employed in the construction of various monuments other than Saiva shrines, there is unmistakable epigraphic and archaeological evidence. In many of the buildings where they were employed, Tamil artisans have left their signatures in the form of Tamil letters used as masons' marks. Paranavitana, who conducted restoration work at Polonnaruva for several decades, has drawn attention to these masons' marks.[49] The recent excavations at the Ālāhana Parivena, conducted under the UNESCO-sponsored Cultural Triangle Project, have also brought to light stone blocks with masons' marks in Tamil.[50]

Testimony of greater significance for the joint work of Tamil and Sinhalese artisans comes in the form of the actual monuments created by them. While there is no doubt that earlier Sinhalese architectural traditions continued into the eleventh and twelfth centuries, one cannot fail to see influences of contemporary Tamil architecture in some of the monuments of this period. Senake Bandaranayake, the foremost authority on Sinhalese monastic architecture, has pointed out that the Thūpārāma Temple at Polonnaruva, which is 'seemingly a product of the continuing Sinhalese traditions', displays features of contemporary south Indian architecture. 'In the design of the superstructure, however, with its four-faceted dome or Nagaraśikhara and the row of *kūṭas* and *sālas* along the periphery of its roof, the Thūpārāma is clearly related to the stone temples of Pallava, Cālukya and Coḷa architecture'.[51]

Another Buddhist shrine, though not in Polonnaruva, that exhibits unmistakable features of Cōḻa architecture is the Upulvan shrine, dedicated to the god Uppalavaṇṇa, in southern Sri Lanka. Built entirely of stone like the temples of Tamil Nadu, the shrine is the subject of some controversy in respect of its architectural style.

Senake Bandaranayake, who considers this structure to belong more likely to the period under diuscussion, has expressed the view that 'the temple appears to be a minor, provincial example of *Drāviḍa* architecture'.[52]

Sculpture

When it comes to the art of sculpture, it is generally acknowledged that this is a field in which distinctive traditions were deveoped in Sri Lanka, culminating in the achievements of the 10th-12th centuries. The peak of these achievements, it may be claimed, was reached in the eleventh and twelfth crenturies, the period which marks the height of the splendour of Sri Lankan civilization when Polonnaruva was the main centre of political authority.

Once again, it could be argued, the achievements in this art were the result of the joint efforts of Sinhalese and Tamil sculptors. This will apply to both Buddhist and Saiva sculptures. It is well known that some of the finest Saiva bronzes of this period in the island have been unearthed in Polonnaruva, Anuradhapura and other urban centres. Similarly, some of the most exquisite Buddhist bronzes and stone sculptures at Polonnaruva attest to the heights reached by Buddhist sculpture in this period.

Considerable attention has been focused on the Saiva bronzes discovered in Polonnaruva. Brought to light during excavations by H.C.P. Bell in 1907 and 1908, the first collection of Saiva images from Polonnaruva drew the attention of scholars, including the reputed critic of South Asian art in the last century, Ananda Coomaraswamy.[53] More Saiva bronze sculptures were discovered during further excavations in 1960, 1982 and 1984 in Polonnaruva as well as in Anuradhapura.[54] The main sculptures are images of Śiva as Naṭarāja, Śiva as Somāskanda-mūrti, Pārvatī, Śivakāmasundarī, Ganeśa, Chaṇḍikeśvara, Sundaramūrti-nāyaṉār and Kāraikkāl-ammaiyār. Of these, one of the Naṭarāja bronzes unearthed in Polonnaruva has been rated among the best examples of its type (see

Appendix III). The image of Somāskandamūrti has also drawn special attention.

The Buddhist sculptures of this period are also classed among the best produced in the island. These reflect a continuation of the high standards achieved by the art of the sculptor in Sri Lanka from about the eighth century. Considering the heights attained by both Buddhist and non-Buddhist plastic art, it is not surprising that some critics have described the period from about the eighth to the twelfth century as 'The Golden Age of Sculpture in Sri Lanka' (van Schroeder).[55] One cannot see any disruption in the practice of this art under Cōḻa rule. There was, on the contrary, close interaction between Sinhalese and Tamil sculptors and there is no doubt that both groups contributed to the creation of Buddhist as well as Saiva-Vaishnava sculptures in this period.

The developments in this art have to be viewed in the light of what was happening in south India. This was the period when sculpture reached great heights, with distinctive regional features, in different parts of south India. In the Tamil-speaking regions, almost completely under Cōḻa rule, the artistic traditions developed under the Pallavas and the Pāṇḍyas in the seventh, eighth and ninth centuries were continued and taken to new levels. These traditions were common to both Saivism-Vaishnavism and Buddhism. By the beginning of the tenth century the conflict between Buddhism and Saivism-Vaishnavism had come to an end but it cannot be said that the former had disappeared from the south Indian scene.[56] Just as a common architectural tradition was used for both Saiva-Vaishnava and Buddhist structures, south Indian sculptors adopted a common basic style with, of course, iconographic variations to suit the different religious images, in the creation of Saiva-Vaishnava and Buddhist icons.

The political anatagonisms amongst the south Indian and Sri Lankan ruling families did not obstruct free interaction among artists. As a result of the religious conflicts of the eighth and ninth centuries, Tamil Buddhists from some parts of the Tamil kingdoms, as discussed earlier, would have sought refuge in Sri Lanka, especially in the centres where Tamil Buddhists were already living in considerable numbers. These centres were mainly in the northeastern region. And it is here that we see see notable influence of south Indian sculptural styles in the Mahayana Buddhist images of the ninth and tenth centuries. This would indicate the presence of south Indian sculptors as well as their interaction with local artists.

Generally there has been a tendency to downplay the extent of this interaction, with statements such as: "Mahayana images of Sri Lanka show reminiscences of South Indian styles of the same period."[57] Taken along with the evidence of Mahayana inscriptions in the south Indian Pallava-Grantha script, the Mahayana images discovered in Tiriyay and other centres along the eastern coast provide clear evidence of the presence of south Indian artists and of close interaction between them and the local artists.

This interaction continued into the eleventh and twelfth centuries. Ulrich van Schroeder, who has made an in-depth study of the Sri Lankan sculpture of this period, has no reservations in accepting this view. 'There can be no doubt', he states, 'that the Buddhist art of the Polonnaruva Period after the liberation [from the Cōḷas] wạs much influenced by the art-styles prevailing mainly in South India...It is possible that artisans of South Indian origin were involved in the renaissance of Buddhist art in Sri Lanka in the late 11th and 12th century.'[58]

If one views the sculptures of the eleventh and twelfth centuries in the background of the larger SISL region, one could move away from the stereotyped attitude of looking at Saiva bronzes as the product of Tamil sculptors and Buddhist images as the creation of Sinhalese artists. Ever since the discovery of the Saiva bronzes in Polonnaruva at the beginning of the last century, a controversy has raged as to whether these were imported from south India or locally made. Since they were non-Buddhist images and because they belonged to a tradition developed in south India, there has been a tendency to view them as foreign to Sri Lanka. But if we look at them as artistic creations in a geographic region where cultural and economic interactions transcended political boundaries, we will see that there is no need to reject them as foreign to Sri Lanka. In recent decades there has been a change in this attitude. In the 1960s, C.E. Godakumbure argued that the Polonnaruva bronzes were made by Sri Lankan artists and, more recently, Sirinimal Lakdusinghe put forward a strong case for a Sri Lankan school being responsible for these bronzes.[59] They were clearly Sri Lankan, reflecting the achievements of both Sinhalese and Tamil (and other south Indian) artists. The Australian scholar, Adrian Snodgrass, has pronounced this dispassionate judgement on this controversy:

> Rather than asking whether the Hindu bronzes unearthed in Sri Lanka were made by Sinhala or Tamil craftsmen, it is perhaps wiser at this stage of scholarly indecision simply to admire the Hindu images for their own intrinsic qualities, viewing them as Sri Lankan, since this is where they were unearthed, rather than as belonging to one group of artisans or another.[60]

Just as the Tamil masons' marks on bricks indicate the participation of Tamil craftsmen in the construction of non-Saiva buildings, there is at least a solitary Sinhalese inscription which provides unequivocal evidence of Sinhala artists being involved in the creation of Saiva images. This valuable evidence seems to have been overlooked in this controversy. The inscription records a grant made by Gajabāhu II, a great patron of Saivism, to an artisan named Dāpera Rangidāge Hinābi for making images of Skanda and other deities for the ceremony of *lakṣapūja.* There is no better evidence than this to show that there were Sinhalese sculptors making Saiva images in Sri Lanka in the twelfth century.[61]

Hydraulic engineering

Of all the elements of the Sri Lankan civilization of the eleventh and twelfth centuries, perhaps the most magnificent was hydraulic engineering. The feats in this field not only gained a covetable place for Sri Lanka among the ancient civilizations of the world but also provided the necessary economic basis without which the cultural achievements of the period would not have been possible. Unfortunately, this is one field in which the co-operative effort of both Sinhalese and Tamils has not been generally recognized. Once again, it was left to a scholar from outside, with an impeccable knowledge in the field and a high reputation, to see this. Joseph Needham, eminent Cambridge professor and historian of science, after studying the major irrigation technologies of the ancient world for his monumental work on the science and civilization of China, paid a rare tribute to the ancient Sri Lankan engineers when discussing one of the finest achievements in ancient hydraulics. He judged 'that the achievements of the Indian civil engineers in ancient and medieval times are quite worthy to be compared with their Chinese colleagues' but concluded that 'it was never in India that the fusion of the Egyptian and Babylonian patterns achieved its most complete and subtlest form. This took place in Ceylon, the work of both cultures, Sinhalese and Tamil, but especially the former.'[62] The failure of many scholars to see this was largely due, it would appear, to viewing the irrigation works of the ancient Sri Lankans within the confines of the island rather than in the context of the larger region of SISL.

In this respect, in recent decades one Sri Lankan historian has broken the trend and done commendable research in this field by widening his geographic area to include south India. Making an exhaustive study of the ancient irrigation works in Sri Lanka and Tamil Nadu, Leslie Gunawardana has sought to establish the nature and extent of the 'intersocietal transfer of hydraulic technology' between the two areas.[63] Just as in the field of the arts, the achievements in Sri Lanka have to be viewed in the context of parallel developments in south India, it is important to assess the developments in hydraulic engineering in the backgound of the whole region of SISL. After all, the separate developments of more than a millennium in the field of irrigation technology in Sri Lanka and Tamil Nadu reached their peaks at the same time, in the eleventh and twelfth centuries, resulting in the creation of the largest human-made reservoir in the world until modern times in Tamil Nadu, and the second and third largest reservoirs in the world in Sri Lanka.[64] These remarkable achievements in two adjoining geographic areas could not have been the result of completely independent developments.

As seen earlier, the development of hydraulic technology in south India and Sri Lanka shared a common heritage. As the technology developed, there was interaction between the two areas. In this respect, Leslie Gunawardana's preliminary observations are notable:

> It appears likely that, while the influence of South Indian irrigation technology spread to Sri Lanka in proto-historic times, there was a reverse flow, from Sri Lanka to South India, in historical times. It would seem that "interaction", rather than "diffusion", is a suitable term to describe this process…Each culture, it would appear, borrowed certain elements of hydraulic technology from the other, but, with regard to a crucial element of this technology [the sluice], preserved its own way of doing things, rejecting attempts at introducing an analogous method from the neighbouring culture.[65]

Though there is no direct evidence in the historical sources of Sri Lanka or south India with regard to interaction between the two areas in the field of hydraulic technology, a strong body of traditional myths relating to a Cōḻa king named Karikālaṉ and a Sinhalese ruler called Gajabāhu seems to preserve some historical information based on such interaction. The historical Karikālaṉ was one of the Cōḻa rulers mentioned in the Tamil Sangam poems and lived probably in the first or second century. Gajabāhu was a ruler at Anuradhapura in the second century. The various versions of the Karikālaṉ myths in south India have one thing in common, namely, that this Cōḻa king was responsible for building dams and embankments connected with the Kaveri River. The Gajabāhu myths of Sri Lanka have at their core the taking away of a large number of people from Sri Lanka as prisoners by a Cōḻa ruler. Some of them state that these prisoners were made to work at the Kaveri River. All of them credit Gajabāhu with the feat of bringing the prisoners back to Sri Lanka.[66] Though these myths cannot be accepted as historically true, the strength of these myths and their persistence for centuries seem to indicate that such stories were based on movement of people, whether as prisoners or free persons, between south India and Sri Lanka for the purpose of employment in irrigation projects. In Leslie Gunawardana's view, 'it seems likely that the legend [about Gajabāhu] reflects the opposition of Sri Lankan rulers to their subjects going to work on South Indian irrigation projects.'[67] Since the Pali chronicle refers to Tamil prisoners from the Pāṇḍya kingdom being brought to Sri Lanka to work on the restoration of Buddhist monuments, it would appear that there was the practice of using prisoners of war in public works. They may have been used in irrigation projects as these constituted some of the largest public works of the eleventh and twelfth centuries, especially in the reign of Parākramabāhu I.

The interactions between Sri Lanka and Tamil Nadu in the field of hydraulic engineering and the extent of the transfer of technology and the participation of Sinhalese and Tamil labour in the irrigation works of the two areas are matters that cannot be easily determined at present. Historians of science and technology may be able to find evidence of technological co-operation in the construction of the large reservoirs in south India and Sri Lanka. For the present, it would appear that at least Sinhalese labour and Tamil labour worked together in some of these constructions, as they did in the case of the architectural monuments. The eleventh and twelfth centuries indubitably marked the peak of the development of hydraulic technology that began in the EIA in the SISL region. This period saw the construction of the largest of all the reservoirs in Tamil Nadu and Sri Lanka. It is difficult to assume that the technological advances in this field in the two regions took place simultaneously without any interaction. When in every other field there was unmistakable interaction, it seems reasonable to conclude that the achievements of the two regions in hydraulic technology were the result of close co-

PLATE 18.

Slab Inscription from Rajaraja-perumpalli. This is one of over fifteen Tamil inscriptions discovered among the ruins recording pious donations by Tamil Buddhist devotees. This is dated in the period of Cola rule.

***Photo** of estampage. **Courtesy:** Department of Archaeology.*

PLATE 19.

Proclamation in Tamil issued by Parakramabahu I, Nainativu, Jaffna District. This relates to foreign trade, particularly the trade in horses and elephants. 12th century. See p.273.

Photo of estampage. ***Courtesy****: Department of Archaeology.*

operation that enabled exchange of ideas as well as participation of skilled and unskilled labour in the hydraulic projects.

Foreign Trade

The economic prosperity of this period was also due in large measure to the expansion of commerce. While this was also a sphere in which both Sinhalese and Tamils jointly participated, the available evidence points to a greater involvement of Tamil mercantile organizations in the foreign trade of the island. The Aiññūṟṟuvar and their associates, who were already wielding much influence at the turn of the tenth century, continued to dominate the economic scene up to the end of the twelfth century. In addition, for the first time we get information about a Muslim mercantile community identifiable as one of the forerunners of the later Tamil-speaking Muslim traders who controlled the ports along the west coast of Sri Lanka.

As seen earlier, Tamil mercantile communities and their associates, including occupational groups and allied commercial groups from other south Indian ethnic communities, were very active in Sri Lanka in the eleventh century. An umbrella organization, usually referred to as the Aiññūṟṟuvar, seems to have controlled most of these communities. In the twelfth century, their influence reached its peak and a number of records belonging to them have been discovered in several parts of the island, mainly in the northern half.

The records of the Aiññūṟṟuvar are not dated and have been set up without even any reference to the reigning monarch. On palaeographical and other grounds most of them have been dated in the twelfth century. They are found mainly in places which were important interior market-towns at that time. Though records of the Aiññūṟṟuvar have not come to light so far in the major ports such as Mātoṭa and Gokarṇa, these merchants were no doubt quite active in all the major ports.[68]

The main centres where the inscriptions of the Aiññūṟṟuvar and their associates have been found are: Anuradhapura, Anaulundava, Padaviya, Polonnaruva, Vahalkada, Viharehinna, Budumuttava, Ilakkattu-eba, Ataragalla, Detiyamulla and Galtenpitiya.[69] The provenance of these records indicates a concentration in the northeastern part of the island. This may point to a dominance enjoyed by the Aiññūṟṟuvar in the northeastern ports of Pallavavaṅka and Gokarṇa.

Some light on the activities of the Aiññūṟṟuvar and other mercantile communities in Sri Lanka is thrown by south Indian inscriptions, too. Although these communities operated freely across political boundaries (somewhat similar to modern multinational companies), some of them or sections of them were apparently fully based in certain regions.

One such group was the Teṉṉilaṅkai Valañciyar (the Valañciyar of Sri Lanka).[70] Although inscriptions of the Valañciyar have been found in Sri Lanka, there is no reference to a group called Teṉ-ilaṅkai Valañciyar in these records. But at least two inscriptions referring to this group have been discovered in south India. These provide information about their activities in the Cōḷa and Pāṇḍya kingdoms.[71]

Another important mercantile group of this period, known only from south Indian inscriptions though active in Sri Lanka too, was the Añjuvaṇṇam (Añcuvaṇṇam). As already seen, this was a community of merchants with West Asian origins. Members of this community were active participants in the maritime trade of south India and Sri Lanka. They were mainly Muslim by religion, although it is possible that there were also Jewish and other West Asian merchants among them. What is of greater interest is that the Añjuvaṇṇam could be reckoned among the forerunners of the Tamil-using (and later, if not at this time, Tamil-speaking) Muslim traders who were settled in considerable numbers in south Indian and Sri Lankan port-towns after the twelfth century. The Añjuvaṇṇam are known to have been active in the ports of the Keraḷa, Pāṇḍya and

Telugu kingdoms as far north as the important port of Visakapattinam (Vishakapatnam) in the twelfth century. It is from two Telugu inscriptions found in Vishakapatnam that we get to know about an Añjuvaṇṇam group that had established itself at the Sri Lankan port of Mātoṭa.[72] The Añjuvaṇṇam, it would appear, were major participants in the lucrative West Asian trade.

The dominance of the Tamil mercantile communities in the maritime trade of south India and Sri Lanka sems to have led to the use of Tamil as the language of trade in this region in the twelfth century. Apart from the records of these traders being written in Tamil, even a royal proclamation by a Sri Lankan king, relating to overseas traders, is in Tamil. Parākaramabāhu I, the prosperity of whose reign depended to a considerable extent on overseas trade, issued a proclamation relating to merchandise from shipwrecks and this was inscribed in Tamil and set up at the northern port of Ūrātturai (known in modern times in English writings as Kayts). The proclamation refers specifically to traders who brought horses and elephants to the island. Clearly the horses were originating from West Asia and were in all probability brought by Muslim traders such as the Añjuvaṇṇam.[73]

Although influential trading organizations controlled by Sinhalese merchants are not met with in the available sources, one cannot rule out their participation in the internal and external trade of the island at a time when there was a marked expansion in this area of economic activity. While the Pali chronicle provides considerable information about the building of irrigation works, very little is given about trade. However, in the detailed account of Parākramabāhu's reign, there are references to the production of commodities collected for foreign trade and to valuable merchandise being sent in ships. The reason for Parākramabāhu's naval expedition to Burma was, according to the chronicle, the unfavourable treatment accorded to the traders sent by Parākramabāhu.[74] It would appear that Sinhalese traders also participated actively in the foreign trade of the island.

That merchants from the Sinhalese kingdom, like their counterparts from the kingdoms of south India, were involved in the lucrative trade with Southeast Asian states is evident from Javanese inscriptions found in Indonesia. These records provide lists of foreigners who were resident at the ports in Java. As early as the ninth century, traders from Sri Lanka appear to have been included in these lists. The earliest inscription with such a list is that of Kalirungan from Kedu in central Java, dated 883 CE. Among the foreigners in this list are those from a country whose name has been tentatively read as Singhala. A slightly later Javanese inscription, the Palebuhan charter of 927 CE, has the name Singhala in a preserved state. Sinhalese traders continued to participate in the Southeast Asian trade in the eleventh and twelfth centuries as well. The Cane inscription of 1021 from the Brantas region of east Java includes Singhala, along with Drawiḍa (Tamil Nadu), in its list of countries from which traders had arrived. The Balawi inscription dated 1305 has Singhala, along with Karnataka, in its list.[75] There is, therefore, no doubt that Sinhalese traders, along with Tamil merchants, participated actively in the trade between South Asia and Southeast Asia in the eleventh and twelfth centuries.

There is a very strong possibility that some Sinhalese traders were members of the Aiññūṟṟuvar community. Unfortunately, the only Sinhalese record of this community so far discovered is fragmentary, with only the preamble surviving.[76] As a result, it is not possible to ascertain from this record anything about Sinhalese traders in the organization. But the fact that some Aiññūṟṟuvar records were inscribed in Sinhalese is in itself significant. In south India the Aiññūṟ6uvar set up public inscriptions in all the major south Indian languages and proudly made known their supralocal character, often describing themselves as Nānādeśi (Persons from different countries). In such a context, the inclusion of Sinhalese traders in the Aiññūṟṟuvar community in Sri Lanka is only to be expected. The existence of another Sinhalese inscription of this period, though not of the Aiññūṟṟuvar, referring to the Nānādeśi in Anuradhapura who were engaged in activities close to the Jetavanārāma monastery, may lend support to the view that there were links between Sinhalese traders and the Aiññūṟṟuvar.[77] Whether Sinhalese traders were part of the Aiññūṟṟuvar community or not, both Tamils and Sinhalese participated in the commercial expansion of this period and contributed to the achievements in this field.

All told, then, it can be said that the eleventh and twelfth centuries constitute a period of remarkable achievements in various fields towards which the Sinhalese and the Tamils contributed. The period marked the culmination of a long process of evolution for both ethnic groups. Until about the end of the tenth century, it still seemed possible for a single ethnic group to emerge eventually. But the events from the end of the tenth century began to strengthen the Tamil element in the north, northwest and northeast. By the end of the eleventh century, it appeared that the process of two major ethnic groups evolving in the island could not be reversed. From the time Sinhalese rule was restored in the old Anuradhapura kingdom, a new spirit of harmony and co-operation created the right conditions for the efflorescence of a truly Sri Lankan civilization.

CONCLUSION

By the end of the twelfth century, the Tamil element in the island was at its highest point. It was clearly dominant in the areas north and west of Anuradhapura and around Polonnaruva and east of it. In the areas south of Anuradhapura there were scattered settlements as far as Kurunegala. Beyond that there were possibly some isolated settlements in market-towns, consisting mainly of Tamil traders and artisans associated with them.

A complete bifurcation of the island into Tamil-speaking and Sinhala-speaking areas would have taken place only after 1200, especially with the fall of Polonnaruva and the establishment of a new centre of Sinhalese power in the southwest. The shift of the Sinhalese power-centre to areas south of Anuradhapura and Polonnaruva, a movement often referred to as the Drift to the Southwest, can only be seen as a retreat by the Sinhalese-Buddhist group in its contest with the Tamil-Saiva group for assimilation of the rest of the island's population. The Tamil group did not win the contest either. But the retreat of the Sinhalese ensured the consolidation of Tamil habitation in the north, northwest and northeast as well as the assimilation of all non-Tamil elements within that region.

Untill about 900 there was always the possibility of the Tamil-speaking population getting assimilated into the Heḷa majority. But the rise of Cōḻa power and the dominance of south Indian mercantile communities as well as the strong influence of Saivism worked against such a possibility becoming a reality. Not only did these factors lead to a rapid increase in the Tamil population of the island, they also set in motion a process of assimilating Heḷa elements into the Tamil population in the heart of the former Anuradhapura kingdom.

This process continued for centuries after the fall of Polonnaruva. In the seventeenth century, when Robert Knox the English prisoner in the Kingdom of Kandy made his escape through Anuradhapura into the Dutch-occupied northwest, he found that, fluent though he was in Sinhala, he could not converse with the inhabitants of the Anuradhapura region as the people there spoke 'the Malabar language' (Tamil). When he managed to communicate to them through sign language about his plight, they exclaimed, "Tombrane" (Tamil, *tampirānē*, meaning 'Oh, God'), with amazement. Even the rendering of the name Anuradhapura by Knox as Anarodgburro, is obviously from the colloquial Tamil form Anrājapuram/ Anrācapuram, still current among Sri Lankan Tamils. Knox, in fact, clearly states that the Territory of Anarodgburro is inhabited by Tamils:

> It is a vast great plain, the like I never saw in all that Island...This plain is encompassed round with woods, and small Towns among them on every side, inhabited by Malabars, a distinct people from the Chingulayes.[78]

In the nineteenth century, British colonial officers had a similar observation to make.

For the Sinhalese, too, their retreat ensured the consolidation of Sinhalese habitation in the southern half of the island and the assimilation of non-Sinhalese elements within that region. As Anuradhapura and Polonnaruva were abandoned forever, a thick belt of jungle separated the Tamil north from the Sinhalese south and, what is more, provided a buffer against any further political interruptions in the form of invasions from south Indian empires. Relations with south India, however, were not interrupted. Migrations from south India continued but the migrants were soon assimilated into the Sinhalese ethnic group whose language and religion did not face any threat until the arrival of the Europeans.

EPILOGUE

"Historians should not write only for other historians." Eric Hobsbawm, 2002: 282.

Two inspiring lines from Kipling's immortal 'If' urged me on and helped me to complete this task:

> (If you can) … watch the things you gave your life to, broken,
> And stoop and build 'em up with worn-out tools.

I have watched what I gave my life to, being broken, and twenty years later I have tried to build something with worn-out tools. With poetic brevity and imagery, the Nobel laureate's lines describe my work in the last three years that has resulted in this book. I intended to write this many years ago when I was in Sri Lanka. Some of the main ideas presented in this book formed the subject of a series of popular articles in the press in 1969.[1] I have waited long to write this book and now accomplished it in a distant land. Looking back, the distance in time and space has been worthwhile.

Those who have read the whole book may turn round and ask, "Has this writer said anything new?" I do not claim to have said anything new. What I have stated is what was already there, what some respected scholars have said, what many have forgotten, what some have chosen to ignore. If I may borrow the words of that great art critic and leading expositor of the *Philosophia Perennis* in the last century, Ananda Coomaraswamy, 'what I have sought is to understand what has been said'.[2] Unlike that savant who was referring to what has been said in the perennial Tradition, I have sought to understand what the more mundane archaeological and literary materials have to say and the interpretations of reputed scholars.

This book is written for the purpose of drawing attention to some of the important aspects of Sri Lanka's distant past. It is written for the Sri Lankan audience and for this reason detailed notes and quotations have been included, as articles in international journals as well as foreign publications are not easily accessible to the average reader. It is for the same reason that a Glossary and Apendices have been added.

In this book, the narration of the historical developments leading to the emergence of two separate ethnic identities ends in 1200. But the story does not end there. The dialogue between the two major ethnic groups in Sri Lanka continues into the centuries that follow. The dawn of the thirteenth century marks the beginning of the political separation of the two groups. Most of the non-Sinhalese elements in the population of the island came to be concentrated in the north, while most of the Sinhalese were confined to the south. The forces that held power in the north aspired to the overlordship of the entire island and did not consider themselves to be ruling a smaller kingdom in the area under their control. The forces in the south, too, claimed to be ruling the whole island. The King of Lanka (Te<u>n</u>-ilaṅkai-k-kō<u>n</u>) was one of the epithets applied to rulers in the north while Lord of Lanka (Laṅkeśvara) continued to be one of the titles used by the rulers in the south.[3]

While the rulers of the north and the south claimed to rule the whole country, although they were de facto rulers of separate kingdoms, the Tamils of the north and the Sinhalese came to be isolated from each other. A stretch of jungle that covered the ancient cities of Anuradhapura and Polonnaruva right across the middle of the island separated the Tamils of the north from the Sinhalese. Migrations from south India, however, continued unabated bringing not only Tamils but also Keralas and other south Indians to the north and the south. There is absolutely no evidence of enmity between the Sinhalese people and the Tamil people in the centuries after the fall of Polonnaruva, although there were occasions when the Tamil and Sinhalese rulers invaded each other's territory.

The close relations between the Tamils and the Sinhalese in the Sinhalese kingdom up to the beginning of European colonial rule are to be seen in many areas of activity. Perhaps the one area in which such relations were never to be seen again is religion. Nevertheless, Theravada Buddhist monks from the Cōḷa kingdom continued to have close connections with the Buddhist establishments in the Sinhalese kingdom.[4] As already mentioned, 'many respected Coḷa bhikkhus who had moral discipline and were versed in the three Piṭakas' were invited by the Sinhalese ruler Parākramabāhu II in the thirteenth century to strengthen the Buddhist Order in his kingdom.[5] One of his successors in the next century, Parākramabāhu IV (1302-1326), paid a high tribute to the Coḷa Sangha by appointing to the respected office of Royal Teacher (*rājaguru*) 'a Grand thera from the Coḷa country, a self-controlled man, versed in various tongues and intimate with philosophic works.'[6]

Saivism continued to be practised in the Sinhalese kingdom. Saiva temples were venerated in many places predominantly settled by Sinhalese Buddhists. Two of the most venerated temples dedicated to Siva were the Nagarīsa-kōvil at Devinuvara (the southernmost point in the island) and Muṉṉīsvaram at Chilaw (on the western coast). An officer in the service of Vijayabāhu VI (1513-1521) was a patron of the former while Parākramabāhu VI (1412-1467) was a patron of the latter shrine.[7] There was another Siva temple just outside the capital city of Kotte in the fifteenth century.[8] In the next century, a Sinhalese king, Rājasiṅha I, became a convert to Saivism and built a Saiva temple, the Berendi-kovil, at his capital, Sitawaka.[9]

From the thirteenth to the nineteenth century, the arts of the Tamil country came into intimate contact with those of the Sinhalese kingdom, both at the elite and folk levels, resulting in an interesting cultural dialogue that helped to shape the late medieval arts of the Sinhalese. This dialogue relates especially to dance, music and drama. Ediriweera Sarachchandra has shown how two of the traditional forms of Sinhalese music, *Vannam* and *Viraha*, and two of the major genre of Sinhalese folk drama, *Nāḍagama* and *Kōlam*, arose as a result of contact with Tamil music and folk theatre.[10] In a kingdom where Buddhism influenced the life of the people, 'song and dance could not form a part of Buddhist worship in the way in which these arts formed part of, for example, Hindu worship'.[11] But non-Buddhist court rituals and village folk rituals allowed room for the arts of song, dance and drama to be fostered. Tamil artistes were able to provide the inspiration for these arts well into the early modern period.

The classical dance form fostered in the royal courts and temples of the Tamil country, better known by its Sanskrit name *Bharata Nāṭya*, had already arrived in Sri Lanka in the eleventh century.[12] Possibly it was performed in the Sinhalese courts at Polonnaruva in the twelfth century. King Niśśaṅka Malla watched dance performances at Saiva institutions.[13] From the thirteenth century, it was clearly an art appreciated by the elite. 'Evidence from sculpture and painting', as Sarachchandra argues, 'strengthens the view that Bharata Nāṭyam constituted the entertainment of royalty and the lay elite'.[14]

As in the eleventh and twelfth centuries, architecture continued to be an art where influence of Tamil artisans made an impact on secular as well as religious buildings in the new capitals. The archaeological remains in these sites bear witness to this. At Yapahuva, one of the capitals in the thirteenth century, the remains of what is assumed to be the royal palace show features that, in the words of Paranavitana, 'differ from corresponding features in Sinhalese buildings of earlier periods, and are clearly derived from contemporary Dravidian schools in South India'.[15] This structure demonstrates the continuing presence of Tamil architects in the Sinhalese kingdom and the ways in which late medieval Sinhalese architecture received new influences.

In the fourteenth century, artisans versed in the south Indian Vijayanagara style of architecture built two impressive Buddhist structures which still stand at Gadaladeniya and Sinduruvana, in the central highlands. Described by Paranavitana as the 'most outstanding architectural monuments of the period' (thirteenth to the fifteenth century), they were created by south Indian architects whose names are preserved in Sinhala inscriptions at the two sites.[16] The chief architect of the Gadaladeniya temple was Gaṇēśvara Ācārya while the architect of the Laṅkātilaka temple at Sinduruvana was Sthapati Rāyar. The mingling of Tamil and Sinhalese architectural features continued over the ensuing centuries with the Nāyakkar style being adopted for various elements of the structures erected under the Kotte and Kandyan rulers. In the eighteenth century, Devendra Mūlācārya was one of the architects who introduced some of these elements into a few of the Kandyan structures.

Architecture and sculpture are inseparable in traditional art. If one looks for sculptures in the style cultivated by Tamil artisans in the thirteenth and fourteenth centuries, one will find them in the architectural monuments. At Yapahuva, for instance, are to be seen some fine examples of relief sculptures of dancers and musicians revealing south Indian influence. In the later Kandyan buildings, too, stone doorways have relief sculptures of dancers and musicians as well as the figure of Gajalakṣmī.[17]

The status of the Tamil language in the Sinhalese kingdom in the pre-colonial period would be an eye-opener to many. Where necessary, Sinhalese kings or other authorities used the Tamil language for their epigraphic records. In the fourteenth century, a record inscribed in Sinhala on the walls of the Laṅkātilaka Temple was provided with a full Tamil translation on the same walls, as if setting an example to future rulers of the country. This Tamil inscription, incidentally, is the longest Tamil epigraph in the island. What is even more interesting is the teaching of the Tamil language in the Buddhist *pirivenas* (religious schools). Some of the products of these institutions who became leading scholar monks were well-versed in Tamil. Perhaps the most reputed among them was Toṭagamuvē Śrī Rāhula who quoted from Tamil writings in his commentaries.[18] Another Sinhalese monk, as Leslie Gunawardana points out, 'spoke proudly of his ability to preach in both Sinhala and Tamil'.[19] One Sinhalese poet, who obviously felt very proud of his knowledge of Tamil (and other languages), even went to the extent of sneering at those who were not fortunate like him to acquire such language skills.[20] In such an atmosphere, it would appear that Sinhalese monarchs extended their patronage to Tamil poets, too, just as they did to Sinhalese poets. Parākramabāhu IV (1302-1326) was the patron of the Tamil poet, Pōcarācar, who composed his work, *Caracōtimālai*, at the behest of the king and presented it to the king's court.[21] Gunawardana draws attention to a line in the Sinhala poem, *Kōkila Sandeśaya*, according to which 'poems composed in Sinhala, Tamil, Pali and Sanskrit were recited at the court of Parākramabāhu VI'.[22] As is widely known, Tamil was used in the court of the last kings of Kandy (early in the nineteenth century). When the British finally conquered the Kingdom of Kandy in 1815, the treaty they entered into with the Sinhalese chiefs shows the signatures of some of them in Tamil. Even before this, as Gunawardana has stated, 'It is particularly interesting to note that some leading Sinhala officials in the Kandyan kingdom used the Grantha and the Tamil scripts in their signatures'.[23]

It was not all one way in the area of language and literature. There were also Tamils who showed their skills in the Sinhala language. The Tamil Buddhist monks who came to reside in the monasteries of the Sinhalese kingdom in the thirteenth and fourteenth centuries were probably versed in Sinhala as much as they were in Pali, although their literary output was in the latter language. In the fifteenth century, we hear of a Tamil Buddhist poet named Nallurutunu-mini who wrote the Sinhalese work *Nāmāvaliya* (usually called the *Purāṇa-nāmāvaliya*). He is generally identified as Nallurutunayan, the son-in-law of King Parākramabāhu VI.[24]

It was not only learned monks, skilled artisans and accomplished artistes who were moving into the Sinhalese kingdom from south India. Ordinary people came in notable numbers to provide various services or to fulfil diverse needs or to escape from social and economic pressures in their villages. A study of Sinhalese folk literature, as done by the literary scholar Hevawasam and the anthropologist Obeyesekere, shows the extent to which there was interaction between Sinhalese villagers and south Indian folk ritual specialists.[25] Using 'indirect historical and sociological data', Obeyesekere has 'made a strong case for Buddhist migrations from South India'. To this renowned anthropologist, the 'cultural data in Sri Lanka leaves no doubt that migrations occurred'. Using the evidence of folk literature and rituals extensively, he has argued that there were notable migrations of mendicants, merchants and folk specialists from south India to the Sinhalese kingdom.[26]

There were also other ordinary people who migrated to perform economic functions. It is well known that the origin of some of the major castes in the Sinhalese society is to be traced to such migrations from south India. In the fourteenth century, when the lucrative trade in cinnamon began to expand, the Sinhalese kings encouraged members of the Tamil *Cāliyar* (weavers) caste to migrate. In time, this community became the caste of cinnamon-peelers and was absorbed into the Sinhalese population as a service caste with the name of *Salāgama*.[27] As Gunawardana has stated, 'there were several waves of immigration which brought not only linguistic groups like Demaḷa, Malala, Kaṇṇaḍa and Doḷuvara (Tulu) from south India but also the Jāvakas from south-east Asia', and these 'groups of immigrants who originally spoke different languages came to be absorbed into the two main linguistic groups in the island'.[28]

The result of all this interaction was a mingling of peoples that led some to caution those who talked about 'racial' purity or exclusivity or superiority in modern times. Prof. K.W. Goonewardene, while endorsing the view that " 'Sinhala' had become an umbrella-like term giving shelter under to persons of diverse linguistic origins", quotes a cautionary statement by W.A. de Silva, made early in the twentieth century. Analysing the evidence of the class of Sinhala writings called *vittipot*, de Silva pointed out that one *vittipota* states that from very early times the island was colonised by people from all parts of India who mixed freely to form one nation. Concluding his analysis, de Silva added: 'Therefore those inhabiting this Sinhala (country) should not say that they belong to some one particular family or race.'[29]

The story of ethnic interaction becomes even more interesting after the fall of Polonnaruva because of the emergence of a third major group, namely the Muslims. Their origins go back to the West Asian as well as Indian Muslim trade settlements at the ports and market-towns of the island. These Muslim traders, it must not be forgotten, married local women and, therefore, their descendants share the ancient ancestry of the Sinhalese and Tamils. Since the Malay soldiers and the Portuguese who came later did not bring their womenfolk with them but married locally, the Malay and Burgher communities, too, share the ancestry of the others.

Anyone turning such a fascinating story of ethnic interaction in a hospitable island with an exceptionally long record of human habitation into a woeful tale of communal conflict and confrontation is surely misinterpreting history for whatever purposes it may be. In this enthralling story, the myth of the monocultural, monolingual people who migrated from some part of north India to settle in the island of Lanka, where only demons lived, confronts the historical reality of prehistoric communities who received new cultural and linguistic influences from the subcontinent that set in motion the evolution of the people of modern Sri Lanka. Out of the complex interplay of cultures, languages and religions, there emerged the modern ethnic groups.

SELECT BIBLIOGRAPHY

Abraham, Meera, 1988. *Two Medieval Merchant Guilds of South India*, Manohar: New Delhi.

Agrawal, D.P., 1982. *The Archaeology of India*, Curzon Press: London.

Allchin, F.R., 1995. *The Archaeology of Early Historic South Asia*, Cambridge University Press.

Allchin, F.R. and Allchin, B., 1982. *The Rise of Civilization in India and Pakistan*, Cambridge University Press.

Bandaranayake, Senake, 1974. *Sinhalese Monastic Architecture*, Leiden.

______1978. The External Factor in Sri Lanka's Historical Formation, *The Ceylon Historical Journal*, 25, 1-4 Colombo.

Banadaranayake, Senake and Mogren, Mats, (ed.) 1994. *Further Studies in the Settlement Archaeology of the Sigiriya-Dambulla Region*, Post-Graduate Institute of Archaeology, University of Kelaniya.

Basham, A.L., 1971. *The Wonder that was India*. Calcutta: Fontana Books.

Begley, Vimala, 1967. Archaeological Exploration in Northern Ceylon. *Expedition*, 9, 4, Bulletin of the University Museum of the University of Pennsylvania, Philadelphia: 21-29.

______ 1981. Excavations of Iron Age Burials at Pomparippu 1970, *Ancient Ceylon* 4: 49-96.

Bell, H.C.P., 1904. *Report on the Kegalla District of the Province of Sabaragamuva*, Colombo.

Bopearachchi, Osmund, 1990. Some Observations on the Roman Coins Found in the Recent Excavations at Sigiriya, *Ancient Ceylon*, Colombo: 20-37.

______1995. Sea-borne and Inland Trade of Ancient Sri Lanka: First Results of the Sri Lanka-French Exploratory Programme. *South Asian Archaeology*: Proceedings of the 13th Congress of the European Association of South Asian Archaeologists, Cambridge: 377-391.

______1997. Foreword to Weerakkody 1997: ix-xxii.

Bopearachchi, Osmund and Wickremasinghe, Rajah M., 1999. *Ruhuna: An Ancient Civilization Re-visited*, Colombo.

Carswell, J., 1991. The Port of Mantai, Sri Lanka, *Rome and India: The Ancient Sea Trade*, ed. Vimala Begley and Richard Daniel De Puma, Madison.

Carswell, J.and Prickett, M, 1984. Mantai, 1980: a Preliminary Investigation, *Ancient Ceylon* 5:3-80.

Champakalakshmi, R., 1996. *Trade, Ideology and Urbanization: South India 300 BC to AD 1300,* New Delhi: Oxford University Press.

Christie, Jan Wisseman, 1998. The Medieval Tamil-language Inscriptions in Southeast Asia and China, *Journal of Southeast Asian Studies*, 29, 2: 239-268.

Coningham, R.A.E. & Allchin, F.R., 1992. Anuradhapura Citadel Archaeological Project: Preliminary Report of the Third Season of Sri Lanka-British Excavations at Salgaha Watta, July-September 1991, *South Asian Studies 8*, 155-167.

Coningham, R.A.E., Allchin, F.R., Batt, C.M. & Lucy, D., 1996. Passage to India? Anuradhapura and the Early Use of the Brahmi Script, *Cambridge Archaeological Journal* 6:1, 73-97.

Coningham, Robin, 1999. *Anuradhapura: The British-Sri ·Lankan Excavations at Anuradhapura Salgaha Watta 2*, I and II, BAR International Series 824, Oxford.

Coningham, R.A.E. & Lewer, N., 2000. The Vijayan colonization and the archaeology of identity in Sri Lanka, *Antiquity* 74, 707-712.

Davies, Norman, 2000. *The Isles: A History*, London.

Deraniyagala, S.U., 1992. *The Prehistory of Sri Lanka: An Ecological Perspective.* Colombo: Department of Archaeological Survey.

______1998. Pre- and Protohistoric Settlement in Sri Lanka. Paper read at the Proceedings of the XIII Congress of the International Union of Prehistoric and Protohistoric Sciences, Forli', Italy, September 1996. Published in Vol 5 of the Proceedings, 1998 Forli'. The version used here appeared online: www.lankalibrary.com/geo/dera1 - 28/11/2001.

De Silva, K.M., 1991. *A History of Sri Lanka,* Oxford University Press.

De Silva, M.W.S., 1979. *Sinhalese and other island languages in South Asia*, Tübingen.

Geiger, Wilhelm, 1938. *A Grammar of the Sinhalese Language,* Colombo.

______1950. English tr. *The Mahāvaṃsa*, Colombo.

______1958. ed. *The Mahāvaṃsa*, Pali Text Society, London.

Godakumbura, C.E., 1955. *Sinhalese Literature,* Colombo.

Gunawardana, R.A.L.H., 1971. Irrigation and Hydraulic Society in Early Medieval Ceylon, *Past and Present*, 53: 3-27.

______1979. *Robe and Plough*, University of Arizona Press, Arizona.

______1981. Social Function and Political Power: A Case Study of State Formation in Irrigation Society. *The Study of the State*, ed. Henri J.M. Claessen and Peter Skalnik, The Hague: 133-154.

______1984. Intersocietal Transfer of Hydraulic Technology in Precolonial South Asia: Some Reflections Based on a Preliminary Investigation, *South East Asian Studies* (*Tonan Ajia Kenkyu*), 22, 2, Tokyo: 115-142.

______1985. Total Power or Shared Power? A Study of the Hydraulic State and its Transformations in Sri Lanka from the Third to the Ninth Century A.D., *Development and Decline: The Evolution of Sociopolitical Organization*, ed. Henri J.M. Claessen, Pieter van de Velde, and M. Estellie Smith, Massachusetts: 219-245.

______1989. Anuradhapura: ritual, power and resistance in a precolonial South Asian city, *Domination and Resistance*, ed. Daniel Miller, Michael Rowlands, Christopher Tilley, London: 155-178.

______1990a. The people of the Lion: the Sinhala identity and ideology in history and historiography, *Sri Lanka: History and the Roots of Conflict*, ed. Jonathan Spencer, London and New York: 45-86.

______1990b. Seaways to Sielediba: Changing Patterns of Navigation in the Indian Ocean and their Impact on

Precolonial Sri Lanka, *Sri Lanka and the Silk Road of the Sea*, ed. Senake Bandaranayake, Lorna Dewaraja, Roland Silva and K.D.G. Wimalaratne, Colombo.

______1992. Conquest and Resistance: Pre-state and State Expansionism in Early Sri Lankan History, *War in the Tribal Zone: Expanding States and Indigenous Warfare*, ed. R. Brian Ferguson and Neil L. Whitehead, Santa Fe New Mexico: 61-82.

______1994. Colonialism, Etnicity and the Construction of the Past: The Changing 'Ethnic Identity' of the Last Four Kings of the Kandyan Kingdom, *Pivot Politics: Changing Cultural Identities in Early State Formation Processes*, ed. Martin van Bakel, Rene Hagessteijn and Pieter van de Velde, Amsterdam: 197-221.

______1995. *Historiography In A Time Of Ethnic Conflict: Construction of the Past in Contemporary Sri Lanka*, Colombo.

______2000. Warfare, the State, and the Proto-World Economy: Armed Struggles and the Economy in Ancient and Early Medieval Sri Lanka, *Reflections on a Heritage*, Colombo: 527-560.

______2001. Cosmopolitan Buddhism on the move: South India and Sri Lanka in the early expansion of Theravada in Southeast Asia, *Fruits of Inspiration: Studies in Honour of Prof. J.G. de Casparis*, ed. Marijke J. Klokke and Karel R. van Kooij, Groningen: 135-155.

Guruge, A.W.P (Tr.), 1989. *Mahāvaṃsa: The Great Chronicle of Sri Lanka*, Associated Newspapers of Ceylon Ltd. Colombo.

Indrapala, K. 1961. *Samāja Toraturu* [Social conditions], *Anurādhapura Yugaya* (Sinhala), ed. A. Liyanagamage and R.A.L.H. Gunawardana, Vidyalankara University, Kelaniya.

______1963. The Nainativu Tamil Inscription of Parakramab1hu I. *University of Ceylon Review,* XXI: 1:63-70.

______1968. *Anurātapurattiluḷḷa Nānkunāṭṭār Kalveṭṭu* [Inscription of the Nānkunāṭṭār at Anuradhapura]. *Cintaṉai* (Tamil) I, 4: 31-35.

______1970. Some Medieval Mercantile Communities of South India and Ceylon, *Journal of Tamil Studies*, II, 2, Madras: 25-39.

______1971. South Indian Mercantile Communities in Ceylon, circa 950-1250, *The Ceylon Journal of Historical and Social Studies*, New Series, I, 2: 101-113.

______1971a. Two Tamil Inscriptions from the Hindu Ruins, Anuradhapura, *ET*, I, 1:1-5.

______1971b. A Pillar Inscription from Mahakirindegama, *ET*, I, 1:6-9.

______1971c. A Fragmentary Inscription from Fort Hammenheil, Kayts, *ET*, I, 1:10-13.

______1971d. An Agampadi Inscription from Hingurakdamana, *ET*, I, 1:14-18.

______1971e. An Inscription of the time of Rājarāja Cōḻa I from Padaviya, *ET*, I, 1:32-36

______1971f. Fourteen Cōḻa Inscriptions from the Ancient Rājarāja-perumpaḷḷi (Velgam Vehera/Natanar Kovil) at Periyakulam, *ET*, I, 1:37-51.

______1971g. A Cōḻa Inscription from the Jaffna Fort, *ET*, I, 1:52-56.

______1973. A Brāhmī Potsherd Inscription from Kantarodai, *Purvakala*, Jaffna Archaeological Society Magazine, I, 1, Jaffna: 18-19.

______1975. *Vavuniya māvaṭṭattil kaṇṭeṭukkappaṭṭa mutalāvatu tamiḻ kalveṭṭu.*, *Vīrakēcari* 25/05/75 Colombo: 3.

______1978. An Inscription of the Tenth Year of Cōḻa Laṅkeśvara Deva from Kantalay, Sri Lanka, *Senarat Paranavitana Commemoration Volume* ed. L. Prematilleke, K. Indrapala and J.E.Van Lohuizen de Leeuw. Leiden: E.J.Brill.

______1979. Epigraphical Discoveries in Ceylon in the Last Decade (1959-1969), *Ancient Ceylon*, 3, August 1979 – Proceedings of the 2nd International Conference Seminar on Asian Archaeology, Colombo 1969: 153-160.

______1980. A Tamil Inscription from Nilaveli, Trincomalee District, *James Thevathasan Rutnam Felicitation Volume*, ed. Indrapala, K., Jaffna Archaeological Society, Jaffna: 164-169.

______1981. Is it an Indus-Brahmi Epigraph? *The Hindu*, Madras 26/04/1981: 19. Reproduced in Ragupathy 1987: 200-202.

______1983. The Recovery of the Pandya Regalia from Sri Lanka, *Journal of Archaeological Studies,* VII, Mysore: 9-16.

______1991. Inscription No.2 from Fort Hammenheil, Kayts, *Epigraphia Zeylanica*, VI, 2 Colombo: 154-160.

Indrapala, K. and Prematilleke, P.L. 1971. A Cōḷa Inscription from Medirigiriya, *ET*, I, !:25-28.

Jayakumar, P., 2001. Carnelian Beads from the Kodumanal Megaliths, *Kaveri*, ed. S.Rajagopal. 248-255.

Karashima, N., 2002. Tamil Inscriptions in Southeast Asia and China, In Karashima (ed.) 2002: 10-18.

Karashima, N. (ed.), 2002. *Ancient and Medieval Commercial Activities in the Indian Ocean: Testimony of Inscriptions and Ceramic-sherds,* Tokyo: Taisho University.

______(ed.) 2004. *In Search of Chinese Ceramic-sherds In South India and Sri Lanka*. Taisho University Press: Tokyo.

Karashima, N. and Subbarayalu, Y. 2002. Aiññūṟṟuvar: A Supra-local Organization of South Indian and Sri Lankan Merchants, Chapter 9 in Karashima N. (ed) 2002.

Karunaratne, Saddhamangala, 1984. *Epigraphia Zeylanica*, VII (Special Volume on the Brahmi Inscriptions of Sri Lanka), Archaological Survey of Ceylon, Colombo.

Kennedy, K.A.R., 1975. *The Physical Anthropology of the Megalithic-builders of South India and Sri Lanka,* Canberra: ANU

______1990. Palaeodemography of Sri Lanka and Peninsular India: A Cross-regional Survey, *Perspectives in Archaeology: Leelananda Prematilleke Festschrift 1990*, ed. Sudharshan Seneviratne et al, Peradeniya: 29-37.

Kenoyer, K.M., 1998. *Ancient Cities of the Indus Civilization,* Karachi: Oxford University Press.

Krishnamurti, Bhadriraju, 2003. *Dravidian Languages*, Cambridge University Press.

Lakdusinghe, Sirinimal, 1994. Hindu Bronzes of Sri Lanka, *Sacred Images of Sri Lanka*, The Art Gallery of New South Wales, Sydney: 20-23.

Liyanagamage, A., 1978. A Forgotten Aspect of the Relations between the Sinhalese and the Tamils, *Ceylon Historical Journal*, XXV, Colombo: 95-142.

______2001. *Society, State and Religion in Premodern Sri Lanka*, Kelaniya.

Ludden, David, 2002. *India and South Asia: A Short History*, One World Oxford.

Mahadevan, Iravatham, 2003. *Early Tamil Epigraphy: From the Earliest Times to the Sixth Century A.D.*, Harvard Oriental Series 62, Chennai.

Mahalingam, T.V., 1988. *Inscriptions of the Pallavas*, Delhi.

Markoe, Glenn E., 2000. *Phoenicians*, London: British Museum Press.

Nilakanta Sastri, K.A., 1955. *The Coḷas*, Madras: University of Madras.

Obeyesekere, Gananath, 1984. *The Cult of the Goddess Pattini*, Chicago: University of Chicago Press.

Paranavitana, S. 1926. Polonnaruva Inscription of Vijayabāhu I. *EI*, XVIII, 38: 330-338.

______194 Two Tamil Inscriptions from Budumuttava, *EZ*, III: 302-312.

______1949. On the Panakadu Inscription, *ASCAR for 1949*: 28-32.

______1959. Aryan Settlements: The Sinhalese, *UCHC*, I, 1: 82-97.

______1970. *Inscriptions of Ceylon*, I. Colombo.

Pushparatnam, P., 1993. *Pūnakari Tolporuḷāyvu* (Tamil: Pūnakari An Archaeological Survey), Tirunelveli (Jaffna).

Ragupathy, P., 1987. *Early Settlements in Jaffna: An Archaeological Survey*. Madras.

Rahman, Tariq, 2001. Peoples and Languages in Pre-Islamic Indus Valley, On-line article. 11/29/2001. http://link.lanic.utexas.edu/asnic/subject/peoplesandlanguages.html.

Rajagopal, S., ed., 2001. *Kaveri: Studies in Epigraphy, Archaeology and History*, Chennai: Panpattu Veliyiittakam.

Rajan, K., 1991. Archaeology of Dharmapuri District, Tamil Nadu, *Man and Environment*, 16, 1: 37-52.

______2001. Recent Advances in Early Historic Archaeology of Tamil Nadu, *Kaveri: Studies in Epigraphy, Archaeology and History*, 228-247, ed. S.Rajagopal, Chennai.

Rajan, K. and Bopearachchi, Osmund, 2002. Graffiti Marks of Kodumanal (India) and Ridiyagama (Sri Lanka) – A Comparative Study, *Man and Environment*, XXVII (2): 97-105.

Rajendran, P., 1984. Tenmalai Mesolithic Rockshelter – A Landmark in the Prehistoric Research in Kerala, *Journal of Indian History*, LXII, 1-3, Trivandram: 7-9.

Ramesh, K.V., 2002. Reconsidering Cultural Intercourse between India and Southeast Asia: An Epigraphical Report, in Karashima 2002: 147-163.

Renfrew, C., 1998. *Archaeology and Language: The Puzzle of Indo-European Origins*, London: Pimlico.

Renfrew, C. and Bahn, P., 1996. *Archaeology: Theories Methods and Practice,* London: Thames and Hudson.

Rutnam, J.T., 1988. *The Tomb of Elara at Anuradhapura*, Jaffna Archaeological Society: Jaffna.

Sarachchandra, E.R., 1966. *The Folk Drama of Ceylon*, Dept. of Cultural Affairs: Colombo.

Selvakumar, V., 2001. Culture and Chronology of the Lithic Industries from Southern Tamil Nadu, *Kaveri*: *Studies in Epigraphy, Archaeology and History,* ed. S.Rajagopal. 256-266.

Seneviratne, S., 1984. The Archaeology of the Megalithic – Black and Red Ware Complex in Sri Lanka, *Ancient Ceylon* 5, 237-307.

______1985a. *Social Base of Early Buddhism in South East India and Sri Lanka* (C. 3rd Century B.C. – 3rd Century A.D.), Jawaharlal Nehru University, New Delhi: Ph.D. Thesis, Department of History. Unpublished.

______1985b. The Baratas: A Case of Community Integration in Early Historic Sri Lanka, *Festschrift 1985: James Thevathasan Rutnam*, ed. A.R.B Amerasinghe & S.J. Sumanasekera Banda. Colombo: Sri Lanka UNESCO National Commission, 49-56.

______1992. Pre-State Chieftains and Servants of the State: A Case Study of Parumaka, *Sri Lanka Journal of Humanities* 15: 99-131.

______1996. State Formation in Peninsular India and Sri Lanka, *History of Humanity* III. New York: UNESCO, 378-384.

______2003. *The Philosophical and Social Role of Early Buddhism in South India*, Chennai

Shanmugam, P. 2004. Kantalay Inscriptions, in Karashima 2004: 75-80.

Srinivasa Iyengar, P.T., 1929. *History of the Tamils: From the Earliest Times to 600 A.D.*, Madras.

Subbarayalu, Y. 2004. Padaviya Inscriptions, in Karashima 2004: 66-74.

Subbarayalu, Y. and Karashima, N., 2002. A Trade Guild Inscription from Viharehinna in Sri Lanka, Karashima 2002:27-35.

Subbarayalu, Y. and Shanmugam, P., 2002. Texts of Select Inscriptions of the Merchant Guilds, Karashima 2002: 227-284.

Thapar, R. 1977. *A History of India*, I, Penguin: Harmondsworth England.

______2000. *History and Beyond*, New Delhi: Oxford University Press.

______2002. *Early India: From the Origins to AD 1300*, Allen Lane London.

Vacek, Jaroslav, 2002. *Dravidian and Altaic 'Water – Viscosity – Cold': An Etymological and Typological Model*, Charles University, Prague.

Van Lohuizen-De Leeuw, J.E., 1971. The Rock-Reliefs at Isurumuni, *Acta Orientalia Neerlandica: Proceedings of the Congress of the Dutch Oriental Society* May 1970, E.J.Brill Leiden: 113-119.

Weerakkody, D.P.M., 1997. *Taprobane: Ancient Sri Lanka as known to Greeks and Romans*, Turnhout: Brepols.

Zvelebil, Kamil, 2003. Dravidian Languages, *The New Encyclopaedia Britannica*, 22: 697-700.

GLOSSARY

Āḻvārs: Vaishnava saints belonging to the Bhakti movement in Tamil Nadu.

Austroasiatic: This is the language family to which the major laqnguages of mainland Southeast Asia belong. There are two subfamilies: Mon-Khmer (about 80 languages) and Munda (about 16 languages). The Austroasiatic language stock is considered to be a substratum for all Southeast Asian languages.

Austronesian: This is a large language family in which there are about 1200 languages (about a fifth of the world languages). It is spoken virtually in all the islands of Southeast Asia, as well as in Melanesia, Polynesia and the Indian Ocean island of Madagascar.

Before Present (BP): Before 1950 CE. Any time scale in years has to be counted from a fixed point in time. Scientists who calculate dates using radioactive methods have preferred to use a neutral international system that is not associated with any sectarian system like the Christian calendar. Choosing to count years back from the present (BP = Before Present), they take BP to mean 'Before 1950'. The year 1950 is the firm fixed point for this calculation. This is the approximate year when the first radioactive method, namely radiocarbon dating, was established by the scientist Willard Libby. (Renfrew and Bahn 1996: 112, 132)

Cetiya: Pali, from the Sanskrit *caitya*, meaning a shrine or religious building.

Chiefdom: 'A term used to describe a society that operates on the principle of ranking, i.e. differential social status. Different lineages are graded on a scale of prestige, calculated by how closely related one is to the chief. The chiefdom generally has a permanent ritual and ceremonial center, as well as being characterized by local specialization in crafts.' (Renfrew and Bahn 1996: 540)

Common Era: The same as the Christian Era. The names Common Era (CE) and Before the Common Era (BCE) do not have any sectarian association.

Holocene epoch: The period of warmer climate, the second epoch of the Quaternary Period, after the Pleistocene Epoch, beginning approximately 10,000 years ago and continuing to the present.

Interglacial: The name given to the warmer interludes separating the four major *glacials* or periods of glacial advance in the Ice Age.
Iron Age: This term was first used in the nineteenth century by the Danish scholar C.J. Thomsen when he proposed the Three Age System (Stone Age, Bronze Age and Iron Age). Archaeologists found this to be a convenient conceptual device offering a framework for studying the past. The Iron Age covers different periods in different countries.
Lineage: A group that claims descent from a common ancestor.
Nāyaṉārs: Saiva saints belonging to the Bhakti movement in Tamil Nadu.
Pleistocene epoch: The name given to the Ice Age when large parts of the earth's surface were covered with ice. This epoch began about two to three million years ago and lasted till about 10,000 years ago.
Prakrit: This name refers to a number of languages and dialects spoken in South Asia about 2000 years ago and of which we have record from about the sixth century BCE. These languages were lineal descendants of Old Indo-Aryan (Sanskrit) and belong to the Middle Indo-Aryan group. In Sanskrit, *prākrta* refers to what the Indian linguist S.M. Katre has defined as the "natural languages of the 'people' uncontrolled by the normative rules of grammarians…as opposed to Sanskrit, the refined language of the gods and the learned." (Quoted in Sjoberg 1992: 518)
Quaternary Period: Geologists use a Geologic Time Scale which organizes all of Earth history into blocks of time. The largest time span on this scale is the eon. Eons are subdivided into eras, eras into periods and periods into epochs. The Quaternary Period is the second period of the Cenozoic Era, beginning two to three million years ago and continuing to the present time.
Radiocarbon dating: 'Radiocarbon is the single most useful method of dating for the archaeologist'. Radiocarbon from the atmosphere is passed on uniformly to all living things through carbon dioxide. When a plant or animal dies, the uptake of radiocarbon stops and the concentration of radiocarbon begins to decline through radioactive decay. The decay takes place at a regular rate which has been estimated to be 5730 years for half the radiocarbon in any sample to decay (its half-life). The age of dead plant or animal tissue could be

calculated by measuring the amount of radiocarbon left in a sample. (Renfrew and Bahn 1996: 132)

Sanskritisation: This term is used here in place of 'Indianisation', 'Hinduisation' and 'Aryanisation' that were widely used in earlier historical writings on South and Southeast Asia to refer to the spread of elements of Indian culture. 'Indianisation' has a tinge of colonialism in its connotation while 'Aryanisation' smacks of racialism. 'Hinduisation' has a religious association. What these terms have been used to refer to is basically a cultural dialogue through which various elements of the culture that developed in north India in the first millennium BCE spread to other parts of South Asia and then to Southeast Asia. As the French scholar G. Coedes has defined it, this process 'must be understood essentially as the expansion of an organized culture that was founded upon the Indian conception of royalty, was characterized by Hinduist or Buddhist cults, the mythology of the *Puranas*, and the observance of the *Dharmasastras*, and expressed in the Sanskrit language.' (Coedes 1968: 15-16). It was essentially a cultural influence that spread among the elite in the chiefdoms of peninsular India, Sri Lanka and Southeast Asia. The chiefs adopted and adapted various elements, including Sanskrit names and titles, the practice of appointing Brāhmaṇa advisers (*purohita*), Brahmanical court rituals, linkage of their lineages with north Indian mythical and epic heroes, worship of Brahmanical deities or the Buddha, and the use of the Sanskrit language and Prakrits. Trade with north India played an important role in the spread of this culture. The term Sanskritization has cultural and linguistic connotations, free from any colonial or racial bias, and is, therefore, preferred as the most suitable of the terms used so far by scholars to describe this process. The eminent Indian sociologist, M.N. Srinivas, has used this term to refer to the process of social mobility in modern India through which "'lower' castes which have become prosperous or powerful or educated like to assert their claim to a higher place in the hierarchy by taking on a new name and by Sanskritizing their ritual" (M.N. Srinivas, 1992, *On Living In A Revolution and Other Essays*, OUP Delhi: 119).

Segmentary society: This is used in place of the term 'tribe' which is considered by some scholars to be rather vague. 'Tribe' implies a larger grouping of smaller units and 'carries with it the assumption that these communities share a common ethnic identity and self-awareness, which is now known not generally to be the case. The term "segmentary society" refers to a relatively small and autonomous group, usually of agriculturists, who regulate their own affairs: in some cases, they may join together with other comparable segmentary societies to form a larger ethnic unit or "tribe"; in other cases, they do not.' (Renfrew and Bahn 1996: 169)

APPENDIX 1

A Note on Īḻam (Coconut)

An ancient Tamil word for coconut is *īḻam*. The element *īḻa* is found in several archaic or old Tamil words. All of them may be ultimately associated with Īḻam, the name of Sri Lanka. In that sense, the occurrence of the word *īḻam* for coconut may also be in some way connected with the history of coconut. This palm is native to Southeast Asia and researchers now seem to think that it is from there that the palm was introduced to the Pacific islands where it is found in abundance today. Without doubt the coconut was introduced to Sri Lanka from Southeast Asia, possibly earlier than its introduction to the Indian mainland. The names given to coconut in Tamil appear to confirm this.

While most of the Indian languages use the word *nārikela* or its derivatives for coconut, the names given for this nut in Sinhala and Tamil are different. In Sinhala it is known as *pol* (which is surmised to be of Austroasiatic origin[1]). In modern Tamil, the words *teṉṉai* and *teṉṉa-maram* are used for the palm. Another word, *teṅku*, occurs in literature. The word for the nut, *tēṅkāi*, may be derived from *teṅku*. The root of these seems to be *teṉ*, meaning south. *Teṉṉa-maram* literally means 'the tree of the south' or 'the tree from the south' (cf. *teṉṉavaṉ* = He of the South, and *teṉṉakkōṉ* = King of the South, both meaning the Pāṇḍya king). *Teṅku* is a variant of *teṟku* (=south) and occurs in the early Tamil Brāhmī inscriptions. *Teṅku-maram* would also mean 'the tree of the south' and *tēṅkai* (coconut) would originally have been *teṅku-kāi*, the fruit of *teṅku* (cf. *miḷaku+kāi* = *miḷakāi*). It is not difficult to infer that the palm introduced from the island in the south (Sri Lanka) or first known as a tree found in the island to the south of the Tamil land acquired the name *teṉṉa-maram*. Though not in vogue now, more than a thousand years ago, possibly about two thousand years ago, there was also another word in Tamil for coconut and that was *īḻam*. Just as *teṉṉa-maram* was a name given to the palm on account of its place of origin (insofar as south India was concerned), *īḻa-maram* may have been used in the sense of 'the tree from Īḻam' (Sri Lanka). *Īḻak-kāi* would then be the nut and *īḻa-nīr* (*īḻa* water) the water in its kernel (scientifically termed coconut milk). *Īḻa-nīr* has, however, survived to this day in the corrupted (or original?) form *iḷa-nīr* and is commonly understood as 'tender water'. But it should be noted that this term is used not just for the water of the young or tender coconut but for the water of any coconut, tender or mature. And what is more, it is used exclusively for the water in the coconut. It must have, therefore, been originally *īḻanīr* (coconut water). On the other hand, *iḷanīr* may have been the original form, since the forms *iḻa* (identified with *īḻa*) and *iḷa* (possibly an alternative form) occur in the earliest Tamil-Brahmi inscriptions (see p.124 for a discussion of these words).

More than a thousand years ago, the name Īḻavar was used in Tamil to refer to the caste associated with climbing the coconut palm (a specialized occupation in Sri Lankan and South Indian societies). Until modern times, in Kerala as well as in Tamil Nadu, the caste of coconut-climbers have been called Īḻavar and, particularly in Kerala, their traditions refer to their original home as Sri Lanka. In the name Īḻavar, too, the association of Īḻa with coconut is significant. The earliest occurrence of this caste name is in the Tamil inscriptions of the ninth century (such as the Velurpalaiyam Plates of Nandivarman III and the Sthāṇu Ravi Plates from Kerala). About the same time, in Tamil epigraphy one comes across the words Īḻam (coconut), Īḻam-pūṭci (a tax on coconut), Īḻam-puñcey (possibly land where coconut was grown, although in later times it seems to refer to the Īḻavar caste), Īḻac-cēri (section of a village where the caste of Īḻavar resided) and Īḻac-cāṉṟāṉ (presumably a prominent member of the Īḻavar caste).

Īḻam also acquired another meaning in Tamil, presumably in the time of the Cōḻa empire. This new meaning was 'gold', derived from a gold coin from Sri Lanka known as Īḻak-kācu (the Sri Lanka coin) that had gained currency in south India. The comment of Nilakanta Sastri on this subject is worthy of note:

The standard *kāśu*, moreover, derived ultimately from Ceylon which had a more ancient and continuous currency tradition than the Cōḷa kingdom which came up in the ninth and tenth centuries. The *īḻak-kāśu*, Ceylon *kāśu*, which was also half-a-*kaḻañju* of the fineness of the *māḍai*, was current in the island as early as the seventh and eighth centuries; it is also mentioned in Coḷa inscriptions from about A.D. 937 in the reign of Parāntaka I.[2]

Since the *Īḻakkācu* was a gold coin, the word *īḻam* also came to be used for gold. This is comparable to the way in which other words came to be adopted in Tamil for gold from the names of gold currency in later times. For instance, the gold coin *Tanka* paved the way for the use of *taṅkam* as a word for gold. In the time of British rule, the English Pound introduced another word in Tamil for gold, namely *pavuṇ*, which is still in use (sometimes in a tautological compound *taṅka-pavuṇ*). Besides the *Īḻakkācu*, there was also another coin from Sri Lanka, the *Īḻakkaruṅkācu* that was in use in the Cōḻa kingdom.

Although it may be debatable whether the name *īḻam* (or its root of which we do not know anything) for coconut came first or whether it was first applied to an ethnic group in the island (or even the island itself), it seems likely that the Tamil word for coconut came later.

---

1. Prof. D.E.Hettiarachchi in *UCHC*, 1, 1:36; P.C.Bagchi, 1929, *Pre-Aryan and Pre-Dravidian in India*: xxviii (Calcutta).
2. Nilakanta Sastri 1955: 617.

APPENDIX II

A Note on the Vēḷaikkārar

One of the significant sections of the armed forces of the Cōḷa and Sinhalese rulers in Sri Lanka in the eleventh and twelfth centuries was the warrior community named Vēḷaikkārar. Much has been written about this community but there are certain misconceptions regarding them among writers on Sri Lankan history. There will always be some controversy relating to the origin of the name and the organization of the community as well as its role in the army and in the security services to individuals and institutions.

The best source of information on this subject is undoubtedly the well known Polonnaruva Tamil inscription set up by the Vēḷaikkārar themselves some time in the latter half of the eleventh century. Besides this, there are at least two other Tamil inscriptions in the island, from Gal Oya and Palamottai, and some notices in the Pali chronicle *Cūḷavaṃsa* that provide some information about the activities of this group.

Nilakanta Sastri has explained that the word *Vēḷaikkārar* is derived from the word *vēḷai* (= time, occasion, moment) and that it stands for the 'time or occasion indicated in an oath by the soldier who binds himself by the oath to lay down his life in certain contingencies'.[1] He has also given the alternative interpretation that 'their designation implies that they were ever ready to defend the king and his cause with their lives when occasion (*vēḷai*) arose'.[2] One cannot, however, be certain that the element *vēḷai* in the name Vēḷaikkārar is the same as the Tamil word meaning time or occasion. It is quite possible that it is derived from some other word now unknown to us (cf. the Indonesian word *bela*, 'to defend').

References to the Vēḷaikkārar occur in Tamil epigraphy and literature from the eleventh century. Although they are better known as constituting sections of the armies of rulers, the members of this community were not all in the employ of kings. Many were in the

PLATE 20.
Tamil inscription from Panduvasnuvara, dated in the reign of Nissanka Malla. 12th century. It records the establishment of certain Buddhist institutions in the town of Sripura. The record is in Tamil verse and is the second oldest Tamil verse found on stone slabs in Sri Lanka.

***Photo** of estampage. **Courtesy**: Department of Archaeology.*

PLATE 21.
Bharata Natya at the Sinhalese court, Yapahuva. 13th century. Dance friezes carved on either side of the main entrance to the royal palace at Yapahuva. This evidence 'strengthens the view that Bharata Natyam constituted the entertainment of royalty and the lay elite' (Prof. E.R. Sarachchandra). See p. 281.

***Photo:** March 2005, by author. **Courtesy:** Department of Archaeology.*

PLATE 22.
Bharata Natya relief sculpture, Yapahuva.

service of village assemblies and other institutions. They seem to have been divided into different types, apparently according to the nature of the duty performed by them. We meet with the following types, for instance, in our sources: a) Pū-Vēḷaikkārar (Tamil *pū* = flowers), b) Kaḷḷa-Vēḷaikkārar (Tamil *kaḷḷar* = robbers), c) Rākṣasa-Vēḷaikkārar (Skt. *rākṣasa* = giant), d) Tacca-Vēḷaikkārar (Tamil *taccar* = carpenters), e) Tiru-cūla-Vēḷaikkārar (Tamil *tiru* = sacred, *cūlam* = spear), and f) Tiru-ciṟṟampala-Vēḷaikkārar (*ciṟṟampalam* = hall of wisdom). The exact functions of these different Vēḷaikkārar groups or regiments are not clear from their names. Pū-Vēḷaikkārar may have been those who guarded the flower garden in a temple. Kaḷḷa-Vēḷaikkārar may have been employed to guard a place against thieves. One can only speculate on their functions from the names born by their groups.

A number of divisions of Vēḷaikkārar, probably in the service of kings, were named after kings and princes. Among them were the a) Nittavinota-Vēḷaikkārar, b) Jananāta-teriñca-Vēḷaikkārar, c) Aḻakiya Coḻa-teriñca-Vēḷaikkārar, d) Aridurga-lānghana-terinta-valaṅkai-Vēḷaikkārar, e) Candra-parakrama-terinta-valankai-Vēḷaik-kārar, and f) Iḷaiya-rāja-terinta-valaṅkai-Vēḷaikkārar. The epithet *valaṅkai* or *iṭaṅkai* denoted their caste group. In Sri Lanka, too, there were similarly named Vēḷaikkārar divisions, such as the Vikkirama-calāmēka-terinta-valaṅkai-Vēḷaikkārar.

From the evidence that is available, it is clear that these soldiers were not a ‘warlike tribe or a clan or a military community’, as Wilhelm Geiger thought,[3] but were more ‘a type of troops bound by specific oaths of loyalty which they were bound to keep at the risk of their own lives’, as surmised by Nilakanta Sastri.[4] They were closely associated with the south Indian mercantile communities and appear to have been organized as a military guild. They were drawn from different castes but may have observed caste distinctions between the broad categories of Valaṅkai and Iṭaṅkai (the Right Hand and Left Hand caste divisions of south Indian society).

The Vēḷaikkārar played an important role in Sri Lanka in the battles of the eleventh century and in the provision of security to various religious institutions and possibly commercial establishments. Very little information is given about them in the chronicles but there is interesting information in the Tamil records about their activities in the island. They were without doubt among the various forces that strengthened the Tamil and other south Indian elements in northern Sri Lanka.

The Vēḷaikkārar appear to have been in the Sinhalese kingdom as early as the tenth century. The ninth and tenth centuries constituted a period when the Anuradhapura rulers, and aspirants to power, recruited Tamil soldiers to strengthen their troops. These soldiers are commonly referred to in Sinhalese inscriptions as *mey-kāppar* (literally, 'bodyguards'; Tamil *mey* = body, *kāppar* = guards). Interestingly, south Indian Tamil rulers also, it appears, recruited Sinhalese soldiers as *meykāppar* to serve in their kingdoms. Such a practice of recruiting security personnel from an alien ethnic group is not surprising, as it was common among other ancient rulers as well. The Celtic ruler of Britannia, some time in the middle of the fifth century, plagued by the raids of the Irish and the Pictish, invited a band of mercenaries from the Continent under the leadership of Hengest and Horsa. The Germanic settlements soon followed. In south India, the Tamil rulers of the Pallava, Pāṇḍya and Cōḷa kingdoms recruited Telugu and Keraḷa soldiers (*Vaṭukar* and *Malaiyāḷar*). That the Pallava rulers employed Sinhalese soldiers (*Ciṅkaḷa meykāppar*), too, is know from one of their inscriptions. The Sinhalese kings of Anuradhapura, on the other hand, relied on Telugu, Keraḷa, Kannaḍa and Tamil soldiers. In recent times, we have the example of the Dutch colonial rulers of Sri Lanka recruiting Malays from their Indonesian colonies to serve as a specially dependable regiment in the island. The rationale behind this practice is not difficult to seek. The local soldiers, in times of conflict with other local leaders, were less dependable than complete outsiders who had no special loyalty or attachment to anyone other than their employer.

An inscription of the Anuradhapura king Kassapa IV (898-914) gives information about a certain Veḷakkā who was a *meykāppar*.[5] The name is so close to the Pali form Veḷakkāra, given to the south Indian regiments in the Pali chronicle *Cūḷavaṃsa*, and the profession of the person concerned is that of the Vēḷaikkārar that it is difficult to dismiss this epigraphic reference as not related to a Vēḷaikkārar soldier. Considering the fact that Tamil *meykāppar* were numerous in the Anuradhapura kingdom in the tenth century, it would appear that Vēḷaikkārar were among these soldiers.

In the eleventh century there is ample evidence about the activities of the Vēḷaikkārar in northern Sri Lanka. Since the Cōḻa rulers Rājarāja I and Rājendra I had several Vēḷaikkārar regiments in their service, the Cōḻa armies that invaded the island in the eleventh century may have included the Vēḷaikkārar. There is, however, no direct evidence on this. On the other hand, there is evidence that Sinhalese leaders employed the Vēḷaikkārar in their armies. In addition, these soldiers were also employed by non-political organzations. The most valuable record we have about their activities is the Tamil inscription from Polonnaruva, generally referred to as the Vēḷaikkāra Inscription.[6]

It is from this Polonnaruva inscription that we know many details about the organization of the Vēḷaikkārar in Sri Lanka. This record in Tamil was inscribed by the Vēḷaikkārar not long after the death of Vijayabāhu I (i.e., after 1070) proclaiming their undertaking to protect the Buddhist Temple of the Tooth Relic at the request of a leading Buddhist High Priest and some officials. It refers to the different sections that composed the group. Among them were the Valaṅkai, Iṭaṅkai, Ciṟutaṉam, Piḷḷaikaḷtaṉam, Vaṭukar, Malaiyāḷar and Parivārakoṇṭam. This mixed composition of the Vēḷaikkārar clearly shows that they were not members of one military caste or community but were organized more like a military guild. Of these different sections, the Vēḷaikkārar of the Valaṅkai and Iṭaṅkai were obviously soldiers drawn from the two categories of south Indian castes known by those names. The Vaṭukar and Malaiyāḷar refer to the Telugu soldiers and Kerala soldiers respectively. It is evident that the organization consisted of different linguistic or ethnic groups.

The Polonnaruva inscription also helps to establish the link between the mercantile communities and the Vēḷaikkārar organization. The mercantile community named Valañciyar is explicitly mentioned here as the *mūtātaikaḷ* of the Vēḷaikkārar. While different interpretations could be given to the term *mūtātaikaḷ*, the most suitable meaning is 'leaders'. That the mercantile communities themselves employed these regiments to protect their properties and supplied Vēḷaikkārar troops to the rulers seems very probable. There is little doubt that the mercantile communities exercised influence over the Vēḷaikkārar.

Besides the Polonnaruva inscription, there are also some short Tamil inscriptions of the eleventh century referring to the Vēḷaikkārar.

---

1. Nilakanta Sastri, K.A, Vijayabāhu I, The Liberator of Ceylon, *JRASCB*, IV, NS, 1954: 68.
2. Nilakanta Sastri 1955: 454
3. Geiger, W., *Culture of Ceylon in Medieval Times*, 1960: 152.
4. Nilakanta Sastri 1954: 58.
5. *EZ*, III: 276.
6. *EI,* XVIII: 330-338.

APPENDIX III

The Saiva bronze sculptures of Sri Lanka

The many metal images unearthed in the ancient cities of Anuradhapura, Polonnaruva and elsewhere are unquestionably among the artistic treasures of Sri Lanka. 'The bronze images of Buddhas, Bodhisattvas, Hindu gods and goddesses coming from the earth of Sri Lanka', as Adrian Snodgrass describes, 'are priceless additions to the world's heritage of historical and aesthetic treasures'.[1] Among these are some of the finest Saiva images found anywhere. A few of them have drawn the attention of art critics ever since their discovery almost a century ago. All of them are the subject of a controversy about their origin.

These Saiva bronzes belong to about the 11th-12th centuries. Many of them were discovered in 1907 when H.C.P. Bell (Archaeological Commissioner) conducted excavations at Polonnaruva.[2] A few more were discovered by him the next year.[3] Many more remained undiscovered in that ancient city until 1960 when C.E. Godakumbure conducted excavations.[4] In 1982 and 1984, when work under the UNESCO-sponsored Cultural Triangle Project led to fresh excavations, important Saiva bronzes came to light at Anuradhapura as well. Outside these two ancient cities, some Saiva bronzes of considerable importance were unearthed at Trincomalee, near the site of the ancient Konesvaram temple.[5] However, it is the Polonnaruva bronzes that have always been in the limelight.

Among the Polonnaruva bronzes, the images of Naṭarāja, Śiva as the Lord of Dance, have been the focus of much attention. There are several good examples of them and they are now in the Colombo Museum. The Naṭarāja images numbered 1, 2 and 15 are considered to be among the best.[6] One of the images discovered in 1960, with a height of 146.8 cm, is among the largest Naṭarāja statues. Of the statues of goddesses, those of Pārvatī and Śivakāmaṉsundarī are worthy of mention. There is also a large image of Ganeśa. Among the other notable bronzes from Polonnaruva are those of five Saiva saints, namely Kāraikkāl Ammaiyār, Appar, Cuntarar, Campantar and Māṇikkavācakar.

The Saiva bronzes discovered at Anuradhapura come from the Jetavanārāma site. Of the bronzes found here, three are images of Śiva and one is that of Pārvatī. It has been pointed out that these bronzes display certain distinctive characteristics indicating that they belong to a Sri Lankan school of sculpture. An earlier and more interesting bronze sculpture comes from the site of the Abhayagiri monastery. It is the image of Ardha-nārīśvara (composite male and female figure). This image is datable to the 7th-8th century and shows some characteristics of Pallava sculpture.[7]

The bronzes from Trincomalee were unearthed in 1950 at two different sites in private properties. There are five of them and these are now kept in the new Konesar Temple at Trincomalee. Two are statues of Śiva, two of Pārvatī and one of Ganeśa.[8]

From the time of the discovery of the first group of Polonnaruva bronzes in 1907, there has been a controversy about their origin. Some scholars have expressed the view that these bronzes, or some of them at least, were imports from south India while some others have argued that they were locally made. After the discovery of more bronzes in 1960, the view that these were produced locally has strengthened. In recent years, Lakdusinghe has adduced valid arguments to show that there existed a Sri Lankan school of Hindu sculpture.[9] An eminent Indian art critic, C.Sivaramamurti, has also put forward emphatic views in support of this theory.[10]

---

1. Snodgrass, Adrian, 1994. 'Introduction', *Sacred Images of Sri Lanka*, The Art Gallery of New South Wales, Sydney: 10.
2. *ASCAR for 1907.*
3. *ASCAR for 1908.*

4. *ASCAR for 1960*: 23; Godakumbure, C.E., 1961. 'Bronzes from Polonnaruva', *JCBRAS*, NS, VII, 2, 1961: 239-253.
5. Balendra, W., 1953. 'Trincomalee Bronzes', *Tamil Culture*, II, 2: 176-198.
6. Commenting on Naṭarāja bronzes in general, Vincent Smith gives a high rating for No.1 and No.15: 'Among good examples may be classed Dr.Coomaraswamy's favourite in the Madras Museum, the Tanjore specimen, and No.1 from Polonnaruva. The No.15 image, without the ring of fire, is the most artistic of all. It is described as being 'the best finished of all the bronzes', and is deserving of the care spent on its production.' *A History of Fine Art in India and Ceylon*, Oxford, 1930: 254. Benjamin Rowland's comment about this image is also worthy of note: 'One of the greatest Nataraja images is preserved in the museum at Colombo…The figure, a perfect fusion of serenity and balance, moves in slow and gracious rhythm, lacking the usual violence of the cosmic dance; this is a cadenced movement communicated largely by the centrifugal space-embracing position of the arms and the suggestion of the figure's revolving in space. The turning effect that comes from the arrangement of the multiple arms, one behind another, and the torsion of the figure, emphasized by the direction of the limbs give something of the effect of the *figura serpentinata* in Mannerist sculpture that seems to coerce the beholder into a consecutive inspection of the image from every angle.' *The Art and Architecture of India*, Penguin Book, 1977: 330, 332.

7. Wickramagamage, Chandra, *Second Report of the Archaeological Excavations at the Abhayagiri Vihara Complex*, Apr.-Oct. 1982: 141-142; Lakdusinghe 1994: 51, 53; Pathmanathan, S., 2003, 'Some Bronzes from the Jetavanarama Site of Anuradhapura', *Glimpses of Hindu Heritage, 2nd World Hindu Conference Souvenir*, ed. Patrick Harrigan et al, Colombo: 151-156.
8. E.Krishna Iyer has made the following comment on one of them: 'The fine combination of easy pose, significant hand mudras, and engaging facial expression in the sitting Siva icon makes it appear as Karunamurti lovingly beckoning to his devotees to come and receive His unbounded grace and blessings.' Newly Found Trincomalee Icons, *The Madras Hindu*, 4 November 1951: 12.
9. Lakdusinghe 1994: 22.
10. Seeing certain special features in the four images of the Saiva saints, Sivaramamurti comments: 'Intoxicated by the soul-stirring hymns of these great saints the sculptors in metal from Ceylon created these strikingly beautiful bronzes of the saints. They are somewhat different from what we normally know in the mainland itself, but, at the same time, are so full of the spirit of the *Tevāram* hymns, which give a deeply religious halo, that they must at once be pronounced as distinct, and undoubtedly a speciality of Ceylon'. Sivaramamurti discerns distinctive features in the other Saiva bronzes as well, especially those of Naṭarāja, Pārvatī, Śivakāmasundarī and Kāraikkālammaiyār: 'It is not in the fashioning of these

[saints] alone but in some other figures also, there is a distinctiveness noticed which should undoubtedly be pronounced as the work of Ceylonese craftsmen inspired by the craft from the mainland.' Sivaramamurti, C., 1974, *Nataraja in Art, Thought and Literature*, New Delhi: 371-372.

APPENDIX IV

South Indian Mercantile Communities

Aiññūṟṟuvar (Nānādeśī)

The most prominent of the mercantile communities that operated in south India and Sri Lanka in the eleventh and twelfth centuries was the Aiññūṟṟuvar. Despite the large number of records left behind by members of this community, it is not easy to establish whether the name Aiññūṟṟuvar refers to a single mercantile group or to several communities and professional groups that were bound together by some kind of sectarian commercial code. The evidence of the inscriptions is insufficient to determine the nature of the organization of this community and its relations with the other bodies associated with it. The most recent study about the activities of this community concludes that 'the *aiññūṟṟuvar*, otherwise known as *padineṇ-vishayam/ padineṇ-bhūmi* or *nānādēsi*, is a concept of the merchant organization which overarches all the substantial merchant organizations formed in some particular area, locality or town.'[1] This may well be the case.

An analysis of the epigraphic records of the Aiññūṟṟuvar, numbering more than six dozen and ranging from the eighth to the seventeenth century, shows that the community possibly originated in Aihole (ancient Ayyāvoḷe, Tamil Ayyappoḷal) in Karnataka, and was bound by a code known as *Banañju Dharma*. The significance of the numerical name '*Aiññūṟṟuvar*' (Five Hundred Persons) is not clear. Such numerical names were common for mercantile and other professional bodies in India.[2] The community was not a single unified corporation of merchants. It is more appropriate to call it a community of merchants with common interests and beliefs, bound together by the *Banañju Dharma*.[3]

Members of the Aiññūṟṟuvar were primarily traders in various types of merchandise. They claimed to have visited a large number of countries and their records have been found in Sri Lanka and Southeast Asia as well.[4] In many trading centres and market-towns, they seem to have occupied a supreme position among the large number of professional groups in those places and acted as their leaders, exercising considerable power and influence over them.

Añjuvaṇṇam

The Añjuvaṇṇam (Añcuvaṇṇam) is another of the major mercantile communities that were active in south India and Sri Lanka as well as Southeast Asia in the period 9th-13th centuries. Unlike the Aiññūṟṟuvar, this community was of West Asian origin and possibly included Muslim as well as Jewish merchants. Going by the epigraphic records referring to the community, it appears to have worked harmoniously with mercantile groups whose religious affiliation was Saiva or Vaisnava. The early activities of the community seems to have begun on the west coast of India, particularly the Kerala ports. Later, its activities spread to the east coast, Sri Lanka and Southeast Asia.[5]

The name Añjuvaṇṇam appears to be derived ultimately from the Persian *hañjamana* /*añjuman.* Subbarayalu very convincingly argues that it is not a name of Indian origin. 'Like the term Yavana/Yona/Sonaka', he concludes, 'this term also seems to have denoted collectively the West asian traders, Arabs, Jews, Christians, Parsees, etc.' and that it may be inferred from the available evidence 'that Arab Muslims figured more prominently than others'.[6]

The Añjuvaṇṇam merchants were doubtless the ancestors of the Muslim communities of Sri Lanka and some parts of south India. In Sri Lanka, the language of the Muslim communities has traditionally been Tamil and the names given to them in the local languages, in common parlance, are *Marakkala minissu* (the Marakkala people) in Sinhala and *Cōṉakar* (Sonakar, from Yona/Yavana) in Tamil. In the south Indian sources, the Añjuvaṇṇam is associated with the names *Marakāla* and *Cōṉakar*, and already in the ninth century the use of Tamil by this community is evidenced in Kerala inscriptions.[7] From Telugu inscriptions we get to know that there was a community of Añjuvaṇṇam merchants established at Mātōṭṭam (Mātoṭa), the ancient port on the northwest coast of Sri Lanka, in the twelfth century.[8]

Maṇigrāmam

The Maṇigrāmam (Maṇikkirāmam), as a mercantile community, finds mention in inscriptions from about the ninth century. We find them active on the Kerala coast, in association with the Añjuvaṇṇam, as well as in Takua-pa in Thailand in that century. They are found in Sri Lanka in the tenth century. Members of this community continued to be active in south India for several centuries and their inscriptions are available as late as the fourteenth century.[9]

The origin of this mercantile community is as obscure as that of the other south Indian merchant groups. It has been suggested that a community by the name of Maṇigrāmam may have existed in the ancient port of Kavirippūmpaṭṭiṉam (Kaveripaṭṭina) in the early centuries CE.[10] There is, however, no mention of a commercial group with this name until the time of the well-known copper plates of Sthāṇu Ravi (ninth century). From these copper plates it is known that this community was operating at the Kerala port of Kollam in the ninth century.[11] In the same century, members of this community were active in the Southeast Asian port of Takua-pa where they were given custody of a reservoir and were possibly responsible for its maintenance. The fact that the reservoir was named Avanināraṇam, after a Pallava ruler, and the discovery of a Viṣṇu and other statues in the Pallava style in association with the Tamil inscription mentioning the Maṇigrāmam may mean that this community had established a trading settlement at the Thai port in the ninth century.[12] It would appear that members of this community had also penetrated into the early Malay and Sumatran states of Indonesia about this time or somewhat later, for we come across the name Baṇigrāma in the epigraphic records of Java and Bali. 'These inscriptions', explains Christie, 'also indicate that while the term *baṇigrāma* (the Javanized version of *vāṇigrāma*) was used in Javanese and Balinese port texts for a time, these *baṇigrāma* appear to have been rather fluid, port-based groupings that incorporated both local and foreign merchants, some of whom were acting as tax farmers under licence from local rulers.'[13] In Sri Lanka, we get evidence of the activities of the Maṇigrāmam in the interior market-town of Hopiṭigamu in the middle of the tenth century.[14]

Although later inscriptions mentioning the Maṇigrāmam in Sri Lanka have not come to light, a south Indian record of the thirteenth century refers to them in association with other mercantile communities connected with Sri Lanka (the Añjuvaṇṇam and the Tenṉilaṅkai Valañciyar).[15] Possibly they continued to be a trading community in Sri Lanka even in the thirteenth century.

---

1. Karashima and Subbarayalu 2002: 87.
2. Cf. Eḻunūrukar (700) and Aññūrukar (500) divisions in the Syrian Christian community of Kerala, the Munnūruvaru (300) of Karnataka, and the Tillai Mūvāyiravar (3000) Brahmins of Cidambaram.
3. Indrapala 1970.
4. Indrapala 1971j; Karashima and Subbarayalu 2002; Karashima 2002: 3ff.; Christie 1998: 239ff.
5. Subbarayalu, Y., 2001, Añjuvaṇṇam A Maritime Trade Guild of Medieval Times, *Kaveri: Studies in Epigraphy, Archaeology and History*, ed. S.Rajagopal, Chennai; Abraham 1988.
6. Ibid: 149.
7. Ibid: 144-147, 149.
8. Subbarayalu and Shanmugam 2002: 236-237.
9. Abraham 1988: 13ff.
10. Champakalakshmi 1996: 49.
11. Ibid: 20.

12. Karashima 2002: 11; Christie 1998: 251.

13. Christie 1998: 244.

14. *EZ*, V: 182. In this inscription from Badulla the community is referred to as Vaṇigrāma, which is a variant form of Maṇigrāmam. This variant occurs in contemporary Tamil literature as *vaṇikkirāmam* (also read as *vaṇikakirāmam*) – *Tolkāppiyam: Naccin̲ārkkin̲iyar Urai*, Tañcāvūr 1962: 173.

15. Subbarayalu and Shanmugam 2002: 269.

APPENDIX V

Sanskritisation legends of South India, Sri Lanka and Southeast Asia

1. The Agastya Legends

These are among the earliest legends connected with the spread of Sanskritisation in south India. These legends are found in the epics, *Mahābhārata* and *Rāmāyaṇa*, as well as in the *purāṇas*. Many shrines in Kerala and Tamil Nadu have their own legends claiming some connection with Agastya. The central figure in these legends is the sage (*rishi*) Agastya.

Agastya, a Brāhmaṇa by caste, is credited with the feat of subduing the insurmountable Vindhya Mountains and crossing over to the south where he established his hermitage on Mount Kuñjara. He married Lopāmudra, who, according to some legends, was the daughter of the sage Kāvera, while other legends treat her as the adopted daughter of the king of Vidarbha, a kingdom in the south. According to the legends in the *Mahābhārata*, Agastya kept the Rākṣasas (demons), who were found everywhere in the south, under control. He even ate a troublesome Rākṣasa named Vātāpi who assumed the form of a ram. When that Rākṣasa's brother, Ilvala, tried to take revenge, Agastya destroyed him. The sage is also credited with introducing literature to the south and writing the first grammar of the Tamil language.

2. The Parasurāma legends

These legends are associated with the process of Sanskritisation in Kerala. A Brāhmaṇa by birth, Parasurāma (Rāma who wields the Axe) is considered as one of the *avatārs* of the god Viṣṇu. His use of a powerful axe (*parasu*), given to him by Śiva, dominates the legends about him. He is depicted as a warrior who instructed Arjuṇa (a hero of the *Mahābhārata*) in the use of arms. He was hostile to the Kṣatriyas and was responsible for settling Brāhmaṇas from the north in Kerala. To protect the Brāhmaṇas from their enemies, Parasurāma created the land of Kerala. He threw his divine axe across the sea from Gokarṇa (on the west coast of India). The weapon fell in the region of Kanyākumari (Cape Comorin) and all the sea between Gokarṇa and Kanyākumari became dry land which Parasurāma donated to the Brāhmaṇas.

3. The Arjuṇa legends

The third of the five Paṇḍu princes (Pañca-Pāṇḍava) of the *Mahābhārata*, Arjuṇa was a skilful warrior who was successful in many of his encounters with tribal people in different parts of the subcontinent. He spent some time in these places during his twelve-year exile. On one of these sojourns, he met a Nāga princess named Ulupi and by her had a son named Iravat. He penetrated into south India, fought with Niṣīdas and other tribes and defeated many rulers.

4. The Vijaya legends

Prince Vijaya and his followers were exiled from their kingdom on account of their violent behaviour. They arrived in Sri Lanka where they encountered the machinations of *yakkhas* (spirits). Kuvaṇṇā, a *yakkhinī* (female spirit) lured the followers of Vijaya and imprisoned them. Vijaya confronted Kuvaṇṇā and, after subjugating her and defeating the *yakkhas* with her help, married her. A son and a daughter were born to them. She was later sent away with her children and Vijaya married a princess from the Pāṇḍya family.

5. The Kauṇḍinya legends

The foundation of several Southeast Asian kingdoms is associated in legends with the arrival of Brāhmaṇas or other adventurers from India. Among these, the most popular are the legends connected with the Brāhmaṇa named Kauṇḍinya. The foundation of the ancient Cambodian kingdom of Funan is ascribed to him. Chinese sources as well as ancient Cambodian inscriptions give versions of this legend. Kauṇḍinya arrived from India with a powerful bow. He encountered a Nāga princess named Soma, shot at her yacht, defeated her and then married her. With her as his queen, he became ruler of Funan and founded a new dynasty. 'This legend of the mystical union between the Brahman and the serpent [*nāga*], giving the dynasty a dual legitimacy of an Indian origin as well as roots in the popular indigenous mythology in which belief in earth, water, and snakes was important, was adopted by several Southeast Asian kingdoms, including Champa, Angkor, and Kedah, to name only a few.' (SarDesai, D.R., 1997. *Southeast Asia: Past & Present*, Colorado: 23).

There are also other legends linking prominent families with Nāga maidens: Rama's son Kuśa married a Nāga princess named Kumudvati, according to the *Raghuvaṃsa*. In the *Harivaṃsa*, it is said that Yadu, the founder of the Yādava family, married the five daughters of the king of the Nāgas (Dhumavarṇa) and from them sprang seven distinct families (*kula*).

APPENDIX VI

[Reproduced from Pūrvakalā, Bulletin of the Jaffna Archaeological Society, I, 1, 1973, Jaffna: 18-19.]

A Brahmi potsherd inscription from Kantarodai

K.Indrapala

In July 1970 a team of archaeologists from the University of Pennsylvania Museum excavated an inscribed potsherd from a pit at what they termed the 'Woodapple Site' at Kantarodai (Jaffna District)[1] This find was given the number KTD A14. The potsherd, belonging to the rouletted variety, presumably formed part of the begging bowl of a mendicant monk. The inscription is in Brāhmī characters.

Although similar potsherds with Brāhmī inscriptions have been discovered at Anuradhapura and elsewhere[2] in Sri Lanka as well as at such Indian sites as Arikamedu[3], this potsherd inscription is of some significance. This is the earliest inscription so far discovered in the Jaffna District. It is also the only proper Brāhmī inscription found in that district, the other known examples being potter's marks and mason's marks in Brāhmī characters[4].

The inscription consists of six Brāhmī characters and is presumably a complete record, the text being similar to those of the Anuradhapura potsherd inscriptions mentioned above. The first character may be read as 'mā', but Dr. W. Saddhamangala Karunaratne, the Assistant Archaeological Commissioner (Epigraphy) of Sri Lanka, is inclined to take it as a symbol. The present writer understands that the late Prof. S. Paranavitana also read it as a symbol[5]. As the present writer has a high regard for the knowledge of these two scholars in the field of Brāhmī inscriptions and as such symbols do occur in the Brāhmī inscriptions of Sri Lanka, this interpretation is adopted by him in this article, although he would prefer to read it as the letter 'mā'. A similar symbol occurs at the beginning of some of the Brāhmī cave inscriptions at Periya Puliyankulam, Naṭṭukanda, Tonigala, Paramakanda and other places[6]. That this symbol is in some way related to the inscription is obvious, but so far it has not been possible to explain its significance satisfactorily.

There is no difficulty in reading the inscription proper, as the letters are very clearly incised. The reading is 'Dataha pata'. The letters are similar to those of the early cave inscriptions of Sri Lanka and may be said to belong to about the second century B.C. The language is the same as that of the pre-Christian cave inscriptions of Sri Lanka, namely a form of Prakrit generally referred to as Sinhalese-Prakrit. 'Dataha pata' means 'The bowl of Data'.

The proper name Data occurring in this inscription is the Prakrit form of the Sanskrit Datta. It must have been a fairly common name in ancient Sri Lanka for it occurs in a number of Brāhmī cave inscriptions in the island[7]. The word 'pata' does not occur in the cave inscriptions but occurs in the potsherd inscriptions from Anuradhapura. [8] It is the Prakrit form of the Skt. pātra.

Text of the inscription

Dataha pata.

Translation

The bowl of Data.

---

1. The present writer is indebted to Dr. Vimala Begley and Mr. Bennet Bronson of the University of Pennsylvania Museum team for allowing him to inspect this potsherd and to Dr.

R.H. de Silva, the Archaeological Commissioner, for granting him permission to publish the photograph of this potsherd. News of the discovery of this inscription and its text were first published in the Tamil journal *Cintanai.* K.Indrapala (Editor), 'News and Notes', *Cintanai,* III, 2, July 1970, p.158 (Peradeniya).

2. S. Paranavitana, *The Excavations in the Citadel of Anuradhapura*, Memoirs of the Archaeological Survey of Ceylon, Vol. III, pp. 11-12 (Colombo 1936); H. Parker, 'Report on Archareological Discoveries at Tissamaharama', *Journal of the Ceylon Branch of the Royal Asiatic Society*, Vol. VIII, No. 27, pp. 67-68.
3. R. E. M. Wheeler, A. Ghosh and Krishna Deva, 'Arikamedu: An Indo-Roman Trading Station on the East Coast of India, *Ancient India* Bulletin of the Archaeological Survey of India, No. 2, July 1946, pp. 111-114.
4. Mr. S. Ponnampalam of Alaveddy has, in his remarkable collection of antiquities from Kantarodai, a potsherd and a brick with Brahmi characters marked on them
5. I am indebted to Dr. W. S. Karunaratne for this information.
6. S.Paranavitana, *Inscriptions of Ceylon*, Vol. I, p. xxvi (Colombo 1970).
7. Ibid., Inscr. Nos. 70, 86, 122, 123, 146, 154, 159, 185, 206, 230, etc.
8. S.Paranavitana, The Excavations in the Citadel of Anuradhapura, p.11

APPENDIX VII

A note on a carnelian seal inscription from Kantarodai

An inscribed carnelian seal, discovered at the archaeological site of Kantarodai (Jaffna District), was brought to the notice of the late Prof. S. Paranavitana in 1958. The only published information about this seal inscription is to be found in a Tamil article written by the present writer in 1959, when he was an undergraduate student at the University of Ceylon (now University of Peradeniya). In view of the usefulness of this information for researchers, a translation of the relevant portion of the article is provided below:

"In chronological order, the next [inscription from Jaffna] is the recently found seal from Kantarodai. Since no information about this is available anywhere, it is deemed appropriate to provide it here. Kantarodai is the most important of the archaeological sites in Jaffna. A small seal, said to have been discovered at Kantarodai, was brought to our university for the purpose of having the tiny letters on it deciphered by our archaeology professor, Dr. Paranavitana. Its owner was said to be the son of the American, Dr.W.R.Holmes, lecturer in history at Jaffna College. According to this boy, this seal was obtained from a boy at Kantarodai. The professor, who read easily the letters on the seal, explained its significance.

"This seal is made of red carnelian, a semi-precious stone. Its length is 1.02 cm and width 1 cm. The inscription on it is a Sanskrit name in the possessive case: Vi\0ubh3ti/ya. This inscription is in a developed form of the Southern Brahmi script. The letters are similar to those in the inscriptions at Nagarjunakonda, belonging to the 3rd/4th centuries. For this reason, Prof. Paranavitana was of the view that this seal probably belonged to the 3rd or 4th century A.D. and that it was probably brought from south India at that time. As far as he knew, this was the only inscribed seal found in Sri Lanka. It is at present with the Department of Archaeology.[1]

1. Indrapala, K., *Yāḻppāṇattuc Cācaṉaṅkaḷ* (Inscriptions of Jaffna), *Iḷaṅkatir*, Magazine of the University Tamil Society, Peradeniya 1959: 26. For the record, it may be added that the person referred to as the owner of the seal was Robert Holmes Jr. Anxious to find the reading of the inscription on the seal, he gave the seal to V.Sivasamy (an undergraduate student at Peradeniya at that time) in order to have it deciphered by Prof. Paranavitana. Sivasamy and the present writer then took it to Prof. Paranavitana, who, after deciphering the inscription and making casts of the seal, requested them to persuade Robert Holmes to part with the seal so that it could be kept in the country, on account of its importance. Prof. Paranavitana said that he would be giving it to the Department of Archaeology. The translation of the inscription is: [The seal] of Viṣṇubhūti.

APPENDIX VIII

A note on the Anaikoddai seal inscription

A steatite seal (earlier mistakenly referred to as a metal seal) was among the artefacts excavated at the megalithic burial site at Anaikoddai, Jaffna District, in December 1980. The legend on the seal has two lines. The first line consists of three non-Brāhmī symbols. The second line has three Brāhmī letters. Soon after its discovery, the present writer proposed two possible readings of the Brahmi inscription on the seal: kōvētaṉ and kōvēnta[1]. The readings were the result of taking the dot above the letter ta as an anusvāra. But after further analysis of the inscription and consideration of the evidence of the Tamil Brāhmī inscriptions, the present writer is now of the view that the dot may not be an anusvāra but a part of the non-Brahmi symbols. Consequently, it is only the three Brahmi letters that have to be read as the name on the seal. The reading of the Brāhmī letters is, therefore, kōvēta.

The name Kōvēta is not Prakrit. It is comparable to such names as Kō Ātan̲ and Kō Pūtivira occurring in the contemporary Tamil Brāhmī inscriptions in south India and has to be read as Kō Vēta[2]. It is to be taken as Early Tamil, although one cannot rule out the possibility of it being some other unknown Dravidian language. Kō in Tamil and Malayalam means 'king' and no doubt refers to a chieftain here. Being a seal inscription, the name Kō Vēta can be taken to be in the genitive case. This would mean that the final consonant -ta or the final vowel -a is the genitive suffix. In Early Tamil as well as in certain other South Dravidian languages the suffix –a occurs as a genitive case ending[3]. In the Tamil Brāhmī inscriptions, -a occurs as a genitive suffix[4]. Here, too, the genitive suffix is –a. On this basis, Kō Vēta could be split as Kō+Vētu+a (= of Kō Vētu)[5].

---

1. Indrapala 1981.
2. Mahadevan 2003: 434, 435
3. Krishnamurti 2003: 233-234. It occurs in some of the Sangam poems (Kur̲untokai 99.4) and in the Irula, Badaga and Tulu languages in the South Dravidian group.
4. Ibid: 290; this suffix also occurs in legends on coins in Tamil Nadu (Centan̲ a in Nagaswamy, R., 1981, Tamil Coins: A Study, Madras: 141) and Sri Lanka (Ūtiran̲a in Bopearachchi and Wickremasinghe 1999: 56). The genitive case in these coins is comparable to the genitive case (sa) of the Prakrit legends, such as Siri Pulumāvisa and Siri Sātakaṇisa, in the Sātavāhana coins of Andhra Pradesh (Nagaswamy, op.cit. 131).
5. Cf. pāṅkāṭa, split as pāṅkāṭu+a (= of Pāṅkāṭu) – Mahadevan 2003: 552; maratta kōṭu split as marattu+a (= of the tree) kōṭu in Kur̲untokai 99.4. This interpretation of taking the final – a of Kō Vēta as a genitive suffix was first suggested by Ragupathy (Ragupathy 1987: 202).

END NOTES

Preface

When the *History of Ceylon* was planned by the University of Ceylon, there was no qualified historian in that university to write some of the chapters. Scholars from outside were invited to write these sections. Mr.S. Natesan (an educationist, Tamil scholar and politician who was the son-in-law of Sir Ponnambalam Ramanathan) was invited to write the chapter on the Jaffna kingdom. But his contribution was not published in full and the chapter (twelve pages) began abruptly. The following footnote was added by the editor: "This Chapter, as it was sent to the Editor by its author, began with an account of the Early History of Jaffna and contained arguments for the existence of a kingdom of the Arya Cakravartis earlier than the thirteenth century. As these matters fall outside the period dealt with in Book V and as, due to the author's ill health, it was not possible for the Editor to discuss with him and settle certain points which required clarification, only the portion of his contribution relating to the period 1215-1505 has been published." *UCHC*, 1, 2: 690. Soon after the appearance of the *History of Ceylon*, the editor, Paranavitana, published a lengthy article (51 pages) on the Jaffna kingdom ('The Arya Kingdom in North Ceylon', *JRASCB*, NS, VII, 2: 174-224).

Introduction

[1] Renfrew1996: 181. Renfrew himself is quoting from Dragadze.

[2] Ibid.

[3] In his comprehensive study of the ethnic origins of nations, A.D. Smith chooses the French term *ethnie* for an ethnic group or community, as the one 'which unites an emphasis upon cultural differences with the sense of an historical community.' In his view, it is 'this sense of history and the perception of cultural uniqueness and individuality which differentiate populations from each other and which endows a given population with a definite identity, both in their own eyes and in those of outsiders.' The chief features that distinguish *ethnie* from other collectivities of human beings, according to Smith, are: a collective name, a common myth of

descent, a shared history, a distinctive shared culture, an association with a specific territory, and a sense of solidarity. As claimed by Smith, these components of *ethnie* afford a working definition of ethnicity. In the case of defining the Sri Lankan Tamil ethnic group, all these, with the possible exception of a common myth of descent (which applies to the Sinhalese), will apply. Smith, A.D., 1989, *The Ethnic Origins of Nations*, Oxford: 21-31.

[4] Gunawardana 1995: 4-5.

[5] Paranavitana 1970: 7, 28, 37. The Brāhmī inscriptions referring to Dameḍa persons published by Paranavitana are from Anuradhapura, Periyapuliyankulam and Kuduvil. A hitherto unpublished Brāhmī inscription (copied in 1973) from Seruvila referring to Gapati Dameḍa Cuḍa is reported by Dias (Dias, Malini, 1991, *Epigraphical Notes* Nos.1-18, Department of Archaeology, Colombo: 68). Also, Karunaratne 1984: 71. The ethnic name in the Periyapuliyankulam inscription is read by Karunaratne as *Dameḷa* and not *Dameḍa.*

[6] Queyroz, Fernao de, *Conquista Temporal e Espiritual de Ceilau*, Colombo. Translated into English in three volumes – Perera, S.G., 1930, *The Temporal and Spiritual Conquest of Ceylon*, Colombo.

[7] Ribeiro, Joao, 1909, *History o Ceilao with a summary of de Barros do Couto Antonio Bocarro and the Documentos Remettidos with Parangi Hatana and Kustantinu Hatana*, translated into English by Paul E. Pieris, Colombo.

[8] Baldaeus, Philippus, 1672, *Naauwkeurige beschryvinge van Malabar en Choromandel…en het machtige Eyland Ceylon*, Amsterdam. Translated into English – Brohier, P. 1960, *A True and Exact Description of the Great Island of Ceylon by Baldaeus, P.A., Ceylon Historical Journal*, Vol III, Nos.1-4, Colombo.

[9] Nissan, E. and Stirrat, R.L., 1990. 'The generation of communal identities', in Spencer 1990, 19-44; Gunawardana 1990 and 1994. Nissan and Stirrat 'have argued that the kind of confrontation that we see today between Sinhala and Tamils in Sri Lanka is the outcome of processes set in motion during the colonial era.' The two anthropologists have shown how British ideas contributed to the generation of the modern identities seen in the island: "British policy was deeply influenced by the racial theory that had developed from the relationship between contemporary

studies of language, etymological and historical, and of evolutionary theory. The 'Aryan Myth', as Poliakov has called it, had a particularly strong hold in European thought of that period, and in Indology. In England in particular the myth of Anglo-Saxonism, in which exclusivity was stressed, had developed from the time of the Reformation. It is associated with the rise of England as a nation-state, and its subsequent spread in empire – justified in part by ideas of inherent Anglo-Saxon superiority over other races, and by the idea of the civilizing mission. European scholarship on Sri Lanka (as on other colonies) was structured by these interests, too, and they conditioned colonial historiography. 'Aryans' (Sinhala) came to be opposed in absolute terms to 'Dravidians' (Tamils) historically. Language and race were conflated..." (pp.29-30). Tracing the development of the Aryan theory in European scholarship in the nineteenth century, Gunawardana has shown how this idea influenced the creation of a theory that the Sinhalese were also Aryans. Analysing the presentation of this theory by James de Alwis in 1866, Gunawardana points out how, 'at a time when the Aryan theory was gaining general acceptance in Europe and south Asia, he was claiming Aryan status not only for the Sinhala language , but also for the speakers of that language.' (Gunawardana 1990:73). By the 1920s, Gunawardana indicates, colonial writings on Sri Lankan history had begun to accommodate the new Aryan theory (L.E.Blaze in 1920 and H.W.Codrington in 1926).

[10] Blaze, L.E., 1931, *A History of Ceylon for Schools*, Colombo (first edition published in 1900). Codrington, H.W., 1926, *A Short History of Ceylon*, London.

[11] S.F. de Silva; Horace Perera and Ratnasabapathy.

[12] Mendis, G.C., 1932, *The Early History of Ceylon*, Calcutta.

[13] De Silva, K.M., 1991, *A History of Sri Lanka*, Delhi, p.7. Surprisingly, de Silva unquestioningly accepts the *Mahāvaṃsa* version of Sri Lankan history and states: 'Their [Aryan colonists'] seat of government was Upatissagama where the 'first' kings of the Vijayan dynasty reigned.'

[14] This is the view based on the Vijaya myth as presented in the Pali chronicle, *Mahāvaṃsa*. According to this myth, Vijaya, a prince from the Indian kingdom of Lāḷa (near Vaṅga), arrived in Sri Lanka with five hundred other male compatriots on the day the Buddha attained *nirvāṇa*, and founded the first kingdom in the island. *Mv*, VI. See Appendix V.

[15] Ludden 2002: 7.

[16] Lakshman S. Perera was the student. After completing his Ph.D., he was on the staff of the Department of History at Peradeniya and was later Professor of History at the University of Colombo. His monumental thesis on the institutions of ancient Sri Lanka, based on inscriptions, remained unpublished for a long time. It was published in 2001: *The Institutions of Ancient Ceylon from Inscriptions (from 3 rd century BC to 830 AD)*, 1, International Centre for Ethnic Studies, Kandy.

[17] Prof. Hem Chandra Ray, a specialist in ancient Indian dynastic history.

[18] S.Kiribamune, 'Some Reflections on Professor Paranavitana's Contribution to History', *Ceylon Journal of the Humanities*, 1, 1, 1970, Peradeniya: 76-92. In this article Prof. Kiribamune has given an account of the writings of Professor Paranavitana and traced his 'transformation from a very cautious researcher to an intrepid theorist'. It does not, however, deal with the nature and extent of his influence on Sri Lankan historiography.

[19] *UCHC*, I, 1: 82-97.

[20] For instance, S. Arasaratnam, one of the leading historians produced by the University of Ceylon, refers to 'Aryan colonists', 'Aryan settlements' and 'Aryan colonization' (*Ceylon*, Prentice-Hall Inc. New Jersey, 1964: 43, 45, 99). K.M. de Silva, another distinguished product of the University of Ceylon and the Foundation Professor of Ceylon History at the same university, writes about 'Aryan migration' and 'Aryan colonization' in ancient Sri Lanka (see Note 13 above). Even a very cautious historian like Leslie Gunawardana, in one of his early writings, could not resist from referring to 'Aryan immigrants' in ancient Sri Lanka (Gunawardana 1971: 4).

[21] In a series of lectures delivered in the mid-sixties, mainly at Peradeniya, Prof. Paranavitana claimed that he had discovered lengthy documents containing very detailed information relating to the ancient history of Sri Lanka, including the island's relations with foreign countries, on stone slabs in different locations ('An Account of Alexander the Great and Greek Culture in a Universal History Written in the Reign of Mahasena', Paper read on 31.10.1964 at the University of Ceylon, Peradeniya; 'Newly Discovered Historical Documents Relating to Ceylon, India and South-east Asia', Paper read on 4.11.1964 at the University of Ceylon,

Peradeniya). What was most incredible about these revelations was the claim that the documents were written in minute characters (not easily visible to the naked eye) in between the lines of existing stone inscriptions. For this reason, these documents were termed interlinear inscriptions. Had this claim been made by anyone else, it would have been laughed at, but Paranavitana's standing as an epigraphist compelled scholars to take serious note of it. The evidence of these so-called inscriptions was used in several of Prof. Paranavitana's latest writings, especially *Ceylon and Malaysia* (Colombo 1966), *The Greeks and the Mauryas* (Colombo 1971) and *The Story of Sigiri* (Colombo 1972).

[22] The present writer was working on his doctoral thesis in London when Prof. Paranavitana made the claims about the existence of valuable interlinear inscriptions. Unable to accept these claims, he cast doubts on their validity in his thesis, submitted in 1965 (p.401). In 1967, when reviewing Prof. Paranavitana's *Ceylon and Malaysia* for the *Journal of the Royal Asiatic Society Ceylon Branch* (XI: 101-106), the present writer again questioned the evidence of the interlinear inscriptions. In 1969, after examining (along with Sirima Kiribamune and Leslie Gunawardana) the stone slabs on which, according to Prof. Paranavitana, the interlinear inscriptions were indited, the present writer concluded that the interlinear inscriptions were non-existent (Paper read at the Second International Conference Seminar on Asian Archaeology, Colombo 1969, Indrapala 1980b). After a very detailed examination of the stone slabs, Leslie Gunawardana also concluded that the interlinear inscriptions were non-existent ('Ceylon and Malaysia: a Study of Professor S.Paranavitana's Research on the Relations between the Two Regions', *The University of Ceylon Review*, XXV, 1&2, April-October 1967: 1-64).

[23] It is indeed very sad that such an eminent epigraphist who enjoyed for several decades a great reputation for his expertise had to end his days as a discredited scholar in respect of his final publications. The present writer does not believe that Prof. Paranavitana attempted to foist a hoax (as hinted by the renowned science fiction writer Arthur Clarke in a letter to the Editor that appeared in the Colombo newspaper *Sunday Observer*, 12/10/1997) on the world of scholarship when he made the claims about the existence of interlinear inscriptions. As an archaeologist and epigraphist who spent a lifetime researching, exploring and excavating,

Prof. Paranavitana probably had dreams of discovering valuable epigraphs. In his late years, he probably believed that he had at last hit upon some important discoveries. All archaeologists must be experiencing similar dreams. As a layman who cannot fathom the mysterious workings of the human mind, the present writer can think of only such an explanation. Whatever the causes that led Prof. Paranavitana to believe in the existence of the interlinear inscriptions, this unfortunate controversy should not blind us to the admirable contributions to Sri Lankan scholarship that Prof. Paranavitana had made for over four decades. Born on 26 December 1896, he joined the Archaeological Survey of Ceylon as an Epigraphical Assistant in 1922, obtained his Ph.D. degree from the University of Leiden in 1936 and became the first Sri Lankan Archaeological Commissioner (1940-1956). Retiring in 1956 from the Archaeological Survey, he joined the University of Ceylon as Research Professor of Archaeology. He died on 4 October 1972.

[24] Prof. R.A.L.H. (Leslie) Gunawardana was (along with the present writer) in the last batch of students, specialising in Ancient History for their B.A. degree, to be taught by Prof. H.C. Ray at Peradeniya. He obtained his Bachelor of Arts degree in 1960 and has been a member of the teaching staff of the Department of History at Peradeniya from that year. He obtained his Ph.D. degree from the University of London (School of Oriental and African Studies) in 1965. His thesis was published in 1979 under the title *Robe and Plough: Monasticism and Economic Interest in Early Medieval Sri Lanka* (University of Arizona Press).

[25] Prof. Sudharshan Seneviratne's contribution to the understanding of the Early Iron Age in Sri Lanka and south India is outstanding. His doctoral thesis (Seneviratne 1985a) submitted to the Jawaharlal Nehru University (New Delhi) still remains the most comprehensive study of this subject, with a thorough analysis of the Sri Lankan and south Indian sources, including the Tamil Sangam poems. The insular approach to the study of the Early Iron Age in Sri Lanka was altered and the earliest phase of the island's history was viewed in the background of south Indian developments.

[26] For a discussion of these developments in the media and some academic publications, see Gunawardana 1995 and Serena Tennekoon, 'Newspaper

nationalism: Sinhala identity as historical discourse', in Spencer 1990: 205-226.

[27] Gunawaradana 1995:1.

[28] Davies 2000: 35-36.

[29] All quotations in this paragraph are from Hobsbawm 1997: 270.

[30] The quotations in this paragraph are from Renfrew and Bahn 1996: 509, 510, 533.

[31] The quotations in this paragraph are from Hobsbawm 1997: 6, 273, 277. G.R. Elton, another well-known British historian, endorses Hobsbawm's view when he says: "Historical writings can do harm; they have done so…" G.R. Elton, 2002, *The Practice of History*, Oxford: 5.

[32] Sudharshan Seneviratne, 'Situating history and 'The Historian's Craft'', Book Review in *The Island*, Colombo 04/08/2001. Prof. Seneviratne echoes the sentiments of Prof. Gunawardana (quoted earlier in this chapter) when he concludes this review article with the indignant observation that 'Anti-Orwellian' historians in Sri Lanka are 'in the process of subverting the study of history for personal ends and political expediency'. See Preface, above, for a fuller quotation.

[33] Thapar 2000: xxiv.

[34] Prof. Seneviratne has made the following comment about these scholars: "Colonial administrators and Orientalists and later Nationalists used the classical texts as a primary point of entrée to the history of Sri Lanka. What some contemporary local and overseas anthropologists, archaeologists and historians have done at the other end of the spectrum is no better. They have not only 'anthropologised' the texts but have used the codified history found in the classical texts (often read in translations) in taking a reverse view of history. This stems from the false notion that contemporary ethno-nationalism is rooted in the ideology of the classical texts. Such scholars have resorted to a 'fashionable' form of critique, what we have identified elsewhere as 'Mahāvaṃsa-bashing'. This is linear history at its best. Ironically enough, this has only enmeshed such scholars in the historicity of the very source they set off to negate." Seneviratne 2002: 4.

[35] The *Mahāvaṃsa* is the product of a long historical tradition preserved in the Buddhist monasteries of Anuradhapura from the time of the mission of Mahinda in the third century BCE which resulted in the conversion of

the Anuradhapura ruler, Devānaṃpiya Tissa, and the establishment of Buddhism as the official religion of the Anuradhapura kingdom. The monks of the Mahinda mission brought with them the Pali Buddhist scriptures as well as the historical traditions connected with the life and teachings of the Buddha and the succession of teachers after the Buddha. This body of historical traditions formed the core of the history preserved in the Buddhist monasteries. To this were added, from time to time, information about major Buddhist events, especially at Anuradhapura, such as the founding of the first main monastery called the Mahāvihāra and the building of Buddhist monuments. In order to give a chronological framework for this history, the reigns of the Anuradhapura rulers were added with basic details such as the succession and length of reigns. When commentaries came to be prepared in Heḷa (Old Sinhalese) for the Pali scriptures, the historical traditions were brought together and added to the commentaries in the form of an historical introduction. This came to be known as the *Aṭṭhakathā Mahāvaṃsa* (*Sīhaḷa-aṭṭhakathā-mahāvaṃsa/Heḷaṭuvā*), which could be loosely translated as the Chronicle of the Commentary. Although originally this historical introduction must have contained only the history of Buddhism and information about the kings of Anuradhapura from Devānaṃpiya Tissa, in time, traditions about the period before this king were gathered from various legends and myths and included in the introduction, giving a more complete picture. Based on this historical introduction, attempts were made later to compile a history of the island in Pali. One of the earliest attempts resulted in the compilation of the *Dīpavaṃsa*, by unknown authors. It was, scholars agree, completed some time in the fourth century CE. A later and more successful attempt resulted in the writing of the *Mahāvaṃsa*, in the fifth century, by a monk named Mahānāma. At the beginning of his work, the author clearly states that he based his compilation on an earlier text which was 'here too long drawn out and there too closely knit; and contained many repetitions'. He had avoided these faults and written his chronicle for 'the serene joy and emotion of the pious'. For details about the growth of the Sri Lankan historical tradition and the compilation of the various chronicles, see Perera, L.S., 'The Sources of Ceylon History', Chapter IV of *UCHC*, I, 1: 46-51; Geiger, W., 1908, *Dipavamsa and Mahāvaṃsa*, Colombo; Mendis, G.C., 'The Pali Chronicles of Ceylon, An Examination of the Opinions Expressed About Them Since 1879', *University of Ceylon Review*, IV, 2:1-24.

[36] The Mahāvihāra, established in the reign of Devānaṃpiya Tissa (third century BCE) as the main monastery for the Buddhist monks at Anuradhapura, developed into one of the greatest monastic establishments of Buddhism in ancient times. Monks from India, China and Southeast Asia came to reside in the monastery for lengthy periods. It was renowned as a centre of Pali learning and attracted Indian and Chinese scholars who came there to copy and translate some of the commentaries on the Buddhist canon. Among the famous Indian Buddhist monk scholars who came to study the Pali and Sinhalese texts in the Mahāvihāra in the fifth and sixth centuries were Buddhaghosa from north India, the Tamil monk Buddhadatta and another south Indian monk Dhammapāla. Among the Chinese monks was the celebrated pilgrim Fa-Hsien who stayed in Sri Lanka in the fifth century for about two years. He came in search of Buddhist scriptures and would have made extensive use of the texts in the Mahāvihāra. Like all great establishments, the Mahāvihāra had its rivals and enemies, too. The monks of the Mahāvihāra always claimed that their interpretation of the Buddhist canon was the orthodox one, going back to Mahinda who founded the Buddhist church at Anuradhapura. This was not always accepted by everyone and often led to conflicts with the rival monastery at Anuradhapura, the Abhayagiri-vihāra. In its long and memorable history, the Mahāvihāra suffered seriously for about a decade when these conflicts culminated in a major confrontation with the Abhayagiri-vihāra. This was at the end of the third century when its buildings were destroyed and the monastery was abandoned for nine years.

[37] Reading the *Mahāvaṃsa*, one does not get to know that there were Jains in the island in the period after Mahinda's mission. But an incidental reference in the chronicle in the reign of Khallāṭa Nāga (second century BCE) helps us to find out that there was a Jain monastery in Anuradhapura at that time. *Mv*: XXXIII.

[38] *Mahāvaṃsa*: End of every chapter.

[39] The account of Eḷāra's reign is completed in Chapter XXI and the epic section is introduced abruptly in the next chapter. Chapter XXI deals with the reign of Eḷāra in the same chronicle style in which the reigns of the

PLATE 23.
Bharata Natya relief sculpture, Yapahuva.

PLATE 24.
Bharata Natya relief sculpture, Yapahuva.

kings after Devānaṃpiya Tissa are recounted: "A Damiḷa of noble descent, named Eḷāra, who came hither from the Coḷa country to seize on the kingdom, ruled when he had overpowered king Asela forty-four years, with even justice toward friend and foe, on occasions of disputes at law". The four legends illustrating Eḷāra's justice are narrated and the chapter closes with the usual ending: "Here ends the twenty-first chapter, called the 'Five Kings', in the Mahāvaṃsa, compiled for the serene joy and emotion of the pious." The next chapter, XXII, begins in the usual chronicle style: "When he had slain Eḷāra, Duṭṭhagāmanī became king. To show clearly how this came to pass the story in due order is this." In this manner is introduced the entire epic of Duṭṭhagāmanī, from Chapter XXII to XXXII. The present writer is inclined to think that the whole epic is an interpolation.

40 *Mv*. The translation is from Guruge 1989:609.

41 *UCHC*, I,1: 144-163.

42 An example of Paranavitana's description relates to the final stage of the war when the Tamil general Dīghajantu marched against Duṭṭhagāmanī: "...he [Dīghajantu] finally came to where Duṭṭhagāmanī really was. There, the Sinhalese champion Sūranimila was ready to defend the king; he drew Dīghajantu from the king towards himself by fulsome abuse of the Tamil champion. Sūranimila parried the sword thrust of Dīghajantu with his shield, which he let go when the Tamil champion's sword pierced it, and himself stepped aside. The sword with the shield fell to the ground and, as Dīghajantu bent down to pick it up, a mighty blow from Sūranimila's spear put an end to his career. Phussadeva blew the conch as he alone could blow it. The Tamil soldiers, seeing their champion fall and hearing the thunderous peals of Phussadeva's conch, broke ranks and took to flight. The Sinhalese pursued them and caused great havoc among the fleeing enemy." *UCHC*, I, 1: 160.

43 Geiger considered the *Mahāvaṃsa* as a work 'worthy of a true epic' and Winternitz described it as 'a completed epic', while Guruge disagreeing with both Geiger and Winternitz, concedes that 'The life and career of Duṭṭhagāmanī Abhaya becomes an independent epic poem by itself.' Guruge 1989: 65.

44 See Chapter 5 for details.

[45] *Mv*, XXV: 72-74. 'In the city he [Duṭṭhagāmaṇī] caused the drum to be beaten, and when he had summoned the people from a yojana around he celebrated the funeral rites for king Eḷāra. On the spot where his body had fallen he burned it with the catafalque, and there did he build a monument [*cetiya*] and ordain worship. And even to this day the princes of Laṅkā, when they draw near to this place, are wont to silence their music because of this worship' (*Taṃ dehapatitaṭṭhāne kūṭāgārena jhāpayi cetiyaṃ tattha kāresi parihāraṃ adāsi ca.*) These are the words in Pali indicating that Mahānāma was referring to a *cetiya* being built over Eḷāra's ashes and not just a monument.

[46] For results of the excavations mentioned here, see the following: Begley 1981; Deraniyagala 1992; Ragupathy 1987; Bandaranayake and Mogren 1994; Coningham 1999; Carswell and Prickett 1984;

[47] *Multicultural Japan: Palaeolithic to Postmodern*, ed. D. Denoon, M Hudson, G. McCormack et al, 1996, Cambridge UP.

[48] Ibid. 50.

[49] Davies: 36.

[50] Coningham's observations are fully relevant to this work: "It is clear that the colonial framework and its preoccupation with culture history has created key identities, and has generated a quest to demonstrate who were the first and most legitimate identities on the island. Communities are being polarized into two main identities Hindu-Dravidian-Tamil and Buddhist-Aryan-Sinhalese (Coningham and Lewer 1999:864) when there is little evidence for such clear identities in the past...Ethnic identities, whilst blurred in the historical period, are invisible in the archaeological record, even though regional traits and dynamics within material culture are identifiable but the concept used to link identities in the past is questioned by many archaeologists (Renfrew 1987). Claims and counter-claims of an Indo-Aryan or proto-Dravidian linguistic foundation for the island (Deraniyagala 1992: 747; Ragupathy 1987: 202) ignore the fact that linguistic changes can occur without recourse to population changes (Coningham et al. 1996:94). Such changes can occur through the creation of a trade language (Sherrat 1988:461-2) or even random processes (Robb 1991: 287). This question is intensely complex, as indicated by the presence of a strong Dravidian element in the Sinhala language (Godakumbure 1946: 827) and genetic evidence linking the Sinhalese

more closely to south India than north Indian communities (Roychoudhury 1984)." (Coningham 2000: 710).

[51] The Brāhmī potsherd inscription is from Kantarodai (Indrapala 1973), the Brāhmī seal inscription is from Anaikoddai (Indrapala 1981) and the other newly discovered Tamil inscriptions are from Fort Hammenheil (Indrapala 1971c), Jaffna Fort (Indrapala 1971g), Kantalay (Indrapala 1978) and Nilaveli (Indrapala 1980).

[52] Karunaratne 1984; Seneviratne 1985a.

[53] Mahadevan 2003.

[54] Rajan and Bopearachchi 2002.

[55] One of the notable developments in the recent writings of scholars from Tamil Nadu on the archaeological finds in that state is the recognition of the flow of influences from Sri Lanka to south India in ancient times. P. Jeyakumar has asserted that 'undeniably cultural elements from Sri Lanka must have spread to Tamiḻakam' and presented evidence from potsherd graffiti showing influences of Sri Lankan Brāhmī and Sinhalese-Prakrit (P. Jeyakumar, *Tamiḻakat Tuṟaimukaṅkaḷ,* Thanjavur 2001: 13, 26). In his monumental work on Tamil epigraphy, Iravatham Mahadevan has drawn attention to several instances of Sri Lankan influence in the Brāhmī inscriptions of Tamil Nadu (Mahadevan 2003). Mahadevan is of the view that, among the inscribed potsherds found in Tamil Nadu, 'A small but significant group of pottery inscriptions is in the Sinhala-Prakrit language written in the Early Sinhala-Brāhmī script (ca. 2nd century B.C. to 1st century A.D.)'. These inscriptions were discovered at Arikamedu, Alangulam, Kodumanal and Poompuhar (Kaveripattinam). Mahadevan 2003: 45-47, 181. Mahadevan has also published a couple of interesting articles on this subject ('An Old Sinhalese Inscription from Arikamedu', *Prof. Kuppuswamy Sastri Birth Centenary Commemoration Volume*, 2: 279-282, ed. S.S. Janaki, Madras 1985; 'Old Sinhalese Inscriptions from Indian Ports – New Evidence for India-Sri Lanka Contacts', *Journal of the Institute of Asian Studies*, 14: 55-65, Madras 1994). A remarkable graffito in Prakrit from the ancient port of Kaveripattinam has been read as a Sinhalese-Brāhmī inscription by S. Iracavelu (*Pūmpukāril Ciṅkaḷa-Pirāmi Eḻuttup Poṟitta Maṭkalattuṇṭu, Āvaṇam* 10:154, Thanjavur 1999).

[56] Pushparatnam 1993: 40; Mahadevan 2003: 61.

[57] Deraniyagala 1992: 741-747; Coningham and Allchin 1992: 155ff.

[58] Weerakkody 1997.

[59] Bopearachchi 1990, 1995 and 1997. This author's researches relate mainly to Graeco-Roman trade and coins.

[60] Bopearachchi and Wickremasinghe 1999: 56.

[61] Pushparatnam 1993: 51.

[62] Godakumbure, C.E., 1946, The Dravidian Element in Sinhalese, *Bulletin of the School of Oriental and African Studies*, 11:837-841; Peter Silva, M.H., 1961. *Influence of Dravida on Sinhalese*, D.Phil. thesis, Oxford University; De Silva, M.W.S., 1979. *Sinhalese and other island languages in South Asia*, Gunter Narr Verlag Tubingen; Gair, James W., 1998. *Studies in South Asian Linguistics: Sinhala and Other South Asian Languages*, Oxford University Press, New York and Oxford.

[63] Gair 1998: 4.

[64] De Silva 1979: 16. See note 80 below, for D.E.Hettiarachchi's comments.

[65] Roychoudhury, A.K., 1984, 'Genetic relationships between Indian populations and their neighbours', in J.R. Lukacs (ed.), *The People of South Asia: the biological anthropology of India, Pakistan and Nepal*, New York: 283-293; Kennedy, K.A.R. 1975. Geneticists, particularly Soviet scientists, are investigating language replacement in Central Asia with the aid of mtDNA and Y-chromosome evidence: see, for example, Ivan Nasidze, Tamara Sarkisian, Azer Kerimov and Mark Stoneking, 'Testing hypotheses of Language replacement in the Caucasus: evidence from the Y-chromosome', *Human Genetics*, 112, 2003: 255-261 (published online Dec. 2002).

[66] Maloney, Clarence, 1980, *The People of the Maldive Islands*, Madras.

[67] Seneviratne 1985a: 59.

[68] Renfrew 1998: 124.

[69] Ibid: 131-133; Renfrew and Bahn: 447.

[70] Renfrew 1998: 132.

[71] Coningham et al 1996: 94; Sherratt 1988: 461-462.

[72] Coningham et al 1996: 94.

[73] Ibid.

[74] Thapar 2002: 113. Discussing the spread of Vedic Sanskrit from the northwest of the subcontinent into the Gangetic valley, Thapar summarises the process of language change in the following manner: "Indo-Aryan was introduced and adopted, so evidently those who spoke it

or adopted it associated it with some advantage, such as authority, technological change or ritual power. At the same time Vedic Sanskrit itself underwent changes. Linguistic elements from Dravidian and Austro-Asiatic (for example, Munda) were introduced into Vedic Sanskrit. A period of bilingualism has been suggested when more than one language was used in the communication between various communities. Alternatively, the non-Indo-Aryan languages could have been substratum languages, elements from which were absorbed into Indo-Aryan. The Vedic corpus is the statement of the dominant group, but this does not preclude the presence of others."

[75] The genetic continuity from prehistoric times seems to be indicated by some recent researches (Kennedy 1975). Kennedy, whose doctoral thesis was on the biological and cultural affinities of the prehistoric Balangoda people with the Veddas, argues here in favour of a biological continuum from the Mesolithic humans to the modern Vedda. A.K.Roychoudhury's researches have shown that the 'genetic distances among the Toda, Irula, Kurumba [tribal people of Tamil Nadu], and the Veddah [of Sri Lanka] are small'. These groups, in his view, cluster together. This may indicate that these groups had common ancestors in prehistoric times.

[76] Bandaranayake 1978: 83.

[77] Bellwood, Peter, 1999. 'Southeast Asia before History', *The Cambridge History of Southeast Asia*, I, 1: 55-56.

[78] Deraniyagala 1992: 31-33.

[79] Grierson, G.A., 1967. *Linguistic Survey of India*, IV, Delhi: 9. Vaiyapuri Pillai, S., 1956. *History of the Tamil Language*, Madras.

[80] Deraniyagala 1992: 748. . Prof. D.E. Hettiarachchi has drawn attention to a number of words in Sinhala that are not traceable to Indo-Aryan or Dravidian. Some examples given by him are: *äpaya* (surety), *oluva* (head), *kakula* (leg), *kaṭa* (mouth), *kalava* (thigh) *UCHC,*1, 1: 35. He identifies the commonly used word for coconut (*pol*) as an Austric word. Several other Austric words, in his view, may have infiltrated into Sinhala through Indo-Aryan. Ibid: 36. M.W.S. de Silva and James Gair have also pointed out this non-Indo-Aryan/non-Dravidian element in Sinhala. See note 64 above.

Chapter 1

[1] Deraniyagala 1998: 1. 'During the last one million years, when humans are known to have existed in various parts of India (v. Mishra 1995), Sri Lanka was connected to the sub-continent on numerous occasions. The rise and fall of sea level (due to cold/warm fluctuations in the global climate) determined the periodicities of these connections, the last separation having occurred at ca. 7000 BP (Deraniyagala 1992: 167). Hence it is impossible to view Sri Lankan prehistory in isolation from India.' The work cited by Deraniyagala is Mishra, S., 1995, Chronology of the Indian Stone Age: The impact of recent absolute and relative dating attempts, *Man and Environment*, 20 (2): 11-16.

[2] Deraniyagala 1992: 61.

[3] Kennedy 1990: 29.

[4] Thapar 2002: 80.

[5] Allchin and Allchin 1982: 33.

[6] Ibid: 36, 45, 47, 57.

[7] Ibid:35.

[8] Thapar, Romila, 1977, *A History of India*, I: 26.

[9] Bellwood 1999: 78.

[10] Ibid: 74.

[11] Ibid: 55.

[12] Ibid.

[13] Deraniyagala 1992: 167.

[14] Kennedy 1990: 29.

[15] Selvakumar 2001: 259.

[16] Ibid: 258; Rajan 1991: 37

[17] Rajendran 1984: 9.

[18] Rajan 1991: 37ff.

[19] Selvakumar 2001: 260.

[20] Ibid.

[21] Agrawal 1982: 75.

[22] Deraniyagala 1992: 107, 269.

[23] Selvakumar 2001: 260.

[24] Ibid: 261.

[25] Ibid: 264.
[26] Deraniyagala 1998: 2.
[27] Deraniyagala 1992: 469.
[28] Ibid: 300.
[29] Ibid: 118.
[30] Deraniyagala 2001: 1.
[31] Ibid: 2.
[32] Ibid: 3.
[33] Ibid.
[34] Ibid: 2.
[35] Coningham 1999: 135.
[36] Kennedy 1990: 30.
[37] Ibid.
[38] Seneviratne 1985: 149.
[39] Ibid.
[40] Deraniyagala : 3
[41] Deraniyagala : 271, 272, 487.
[42] Kennedy 1990: 34.
[43] Kennedy 1990: 29-30.
[44] Selvakumar 2001: 260.
[45] Seneviratne 1985a: 148; Deraniyagala 1992: 707.
[46] Seneviratne 1985a: 156.
[47] Deraniyagala 1998.
[48] Deraniyagala 1992: 734 (also Deraniyagala 1998).
[49] Ibid: 748.
[50] De Silva 1979:16.
[51] See Introduction, notes 63, 64 and 80.
[52] There are a number of islands in the Krishna-Godavari Delta of Andhra Pradesh with names ending in *–laṅkā*: for example, Bobbar-lanka (Guntur District), Agadala-lanka, Gudivaka-lanka (West Godavari District) and Nagaya-lanka (Krishna District). There is also a placename Lanka in Assam.
[53] Of the Sangam poems, *Puṟanāṉūṟu* v. 176 refers to Peru-Māvilaṅkai and *Ciṟupāṇāṟṟuppaṭai* (ll.119-120) refers to Toṉmāvilaṅkai, Kīḻmāvilaṅkai and Naṭunāṭṭumāvilaṅkai. Another verse (No.379) in the former text refers to *Ilaṅkaik-kiḻavōṉ* (Lord of Ilaṅkai). It is hard to establish whether

this is a reference to a chief in Sri Lanka or in another Lanka. There was also a Māyilaṅgai in Karnataka (*Epigraphia Carnatica*, III: 147-148). It has been pointed out that *laṅkā* is a word in the Mundari language (Austroasiatic family), meaning 'a distant land beyond the sea'. The present writer has been unable to trace this reference or to confirm this.

[54] Nilakanta Sastri 1955: 443, n.83; *Madras Epigraphical Report for 1913*, No.77 of 1913.

[55] Teṉṉilaṅkai occurs in a number of Tamil texts from about the seventh century: in the hymns of Campantar, Cuntarar and Māṇikkavācakar and in inscriptions of the twelfth and thirteenth centuries.

[56] *UCHC*, I, 1:97.

[57] Renfrew 1998: 3ff.

Chapter 2

[1] Deraniyagala 2004: Deraniyagala 2001: 5; Deraniyagala 1992: 734 n.3.

[2] Seneviratne 1985: 8-9.

[3] Thapar and Rahman 1996: 274.

[4] Hegde 1996: 357.

[5] Seneviratne 1996: 378.

[6] Seneviratne 1985: 8.

[7] The name Matirai is the original Tamil form, later Sanskritized as Madurai.

[8] Ibid: 9.

[9] Thapar and Rahman 1996: 274.

[10] Ibid.

[11] Deraniyagala 1992: 709,734. Possehl has assigned very early dates for Iron Age sites in south India. For example, Hallur in Karnataka at 1255 cal BC, Veerapuram in Andhra Pradesh at 1035 cal BC and Korkai in Tamil Nadu at 828 cal BC (Possehl, G. *Scientific Dates for South Asian Archaeology*, University of Pennsylvania 1990, quoted in Deraniyagala 1992: 734).

[12] Megalithic monuments of various types have been erected in ancient times in different parts of the world. In Western Europe they have been

found widely along the Atlantic coasts. Most of these belong to the Neolithic period. Archaeologists have attempted to give explanations to many questions about these monuments, particularly how and why the Neolithic people erected such big lithic structures. These monuments are, of course, unrelated to the South Asian megaliths. Scholars have been attempting to find the origin of the megalithic burial practice that spread in peninsular India towards the last quarter of the second millennium BCE. Some have argued that this culture spread to India from West Asia but no definite links have been as yet established between the two areas on this score.

[13] Seneviratne 1985: 24ff; Rajan 1991: 37-52. Fixing a satisfactory chronology for the Iron Age sites in Tamil Nadu is a problem in the absence of Cabon 14 dates for most sites. South Indian archaeologists are cautious about suggesting dates and tend to give late dates compared with the dates given by Possehl for the Hallur (Karnataka) and Korkai (Tamil Nadu) sites (see fn. 3 above). With regard to the sites in the Dharmapuri District, for instance, Rajan is inclined to adopt the view that these 'can be dated to a period anywhere between 1000 B.C.-A.D.100' and favours the conclusion that 'one can safely place the beginning of the Dharmapuri Megalithic culture to c. 4th century B.C.' (Rajan 1991: 46).

[14] Seneviratne 1985: 26-27.

[15] European scientists have shown interest in the urn burials at Adichchanallur from the 1870s. The German A.F. Jagor conducted excavations at this site from 1873 to 1877 and carried away some skeletal remains for study in Germany. These are still in Berlin. The British archaeologist A. Rea conducted studies at Adichchanallur and Perumbair from the 1880s. For an interesting account of these investigations since the 1870s and the fate of skeletal remains taken from these sites to western museums, see K.A.R. Kennedy 1975: 11-14.

[16] Seneviratne 1985: 52.

[17] Ibid: 34.

[18] Ibid: 59.

[19] Ibid.

[20] Ibid: 164.

[21] Ibid: 60.

[22] Carswell 1991: 198; Deraniyagala 1992: 732; Carswell and Prickett 1984: 62.

[23] Seneviratne 1984: 245.

[24] The urn burials at Pomparippu were first examined in the early 1920s by A.M.Hocart. But it was not until 1956 that a systematic, though by no means extensive, investigation of the site was carried out by the Department of Archaeology. The results of these early studies helped to identify the burials as those belonging to the south Indian urn burial complex and to establish the similarities between Adichchanallur and Pomparippu. In 1970, an expedition from the University of Pennsylvania Museum, headed by Vimala Begley, conducted excavations at Pomparippu. Bennett Bronson, K.A.R. Kennedy, B.A. Hussainmiya, M.H.M. Maharoof and the present writer were among those who participated in the excavations. Begley's reports and Kennedy's writings on the skeletal remains are the latest scientific data from the site.

[25] Seneviratne 1984: 247.

[26] Ibid. 246.

[27] Seneviratne 1984: 282.

[28] Ibid: 283.

[29] Ibid: 246-260.

[30] Ragupathy 1987: 57-62; Begley ; Deraniyagala 1992.

[31] Ragupathy 1987: 63-78, 199-204; Indrapala 1981.

[32] Ragupathy 1987.

[33] Pushparatnam 1993.

[34] *Mv*. 19: 60; *Sammohavinodanī*: 445-446 (ed. A.P.Buddhadatta, London 1923). The port Kolapaṭṭana, referred to in the *Milindapañha*, appears to be Jambukola-paṭṭana (Gunawardana 1990b: 27).

[35] Deraniyagala ; Ragupathy

[36] Coningham 1999: 137; Deraniyagala 1992: 730-732.

[37] Deraniyagala 1992: 363, 735. Stories about the Nāgas in the northern and western parts of Sri Lanka are found in the *Mahāvaṃsa* and the *Valāhassa Jātaka*.

[38] Seneviratne 1984: 260-262.

[39] Bopearachchi and Wickremasinghe 1999: 7.

[40] Ibid.

[41] Deraniyagala 1992: 715-730; Coningham 1999; Coningham and Allchin 1992; Coningham, Allchin et al 1996.

[42] Seneviratne 1985a: 65.

[43] Ibid: 66

[44] Deraniyagala 1992: 709; Coningham 1999: 136.

[45] Seneviratne 1985a: 66.

[46] Lukacs and Kennedy 1970: 74-76 (?)

[47] *UCHC*, 1, 1: 106-109. See below, note 72 and Appendix V on Sanskritisation legends.

[48] Deraniyagala 1992: 729.

[49] Coningham 1996: 79.

[50] Deraniyagala 1996: 4.

[51] Ibid.

[52] Deraniyagala 1992: 732; Bandaranayake and Mogren 1994: 40.

[53] Deraniyagala 1992:732.

[54] Begley 1981: 95; Seneviratne 1984: 287.

[55] Seneviratne 1984: 287.

[56] Champakalakshmi 1996:184; Maloney 1970: 604.

[57] Scholars are now agreed that the Phoenicians, who originated in the land that is modern Lebanon, were among the most impressive navigators and long-distance traders of the ancient world. 'They were celebrated – as learned scribes, who passed on the modern alphabet; as vaunted seafarers and intrepid explorers, who redefined the boundaries of the ancient world; as skilled engineers, who built monumental harbours and cities; and as gifted artisans, whose skilful creations were the envy of royalty' (Markoe: 10). Although their maritime activities were mainly concentrated in the Mediterranean area, it is an established fact that they also travelled down the Red Sea and brought back gold from a land called Ophir in the tenth century BCE. Most modern scholars are inclined to support the view that Ophir was a place in the northeastern coast of Africa, either in the Sudan or further south in the Eritrean/Somalian coast (Glenn E. Markoe, *Phoenicians*, London: 2000). Some have suggested southern Arabia as a likely location while others have proposed India. Whatever the location of Ophir, the Phoenicians were doubtless active in the Arabian Sea. These daring sailors, who are credited with having circumnavigated the African continent, had probably reached the shores of India in quest of trade.

[58] Weerakkody 1997: 33.

[59] The *Arthaśāstra* refers to pearls from Pāṇḍya Kavāṭa and Tāmraparṇī. *The Kautilya Arthasastra*, II, ed. and tr. R.P.Kangle, Delhi 1986: 97. In the *Rāmāyaṇa* (*Kavāṭaṃ Pāṇḍyānaṃ*) and the *Mahābhārata*, too, there are references to Pāṇḍya Kavāṭa (quoted in Srinivasa Iyengar 1929: 53 and Paranavitana *UCHC*, I,1: 94).

[60] Koṟkai. For example, *Akanāṉūṟu* 350: 13 refers to Paratavar diving for pearls at Koṟkai.

[61] The origin of what may be called the chank cult in South Asia is lost in antiquity. It is closely associated with Hindu rituals and beliefs. One of the major deities of Hinduism, Viṣṇu, is portrayed holding the chank. There are references in early lieterature, including the Sanskrit epics, to the chank being used as a battle trumpet. In Tamil tradition, the rare *valampuri* chank (abnormally spiralling anti-clockwise) is especially venerated and fetches a high price. As the chank is considered to bring good luck (an auspicious symbol), it is a Tamil custom to bury a chank, leaving part of the shell exposed, in front of the main threshold or doorway to a house. For thousands of years, several chank products, such as bangles, finger and toe rings, ear-rings, necklaces of chank beads, little containers and chank powder for medicinal and cosmetic purposes, have been and continue to be used in traditional Tamil society. Heppell, David, 2001. 'The Chank Shell Industry in Modern India', *Princely States Report* (Journal of Indian States History, Philately and Numismatics), II, 2 (online: princelystates.com 30/12/2001).

[62] Seneviratne 1984: 278.

[63] Weerakkody 1997: 37.

[64] There are numerous references to *maṇi* (gems) in the Sangam poems. Beads of sapphire, beryl, agate, carnelian, amethyst, lapis lazuli, jasper, garnet, soapstone, quartz, onyx and other precious and semi-precious stones were unearthed in the course of the excavations at Kodumanal about twenty years ago. Rajan 2001: 241; Jayakumar 2001: 248ff.

[65] For a long time, several writers have drawn attention to words of Sanskrit or Tamil origin, referring to imported items, in the Hebrew language found in the *Bible*. One of them, cited by the historical linguist Zvelebil, is *tukkhiyīm* (peacocks). This word is considered to be related to the Tamil word *tōkai* (tail of the peacock). Zvelebil, *The New Encyclopaedia*

Britannica, 22: 699 (2003). P.T.Srinivasa Iyengar argued, as early as 1929, that some of the items of foreign merchandise brought to the domain of King Solomon and mentioned in the *Bible*, such as ivory, apes and peacocks, reveal Sanskrit or Tamil origin in their Hebrew names. *History of the Tamils*, Madras 1929: 129-131 (Reprint New Delhi 2001).

[66] Gunawardana 2000: 529.

[67] *Iṟaiyaṉār Akapporuḷ Urai* is the commentarial text in which this legend is recorded. P.T.Srinivasa Iyengar provides a very literal translation of the relevant portion. Srinivasa Iyengar 1929: 230-232.

[68] *UCHC*, 1,1: 95.

[69] Davies 2000: 156.

[70] Sanskritisation is the term preferred in this work to refer to the process by which north Indian influences spread in south India, Sri Lanka and Southeast Asia. From time to time, various terms have been used by scholars to describe this process, including Aryanisation, Indianisation and Hinduisation. The first smacks of racialism, the second connotes colonial association, while the third presents religious overtones. Sanskritisation is more neutral, indicating a linguistic and cultural influence. This term was proposed and popularised by the eminent Indian sociologist, M.N.Srinivas, in relation to the modern process of social mobility in India. Srinivas offers the following explanation of the term: "Sanskritization refers to a cultural process but it is essential to realize that it is usually a concomitant of the acquisition of political or economic power by a caste. Both are parts of the process of social mobility…'lower' castes which have become prosperous or powerful or educated like to assert their claim to a higher place in the hierarchy by taking on a new name and by Sanskritizing their ritual." *On Living In A Revolution and Other Essays*, Delhi, 1992: 119. Srinivas first proposed this term in his *Religion and Society among the Coorgs of South India*, Bombay 1952 (Reprint 1965): 30. When north Indian cultural influences spread in south India, Sri Lanka and Southeast Asia, elite groups with political or economic power in these areas took on Sanskrit/Prakrit names, adopted the ritual use of Sanskrit/Prakrit and Brahmanical rituals and ideology. The name 'Sanskritisation' is used here for this process.

[71] See Appendix V on Sanskritisation Legends of South India, Sri Lanka and Southeast Asia.

[72] The Paṇḍukābhaya cycle of legends are to be found in the two early Pali chronicles, the *Dīpavaṃsa* and the *Mahāvaṃsa*. Many of the elements were borrowed from Indian stories, especially those relating to Krişṇa, as found in the *Mahābhārata* and the *Harivamsa*. For an analysis of these legends, see L.S.Perera, 'The Early Kings of Ceylon Up to Muṭasiva', *UCHC*, I, 1: 106-111. The central figure in these legends is Paṇḍuka Abhaya (often written as Paṇḍukābhaya). The element 'Paṇḍu' occurs not only in his name but also in the names of several other important characters in these legends (Paṇḍu Vāsudeva, Paṇḍu Sakka, Paṇḍula) as well in a placename (Paṇḍulagāma). Paṇḍu is the name given to the Pāṇḍyas in the Pali chronicles and in other Pali and Prakrit sources. It is also the name given to the father of the Pāṇḍava brothers in the *Mahābhārata*. In these legends, Paṇḍukābhaya appears as a rebel hero who waged war to win the kingdom of Tambapaṇṇi. After his victory, he is credited with the foundation of a new capital at Anurādhagāma, later renamed Anurādhapura. L.S.Perera's conclusion is worthy of note: "In the story of Paṇḍukābhaya, there is little doubt that the war he waged to win the kingdom and the foundation of Anurādhapura constitute the core of the historical tradition. He was for a long time a rebel who lived probably by pillage. He gathered round him a band of followers and lived in the eastern parts of the Island. After a series of battles, he defeated his rivals and established himself as king with Anurādhapura as his capital." *UCHC*, I, 1: 110-111. The Paṇḍu association in these legends appears to indicate a connection with the Pāṇḍya lineage in south India. Some members of that lineage were possibly involved in the contest for power in the new chiefdoms of the island, as they indeed were in the later centuries at Anuradhapura.

[73] Kennedy 1975 .

[74] Coningham rightly concludes that 'such non-scriptural graffiti are commonly held to indicate ownership whether of a personal or more corporate nature, and that as such represent a continuity in function with the later vessels inscribed in Brāhmī and Kharoshti' (1996: 90). Potsherds from the bowls used by monks and others have been discovered with graffiti clearly establishing ownership (for instance, *Dataha pata*, the bowl of Data): Indrapala 1973: 18-19 (see Appendix VI).

[75] The discovery of these potsherds with Brāhmī writing was clearly of great significance that the excavator, an experienced and highly respected prehistoric archaeologist, was so carried away with excitement particularly at the name Anurādha on one of the sherds and the language of the graffiti that he rushed to conclude that the potsherd "evidence does indeed vouch for the accuracy of the Mahāvaṃsa" (in respect of what this chronicle tells us about Anurādha, a maternal great-uncle of King Paṇḍukābhaya!). Not stopping with this, he went on to claim that the inscriptions on the potsherds "certainly support the hypothesis of a major Indo-Aryan impulse", no doubt leaving many of his genuine admirers dumb-founded. Deraniyagala 1992: 747. . 'As these inscriptions represent names in their dative and genitive cases', comments Coningham, 'it is assumed that they refer to the owner of the pot and whatever objects were contained or transported in it' (1999: 138). Clearly the graffiti were labels used by traders and the conclusion is that Prakrit-using traders were present in Anuradhapura in the period to which these potsherds belong. The evidence is inadequate to claim that it validates the *Mahāvaṃsa* story or supports the hypothesis of a 'major Indo-Aryan impulse'.

[76] Wilhelm Geiger was one of the first to make a proper historical analysis of the Sinhala language. In his account he gives the name Sinhalese-Prakrit to the earliest form as found in the Br1hm2 inscriptions. The period of this Sinhalese-Prakrit is dated by him to c.200 BCE to the 4th/5th century CE. Geiger 1938: 2.

[77] *UCHC*, I, 1:36-38; Karunaratne 1984: 42.

[78] Karunaratne 1984: 42-43.

[79] Renfrew 1998: 123-124.

[80] Allchin and Allchin 1988: 299.

[81] Renfrew 1998: 132-133.

[82] Ibid: 132.

[83] Sena and Guttaka, sons of a horse-freighter, seized power at Anuradhapura and ruled for twenty-two years in the second century BCE.

[84] Coningham et al 1996: 94; see also, Introduction: Concepts, above.

[85] Ibid.

[86] Robins, H.R. (Emeritus Professor of General Linguistics, University of London), 'Linguistic change', *The New Encyclopaedia Britannica*, 22, 2003: 569-570.

[87] Renfrew 1998: 285.

[88] Seneviratne 1985: 162.

[89] Ibid.

[90] Ibid: 162-163.

[91] While early Tamil texts, especially the grammatical treatise *Tolkāppiyam*, have oblique references to different dialects of Tamil spoken in different regions, there is no specific mention about different languages. However, a rare reference to the language of the Nāgas is found in a story included in the Buddhist Tamil epic *Maṇimēkalai.* In this story, a Tamil maritime trader is shipwrecked in the land of the Nāgas (presumably Nāgadīpa) but manages to get assistance 'because he had thoroughly learnt their language' (XVI: ll.60-61). Such a statement implies knowledge among Tamil-speakers that the Nāgas spoke a different language.

[92] Markoe 2000: 10. A casual glance at the Phoenician alphabet and Brāhmī will strike anyone with their similarity. There is, of course, no one-to-one equation between the letters of the two alphabets. But it is hard to rule out the possibility of one having influenced or inspired the creation of the other. The first letter of the Phoenician alphabet, which looks like an upper case K and which evolved later into the A of the modern Roman script, is the mirror-image of the first letter of the Brāhmī script. The Brāhmī letters for 'ka', 'e', 'ya', 'na', 'ga', 'u', 'tha' are similar to letters in Phoenician. It is not difficult to imagine local traders in the western coast of the subcontinent or in SISL drawing inspiration from the Phoenician traders who were making effective use of writing. Once the principle was understood, with or without the help of some Phoenician traders, an intelligent local trader or other elite member or even a group of them could have devised an alphabet which they found useful for keeping a rudimentary record of transactions and for labels (indicating ownership) to be scratched on the earthenware pots containing various merchandise. In fact, the Greeks who learnt the alphabet from the Phoenicians used the new alphabetic writing early on for graffiti on pottery (the earliest of these potsherds date to the second quarter of the eighth century BCE). It is surmised that the process through which the Greeks received the alphabet from the Phoenicians 'was probably the product of a direct exchange between two individuals – a Greek recipient and a literate or

semi-literate Phoenician (priest, scribe, merchant or artisan).' Markoe 2000:112-113.

[93] Cook, M., *A Brief History of the Human Race*, London 2004: 45.

[94] Seneviratne 1984: 293. Deraniyagala 2004: *Frontline* interview – 'end of the Stone Age is around 1,000 BC as far as Sri Lanka is concerned, and the Iron Age set in roughly around that time.' June 2004.

Chapter 3

[1] Renfrew 1998: 9-19.

[2] The findings of European linguists from the comparative study of European and north Indian languages early in the 19th century soon led to the promulgation of racist theories. Prominent among those who propounded these new theories was the French writer, Comte de Joseph Arthur Gobineau (1816-1882), whose racist interpretations of history had a great influence on the development of the concept of race in Europe in the 19th century. In his well-known *Essay on the Inequality of Human Races* (*L'Essai sur inegalite des races humaines*), published in several volumes in 1853-55, Gobineau claimed superiority for the white 'race' as far as intellectual and spiritual qualities were concerned. He also claimed supremacy for the Aryans among the white people. There were also others who put forward similar claims, but Gobineau's most important follower was the Englishman H.S.Chamberlain (who lived mostly in Germany and wrote in German). Gobineau and Chamberlain are considered to be the intellectual forerunners of those who spelt out the racial theories on which German Nazism was founded. Even some of the reputed scientific scholars of the twentieth century, including linguists, historians and archaeologists, fell into the trap of racialist thinking when writing about the Aryans. One of the leading archaeologists of the early twentieth century, V.Gordon Childe, could not resist the temptation of giving a racialist interpretation to his ideas about the spread of Aryan languages: "…the fact that the first Aryans were Nordics was not without importance. The physical qualities of that stock did enable them by the bare fact of superior strength to conquer even more advanced peoples and

so to impose their language on areas from which their bodily type has almost completely vanished. This is the truth underlying the panegyrics of the Germanists: the Nordics' superiority in physique fitted them to be the vehicles of a superior language." (Childe, V.G., *The Aryans – A Study of Indo-European Origins*, London 1926: 212). In fairness to Childe, it must be said that he later regretted this interpretation. For a very comprehensive analysis of the Aryan theory, see Leon Poliakov, *The Aryan Myth*, New York: 1996.

[3] Renfrew 1998: 41.

[4] Ibid: 75, 76. The method of linguistic palaeontology was used to identify cognate or related words in the different Indo-European languages and then to establish the original of those words in the parental language (Proto-Indo-European). Using this so-called protolexicon, scholars attempted to recreate a physical description of the homeland. For example, in the protolexicon there are names of certain animals, birds and trees. These words were used as clues to identify the natural environment of the people who spoke Proto-Indo-European. To quote Renfrew, "If, then, we can point to some region in Europe or Asia where it can be demonstrated that these species were living a few thousand years ago, and if that is the only area where they could all be found, then that must be the homeland, so it is argued, and the problem is solved." Ibid: 79-80.

[5] Ibid: 94.

[6] Renfrew does not suggest a model of diffusion or acculturation for the spread of farming in Europe. In such a model, the existing hunter-gatherer population comes into contact with other people in neighbouring areas with a knowledge of farming and learn the farming practices as well as acquire the domesticated plants and animals. In this manner they come to take up farming and the process spreads far and wide. Instead Renfrew suggests that farming spread in Europe by a process similar to what is known as the wave of advance model (on which movements of people are involved but only over very short distances). Renfrew 1998: 148.

[7] Ibid: 174.

[8] Ibid: 189.

[9] Ibid: 190.

[10] Ibid: 205.

[11] A good example of the view generally held by Western Indologists is to be seen in *The Wonder that was India*, written by A.L.Basham (first published in 1954, Fontana edition Calcutta 1971), one of the leading British historians of ancient India. Basham writes: "The invaders of India called themselves *Aryas*, a word generally anglicized into Aryans…The Aryan invasion of India was not a single concerted action, but one covering centuries and involving many tribes, perhaps not all of the same race and language. It seems certain that many of the old village cultures of the western hills were destroyed before the cities of the Indus vanished…Evidently the invaders did not take to living in cities, and after the fall of Harappa and Mohenjo Daro the Panjab and Sind became a land of little villages."(Basham 1971: 29-31). In his view, the Aryans originated in 'the great steppeland which stretches from Poland to Central Asia' and were 'semi-nomadic barbarians, who were tall, comparatively fair, and mostly long-headed'. From their homeland, 'They migrated in bands westwards, southwards and eastwards, conquering local populations, and intermarrying with them to form a ruling class.' *Ibid.*

[12] Thapar 2000: 82

[13] In a lecture on the Aryan Question given at the Academic Staff College, Jawaharlal Nehru University, on 11 Ocotber 1999, Romila Thapar drew attention to the 'language change' that took place as a result of Indo-Aryan, particularly Vedic Sanskrit, spreading among speakers of Proto-Dravidian and Austroasiatic languages. Romila Thapar, 'The Aryan Question Revisited', http://members.tripod.com/ascjnu/aryan.html 1/10/2002.

[14] Thapar : 105.

[15] Ibid: 113.

[16] Thapar has summed up this view in the following words: "…some are now propagating an interpretation of Indian history based on Hindu nationalism and what has come to be called the Hindutva ideology. Since the early twentieth century, this view has gradually shifted from supporting the theory of an invasion to denying such an event, now arguing that the Aryans and their language, Sanskrit, were indigenous to India. The amended theory became axiomatic to their belief that those for whom the subcontinent was not the land of their ancestors and the land

where their religion originated were aliens. This changed the focus in the definition of who were indigenous and who were alien...According to this theory only the Hindus, as the lineal descendants of the Aryans, could be defined as indigenous and therefore the inheritors of the land, and not even those whose ancestry was of the subcontinent, but who had been converted to Islam and Christianity." Thapar: 14.

[17] Renfrew 1998: 182.

[18] The archaeologist Jonathan Mark Kenoyer sums up the current opinion among leading archaeologists in the following statement: "Contrary to the common notion that Indo-Aryan speaking peoples invaded the subcontinent and obliterated the culture of the Indus people, we now believe that there was no outright invasion, the decline of the Indus cities was the result of many complex factors." In his view, 'there is no archaeological or biological evidence for invasions, or mass migrations into the Indus valley between the end of the Harappan phase, about 1900 B.C. and the beginning of the Early Historic Period around 600 B.C.' Kenoyer : 19, 174.

[19] Caldwell, R., 1856, *A Comparative Grammar of the Dravidian or South Indian Family of Languages*.

[20] Krishnamurti 2003: 2. The name *Draviḍa* occurs in the early Sanskrit texts *Tantravārttika*, *Nāṭyaśāstra*, *Manusmriti* and *Mahābhārata*.

[21] The word *Tamiḻ* occurs in the following early Tamil texts: *Puṟanāṉūṟu* 35:2, 50: 19, 58:13; *Patiṟṟuppattu* 63.9; *Ciṟupāṇāṟṟuppaṭai* 66. It occurs in the sense of Tamil language, Tamil country and Tamil people. The Pali equivalent *Damiḷa* occurs in the *Akitti Jātaka* with reference to the Tamil country (*Damiḷaraṭṭhaṃ*).

[22] Among those who have made notable contributions to Dravidian historical linguistics are M.B. Emeneau, T. Burrow, K. Zvelebil, B. Krishnamurti, J. Vacek and F. Southwork.

[23] Parpola, Asko, 1994, *Deciphering the Indus Script*, Cambridge University Press; Heras, Henry, 1953, *Studies in Proto-Indo-Mediterranean Culture*, Bombay; Marshall, John, 1924 (September), 'First Light on a Long Forgotten Civilization', *Illustrated London News*, London: 528-532.

[24] Vacek, Jaruslav, 2002, *Dravidian and Altaic 'Water – Viscosity – Cold': An Etymological and Typological Model*, Charles University, Prague; Ohno, Susumu, 1980, *Sound Correspondence between Tamil and Japanese*, Tokyo; Sjoberg, Andree, 1971, 'Who are the Dravidians? The present state of knowledge' in Andree F.Sjoberg (ed.), *Symposium on Dravidian Civilization*, Austin (Texas).

[25] McAlpin, D.W., 'Elamite and Dravidian: further evidence of relationship', *Current Anthropology*, 16: 105-115.

[26] Zvelebil 2003: 697; Vacek 2002: 8.

[27] Zvelebil 2003: 698.

[28] Ruhlen, Merritt, *A Guide to the Languages of the World*, Stanford University 1976: 83.

[29] Cavalli-Sforza, Luigi Luca, *The Great Human Diaspora: The History of Diversity and Evolution*, tr. from Italian, Addison-Wesley Publising Co. USA 1995: 177. The Czech scholar of Dravidian studies, Kamil Zvelebil, summarises the current scholarly opinion on this subject in the following words: "The circumstances of the advent of Dravidian speakers in India are shrouded in mystery. There are vague linguistic and cultural ties with the Urals, with the Mediterranean area, and with Iran. It is possible that a Dravidian-speaking people that can be described as dolichocephalic (longheaded from front to back) Mediterranean mixed with brachycephalic (shortheaded front to back) Armenoids and established themselves in northwest India during the 4th millennium BC. Along their route, these immigrants may have possibly come into an intimate, prolonged contact with the Ural-Altaic speakers, thus explaining the striking affinities between the Dravidian and the Ural-Altaic language groups. Between 2000 and 1500 BC, there was a fairly constant movement of Dravidian speakers from the northwest to the southeast of India, and in about 1500 BC three distinct dialect groups probably existed: Proto-North Dravidian, Proto-Central Dravidian, and Proto-South Dravidian. The beginnings of the splits in the parent speech, however, are obviously earlier. It is possible that Proto-Brahui was the first language to split off from Proto-Dravidian, probably during the immigration movement into India sometime in the 4th millennium BC, and the next subgroup to split off was Proto-Kurukh-Malto, sometime in the 3rd millennium BC." Zvelebil 2003: 698.

[30] Krishnamurti 2003: 5.

[31] Krishnamurti provides a list of 26 Dravidian languages. They are divided into four major groups. **Southern Group**: 1. Tamil, 2. Malayalam, 3. Irula, 4. Kurumba, 5. Kodagu, 6. Toda, 7. Kota, 8. Badaga, 9. Kannada, 10. Koraga, 11. Tulu; **South Central Group**: 12. Telugu, 13. Gondi, 14. Konda, 15. Kui, 16. Kuvi, 17. Pengo, 18. Manda; **Central Group**: 19. Kolami, 20. Naikri/ Naiki (Chanda), 21. Parji, 22. Ollari, 23. (Kondekor) Gadaba; **Northern Group**: 24. Kurux, 25. Malto, 26. Brahui. Krishnamurti 2003: 19.

[32] Zvelebil 2003: 698.

[33] Parpola, Heras, Knorozov. See note 23 above.

[34] Subbarayarappa, B.V., *Indus Script: Its Nature and Structure*, 1996.

[35] Historical linguists have identified a growing Dravidian influence on Sanskrit from the time of the Rigvedic hymns. Loan words such as *phalam*, *mukham* and *khala* have been pointed out as examples. A greater influence has been noticed in the post-Vedic texts. This includes certain elements in phonology, syntax and vocabulary. The retroflex in the Indo-Aryan languages is seen by linguists as a clear indication of Dravidian influence as the Sanskrit language spread widely among the non-Indo-Aryan speakers. The Sanskrit scholar, T. Burrow, is of the view that the large majority of Dravidian loan-words appear in Classical Sanskrit, being first recorded in such early texts as Panini's Grammar, Patanjali's work and the *Mahābhārata* (Burrow, T., 1955, *The Sanskrit Language*, London: 386). The Pakistani linguist, Tariq Rahman, has expressed the view that the roots of the languages spoken in Pakistan today are both Dravidian and Indo-Aryan. (Rahman 2001)

[36] Thapar 1999: 13. 'One of the interesting aspects of the linguistic study that has been done of Vedic Sanskrit is that a number of words that relate to agricultural processes – some very common words like *langala* which means plough, *khala*, *ulukhala* so on – are all words that come from non-Indo-Aryan languages.'

[37] Zvelebil 2003: 698.

[38] Krishnamurti 2003: 19-20.

[39] Gunawardana 1994: 211.

[40] Ibid.

[41] Ibid.

[42] De Silva, K.M., 1977: 32 'Sinhalese were a people of Aryan origins'; 1981: 7, 13; Arasaratnam, S., *Ceylon*, Englewood Cliffs New Jersey 1964: 45 'Aryan settlements', 99 'Aryan colonization'.

Chapter 4

[1] Paranavitana, S., 'Aryan Settlements: The Sinhalese', *UCHC* I, 1: 89.

[2] Davies 2000: 145-146.

[3] See Appendix I.

[4] A good example is the Tamil lineage name Atiyamāṉ which is rendered in Prakrit in the Asokan inscriptions of the third century BCE as Satiyaputa and, very much later, as Satyaputra in Sanskrit. While the suffix *–māṉ* in the original name meant 'son' and was, therefore, translated as '*puta*', the proper name Atiya, which was no doubt untranslatable, was rendered as Satiya with an initial 's'. In a similar manner, Iḷa may have been rendered as Sīhaḷa in Pali.

[5] The Allahabad Pillar Inscription of Samudragupta (fourth century CE) refers to *Saiṃhaḷa* (*Corpus Inscriptionum Indicarum*, III, ed. J.F.Fleet, Calcutta 1888: 8). An inscription from Java (eighth century CE) refers to *Siṃhaḷa* (*Artibus Asiae*, XXIV, 1962: 241). . *Siṃhaḷa* also occurs in the *Mahābhārata* Sabhā-parva and in the Commentary to the *Arthaśāstra*.

[6] An inscription (circa second/third century CE) from Nagarjunakonda, Andhra Pradesh, refers to a monastery called Sīhaḷa-vihāra (Vogel, J.Ph., 'Nāgārjuṇakoṇḍa Inscriptions', *EI*, XX: 1-37).

[7] *Heḷaṭuvā*, *Heḷabasa* and *Heḷu* in the tenth century literary work *Dhampiyā-aṭuvā gäṭapadaya*; *Heḷadivi* in one of the Sīgiri graffiti; *Heḷekuḷī* in several inscriptions of the ninth century; and *Eḷu* in later centuries, as in *Eḷu-Bodhivaṃsa*.

[8] The Sangam poem *Paṭṭiṉappālai* has a reference to '*īḻattuṇavu*' (food items from Īḻam).

[9] Weerakkody 1997: 23.

[10] Mahadevan 2003: 393.

[11] Ibid: 152. Earlier, Iḻa was interpreted to mean Sri Lanka (the Tamil name Īḻam), giving the words *Iḻa kuṭumpikaṉ* the meaning 'householder from

Sri Lanka'. Such an interpretation is unacceptable as the name of a large region or country was not used as part of a personal name. The only known exception where Īḻa is claimed to be used with a personal name is the case of the Tamil Sangam poet Pūtaṉ Tēvaṉār, who is referred to in a late colophon as Īḻattu (of Īḻam) Pūtaṉ Tēvaṉār but this seems to be a later corruption. Even in this case, the poet is referred to as Maturai Īḻattu Pūtaṉ Tēvaṉār, making it doubtful that the Īlam here indicates Sri Lanka.

12 Mahadevan 2003: 579, 602. Iḷayar (*Iḷa*+personal noun/ group noun suffix *–ar*) is explained by Mahadevan as a clan name. It occurs as Iḷa-makkaḷ (Iḷa people) in later inscriptions. In the Tamil Brāhmī inscriptions, it also occurs in the singular form as *Eḷamakaṉ* (member of the Iḷa clan) and *Iḷavaṉ* (*Iḷa*+personal noun suffix *–aṉ*). Because the name Iḷa is easily confused with the common adjective *iḷa* (young), many other occurrences of this name in inscriptions and literature can be missed. It is interesting to note that in the Tamil Brāhmī inscriptions, in those instances where the meaning of 'junior' or 'younger' is clearly implied, the word used is *ḷa* and not *iḷa.* Since *iḷa* is the known literary form for 'junior' or 'young', Mahadevan offers the explanation that this was probably because the initial *i* was elided in speech (Mahadevan 2003: 405). It appears to the present writer that the explanation may have to be sought elsewhere. *Ḷa* may be an earlier non-literary form which is still found as a prefix (meaning 'young') in a number of Sinhala words from early times. Just as the younger of the two Cēra royalties (father and son) with the same name was distinguished by the epithet *Ḷa* (Ḷaṅ Kaṭuṅkō) in the Pugalur Tamil Brāhmī inscription (ibid), the younger of the two Tamil rulers of Anuradhapura (father and son) with the same name (fifth century) was given the distinguishing epither *Ḷa* (Ḷa Parideva = Parideva the Younger) in an early Sinhala (Heḷa) inscription from Anuradhapura (*EZ*, IV: 114). Among the Sinhala words having the prefix *ḷa* (meaning 'young') are: *ḷamayā* (child, boy), *ḷadaru and ḷapaṭi.*

13 Paranavitana 1970: No.94. It would appear that from the time this inscription was first read, the misreading of *iḷa* as *ilu*, as well as the reading of this name as the prefix of a longer name Ilubarata, misled scholars for a long time. Paranavitana's reading (Ilubarata) was later corrected by Karunaratne and Seneviratne as Iḷabarata. Seneviratne 1985b: 54, n.16; Karunaratne 1984: 33-35.

[14] Paranavitana 1959: 87.

[15] *EZ*, VII: 79.

[16] *Mv.*,XXXV: 15.

[17] *Pūjāvaliya,* ed. A.V. Suravira, Colombo 1961; *Rājāvaliya,* ed. B. Gunasekara, Colombo 1953.

[18] *Mv.*,XXXV: 48.

[19] The date of the data in the Sinhala chronicles, *Pūjāvaliya* and *Rājāvaliya*, is likely to be much earlier than the time when these chronicles were written, for the traditions on which these chronicles are based go back to the commentaries in the local language, known to us as the *Sīhaḷa-aṭṭhakathā* or *Heḷaṭuvā*.

[20] Weerakkody 1997: 23. The relevant statement in Ptolemy's text is: 'Opposite the promontory of Cory in India there lies the extreme point of the island of Taprobane, which in the past used to be called Simoundou, but is now called Salike. Its inhabitants are commonly called Salae…'. Ibid: 230.

[21] Ibid: 244.

[22] Ibid: 245.

[23] Ibid: 24.

[24] Geiger 1938: 82. . "Frequently *s* has changed to *h*. Alternating forms with *s* or *h* are very numerous and it is obvious that those with *h* are more modern and their use in literature is increasing from century to century. The change itself is very old."

[25] Gunawardana 1990: 53.

[26] An inscription of about the third century CE from Nagarjunakonda (Andhra Pradesh) refers to *Sīhaḷa* (*EI*, XX: 1-37). A number of early Sanskrit writings have references to the name Siṃhaḷa. Among them are the *Mahābhārata* (Sabhāparva), tr. P. Chandra Roy, Calcutta 1912: 146; *Kathāsaritsāgara*, tr. C.H. Tawney, *The Ocean of Story*, IV, London 1925: 220. For the references in the Commentary to the *Arthaśāstra*, see H. Raychaudhuri, 'Palaesimundu', *Indian Antiquary*, XLVIII: 195-196.

[27] Much has been written about the origin myth of the lion. See, for example, Gunawardana 1990a; Kapferer, Bruce, 1988, *Legends of People Myths of State: Violence, Intolerance and Political Culture in Sri Lanka and Australia,* Washington: 34.

[28] *EI*, XX, 5: 80.

[29] Nilakanta Sastri 1955: 31.

[30] Ludden 1999: 77.

[31] Gunawardana 1990: 53.

[32] Gunawardana 1995: 35.

[33] Ibid: 25.

[34] Mahadevan 2003: 393.

[35] Pallava inscriptions of about the eighth century have references to the Īlavar community whose main occupation was climbing coconut and palmyrah palms for tapping toddy and plucking nuts (Velurpalaiyam Plates of Vijaya Nandivarman III and the Tandantottam Plates of Vijaya Nandivikramavarman). Cōḻa inscriptions, too, have numerous references to the Īḻavar and their villages (Īḻaccēri). See Appendix I.

[36] Kerala traditions are full of legends about the migration of the Īḻavar from Sri Lanka to Kerala. The community is mentioned in the *Keralotpatti* , the well-known book of historical traditions relating to Kerala. These legends explain how the Īḻavar came from Sri Lanka and introduced the coconut to Kerala. For a discussion of these legends, see A. Aiyappan, *Iravas and Culture Change*, Bulletin of the Madras Government Museum, NS, General Section V, 1, Madras 1944; V. Nagam Aiya, *Travancore State Manual*, I, 1906: 398-402; T.K. Veluppillai, *Travancore State Manual*, II, 1940: 14-15; C.A.Menon, *Cochin State Manual*, 1911: 33, 203.

[37] Nilakanta Sastri 1955: 490, 548, 578.

[38] Coningham et al 1996.

[39] Not all the words in the graffiti seem to be Prakrit. One of the words, *timula*, could be *timul* or *timil*, which occurs in ancient Tamil. Coningham et al 1996: 85. Timil, meaning a fishing boat, occurs in the Sangam poems *Maturaikkāñci* (l.116), *Paṭṭiṇappālai* (l.112), *Puṟanāṉūṟu* (24: 4; 60: 1) and *Kuṟuntokai* (123: l.5).

[40] Coningham et al: 80.

[41] Ibid: 81.

[42] Many south Indian dynasties, like the Āndhras, Śātavāhanas, Ikshvākus and the Pallavas used Prakrit in their earliest epigraphic records.

[43] See Chapter 2.

[44] Paranavitana 1970: No. 94; Seneviratne 1985b: 54 n.10.

[45] Sivaramamurti, C., *Amaravati Sculptures in the Madras Government Museum*, Madras, 1977: 303.

[46] The inscription from Nagarjunakonda is damaged where the word *'Damiḷa'* occurs. The editor of the inscription, J.Ph. Vogel, is inclined to restore the damaged word as *'Damiḷa'*. *EI*, XX: 22. For *'Dhamiḷa-gharinī'*, see Luders, H., *A List of Brāhmī Inscriptions*, Delhi, 1973: Nos. 1014, 1018.

[47] *EI,* XX, 5: 79, 86. The relevant statement in the inscription is: "(he) thoroughly breaks up the confederacy of the T[r]amira (Dramira) countries of one hundred and thirteen years…".

[48] *Jataka* No. 480: Akitti Jataka (the reference is to *Damiḷaraṭṭhaṃ*).

[49] See Chapter 3.

[50] *Tolkāppiyam* and Sangam works, such as *Puṟanānūṟu* 35, 50, 58.

[51] Paranavitana gave much publicity to this inscription. One of his earliest writings on this epigraph appeared in the *Annual Bibliography of Indian Archaeology*, XIII: 13 ff. In 1940, he published another article in the *Journal of the Royal Asiatic Society Ceylon Branch,* XXXV: 54-56, 'Tamil Householders' Terrace, Anuradhapura'. This inscription is included in his *Inscriptions of Ceylon*, I, 1970 (No.94).

[52] Paranavitana 1970: Nos. 356, 357, 480.

[53] Karunaratne 1984: 33, 71.

[54] Davies 2000: 149.

[55] Dutthagāmanī fought his brother Saddha Tissa.

[56] While most history books on Sri Lanka refer to Sena and Guttaka as invaders, even some reputed scholars fall into the trap of considering these two rulers as invaders. Sudharshan Seneviratne (1985 a: 523): 'It is not a coincidence that the earliest recorded invasion from south India occurred around B.C. 200 and it is associated with Sena and Guttaka'. C.R. de Silva (*Sri Lanka: A History*, 2nd edition, Delhi 1997, Reprint 2001: 27): 'In 177 B.C.E., two South Indians, Sena and Guttika, seized power at Anuradhapura and ruled for twenty years.'

[57] *Dv*. 18: 47. '*Sūratissaṃ gahetvāna Damiḷā Sena Guttakā duve dvādasa vassāni rajjaṃ dhammena kārayuṃ.*' The *Dv* does not even refer to Eḷāra as a Damiḷa or as an invader (*Dv* 18: 49).

[58] *Mv* XXI: 10.

[59] Ibid. tr. Geiger

Chapter 5

[1] Deraniyagala 1992: 711-713.

[2] *Mv*: XXV. Several chiefdoms of Tamil rulers, along the Mahaväli River, are referred to in this chapter.

[3] The nine rulers are: Sena, Guttaka, Eḷāra, Pulahattha, Bāhiya, Panayamāra, Piḷayamāra, Dāṭhika and Vaṭuka.

[4] Gunawardana 1982: 7.

[5] Paranavitana is inclined to take this term to mean 'grandson'. Seneviratne, however, prefers the meaning 'nephew/son-in-law': Seneviratne 1985a: 435. In the Sangam poems *marumakaṉ* and its variant *marumāṉ* occur several times with the meaning 'descendant' (for example, *Puṟanāṉūṟu*: 909). In early Tamil inscriptions, the plural form '*marumakkaḷ*' occurs in the sense of 'descendants': Kuram Pallava Grant, l.84 '*Ananta Civa ācāriyār makkaḷ makkaḷ marumakkaḷ*', *South Indian Inscriptions*, I, p.151. M.H. Peter Silva supports the derivation of the Sinhalese word *muṇuburu* (grandson) from *marumakan*, through the intermediate *manumaraka* (op. cit. iv, see above Introduction note 62.), which may indicate that *marumakana* in the Brāhmī inscriptions meant 'grandson'.

[6] Paranavitana *UCHC*, I, 1: 235.

[7] Bell 1892: 69, n.3. Bell does not derive *parumaka* from *perumakaṉ*, but draws a comparison between the two terms: "The word really siginifies 'chief' (Skt. *pramukha*, Eḷu *pāmok*) and is applied to kings. Cf. the inscriptions of 10th and 11th century …and Tamil *perumakan*, a prince, a nobleman." In the Sangam poems, *perumakaṉ* occurs several times with the meaning 'chief' (for example, *Puṟanāṉūṟu*: 88, 90).

[8] Seneviratne 1984: 288, n.46:

[9] Indrapala 1961. That the feminine suffix in the term *parumakalu* (as read by Paranavitana) strengthens the view that the term *parumaka* is closer to the Tamil *perumakaṉ* than to the Sanskrit *pramukha* was put forward in this contribution. Subsequently, the term read as *parumakalu* by Paranavitana was given the reading *parumakaḷa* (also readable as *parumakaḷ*) by W.S. Karunaratne and others.

[10] For instance, the Sangam poem *Perumpāṇāṟṟuppaṭai*, l. 101.

[11] Seneviratne 1992: 103.

[12] Gunawardana 1982: 7. Cf. *ayyā.* The word *ayyā* in Tamil and Sinhalese (as well as in other Dravidian languages like Telugu), denoting 'elder brother', may well have originally meant 'leader' (the older brother as the leader of the younger siblings). It is also still used in Tamil and Telugu as an honorific form of address in the same way as 'sir' in English.

[13] The names Vēḷ and Vēḷir occur in a number of Sangam poems: *Akanāṉ ūṟu* :135, 372; *Kuṟuntokai* :164; *Puṟanāṉūṟu* :24.

[14] Seneviratne 1992: 112.

[15] Paranavitana 1970. The term Barata occurs in nearly two dozen records in this collection. More have been discovered after the publication of this volume – see, Dias, Malini, 1991, *Epigraphical Notes* Nos. 1-18, Colombo; also No.21, June 2001.

[16] Seneviratne 1985b: 49ff.

[17] Ibid: 51.

[18] Ibid: 52.

[19] Ibid.

[20] Seneviratne 1985a: 411.

[21] Gunawardana 1982: 32.

[22] De Silva 1979: 16. A few years earlier, in his study of Dravidian influence on Sinhala, M.H. Peter Silva concluded: 'An analysis of the vocabulary represented by the Sinhalese inscriptions and the literary works shows that there is a stratum of Dravidian loans in it'. Peter Silva, op. cit. 1 (see above, Introduction, note 62).

[23] De Silva 1979: 17: 'The earliest available records show that Sinhalese differed from the Indo-Aryan languages of North India in a number of ways. The most striking difference is in the behaviour of Old Indic aspirate consonants which are phonemic in almost all languages but Sinhalese. Geiger (1935a: XVIII) thought that this peculiarity in Sinhalese might have been the result of Dravidian contact. Dravidian influence might also account for the subsequent intervocalic merger of voiced and voiceless stops, which, in Sinhalese, yields voiced stops only…Sinhalese developed this feature without exception with the increase of Dravidian influence on the land'. Elaborating this further, de Silva gives examples of Dravidian characteristics in Sinhala: 'The non-declinability of the adjective distinguishes Sinhalese from, say, Hindi, but

puts it on the same side as Tamil. In both Tamil and Sinhalese relativised clauses appear on the surface as gerundive phrases while Hindi shows relative clauses both to the left as well as to the right of the head noun phrase. In both Tamil and Sinhalese sentences such as "I can …" and "I want…" take the subject in the dative case, but in Hindi the subject appears in the nominative. There are morphological similarities too. The Sinhalese neuter plural affix *–val* has been stated as a derivation of the Tamil plural affix *–kal* (Wijayaratne 1956). There are similarities in the way verbal categories are recognised in the two languages. In colloquial usage, for instance, both languages use a neutral verb regardless of the number, person, etc. of the subject word. A study of morpho-syntactic typologies of these languages should be very productive.' (De Silva 1979: 22-23).

[24] Thapar 2002: 113.

[25] Some of the early geographical names in the Pali chronicles also seem to indicate the influence of Dravidian languages. The territorial name Malaya, applied to the central highlands of Sri Lanka from the time of the earliest writings, is of non-Indo-Aryan origin. Two leading scholars of Dravidian linguistics, T.Burrow and M.B.Emeneau, treat the word *malai* as Dravidian (*A Dravidian Etymological Dictionary*, Oxford 1961: 314). This word occurs in many of the Sangam poems, both alone and in compounds such as the title *malaiyamān̲* (chief of the mountains), *Puranān̲ūr̲u* 121, 122, 123. The suffix *–paṭṭana* in the names of two ports in the northern part of the island, Jambukola-paṭṭana and Gonagāmaka-paṭṭana, is also worth considering. This suffix occurs in some ancient port names in south India (Kāvīrapaṭṭana/ Kāvirippūmpaṭṭin̲am, Nāgapaṭṭana/ Nākapaṭṭin̲am and Mayūrarūpapaṭṭana) and *paṭṭin̲am* is a word found in the Sangam poems with the meaning 'coastal town', 'coastal region'. It is significant that names of ports in the southern part of Sri Lanka do not have this suffix. Survivals in personal names, such as Kuñca and Kuḍā may also indicate Dravidian influence. These epithets, meaning 'younger' or 'smaller' are given to a king of the second century CE (Kuñca Nāga in Pali and Kuḍā Nā in Eḷu). The word *kuñci/kuñcu* is still used for 'smaller' or 'younger' in Jaffna Tamil as in *kuñciyappu, kuñcācci, kuñcu-petti, Kuñcu Parantan̲. Kuḍā* itself seems to be related to *kuṭṭi* (young one, small).

[26] Bopearachchi and Wickremasinghe 1999: 56. Coin No.A.21 has the legend *ūtira<u>n</u>a* (which could be read as Ūtira<u>n</u>, but as a legend on a coin the name is likely to be in the genitive case, which would mean that the reading Ūtira<u>n</u>a is correct). Comments by authors: "This coin is of utmost importance in that it presents us a personal name in a clear Tamil nominative form with an *akṣara <u>n</u>a*, representing an alveolar nasal, which is not found in Ceylonese Brāhmī rock inscriptions, but which is well-known from South Indian inscriptions in Tamil-Brāhmī." (Ibid). Coin No. A.37 has the legend *(ta)sapijana* and Coin No. A.23 has the legend *tiriha* (Ibid). The authors treat Tasapijana as another Tamil name. *Tiri* is the Tamil form Sri and it is from this the form *tiru* is derived.

[27] Pushparatnam 1993: 47.

[28] Seneviratne 1992: 113.

[29] Seneviratne 1985: 54; Gunawardana

[30] Turnour, G. (ed), *The Mahāvaṃsa*, Colombo 1837: 100.

[31] Seneviratne 1985: 523.

[32] Mv. XXI: 13. '*Coḷaraṭṭhā idhāgamma rajjhattaṃ ujujātiko Eḷāro nāma Damiḷo*'.

[33] Mv. XXI: 14.

[34] Legend 1: "At the head of his bed he had a bell hung up with a long rope so that those who desired a judgement at law might ring it. The king had only one son and one daughter. When once the son of the ruler was going in a car to the Tissa-tank, he killed unintentionally a young calf lying on the road with the mother cow, by driving the wheel over its neck. The cow came dragged at the bell in bitterness of heart; and the king caused his son's head to be severed (from his body) with the same wheel." Legend 2: "A snake had devoured the young of a bird upon a palmtree. The hen-bird, mother of the young one, came and rang the bell. The king caused the snake to be brought to him, and when its body had been cut open and the young bird taken out of it he caused it to be hung up upon the tree." Legend 3: "When the king, who was a protector of tradition, albeit he knew not the peerless virtues of the most precious of the three gems, was going (once) to the Cetiya-mountain to invite the brotherhood of bhikkhus, he caused, as he arrived upon a car, with the point of the yoke on the wagon, an injury to the thupa of the Conqueror at a (certain) spot. The ministers said to him: 'King, the thupa has been injured by

thee.' Though this had come to pass without his intending it, yet the king leaped from his car and flung himself down upon the road with the words: 'Sever my head also (from the trunk) with the wheel.' They answered him: 'Injury to another does our Master in no wise allow; make thy peace (with the bhikkhus) by restoring the thupa'; and in order to place (anew) the fifteen stones that had been broken off he spent just fifteen thousand kahapanas." Legend 4: "An old woman had spread out some rice to dry in the sun. The heavens, pouring down rain at an unwonted season, made her rice damp. She took the rice and went and dragged at the bell. When he heard about the rain at an unwonted season he dismissed the woman, and in order to decide her cause he underwent a fast, thinking: 'A king who observes justice surely obtains rain in due season.' The guardian genius who received offerings from him, overpowered by the fiery heat of (the penances of) the king, went and told the four great kings of this (matter). They took him with them and went and told Sakka. Sakka summoned Pajjunna and charged him (to send) rain in due season. The guardian genius who received his offerings told the king. From thenceforth the heavens rained no more during the day throughout his realm: only by night did the rains give rain once every week, in the middle watch of the night, and even the little cisterns everywhere were full of (water)." *Mv.*: XXI: 15-34.

[35] *Mv.*XXI: 21.

[36] Nilakanta Sastri 1955: 8.

[37] A remarkably similar story, which seems to have been carried to the West from South Asia by ancient traders, is told about Charlemagne. This story is found in modern books of tales for children under the title 'Charles the Great and the Snake'. According to this story, the Emperor often held his court in the palace at Zurich. He was a just judge and ruler, and had a ready ear for any of his subjects who came to him with a wrong to be righted. He wanted the poorest and humblest of his people to be able to appear before his judgement-seat. He, therefore, ordered a pillar to be set up near the palace and from this pillar a bell to be hung. The following proclamation was then issued: 'Whoever has suffered a wrong at the hands of another shall pull this bell and justice shall be done'. One day when the Emperor was sitting with his courtiers, the bell rang. When he came to the pillar, he was astonished to see a snake hanging from the bell-

rope and causing the bell to ring. Then the snake let herself down to the ground and slid down the hill. The Emperor followed the snake and came to a place where she had her nest. A venomous toad was sitting on the little snake's eggs. She could not remove her enemy without crushing the eggs. It was this that had driven her to seek the help of the Emperor, who then had the toad removed from the nest, and condemned it to be burnt alive. When the snake's eggs were hatched, she appeared once again at Charles the Great's banquet-table, slid up to where his drinking-cup was standing, and dropped a sparkling jewel into the Emperor's wine. The Emperor treasured this jewel, had it set in gold and presented it to his wife.

[38] *Mv*. XXV: 69-74

[39] J.T.Rutnam, *The Tomb of Elara at Anuradhapura*, Jaffna Archaeological Society: 1988. In this work, Rutnam gives a detailed account of the references to the veneration paid to the Eḷāra monument at Anuradhapura over the centuries up to modern times. After the *Mahāvaṃsa*, the commentary on the *Mahāvaṃsa* (*Mahāvaṃsa-tīkā*) known as the *Vaṃsatthappakāsinī* provides evidence for the continued veneration given to the monument. According to the commentator, even in his time, when processions drew near the monument not only was the music silenced, circumambulation of the *cetiya* with garlands and perfumes and performance of worship also took place (*Vaṃsatthappakāsinī*, II, ll.15-16, ed. G.P. Malalasekera, Oxford 1935: 484). The date of the commentary is not clearly established. Editing and publishing this work in 1935, G.P.Malalasekera ascribed it to the eighth or ninth century, while another Pali scholar, Wilhelm Geiger, was of the opinion that it belonged to a period between the eleventh and the thirteenth centuries. In either case, it was several centuries after the time of the *Mahāvaṃsa*. The Sinhalese chronicle *Saddharmālaṅkāraya*, written in the fourteenth century, also follows the example of the *Mahāvaṃsa* and states that even at the time of writing this chronicle, the Eḷāra dāgäba (*Eḷāḷa nam dāgäba*) was still being venerated by princes who silenced their drums when they approached this place (*Saddharmālaṅkāraya*, ed. M. Piyaratana, Colombo 1971: 547). After this time, Anuradhapura was in ruins and jungle-covered. However, it continued to be a place of pilgrimage for Buddhists.

[40] That the Eḷāra monument continued to be venerated by Buddhists in the nineteenth century is attested even by British writers. In his translation of the *Mahāvaṃsa*, published in 1837, George Turnour, following the tradition set up by the author of the *Mahāvaṃsa*, adds a footnote saying: "These honours continue to be paid to the tomb of Elara up to the period of the British occupation of the Kandyan territory." (*The Mahāvaṃsa*, I, p.113 fn). An interesting anecdote is to be found in the book *Eleven Years in Ceylon*, by Major J. Forbes, published in 1840, describing the extraordinary manner in which the fugitive Kandyan chief Pilima Talawa paid his respects to the Elara monument in 1818 when he passed through Anuradhapura:

"The ruined tomb of an infidel is now looked upon by many Buddhist pilgrims as the remnant of a sacred edifice, although twenty centuries have elapsed since the death of Elara. I do not believe that the injunctions of his conqueror have ever been disregarded by a native. In 1818 Pilima Talawa, the head of the oldest Kandyan family, when attempting to escape, after the suppression of the rebellion in which he had been engaged, alighted from his litter, although weary and almost incapable of exertion; and not knowing the precise spot, walked on until assured that he had passed far beyond this ancient memorial." J. Forbes, op. cit.: 233.

Writing after Forbes, the British administrator Emerson Tennent, in his major work Ceylon, refers to the Elara monument in the following manner: "... its ruins remain to the present day and the Sinhalese still regard it with respect and veneration." (Emerson Tennent, *Ceylon*, London 1860: 303). At this time, the Elara monument was referred to in common parlance as the Elala-sohona (tomb of Elara) and it is this name that is given in the archaeological reports of the late nineteenth century (Rutnam 1988: 5).

What was referred to as the Elala-sohona or the Tomb of Elara is now identified by the Department of Archaeology as the Dakkhina Thupa.

There is a controversy surrounding the identity of the real Elara monument. See, Rutnam 1988 for details of this controversy.

[41] The *Vaṃsatthappakāsinī* (Commentary of the *Mahāvaṃsa*) describes the location of the battle fought by Eḷāra and Duṭṭhagāmaṇī as lying east of the Eḷāra-paṭhimā-ghara. Op. cit.:.483, ll. 8-10.

[42] As many as twenty-two strongholds of Tamil chiefs are listed in the *Mahāvaṃsa*: Mahiyangana under Damiḷa Chatta, Ambatitthaka under Damiḷa Titthamba, Antarasobbha under Mahakotta, Dona under Gavara, Halakola under Issariya, Nalisobbha under Nalika, Dighabhayagallaka under Dighabhaya, Kacchatittha under Kapisisa, Kotanagara under Kota, Halavahanaka, Vahittha under Damiḷa Vahittha, Gamani under Gamani, Kumbhagama under Kumbha, Nandigama under Nandika, Khanugama under Khanu, Tamba, Unnama, Jambu, Vijitanagara, Girilaka and Maheḷanagara. *Mv*: xxv

[43] *Mv*:xxv

[44] De Silva, C.R.: 29.

[45] *UCHC* 1, 1: 166.

[46] *UCHC* 1, 2: Genealogical Table facing p.850.

[47] Paranavitana 1970.

[48] Seneviratne 1985a.

[49] Gunawardana 1982: 2. Gunawardana attributes the continuation of this framework in Sri Lankan historiography to a new Sinhalese ideology: 'However, the persistence of the influence of the ideological framework provided by the chronicles cannot be satisfactorily explained as the result of a mere lack of refinement in historical methodology. Modern historiography developed in Sri Lanka at a time when a new form of the Sinhala ideology, which drew on such traditional concepts of identity as those based on religion as well as on more recently acquired racist ideas of the Aryan identity, was gaining increasing influence . From about the 1920s, some of the proponents of this ideology began to adopt a markedly hostile attitude towards the Tamil-speaking population in the island…In the 1950s when a particularly virulent form of the Sinhala ideology was at the height of its influence, it was difficult, even for academic historians, to question the ideological framework of the *Mahāvaṃsa*.' Ibid: 3.

[50] Ibid: 8.

[51] Excavations at Anaikoddai in the Jaffna peninsula in 1980 brought to light an EIA burial with a steatite seal on a ring (Ragupathy 1987: 199-204). The seal has a Brāhmī inscription and three non-Brāhmī symbols. The inscription reads: *Koveta*. Whatever the interpretation of this name, it is not Prakrit. *Kō* in Tamil is the equivalent of the Prakrit *raja* and occurs in the contemporary Brāhmī records of Tamil Nadu. It is clear that the name refers to a chieftain. (See Appendix VIII) Commenting on this seal inscription, the reference in the Pali and Brāhmī sources to Dīparāja and the associated Megalthic-BRW sites discovered in the Jaffna peninsula, Seneviratne concludes: 'Kantarodai has yielded several C-14 dates ranging from B.C. 500-450 from the Megalithic-BRW level, which is at an approximate depth of 12 feet below the surface. Thus, this time span and craft/ commercial activity may have given sufficient time for a separate geo-political unit to evolve in the Jaffna peninsula during the Pre-Christian period, where there may have been the emergence of a powerful chieftain, i.e. Dīparajha, over the rest of the chieftains.' Seneviratne 1985a: 403. The Tamil form of this name, Tīpattaraiyaṉ, is found in later south Indian inscriptions.

[52] Gunawardana 1982: 32.

[53] Seneviratne 1985b: 53.

[54] Ibid. Clarence Maloney put forward this identification in his Ph.D. thesis: *The Effect of Early Coastal Sea Traffic on the Development of Civilization in South India*, 1968, University of Pennsylvania.

[55] The word can be read as Veḷ or Veḷa. W. Saddhamangala Karunaratne revised Paranavitana's reading of 'Velu' and read it as 'Veḷa', following the clue provided by the Tamil Brāhmī inscriptions of south India (Karunaratne 1984: 32-33 – though published in 1984, the new reading was included in his Ph.D. thesis much earlier). Seneviratne also adopts this reading (Seneviratne 1985a: 375; Seneviratne 1992: 111).

[56] Seneviratne 1992: 113.

[57] Ibid: 112.

[58] Seneviratne 1985a: 377. 'Some of these names are Paḷikaḍa, Nala, Namara, Veḷa, Naguli, Pola, Hadaka, Nugaya, Sigara Nalu, Ruvala, Raki, Paṭakana śata, Haruma, Ayimara, Poṭimasa, Palaya, Sabili, Kaḍali, Uba, Puda, etc.'

[59] Seneviratne 1985a: 411, 415. '...there is a strict adherence to a practice found in the Dravidian kinship structure, known as *peyaran*, where the grandson takes up the name of his grandfather. This was often followed by the *parumakas*.' *Peyaraṉ* (now more commonly *pēraṉ*) in Tamil means 'namesake' and is the common word for both grandfather and grandson. It is an ancient word occurring in the Tamil Sangam poems.

[60] References to Jambukola-paṭṭana are found not only in the *Mahāvaṃsa* but also in other early Pali texts such as the *Sammohavinodanī*. *Mv*. 19: 60; *Sammohavinodanī*, English Tr. *The Dispeller of Delusion*, Pt.II, tr. Bhikkhu Nanamoli, PTS London 1996: 130, 193. The form Kolapaṭṭana occurs in the *Milindapañha* (Gunawardana 1990b: 27).

[61] Some of the names of ancient south Indian ports mentioned in the Pali sources are: Kāvīrapaṭṭana, Mayūrarūpapaṭṭana and Kaṇṭakasolapaṭṭana. Nāgapattinam, Visakapattinam and Kayalpattinam are other well-known south Indian ports with the *paṭṭiṉam* suffix in their names.

[62] *Mv.* VIII: 25; C.W. Nicholas, 'Historical Topography of Ancient and Medieval Ceylon', *JRASCB*, NS, VI, 1959: 75-81.

Chapter 6

[1] A linguistic study of the influence of Dravidian on Sinhala in the early centuries CE led Peter Silva to infer 'that Tamil had been a medium of communication in Ceylon during the first ten centuries of its history and that Tamil literature was known in the island during the same period.' Peter Silva, op. cit.: 18 (see Introduction, note 62, above).

[2] This is the controversial Vallipuram Gold Plate inscription. Whatever the controversy about its contents and language, the place name Nakadiva occurs in this epigraph from the Jaffna peninsula and is datable to the early centuries of the Common Era. *EZ*, IV: 237; Gunawardana 1995: 10-11.

[3] *Sammohavinodanī*: 443. This is a Pali commentrary attributed to the Indian monk, Buddhaghosa, of the fifth century. According to a story in this text, the ruler of Nāgadīpa bore the title of Dīparāja. It is interesting to note that this story survived among the historical traditions of Jaffna

and found its way into the late Jaffna chronicle, *Yālppāṇa-vaipava-mālai* (*Yvm*), in a different garb. According to this story, a king in ancient Sri Lanka gave a promise to one of his consorts that he would make her son to succed him on the throne. But the prince, before he grew into adulthood, lost one of his eyes in an accident while watching a cock-fight. Later, when the prince's mother reminded the king of his promise, the latter explained that it would be against the custom to make a person with a physical defect to succeed to the throne. But he was happy to make him Dīparāja, the ruler of Nāgadīpa. In the *Yvm*, this story is mixed up with the story based on folk-etymology to explain the name Yālppāṇam (Jaffna). According to this story, a blind lutanist (*yālpāṭi*) came from the Cōḷa country to the court of a king in Sri Lanka, sang the praises of the king and obtained the peninsula of Jaffna as his prize. Thus he became the founder of the kingdom of Jaffna (*Yvm*: 13-22).

4 *Maṇimēkalai*, Canto xxv.

5 Ibid: Canto xxiv.

6 Weerakkody 1997: 87.

7 Deraniyagala 1992: 735.

8 Ibid: 363.

9 That the Nāgas spoke a language different from Tamil is seen from a rare reference to their language in the *Maṇimēkalai.*, 16: ll 60, 70.

10 South Indian historians have been referring to this period as the Kalabhra Interregnum. The Velvikkudi grant of the Pāṇḍyas (*EI*, XVIII: 291 ff) and some Pallava charters (for example, the Kasakkudi Plates, *SII* ii: 356) refer to the Kalabhra rulers. Accuta Vikkanta, a Kalabhra ruler in the Cōḷa kingdom and a patron of Buddhism, is referred to in the Pali Buddhist writings of the south Indian monk Buddhadatta (*Vinayaviniccaya*).

11 Nilakanta Sastri 1955: 100-101.

12 *UCHC* 1, 1: 388.

13 Ibid: 389.

14 Ibid: 391.

15 Dhammaratana Thero, H., *Buddhism in South India* (abridged tr. From Sinhala), Kandy 1968; Ramachandran, T.N., *Nagapattinam and Other Buddhist Bronzes in the Madras Museum*, Madras 1965; Paranavitana, S., 'Negapatam and Theravada Buddhism in South India', *Journal of the Greater India Society*, XI, 1944: 17-25; Malalasekere, G.P., *Pali*

Literature of Ceylon, London 1928: 106-107, 112-116; *Encyclopaedia of Buddhism*, III, Colombo 1972: 192.

[16] Commenting on the role of the Buddhists of Tamil Nadu in the expansion of Buddhism in Southeast Asia, Gunawardana draws attention to the absence of specific information about this aspect: 'One lacuna in the picture that has emerged so far is the relative lack of specific information on the participation of members of Buddhist communities in what is now Tamil Nadu in this process of expansion. Tamil Nadu was another area where Theravada Buddhism was thriving during the period under discussion. The Sanskrit inscription from Vo Canh...certainly attests to the prevalence of relations between the eastern coast of modern Vietnam and South Asia...The name Śrīmāra in the record, reminiscent of names of members of the Pāṇḍya dynasty, may be taken, as Filliozat (1969: 114-116) suggested, as an indication of a South Indian connection. If South Indians from the Tamil Nadu region were active in the eastern coast of the Cam kingdom, it is very likely that they were also among the purveyors of Theravada influences'. Gunawardana 2001: 150.

[17] There is no agreement in the Chinese sources about the dates of Bodhidharma's mission and death. While some Chinese sources place his arrival in China in the last quarter of the fifth century, other accounts state that he went to China in either 520 or 527. Similarly, the dates given for his death range from 495 to 532. At the time of his death, he is said to have been more than 150 years of age. *Encyclopaedia of Buddhism*, III: 191.

[18] Two of the earliest Chinese sources providing information on Bodhidharma agree that he came from a Brahmin family in south India. The earliest of these is the lengthy historical work of Tao-hsuan (seventh century), entitled *Hsu-kao seng chuan* (*Further Biographies of Eminent Monks*), according to which "Bodhidharma, of South Indian Brahman stock, was a person of wonderful wisdom and penetrating clarity who understood everything he heard...He first arrived at Nan-yueh during the [Liu] Sung period [420-479]. From there he turned north and came to the kingdom of Wei. Wherever he stayed he spread the teaching of *dhyana* [Zen]". Dumoulin, H. *Zen Buddhism: A History*: 87.

[19] Nilakanta Sastri 1955: 636.

[20] Seneviratne 2003: 16-17.

[21] With the conversion of Emperor Constantine to Christianity in 312 and the issue of the Edict of Milan by the Emperor in the following year, Christianity began its rise to dominance in Europe. In a similar manner, the conversion of the Anuradhapura ruler, Devānampiya Tissa, to Buddhism no doubt paved the way for the rapid spread of Buddhism in the Anuradhapura kingdom.

[22] This account is based on the *Periyapurāṇam.*

[23] The Saiva religious literature, especially the *Periyapurāṇam,* which recounts the activities of the Nāyaṉārs, refers to the persecution of Jains and Buddhists. The punishment meted out to the defeated antagonists of Saivism included burning on stakes. Nilakanta Sastri is inclined to dismiss such claims and is of the view that these 'stories of persecution are late popular legends that were put into melodious verse by the pious credulity of the author of the *Periya Purāṇam'* (Nilakanta Sastri 1955: 635).

[24] *UCHC*, 1,1: 292.

[25] Ibid: 293.

[26] *EZ* IV: 114.

[27] *UCHC*, 1,1: 364.

[28] Cf. Cōḷa princes ruling northern Sri Lanka in the eleventh century took the consecration names of the Sinhalese rulers and the title Laṅkeśvara. See next chapter.

[29] *UCHC*, 1,1: 293; *EZ* III: 216.

[30] *UCHC*, 1,1: 294.

[31] Ibid: 298.

[32] *EZ* III: 109.

[33] The Ulalur inscription of Pallava Nandivarman II (eighth century) refers to a *Ciṅkaḷa meykāppāṉ.* T.V.Mahalingam, *Inscriptions of the Pallavas*, Delhi 1988: 330.

[34] *UCHC*, 1,1: 312-313.

[35] Ibid: 383.

[36] On grounds of style, this sculpture has been ascribed to the seventh century. The following comments by Paranavitana on this sculpture are noteworthy: "This work has earned the highest encomiums from art critics; and, in the studied restraint which characterizes the form of the man, the paucity of jewellery which accentuates the plastic form, and in

the elongated slender limbs, the work is reminiscent of the sculptures executed under the patronage of the Pallavas of Kanchi." *UCHC*, 1, 1: 403. The Dutch scholar of South Asian art, J.E.Van Lohuizen-De Leeuw, has identified this sculpture as that of the south Indian deity Aiyaṉār. 'The Rock Reliefs at Isurumuni', *Acta Orientalia Neerlandica*, Leiden 1971: 113-119.

[37] *UCHC*, 1, 1: 403.

[38] These, according to Paranavitana, 'exhibit the elongated limbs and the cold severity of expression which distinguish Pallava work.' Ibid.

[39] Van Lohuizen-De Leeuw, op. cit.: 115. As early as 1930, A.M. Hocart identified this relief as an example of Pallava art. *The Ceylon Journal of Science*, Section G, II, 2, 1930.

[40] Bandaranayake 1974: 352.

[41] Ibid: 208-209, 352.

[42] For the Telugu texts, see H.H. Wilson, 1828, *Mackenzie Collection*, I, Calcutta: xliv.

[43] The Kannada inscriptions are: a) from Tirumakudlu-Narasipur taluk, dated 1185, alluding to Akalāṅka's defeat of the Buddhists, and b) from Sravana Belgola celebrating Akalanka for his victory at Kanchi over the Buddhists who were in consequence banished to Sri Lanka. *Epigraphia Carnatica*, II, 54: 42-50.

[44] Approaching Sinhalese folk traditions as an anthropologist, Obeyesekere makes a strong case for Buddhist migrations from south India to Sri Lanka as a consequence of the Saiva-Vaisnava movment against Buddhism and Jainism. 'The cultural data in Sri Lanka leaves no doubt that migrations occurred', he concludes. Obeyesekere 1984: 523.

[45] Using the evidence of Chinese sources, Gunawardana argues that 'between the third and fifth centuries A.D., a change of fundamental importance in navigational technology appears to have taken place, ushering in a transformation in the patterns of navigation which helped to elevate Sri Lanka, with its strategic location in the Indian Ocean, and the southeastern coastal belt of the subcontinent to positions of important intermediaries in the trade between east and west.' Gunawardana 2001: 136.

[46] Notable work has been done in recent years, especially by Meera Abraham (1988), on the activities of the Maṇigrāmam. A leading

historian of south India, R. Champakalakshmi, surmises that this merchant community originated in the ancient Cōḻa port of Kāvēripaṭṭiṉam. In her view, 'The *Maṇigrāmam* was apparently a descendant of the group of traders from Vaṇika-grāma in Kāvērippūmpaṭṭiṇam, who, after the decline of external trade in the early period, moved into the interior to places like Uraiyur and Kodumbalur, where they re-emerged as *Maṇigrāmam*, an organized group of traders, by the ninth century A.D.' Champakalakshmi 1996: 49. Whether they originated in Kāvēripaṭṭiṉam or not, they were a well-known community in the Tamil land and find mention in Tamil literature as well. By the ninth century, members of this community were active from the west coast, in Kerala, to as far east as the coast of Thailand. In a copper-plate inscription of a Kerala ruler named Sthanu Ravi, datable to the ninth or early tenth century, a land grant to a Christian church is recorded. The record, which is in Tamil, names certain communities which 'were enjoined to do everything in their power for the good of the church and its land in accordance with the conditions laid down in the copper-plate document' (*Travancore Archaeological Series*, II: 9). One of these was the Maṇigrāmam. Another Tamil inscription, datable to the ninth century, from the ancient port of Takua-pa, Thailand, records the construction of an irrigation tank that was placed under the protection of three bodies, including the Manigramam. (N. Karashima, 2002: 10ff).

[47] The Badulla Pillar Inscription of Udaya III (946-954) refers to the merchant community as Vaṇigrāma, a variant form of Maṇigrāmam. It is Paranavitana's view that this name is the same as Sanskrit *vaṇig-grāma* and that 'the Tamil Maṇigrāmam ... is doubtless a corruption of Skt. *vaṇig-grāma'* (*EZ*, V:190, n.6). The equation of Vaṇigrāma with Maṇigrāmam need not be contested, for the alternative form of *vaṇikkirāmam* (also read as *vaṇika-kirāmam)* occurs in medieval Tamil literature (*Tolkāppiyam: Nacciṉārkkiṉiyar Urai*, Tañcāvur 1962: 173.). The *va* and the *ma* do sometimes interchange in the Dravidian languages.

[48] This early Tamil inscription from Thailand is reported to have been discovered about a hundred years ago in an ancient site in Takua Pa along with artefacts of the ninth and tenth centuries. This stone inscription (now in the Nakhon Si Thammarat Museum) was found among some ruins, presumably of a Hindu temple, along with a stone Visnu image and other

statues in the Pallava style of south Indian sculpture. The inscription was deciphered at the Office of the Government Epigraphist for India and first published by E. Hultzsch (1913). Later, Nilakanta Sastri gave his interpretations to the inscription and published it in 1932 and 1949. It was published again recently by Karashima (Karashima 2002: 11-13). The beginning of the record is damaged. Cosequently, it is not possible to ascertain the date of the inscription, although it appears to have been dated in the regnal year of a ruler whose name ended in –varma (as in the case of the contemporary Pallava rulers as well as many other Southeast Asian monarchs). It records the fact that a reservoir named Avani-nāraṇam, which was constructed by a personage whose name is damaged in the record, was entrusted to the Maṇikkirāmam, the Cēṉāmukam and another body (whose name is damaged), presumably for management and maintenance. As Karashima has pointed out, only a few references to the Cēṉāmukam are met with in south Indian inscriptions. Since the prefix of this name, Cēṉā (Skt. Sena), means 'army', it appears to refer to a body of soldiers who were associated with the Maṇigrāmam and other mercantile communities. In the eleventh century, we find that the martial communities like the Vēḷaikkārar were associated with mercantile communities like the Valañciyar and were entrusted with the protection of religious institutions.

[49] A Tamil inscription of about the ninth century, from Anuradhapura, records the activities of the mercantile community named Nāṉkunāṭu (Kannada Nālku-nāḍu). Indrapala 1968: 35.

[50] Indrapala 1971a: 4.

[51] The discovery of Hindu and Buddhist sculptures in Pallava style and of Sanskrit inscriptions in the Pallava-Grantha script in Southeast Asian countries has long been known. Recently, a joint Indo-Japanese project was launched under the auspices of the University of Tokyo and the Department of Culture, Government of Japan, led by Prof. Noboru Karashima, to make a reassessment of these Southeast Asian archaeological finds. The results of this project confirmed beyond doubt the spread of Buddhist and Hindu influences from the Pallava kingdom and the use of the Pallava-Grantha script in the major ports of Southeast Asia about the seventh century. No doubt the spread of these influences was greatly assisted by mercantile communities. At the well-known

archaeological site of Oc-Eo in Viet Nam, there is a Sanskrit inscription in late Southern Indian Brāhmī characters of about the 6th-7th century recording the construction of a Viṣṇu temple and some benefactions made to it. Other sites in the Mekong delta have yielded more Hindu artefacts of about the same period, including a set of nearly a dozen gold leaves with embossed figures of Hindu deities and their names written in Sanskrit in late Southern Indian Brāhmī of the 6th-7th century. At Go Xoai, a site belonging to the Oc-Eo culture, a gold plate was unearthed in one of the ruined Buddhist establishments. The inscription on the plate is in Prakrit and the script, derived from Southern Indian Brāhmī, is datable to the 8th-9th century. Another inscription of the seventh century, now in the Ho Chi Minh City Museum, originally belonging to a Saiva institution, is also in a script derived from the southern Indian script of the Pallava kingdom. As was the practice in the Pallava kingdom, the first part of the inscription is in Sanskrit and the main part is in the local language. Ramesh 2002: 150.

52 Ibid: 151.

53 Ibid: 148.

54 Ibid. It is in Thailand that the largest number of Pallava-Grantha and Southern Indian Brāhmī inscriptions of the about the sixth and seventh centuries are found. This is understandable as the famous port of Takua-pa was on the other side of the Bay of Bengal for the merchants from the Pallava kingdom and there must have been very regular traffic between Kanchi, Mamallapuram, Nagapattinam and the ports of eastern Sri Lanka on the western side of the Bay of Bengal and the ports of Burma, Thailand, the Malay Peninsula and Sumatra on the eastern side. Many of the inscriptions in Thailand are now found in the Bangkok National Museum and the Museum at Nakhon Si Thammarat. (Ramesh 2002: 147-157).

55 *UCHC*, 1, 1: 383.

56 Ibid*:* 68.

57 Gunawardana 1984: 117-118. Seneviratne 1985: 8.

58 See note 59.

59 *Paṭṭiṉappālai*: ll.283-284 –'*kāṭu koṉru nāṭākki kuḷam toṭṭu vaḷam perukki'*.

[60] Telugu-Coda plates: The Malepadu Plates of Punyakumāra, a Telugu-Coda king of the seventh or eighth century mentions the raising of the flood-banks of the Kāveri by Karikālaṉ. Telugu-Coda inscriptions of later times elaborate this legend further. Karikālaṉ's constructions of embankments on the Kāveri also find mention in the Tiruvalankadu Plates of Rājendra Cōḷa I. Nilakanta Sastri, 1955: 36.

[61] The Gajabāhụ myths are found in the Sinhalese chronicles written after the twelfth century and in the Sinhalese folk ritual texts relating to the cult of the goddess Pattini. Among the Sinhalese chronicles that cover these myths in great detail are the *Pūjāvaliya* (thirteenth century), the *Rājāvaliya* and the *Rājaratnākaraya.* The accounts of the myths are basically the same. According to these accounts, when Gajabāhu (whose reign falls in the second century) was ruling Anuradhapura, he came to know that in the reign of his father the Cōḷa king had taken 12,000 persons from Sri Lanka to work on bunding the Kāveri river. Angered by what he heard, he invaded the Cōḷa kingdom and brought back the 12,000 prisoners as well as a further 12,000 Tamils who were later settled by him various Sinhalese villages. The Pujavaliya adds that Gajabāhu 'made a law that henceforth the inhabitants of Lanka shall not go to work at Kāveri' (*Pūjāvaliya* 1895: 21).

[62] In his monumental study of the Pattini cult in Sri Lanka, Gananath Obeyesekere has made an anthropological analysis of the Karikālaṉ and Gajabāhu myths preserved in the ritual dramas of the Sinhalese. In the Sinhalese myths, the Cōḷa ruler 'Karikāla raises the banks of the river Kāvēri to prevent floods and foster agriculture, and he constructs rest houses, all for the common weal' (Obeyesekere 1984: 354). Karikālaṉ is the good king in these myths while the Pāṇḍi (Pāṇḍya) ruler is the evil one. Underlying these themes, as Obeyesekere interprets them, is the 'widespread universalistic message of the myths: the just king serves the common weal and brings prosperity to the human community, while the actions of the evil king create a wasteland and destroy fertility and prosperity.' (Ibid: 355). In Obeyesekere's view, these are colonization myths (Ibid: 361-380).

[63] See note 48 above.

[64] *Cv.* 45: 11-16.

[65] Ibid 45: 19, 21.

[66] *EZ*, III: 273.

[67] A *pamuṇu* was 'an estate possessed in perpetuity by a family in hereditary succession, or by an institution like a monastery or a hospital.' *UCHC*,1, 1: 375.

[68] *EZ*, IV: 36.

[69] *EZ*, II: 56.

[70] *EZ*, I: 117.

[71] *Cv*. 50: 15.

[72] *EZ*, II: 38, 56.

[73] For example, in the case of the immunities granted in respect of the village of Kinigama, the term *kuḷī* occurs without the prefix Demeḷe or Heḷe in the Rajamaligawa inscription of Mahinda IV. The same inscription also refers to another village by the name of Demeḷ-Kiṇigam (Tamil Kiṇigama). Presumably, a part of the original village of Kiṇigama where Tamils were settled had become a separate village. This would mean that the Kiṇigama of this record had only a Sinhalese population and, therefore, there was no need to refer to the impost levied there as *Heḷe-kuḷī* (Sinhalese *kuḷī*).

[74] *EZ*, III: 272, 274; *UCHC*, 1, 1: 372.

[75] The survival of Pali-derived words in Jaffna Tamil, a vestige of the period of Buddhist influence, is a phenomenon that should be of great interest to historical linguists studying the Jaffna dialect of Tamil. The word for non-vegetarian food in common parlance in Jaffna is *maccam* (Pali, *macca,* fish). Often it is used with the word *māmicam* (Pali *māṃsaṃ*, meat), as a compund word *maccam-māmicam.* Another word for vegetarian dishes, which may be already out of vogue, is *āratakkari*, the curry of the *arhat* (Pali, *arhat*, a holy person). The survival of the word *kāmam* (Pali, *gāma*, village) as a suffix in some placenames may further indicate the influence of Pali when Buddhism was a dominant religion in Jaffna. It may well be that this reflects a different Prakrit influence from that seen in the Brāhmī inscriptions of the south where the word *gama* occurs. Such an influence may have come from Andhra, which region seems to have been a source of Buddhist influence in Jaffna. Early inscriptions from Amaravati, in Andhra, have placenames ending in *gāma* (Kalavaira-gāma, Ragāma, Nhapitagāma).

[76] Buddhist remains in Neduntivu (Delft): Ragupathy 1987: 17; *JRASCB* XIII, 1969: I; Punkudutivu: Ragupathy 1987: 24; Velanai: Ibid: 25; Kantarodai: Ibid: 57ff. A Bodhisattva head in Graeco-Buddhist style was also found in Kantarodai: *ASCAR 1966/67*, G57 (April 1970).

[77] Vallipuram Buddha image: *Ceylon Antiquary* II, 2: plate x, fig. ii ; *JRASCB* XVI: 43; *ASCAR 1966/67*: G77; EZ IV: 229. Discovered in the nineteenth century, this standing Buddha image was gifted to the king of Thailand by the British governor, Sir Henry Blake, in 1906. It is now in a temple in Bangkok. A few years ago, Prof. Peter Schalk of the Uppsala University, Sweden, visited this temple (popularly known as the Marble Temple, in Wat Benja, Bangkok) and made a study of this statue. In his view, the style of this sculpture is that of the famous south Indian Buddhist centre, Amaravati.

[78] Parts of Buddha images have been discovered in several places in the Jaffna peninsula. Among these are a broken sedent Buddha image from Ponnalai (*ASCAR for 1949*: 28), a Buddha image from Mahiyapitti (P.E. Peiris, 'Nagadipa and Buddhist Remains in Jaffna', *JRASCB*, XXVI, 70, 1917: 26), a limestone Buddha image from Nilavarai, in Navakiri (*ASCAR for 1954*: 32; ASCAR for 1955: 17-19) and Buddha images from Uduvil, Kantarodai and Jaffna town (*JRASCB* XXVI, 70: 25ff, 43; *Ceylon Antiquary and Literary Register*, II, 2: 96; S.Kumāracuvāmi, '*Vaṭamākāṇatiluḷḷa cila iṭappeyarkaḷin varalāṟu*' in *Yālppāṇa vaipava kaumuti* by K.Vēluppiḷḷai, Jaffna, 1918: 14.).

[79] See notes 2 and 77 above.

[80] See Appendix (Kantarodai carnelian seal.)

[81] *Nampota*, M.D. Gunasena and Co., Colombo 1955.

[82] *UCHC,* 1, 1:383.

[83] Ibid.

[84] There is a reference in the *Mahāvaṃsa* to a *sivikāsāla* at Anuradhapura, built in the time of Paṇḍukābhaya in the fourth century BCE (*Mv.* X: 102). That this was possibly a shrine for the worship of Siva is an interpretation one could give on the basis of what is said in the commentary of the *Mahāvaṃsa* (*Mahāvaṃsa-tīkā*, I, ed. G.P. Malalasekera, London 1935: 207).

[85] Ludden (gifts to Br1hma0as).

[86] Chamapakalakshmi 1996: 17.

[87] Ibid: 39.

[88] Ibid.

[89] In the third century CE, the Anuradhapura ruler Mahāsena is said to have destroyed Siva temples (Mv. XXXVII: 41; *Mahāvaṃsa-tīkā*: 685). See below, note 98.

[90] The Chinese Buddhist monk Fa Hsien (Faxian) has noted that Brahmanical rituals were practised at the court of the Sinhalese king (Samuel Beal, *Buddhist Records of the Western World*, I, Boston 1885: lxxiv).

[91] *Cv*. XLVIII: 143-144.

[92] Ibid: XLVIII: 23.

[93] Ibid LI: 65-67.

[94] The seal inscription with the name Sripatigrama in Grantha characters was discovered at Padaviya in 1970. The text and a Tamil translation, together with a plate, of the inscription was published in 1972 by the present writer. K. Indrapala, 1972, *Yālppāṇa Irācciyattiṉ Toṟṟam*, Kandy: 76, 95.

[95] Indrapala 1971.

[96] Indrapala 1978.

[97] *EZ*, IV: 191.

[98] That the Siva temples of Mātoṭa and Gokarṇa existed early in the Common Era may be inferred from certain references in the Pali chronicles. According to the *Dāṭhāvaṃsa* (ed. and tr. B.C. Law, Lahore 1925: 42) , there was a temple of god at the port of Mahātittha (Mātoṭa) in the ninth year of Kitti Siri Megha (310 CE). The existence of a Siva temple at Gokarṇa in the time of Mahāsena (274-301) is vouched for by the *Mahāvaṃsa*, which mentions the construction by Mahāsena of a *vihāra* at Gokarṇa after the destruction of a temple of god there (*Mv*. XXXVII: 41). The commentary on the Mahāvaṃsa states that this temple of god was a Sivalinga temple (*Mahāvaṃsa-tīkā*: 685).

[99] *Tiruñāṉacampantar tēvāra tiruppatikaṅkaḷ*, Tamiḻ Kaḻakam, Ceṉṉai: 810-812.

[100] Cuntarar Tevaram.

[101] *Tiruvācakam* .

[102] *Nikāyasasaṃgrahaya*: 18; *Rājaratnākaraya*: 81-82.

[103] *EZ*, III: 132, 225.

PLATE 25.
Bharata Natya relief sculpture, Yapahuva.

[104] Indrapala 1980.

[105] Excavations at Anuradhapura in 1892 brought to light a number of ruined Hindu shrines. *ASCAR for 1892*: 5. Three Tamil inscriptions were also found among these ruins. Indrapala 1971:4; *South Indian Inscriptions*, IV, Nos. 1403, 1404 and 1405.

[106] *UCHC*, 1, 1: 403.

[107] Ibid.

[108] Ibid.

[109] Van Lohuizen-De Leeuw 1971: 116.

[110] An inscription from Anuradhapura refers to Senavarma. Indrapala 1968: 32. An inscription of the eleventh century from Kantalay refers to the ruler by the name of Caṅkavarma<u>n</u> (Saṅgha-varma for Saṅghabodhi-varma). Indrapala 1978: 94.

[111] Although some kings did meet visiting Mahayana teachers, there is no evidence of their patronage of these teachers. *UCHC*, 1, 1:383.

[112] *UCHC*, 1, 1: 358; Subbarayalu and Shanmugam 2002: 266.

[113] Karashima 2002: 11; Abraham 1988: 45.

[114] Ramesh 2002: 218.

[115] Subbarayalu and Shanmugam 2002: 266.

[116] In her study of urbanization in south India, Champakalakshmi has shown that the *brahmadeyas* or Brāhmaṇa settlements initiated by the Pallava rulers, and continued by the Pāṇḍya and Cōḷa kings, played a major role in the expansion of agriculture. 'Under the Pallavas, i.e. seventh to eighth centuries, agrarian expansion through *brahmadeyas* took place in certain key areas in the Palar-Cheyyar valleys, invariably accompanied by irrigation works (*taṭāka* = reservoir or *ēri* = lake), the region around Kāñcīpuram receiving greater attention' (Champakalakshmi 1996: 375). In this respect, it is of great interest to note that the locality where the Gaṅgā-taṭāka was built not only had a name that emulated the names of Pallava reservoirs but was also the best known *brahmadeya* in Sri Lanka for over two centuries. The earliest Tamil inscription that we get there, belonging to the early part of the eleventh century, informs us that it was a *brahmadeya* with its own village assembly or *Mahāsabhā*, after the fashion of the south Indian *brahmadeyas*. Like its counterparts in south India, this village assembly was concerned with the maintenance of the irrigation facilities in the area. Early in the eleventh century, the Cōḷa

conquest resulted in the *brahmadeya* being named as the Rājarāja-caturvedimaṅgalam, after the Cōḻa emperor. Later inscriptions give more information about this *brahmadeya*. When Vijayabāhu I became king after defeating the Cōḻas, the *brahmadeya* was re-named as Vijayarāja-caturvedimaṅgalam, after the new ruler. Inscriptions of Gajabāhu II, one of the successors of Vijayabāhu I, show that it continued to flourish as a *brahmadeya*. (Indrapala 1978: 81-97). In view of these facts, it is very probable, that this brahmadeya originated in the seventh century when the reservoir was built and that its origin was due to Pallava influence through the medium of mercantile communities.

Chapter 7

[1] Thapar : 365, 366.

[2] Ibid: 382-383.

[3] Needham, Joseph, 1971, *Science and Civilization in China*, 4 (Cambridge): 368, note f. '...it must be remembered that the Cauvery valley had the largest reservoir in the world for nearly a millennium, the Virānam-kulam near Jayamkonda-cholapuram already mentioned, built by the Cholas, a command of 22,000 acres'. Giants' Tank, Sri Lanka: 'Though holding only 4,400 acres of water instead of Parakrama's planned 6,400, it was still at that time the third largest reservoir in the world.' Ibid: 371, note c.

[4] Nilakanta Sastri 1955: 183.

[5] Thapar: 387.

[6] Nilakanta Sastri 1955: 730.

[7] Ibid: 512, 653

[8] As early as 923, the title '*Maturaiyum Īḻamum koṇṭa*' is given to Parāntaka in one of his inscriptions. Nilakanta Sastri 1955: 122. For a discussion of this evidence, see Krishnan, K.G., 1971, Kudumiyamalai Inscription of Parakesarivarman – 33rd Year, *ET*, I, 1: 19-24.

[9] *Cv*. LIII: 41ff.

[10] *Cv*. LIII: 5ff.

[11] Brāhmaṇa villages and settlements were known as *caturvedimaṅgalam*. In the Cōḷa period, more settlements of Brāhmaṇas were established in different parts of the empire and often these had names ending in –*maṅgalam* or *caturvedimaṅgalam*. Nilakanta Sastri 1955: 492-493.

[12] After the death of Parāntaka I, for nearly three decades (955-985) the Cōḷa dynasty faced serious internal problems. 'The relatively short interval of about thirty years from the death of Parāntaka to the accession of Rājarāja I is one of the most difficult passages of Cōḷa history.' Nilakanta Sastri 1955: 140.

[13] Ibid: 154.

[14] Ibid: 172.

[15] *SII*, II, No.92.

[16] All these names are found in Cōḷa inscriptions in Sri Lanka.

[17] Ravikula-māṇikya and Nittavinoda were titles/honorifics used by Rājarāja I. Indrapala 1971f: 34; Indrapala 1971e: 27.

[18] Indrapala 1982; Indrapala 1991.

[19] Ibid. The inscriptions from Fort Hammenheil state that Jayaṅkoṇṭa Cōḷa Mūvēnta Vēḷār 'took away the crown that the Pāṇḍya had deposited as (part of) his family treasure in Īḻam alias Mummaṭicōḷa-maṇṭalam, the crown of the King of Īḻam and the crown of his queen, as well as the ladies and treasures (of the king of Īḻam)'.

[20] Indrapala 1978; Indrapala 1991.

[21] *UCHC*, 1, 1: 413. Two inscriptions of Rājendra I refer to the presence of a Laṅkeśvara in the Cōḷa kingdom (*Annual Report on Epigraphy for 1909*: No.642 and *Annual Report on Epigraphy for 1956/57*: No.166).

[22] Indrapala 1978: 84; Shanmugam 2004: 75.

[23] *EZ*, IV: 195; *EZ*, III: 310.

[24] *EZ*, III: 310.

[25] Indrapala 1971b: 8; Indrapala and Prematilleke 1971: 25.

[26] At the time the Cōḷas were rising to imperial power in south India, the political situation in China became more favourable to the development of close Sino-Indian trade relations. The Sung government paid particular attention to foreign trade by making it a government monopoly abd taking strenuous efforts to increase its volume. Special missions were sent to attract foreign traders to the shores of China (*Chau Ju-kua*, ed. F.Hirth and W.W. Rockhill, Intro. p.6 Amsterdam 1966). The Cōḷa rulers were

not slow in grasping these opportunities, for we find that R1jar1ja I (985-1014), Rājendra I (1012-1044) and Kulottuṅga I (1070-1120) had sent missions to the Chinese court (Sastri 1955:605-606). The result was a brisk trade in the eleventh century in textiles, spices and a number of luxury articles. The trade in luxury articles, however, ran into difficulties in the twelfth century when the drain of Chinese currency and precious metals resulting from the expansion of this commerce led to attempts by the Chinese government to restrict the volume of trade with south India (Nilakanta Sastri 1955: 607-608).

[27] The most recent research into into the activities of the south Indian mercantile communities is the Research Project of the Taisho University 1997-2000, headed by Noboru Karashima. In the report of this Project, N.Karashima and Y.Subbarayalu have made a comparative study of the inscriptions of the Aiññūṟṟuvar found in south India and Sri Lanka and shown some of the problems facing those who try to understand the operations of this organization (Karashima and Subbarayalu 2002: 72-87).

[28] Karashima and Subbarayalu 2002: 76-78.

[29] These records are listed in P.Shanmugam 2002: 297ff.

[30] Teṉ-ilaṅkai (literally, South Lanka) does not mean Southern Lanka. It should be translated as 'Lanka in the South'. The prefix *teṉ* (south) is used to distinguish Sri Lanka from other places named Lanka, particularly Uttara-Lanka (Lanka in the North). The name Teṉ-ilaṅkai has been used in inscriptions as well as in Tamil literature, almost always in poetry, for a long time since the seventh century to refer to the island of Sri Lanka. *Tiruñāṉacampantar Tēvāratiruppatikaṅkaḷ*, Kaḻaka edition, Cennai: No.243 (seventh century); Subbarayalu and Shanmugam 2002: 264, 269 (thirteenth century).

[31] The name Añjuvaṇṇam was earlier interpreted by some to mean an organization of five castes (añcu = five, vaṇṇam/varṇa = castes) See Meera Abraham: 25 n. 51. But recent researches support the interpretation that Añjuvaṇṇam is derived from the word *hañjamana* (Persian *anjuman*?) and refers to an organization of merchants of West Asian origin (Abraham: 25; Subbarayalu in Karashima 2002:24). Among some inscriptions relating to a mosque (*paḷḷi*) discovered in Visakapatnam, in Andhra Pradesh, there are three (dated 1090) that refer to the

Añjuvaṇṇam. Of these, two specifically refer to merchants (*vyāpāri*) who belonged to the Añjuvaṇṇam of Mātoṭṭam (Mātoṭa). One is in Telugu and the other is in Tamil. Subbarayalu and Shanmugam 2002: 236-237. See Appendix IV.

[32] Subbarayalu and Shanmugam 2002: 269.

[33] See Appendix II.

[34] Subbarayalu and Shanmugam 2002: 266.

[35] Ibid:

[36] Ibid: 264.

[37] Indrapala 1971d.

[38] *UCHC*, I, 1: 590.

Chapter 8

[1] *SII*, IV: 489.

[2] For a discussion of the various princes who waged battles against the Cōḻas from the southern part of the island, see *UCHC*, 1, 2: 417ff.

[3] *UCHC*, 1, 2: 424.

[4] Ibid: 425; *EI*, XXI: 243.

[5] *ASCAR for 1949*: 31.

[6] The period of Cōḻa rule in Sri Lanka is still in need of a comprehensive study. Apart from the articles on Cōḻa inscriptions, two of Nilakanta Sastri's contributions are worthy of note: 1) 'Vijayab1hu I, the Liberator of Lanka', *JRASCB* NS, IV: 45-71; 2) 'Ceylon as a Province of the Coḷa Empire', *UCHC*, 1, 2: 411-416. There is also an unpublished thesis on the subject: W.M.K.Wijetunge, *The Rise and Decline of Coḷa Power in Ceylon* (University of London, Ph.D. 1962).

[7] *UCHC*, 1, 2:433; *Cv*. LX: 24 ff.

[8] Two daughters of Kulottunga I are known from inscriptions, namely, Cuttamalli Āḻvār and Ammaṅkai Āḻvār (Nilakanta Sastri 1955: 333). A Tamil inscription from Sri Lanka provides the information that Cuttamalli Āḻvār was married to a prince in Sri Lanka (*EZ*, III: 308 ff; *UCHC*, 1, 2: 441).

[9] *UCHC*, 1, 2: 419.

[10] *EZ*, V: 27.

[11] *Cv*., LX: 25-44.

[12] Kiribamune 1976: 24-25. Citing evidence from the Pali chronicle and the inscriptions, Kiribamune concludes that Vikramabāhu I was not a Buddhist. As for his mother, Tilokasundarī, 'it is very likely that she was not only a non-Buddhist but also that her actions were directed against Buddhism'.

[13] *Cv*.,LXII: 45; LXIV: 13ff. 'From birth to death, the services of Brāhmaṇas were enlisted for the performance of the rites prescribed for Indian royalty at important occurrences in life' (UCHC, 1, 2: 534).

[14] Inscriptions of Vikramabāhu I, Gajabāhu II and Niśśaṅkamalla refer to many Brahmanical rituals being performed. An inscription from Kahambiliyava, in which Vikramabāhu is described as one who received the blessings of Śiva, implies that he performed Brahmanical rituals to receive such blessings (EZ, V, No. 39). In an inscription from Kapuruvaduoya, Gajabāhu is associated with the Brahmanical ceremony of *lakṣapūjā* (*EZ*, V, No.38). Niśśaṅkamalla is associated with the ceremony of *navagrahaśānti* in another inscription (*EZ*, II: 148).

[15] *EZ*, IV: 194.

[16] *EZ*, V: 407. The husband of Pārvatī is Śiva.

[17] Kiribamune 1976: 25.

[18] Ibid.

[19] *Cv*., LXII: 33ff.

[20] *UCHC*, 1, 2:508.

[21] Ibid: 509; *EZ*, I: 130.

[22] *EZ*, II: 137, 174; *UCHC*, 1, 2: 522.

[23] *EZ*, II: 148.

[24] Paranavitana, S., 1965. 'Ramesvaram Inscription of Nissamkamalla', *EI*, XXXVI:23-31.

[25] *UCHC*, 1, 2:571.

[26] Indrapala 1981: 30.

[27] Ibid: 32.

[28] G.P.Malalasekera, *The Pali Literature of Ceylon*, London 1928: 220.

[29] Gunawaradana 1979: 271.

[30] Ibid: 266.

[31] Ibid.

[32] *Sīmālaṅkāra*, ed. Buddhasiri Tissa, Colombo 1904: 42-43.

[33] Gunawardana 1979: 266.

[34] Liyanagamage 1978: 99.

[35] *Cv*., LXXXIV: 7-10.

[36] *UCHC*, 1, 2: 433.

[37] This information is found in an important Tamil record of the Vēḷaikkārar at Polonnaruva. It has interesting details about the reign of Vijayabāhu I and confirms the evidence of the Pali chronicle in some important respects. After the death of Vijayabāhu, a leading Buddhist monk invited a Vēḷaikkārar regiment to undertake the protection of the Temple of the Tooth Relic (See Appendix IV).

[38] S.Pathmanathan, 'Vikramabāhu II and Vikrama Salamevan', *Sri Lanka Journal of the Humanities*, XIX, 1& 2, 1993: 100.

[39] *Cv*. LXIII: 24-29.

[40] *UCHC*, 1, 2: 491ff.

[41] Ibid: 589.

[42] Liyanagamage 1978: 135, 138.

[43] Nilakanta Sastri 1955: 458.

[44] *UCHC*, 1, 2: 591.

[45] In the words of the Pali chronicle, some of the defeated Tamil soldiers in south India, 'at the command of the ruler of Lankā who thought to have all the *cetiyas* formerly destroyed by the Damiḷas rebuilt by them, he [the Sinhalese commander Laṅkāpura] had brought to Lankā and the work of restoration begun on the Ratanavāluka *cetiya*.' *Cv*. LXXVI: 103-104. In another place, the chronicle further states that Laṅkāpura, after having made over the government of the Pāṇḍya kingdom to Vīra Pāṇḍya, 'sent with speed to Sīhaḷa the many horses, men and elephants captured from the Coḷa country and from the Paṇḍu land.' *Cv*. LXXVII: 103. Later, Parākramabāhu I 'also had the Mahāthūpa erected which bore the name of Damiḷathūpa because it had been built by the Damiḷas *who had been brought hither after the conquest of the Paṇḍu kingdom.'* *Cv*. LXVIII: 76-77.

[46] *Cv*. LXXVIII: 76-77.

[47] The inscriptions of the Aiññūṟṟuvar, for instance, refer to various groups of professionals and others associated with them. Among them are artisans and servant groups. Karashima and Subbarayalu 2002: 78.

[48] *UCHC*, 1, 2: 592.

[49] Ibid.

[50] P.L.Prematilleke, *Alahana Parivena Polonnaruva: Third Archaeological Excavation Report*, Colombo 1982: 27.

[51] Bandaranayake 1974: 353.

[52] Ibid: 209.

[53] Bell, H.C.P., 1913, *ASCAR for 1907* and *ASCAR for 1908*; Coomaraswamy, A.K., 1914, *Bronzes from Ceylon, Memoirs of the Colombo Museum*, I; Arunachalam, P., 1915, Polonnaruva Bronzes and Siva Worship and Symbolism, *JRASCB*, XXIV, 68: 189-222; Gangoly, O.C., 1915, *South Indian Bronzes*, Calcutta.

[54] Godakumbure, C.E., 1961, Bronzes from Polonnaruva, *JRASCB*, NS, VII, 2: 239-253; Godakumbure, C.E., 1964, *Polonnaruva Bronzes*, Colombo; Lakdusinghe 1994.

[55] Ulrich von Schroeder, 1992, *The Golden Age of Sculpture in Sri Lanka*, Hong Kong.

[56] Indrapala 1981: 29-30; Ramachandran, T.N., 1965, *Nagapattinam and Other Buddhist Bronzes in the Madras Museum*, Madras.

[57] Chutiwongs, N. and Prematilleke, L., 1994, Buddhist Images, *Sacred Images of Sri Lanka*, Art Gallery of New South Wales, Sydney: 18.

[58] Von Schroeder 1992 (*op. cit*): 98. The bronze Samadhi Buddha from Thirukkovil (Ampara District) is in the Cōḻa style. Ibid: 100.

[59] Lakdusinghe 1994: 21-22.

[60] Snodgrass, Adrian, 1994, Introduction, *Sacred Images of Sri Lanka* (*op. cit*): 15.

[61] Kiribamune 1976: 26; *EZ*, V: No.38.

[62] Needham, Joseph, 1971, *Science and Civilization In China*, 4: 368.

[63] Gunawardana 1984.

[64] See Chapter 7, note 3.

[65] Gunawardana 1984: 140.

[66] Obeyesekere 1984: 361ff. See Chapter 6, note 61.

[67] Gunawardana 1984: 138.

[68] The absence of Aiññūṟṟuvar records at Gokarṇa and Mātoṭa is not difficult to explain. The temples at these two sites were completely razed to the ground by the Portuguese early in the seventeenth century and the bricks and stones of those structures were used to build the Portuguese

forts. Some of the stones with Cōḻa inscriptions have been found in the forts at Trincomalee, Jaffna and Kayts.

[69] Subbarayalu and Shanmugam 2002: 249, 251, 264, 265; Subbarayalu 2004: 69-70.

[70] See Chapter 7, note 30.

[71] Subbarayalu and Shanmugam 2002: 264, 269.

[72] Ibid: 236-237.

[73] Indrapala 1963: 68-69.

[74] *Cv*. LXXVI: 10-35; *UCHC*, 1, 2: 473ff.

[75] Christie 1998: 244.

[76] *EZ*, II: 38.

[77] *EZ*, I: 180. The inscription refers to the *Nānādeśī vyāpārayan* (1.19).

[78] Knox, Robert, 1681, *An Historical Relation of the Island Ceylon in the East-Indies*, London: 167.

Epilogue

[1] A series of thirteen popular articles, under the title 'Tamils in Ancient Sri Lanka' were published in 1969 (May-August) in the Sunday edition of the Sri Lankan Tamil daily *Vīrakēcari*. That there were close relations between the prehistoric peoples of Sri Lanka and south India and that the Sinhalese ethnic group evolved in the island as a result of Prakritic influences that spread among the prehistoric people were among the views presented in these articles.

[2] Ananda Kentish Coomaraswamy (1877-1947), whom many consider as 'exemplar for scholar, critic, and teacher', died within three weeks after his seventieth birthday. Shortly before his death, at his last public appearance, he said: "I should like to emphasize that I have never built up a philosophy of my own or wished to establish a new school of thought. Perhaps the greatest thing I have learned is never to think for myself; I fully agree with Andre Gide, that 'Toutes choses sont dites deja!' and what I have sought is to understand what has been said, while taking no account of the 'inferior philosophers'. Holding with Heraclitus that the Word is common to all, and that wisdom is to know the Will whereby all

things are steered, I am convinced with [Alfred] Jeremias that the human cultures in their apparent diversity are but dialects of one and the same language of the spirit, that there is a 'common universe of discourse' transcending the difference in tongues." Quoted in Ray Livingston, *The Traditional Theory of Literature*, Minneapolis: University of Minnesota Press 1962: 7.

[3] Consider, for example, the reference to one of the rulers of the northern kingdom as '*Teṉṉilaṅkaikkōṉ*' (King of Lanka) in the Tamil source Kailāyamālai, ed. Cā. Vē. Jampuliṅkam Piḷḷai, Chennai 1939: 6. Cf. '*Teṉṉ ilaṅkaikkōṉ*' used for the Polonnaruva ruler Niśśaṅka Malla in the Tamil inscription from Panduvasnuvara (Krishnan, K.G., 'Notes on the Tamil inscription from Panduvasnuvara', *University of Ceylon Review*, XX, 1, April 1962: 15). The title '*Laṅkeśvara*' was used by the Polonnaruva rulers (e.g., Vikramabāhu I and Niśśaṅka Malla) as well as by later Sinahalese rulers even as late as the eighteenth century (e.g., Kīrti Śrī Rājasiṅha).

[4] Liyanagamage 1978; Gunawardana 1979: 262-271; Indrapala 1981.

[5] *Cv* 84: 7-10.

[6] Ibid 90: 80.

[7] Paranavitana, S., *The Shrine of Upulvan at Devundara*, Colombo 1953: 74-78; Pathmanāthan, S., 'The Munnesvaram Tamil Inscription of Parakramabāhu VI', *Journal of the Royal Asiatic Society Sri Lanka Branch*, New Series, XVIII, Colombo 1976: 54-59.

[8] Śrī Rāhula, Toṭagamuvē, *Sälalihinisandēsaya*, v. 22.

[9] De Silva, C.R., The Rise and Fall of the Kingdom of Sītāvaka, *University of Peradeniya History of Sri Lanka*, ed. K.M.de Silva, Peradeniya 1995: 95. There is an interesting book in Sinhala on Berendi Kovil: Gamalath, D.P., *Sītāvaka Bäränḍi Kōvila*, Colombo 1996.

[10] Sarachchandra 1966: 95ff.

[11] Ibid: 9.

[12] *EZ*, IV: 195.

[13] Wickremasinghe, D.M. de Z., 'Kantalay Stone Seat insciption', *EZ*, II: 282-290.

[14] Sarachchandra's comments on the dance sculptures: "In the stone friezes at Yāpahuva and Gaḍalādeṇiya, and the wood carvings at Embekke Devālaya women are represented in traditional dance poses such as are

described by Bharata. The dancing figures at Yāpahuva are similar to the figures on the walls of the Hindu temple at Chidambaram, and among the dance poses one can recognise the Siva Naṭarāja, Catura, Karihasta, Gaṇḍasūci, and Nikuñcita poses. Besides this, a large number of female figures are represented, both in the sculptures as well as in the paintings of various periods, in classical dance poses. Even the female figure in the lamp recently discovered at Dedigama is represented as executing a similar classical dance pose." Sarachchandra 1966: 16.

[15] *UCHC*, I, 2: 780.

[16] Ibid: 782.

[17] Ibid: 792.

[18] Ibid: 776.

[19] Gunawardana 1990: 66.

[20] The poet is Alagiyavanna (which name itself is of Tamil origin), described by K.N.O Dharmadasa as 'the last flicker in the flame of a poetic tradition that had flourished since the *Muvadevdāvata* aand the *Sasadāvata* of the twelfth century' and 'the only learned poet of the 16th century'. *University of Sri Lanka History of Sri Lanka*, II: 473. Alagiyavanna, in his *Subhāṣitaya*, says that he composed this work for the benefit of 'the creatures who are ignorant of Tamil, Sanskrit and Pali' (*demaḷa saku magada nohasala sataṭa*) – *Subhāṣitaya*, Educational Publications Department, Colombo 1979: v.5.

[21] Rasanayagam, C., *Ancient Jaffna*, New Delhi 1984: 350 (Reprint).

[22] Gunawardana 1990: 66.

[23] Ibid: 67, 83. "There are several instances of members of the nobility and the gentry using the Grantha and Tamil scripts in their signatures. See, for instance, the signature of Dumbara Rājakaruṇā Mudiyansē in documents dated in the years 1688 and 1714 of the Śaka era (Sri Lanka National Archives Documents Nos. 5/63/67/-3 and 12)."

[24] Godakumbura 1955: 323. Gunawardana considers the author of *Nāmāvaliya* to be 'a Tamil prince who was married to the king's daughter'. Gunawardana 1990: 66.

[25] Hevawasam, P.B.G., *Pantis Kōlamurakavi*, Colombo 1974; Obeyesekere 1984. The Sinhala term *pantis kōlamura*, meaning 'thirty-five ritual texts' or 'thirty-five songbooks', refer to a compendium of the textual traditions relating to the Pattini cult in Sri Lanka. These texts have been edited and

published by Hevawasam while Obeyesekere has made an in-depth analysis of these for his research on the Pattini cult.

[26] Obeyesekere 1984: 523.

[27] De Silva, C.R., Expulsion of the Portuguese from Sri Lanka, *University of Sri Lanka History of Sri Lanka*, II: 179-180. The weaver caste of *Cāliyar* find mention in the south Indian inscriptions of the Coḷa period. The migration of this caste to Sri Lanka may have begun as early as the eleventh or the twelfth century. De Silva states: '…the *salāgamas*, who were an important group which had migrated from the Malabar Coast between the thirteenth and the sixteenth centuries had originally been primarily weavers. Some of them had been ordered by the king of Kōṭṭe to peel cinnamon. With the rising demand for cinnamon there was a tendency to enlist all of them for cinnamon peeling. In time, members of other castes too were required to peel cinnamon and there are instances of *karāva*, *hunu* and *batgam* people performing this task. In course of time these peelers were absorbed by the *salāgama* caste…By the sixteenth century, the new immigrant *karāva* and *salāgama* groups were developing an identification with an occupation but had not as yet developed a ritual connection with the *goyigamas*.' Obeyesekere is, however, inclined to treat the *Salāgama* as later immigrants: 'The *salāgama* caste were weavers, later cinnamon peelers, from Malabar who were brought to the south coast by the Portuguese…The original settlers of the West and South were Sinhala *goyigama* (farmers), some of them originally from Malabar. Much later, in early Portuguese times, there were immigrations of *karāva* (fishermen, *karaiyār* of South India) and *salāgama*.' Obeyesekere 1984: 527.

[28] Referring to the 'significant changes in the composition of the population of the island' in the period after the fall of Polonnaruva, Leslie Gunawardana notes: 'Myths of this period reflect the distribution of the immigrant population over different parts of the island, especially in the northern, western and southern coastal regions. These groups of immigrants who originally spoke different languages came to be absorbed into the two main linguistic groups in the island. Their incorporation and assimilation seems to have been slow and long-drawn; but it was a relentless process in that few retained their original languages or group identities for any considerable length of time. Nevertheless, this very

process of incorporation did leave its impact on the polity and on what came to be perceived as Sinhala culture.' Gunawardana 1990: 65.

[29] Goonewardene, K.W., *Journal of the Royal Asiatic Society Sri Lanka Branch*, 1995. The founding fathers of some of the leading families in the modern political history of Sri Lanka, it must be remembered, were themselves migrants from south India in the period after the fall of the ancient kingdoms. The founding father of the Bandaranaike family, according to their family traditions, was Nilapperumal, who came to the island in the fifteenth century. Prof. Yasmine Gooneratne, herself a member of the Bandaranaike family, traces the origin of the family name using family traditions in the following manner: '[The founding personage,] serving under the Kings of Kandy and bearing the name Neela Perumal, was made high priest of the Temple of the God Saman, and commanded to take the name of *Nayaka Pandaram* (Chief Record Keeper) in 1454. If the tradition has truth in it, we may surmise that the Indian name of *Nayaka Pandaram* came in time to adopt the form of *Pandara Nayaka*. By the time it had turned into the Sinhalese *Bandaranaike*, the Hinduism of its bearers had been replaced by Buddhism; just as we know, from written genealogical records dating back to the early seventeenth century, that Buddhism was itself replaced in the family by Christianity in its Catholic and later in its Protestant forms.' Gooneratne, Yasmine, 1986, *Relative Merits: A Personal Memoir of the Bandaranaike Family of Sri Lanka*, London: 3. Also, James T. Rutnam, 1957, 'The House of Nilaperumal', *Tribune*, July 19, Colombo. The ancestor of the Jayawardene family, fondly referred to as Tombi (sometimes rendered as Tambi) Mudaliyar in early nineteenth century British documents, arrived in Colombo in the time of Dutch rule. Two eminent professors, one from the University of Peradeniya and the other from Columbia University, have researched into the ancestry of President J.R. Jayawardene and concluded that Don Adrian Wijesinghe Jayawardene (died 1830), a direct paternal ancestor of the President, "was descended from a family of the Chetty community, a community of traders, which had emigrated from the Coromandel coast in India in the early years of Dutch rule in the mid-17th century and settled in the vicinity of Colombo…by the time he [Adrian] himself appears on the stage of Sri Lanka's history at the tail-end of the eighteenth century the process of

‘Sinhalisation’ of his family had been completed.” De Silva, K.M de and Wriggins, Howard, 1988, *J.R. Jayawardene of Sri Lanka: A Political Biography*, London: 22. Coromandel (from Chola-mandala) was the name given in European writings for the Tamil Nadu part of the eastern coast of India. Also, James T.Rutnam, 1957, ‘Tambi Mudaliyar’s legacy’, *Tribune*, August 30, Colombo.

INDEX

ADDENDUM

While this work was in the press, the author had occasion to learn about some very recent developments in field archaeology in Sri Lanka and south India, especially the interesting finds relating to the Early Iron Age at the Jetavanarama site, Anuradhapūra (where Prof. Sudharshan Seneviratne is directing excavations), and at Adichchanallur in Tamil Nadu (where Dr. T. Satyamurthy is directing excavations). No doubt, the results of these excavations, when released in final reports, will have a direct bearing on some of the matters discussed in this work. But there is one announcement, coming from Adichchanallur, that is worthy of mention here. Dr. Satyamurthy, according to the media (*The Hindu*, Chennai 17 February 2005: 13), has unearthed an urn with writing in a 'very rudimentary Tamil-Brahmi' script for which he has proposed, on the basis of preliminary thermo-luminescence dating of the urn, a date as far back as c. 500 BCE.* This is indeed interesting in view of the fact that leading epigraphists are still struggling to come to terms with a similar date assigned to certain potsherd graffiti from Anuradhapura by Dr. Siran Deraniyagala, Dr. Robin Coningham and Prof. F.R. Allchin. The new discovery has great relevance to some of the issues about the Brahmi script discussed in this work.. One has to await the publication of the results of the new Adichchanallur excavations for any further comment.

15 March 2005

* The author is thankful to Dr. Siran deraniyagala for drawing his attention to this news item.